The Military and Political in Authoritarian Brazil

The Portuguese-Speaking World

ITS HISTORY, POLITICS AND CULTURE

The Series Editors
António Costa Pinto (University of Lisbon)
Onésimo T. Almeida (Brown University)
Miguel Bandeira Jerónimo (University of Coimbra)

This new series will publish high-quality scholarly books on the entire spectrum of the Portuguese-speaking world, with particular emphasis on the modern history, culture, and politics of Portugal, Brazil, and Africa. The series, which will be open to a variety of approaches, will offer fresh insights into a wide range of topics covering diverse historical and geographical contexts. Particular preferences will be given to books that reflect interdisciplinarity and innovative methodologies. The editors encourage the submission of proposals for single author as well as collective volumes.

Published

The Lusophone World: The Evolution of Portuguese National Narratives
Sarah Ashby

The Politics of Representation: Elections and Parliamentarism in Portugal and Spain, 1875–1926
Edited by Pedro Tavares de Almeida & Javier Moreno Luzón

Inequality in the Portuguese-Speaking World: Global and Historical Perspectives
Edited by Francisco Bethencourt

The Military and Political in Authoritarian Brazil: The Aliança Renovadora Nacional (ARENA), 1965–1979
Lucia Grinberg

Marcello Caetano: A Biography (1906–1980)
Francisco Carlos Palomanes Martinho

From Lisbon to the World: Fernando Pessoa's Enduring Literary Presence
George Monteiro

The First Portuguese Republic: Between Liberalism and Democracy (1910–1926)
Miriam Pereira

The Portuguese at War: From the Nineteenth Century to the Present Day
Nuno Severiano Teixeira

The Locusts: British Critics of Portugal before the First World War
Gary Thorn

Forthcoming

Politics and Religion in the Portuguese Colonial Empire in Africa (1890–1930)
Hugo Gonçalves Dores

The Eruption of Insular Identities: A Comparative Study of Azorean and Cape Verdean Prose
Brianna Medeiros

Dictatorship and the Electoral Vote: Francoism and the Portuguese New State Regime in Comparative Perspective, 1945–1975
Carlos Domper Lasús

Literary Censorship in Francisco Franco's Spain and Getulio Vargas' Brazil, 1936–1945: Burning Books, Awarding Writers
Gabriela de Lima Grecco

On Guard Against the Red Menace: Anti-Communism in Brazil, 1917–1964
Rodrigo Patto Sá Motta

The Military and Political in Authoritarian BRAZIL

The Aliança Renovadora Nacional (ARENA), 1965–1979

LUCIA GRINBERG

sussex
ACADEMIC
PRESS
Brighton • Chicago • Toronto

Copyright © Lucia Grinberg 2019.

The right of Lucia Grinberg to be identified as Author of this work has been asserted in accordance with the Copyright, Designs and Patents Act 1988.

2 4 6 8 10 9 7 5 3 1

First published in 2019 in Great Britain by
SUSSEX ACADEMIC PRESS
PO Box 139
Eastbourne BN24 9BP

Distributed in North America by
SUSSEX ACADEMIC PRESS
Independent Publishers Group
814 N. Franklin Street
Chicago, IL 60610

All rights reserved. Except for the quotation of short passages for the purposes of criticism and review, no part of this publication may be reproduced, stored in a retrieval system, or transmitted, in any form or by any means, electronic, mechanical, photocopying, recording or otherwise, without the prior permission of the publisher.

British Library Cataloguing in Publication Data
A CIP catalogue record for this book is available from the British Library.

Library of Congress Cataloging-in-Publication Data
Names: Grinberg, Lucia, author.
Title: The military and political in authoritarian Brazil : the Aliança Renovadora Nacional (ARENA), 1965–1979 / Lucia Grinberg.
Description: Brighton ; Chicago : Sussex Academic Press, 2019. | Series: The Portuguese-speaking world : its history, politics and culture | Includes bibliographical references and index.
Identifiers: LCCN 2019015239 | ISBN 9781845199760 (hbk : alk. paper)
Subjects: LCSH: Aliança Renovadora Nacional—History. | Brazil—Politics and government—1964–1985. | Political parties—Brazil—History—20th century. | Dictatorship—Brazil—History—20th century. | Military government—Brazil—History—20th century. | Brazil—Armed Forces—Political activity—History—20th century.
Classification: LCC JL2498.A4 G74 2019 | DDC 324.273/04—dc23
LC record available at https://lccn.loc.gov/2019015239

Typeset & designed by Sussex Academic Press, Brighton & Eastbourne.
Printed by TJ International, Padstow, Cornwall.

Contents

Series Editors' Preface ix
Acknowledgments xi

Introduction 1

Chapter 1
Political Memories of ARENA 6
1 Political memories of ARENA in the 1990s 8
2 The historiography of ARENA 11
3 Political party or scapegoat? 18

Chapter 2
A Time of Conspiracy and Misgivings (1964–1966) 29
1 Opposition to the João Goulart government 30
2 Brazilian politicians stripped of their political rights in 1964 31
3 The extension of Castello Branco's term 34
4 Political party reform 36
5 The formation of a new party system 40
6 The creation of ARENA 44
7 Archives of the ARENA National Committee 65

Chapter 3
A Time of Uncertainty and Divisions (1966–1968) 70
1 Founding ARENA 71
2 The purges of 1966 75
3 Drafting the 1967 Constitution 78
4 Revoking local government autonomy: ARENA and government in discussion 88
5 Daniel Krieger resigns: ARENA and government in transaction 91
6 The Márcio Moreira Alves affair and Institutional Act No. 5: ARENA and government on a crash course 95

Chapter 4
A Time of Silence and Reorganization (1969–1973)   102
1   The alternatives for ARENA   103
2   Reorganization of ARENA   107
3   Reopening of the National Congress   113
4   Membership and party loyalty in ARENA   117
5   The "politics of the governors": Indirect elections and leadership in the state committees   122
6   The ARENA leadership   131
7   The jurists, the "third party" proposal, the "hooded ones"   138
8   The issue of congressional immunity   143

Chapter 5
The Time of Political Détente (1974–1979)   146
1   The meanings of 1974   148
2   Geisel, the politicians, and ARENA   151
3   Congressional recess and political reforms   160
4   Amnesty and party reform   171
5   The "Yes, Sir! Party"   178

Chapter 6
A History of ARENA in Cartoons   185
1   Press, memory, and political humour   185
2   Newspapers and cartoonists   191
3   A history of ARENA in cartoons   196
4   The personification of ARENA and its relations with government   202
5   Threats to political representation   208

Final Remarks: Political Party and Scapegoat   214

Glossary of Political Parties   217
Notes   221
References   247
Index   254

Series Editors' Preface

The Brazilian Military Dictatorship (1964–1985) began after a *coup d'état* by the armed forces. The nature of the new administration has led some social scientists to characterize it as a "Civil-Military" authoritarian regime. This is the first book in English dealing with the *Aliança Renovadora Nacional* (ARENA) as a dominant party, formed in 1965, to back the military dictatorship in power since 1964, making it an excellent contribution to the modern history of Brazil and of military dictatorships in general. Based on original primary sources, Lucia Grinberg's book is a significant contribution to the comparative study of the role of dominant parties in contemporary dictatorships worldwide. Its relevance vastly exceeds its geographical and chronological focus.

The author discusses the participation of politicians in the 1964 coup and the subsequent formation of the ARENA party, the extinction of existing parties in 1965, and the format for the party as proposed by the executive arm of the dictatorship. Key is the analysis of the previous careers of the politicians that formed ARENA. Like other dominant (or single focus) parties, ARENA sought collaboration and endorsement on a wide scale: via the intellectual elite, organizing courses for its new leaders, and the creation of departments to mobilize women, labour, and youth constituencies. The book's central empirical corpus consists of documents from the archives of the ARENA National Committee, congressional debates, and the press. The history presented is enhanced by including press and publisher cartoons of the period that address and encapsulate the issues as the wider polity engaged with this new dictatorial circumstance.

The Brazilian Military Dictatorship did not underestimate the mechanisms of political representation and the formal political rights of citizens. In this sense, the ARENA is a rare case. After all, even if under the dictatorship democratic politicians were heavily marginalized and repressed, a party with the usual political obligations had nevertheless been created to support the 1964 movement. It functioned alongside Congress, which was characterized by a "limited pluralism", implemented by a dominant party and by a party representing in theory the opposition, the Movimento Democrático Brasileiro (MDB). Flores-Macías' definition of "dominant party"* as "a political institution that has the leading role in determining access to most political offices, shares powers over policymaking and patronage distribution, and uses privileged access to state resources or extra-constitutional means to maintain its position in power", defines the Brazilian situation precisely. The case of Brazil undoubtedly contributes to the proper comparative study of dominant parties, and this book demonstrates why and how. For this and many other reasons, we are immensely pleased to welcome Lucia Grinberg's book into the series "The Portuguese-Speaking World: Its History, Politics, and Culture".

ANTÓNIO COSTA PINTO (University of Lisbon)
ONÉSIMO T. ALMEIDA (Brown University)
MIGUEL BANDEIRA JERÓNIMO (University of Coimbra)

---

* Flores-Macías, "México's PRI: The resilience of an authoritarian successor party and its consequences for democracy," in James Loxton and Scott Mainwaring, eds., *Life after Dictatorship: Successor Parties Worldwide* (Cambridge: Cambridge University Press, 2018), p. 260.

Acknowledgments

The idea of studying the political party ARENA first came from Professor Angela de Castro Gomes during the course she gave with Professor Daniel Aarão Reis Filho on *Parties, Elections, and Political Representation* in the Graduate Studies Program in History at Universidade Federal Fluminense (UFF) in Niterói, Rio de Janeiro. At the time, Angela called attention to the contrast between the vast academic production on leftist parties in Brazil compared to the paucity of studies on right-wing parties. She told especially of ARENA, whose last chairman had donated the documental archives of the National Committee to CPDOC/FGV in 1980. Over the years, Angela encouraged me steadfastly, and it was always a privilege to count on an attentive and patient reader for the initial drafts of this work. Daniel Aarão Reis Filho followed my research closely from the onset and urged me on when most people considered the theme rather odd. On numerous occasions he made suggestions and observations that I did my best to incorporate into the work.

I conducted my research for years at four institutions that have always welcomed me with open arms: CPDOC/FGV, the periodicals section of the Brazilian National Library, the Library of the Rio de Janeiro State Legislature (ALERJ), and the Library of the Brazilian Ministry of Finance (in Rio de Janeiro).

In March 2004 I defended my PhD thesis at the Graduate Studies Program in History at Universidade Federal Fluminense. I would thus like to thank the thesis review panel for their careful reading and keen observations: Prof. Dr. Alzira Alves de Abreu (CPDOC/FGV), Prof. Dr. Daniel Aarão Reis Filho (UFF), Prof. Dr. Francisco Carlos Teixeira da Silva (UFRJ), and Prof. Dr. Leôncio Martins Rodrigues (Unicamp). During my doctoral studies I received a three-year grant from CAPES. Publication of the book in English was made possible thanks to financing by the Rio de Janeiro State Research Foundation (FAPERJ) with the support of my colleagues in the Graduate Studies Program in History at the Federal University in the State of Rio de Janeiro (PPGH/UNIRIO). Finally, the book benefited from collaboration by the cartoonists' families (Paola Biganti, Luis Raul Weber Abramo, Cristina Penz, João

Baptista Weber Abramo, Lucas Bernardes Fonseca Weber Abramo and Caio Bernardes Fonseca Weber Abramo), who authorized the reproduction of the cartoons depicting ARENA and MDB, and originally published from 1965 to 1979.

The Military and Political in Authoritarian BRAZIL

The Aliança Renovadora Nacional (ARENA), 1965-1979

Introduction

Democracy as a universal value is still a challenge for Brazilian society. There is a strong tradition of attaching adjectives to democracy as a category: "liberal", "bourgeois", "formal", etc. Democracy as a category *per se* appears insufficient, because it is incapable of solving the country's social issue. As for politicians, Brazilians' common-sense view of them is generally even more negative. Politicians are associated first and foremost with corruption. And the political parties? With one or another exception, in the Brazilian people's eyes they represent nothing, only show up at election time, and multiply indefinitely.

The predominant view in Brazilian political culture is one of disregard for mechanisms of political representation, considered insufficient formalisms for transforming society.[1] In this context, how does one understand the importance of maintaining institutions of political representation that were so disfigured under the dictatorship launched by the "movement of 1964"? From this perspective, to study Brazil's dictatorship places squarely on the order of the day the debate on democracy, the representative system, and citizens' political rights. In the late 1970s, during the national détente (*abertura*, or "opening"), with a new appreciation of political rights after their partial loss and widespread perception of the vote as a tool for struggle, essential academic articles were published on the importance of the representative system's formalisms. The ARENA is an extreme case in this context. After all, the party had been created to support the 1964 movement, but under the dictatorship the politicians were heavily marginalized, and ARENA's history is profoundly linked to the circumstances in which it acted in the political field.

The narrative of the party's history through various plots and the depiction of different characters is largely similar to what has been considered a traditional political history. Yet I found this approach indispensable. Throughout my bibliographic research, I found many articles on Brazil's two-party system, but there were no extensive studies based on primary sources about ARENA itself. I thus began by attempting to systematically compile the existing analyses on the party. During this process I perceived a recurrent disregard for ARENA's political representativeness, an image I found to be well consolidated in the 1980s. From that starting point, I took two complementary paths, one to study the process by which that compact image of the party was constructed, and the other to examine the party's creation in detail, drawing on various sources, always situating the actors in this process: characterizing the individuals, their experiences, their networks of relations, and their political strategies. In this precise sense, beyond the ever-present structural constraints, the study intends to emphasize a political history of the possibilities and choices that shows the politicians' perspectives and attitudes vis-à-vis the events. The narrated facts thus appear as the locus for analysis of the disputes at stake in the political field, where one can observe the practices of those public men. On this scale, one can hear the voices of the politicians that formed the party and observe their individual decisions and the existing alternatives on which they acted, even under numerous heavy constraints.

In the first chapter I present the questions I will address over the course of the thesis. Based on an inventory of the representations concerning ARENA, we observe the force of an image marked by ridicule and *"adesismo"* (rubber-stamp subordination to the regime). This image is part of ARENA's history, having been built through a process of dispute for the legitimacy of its political representativeness. I seek to show how each set of primary sources I consulted has a specific place in the political field and expresses different memories of ARENA.

In chapters 2, 3, 4, and 5, I analyse ARENA's path over the course of the regime observing the different conjunctures, building a chronology based especially on the relations between ARENA and the government.

In the second chapter, focusing on the years 1964 to 1966, I discuss the participation by politicians in the 1964 movement and the formation of the ARENA party, noting the drastic intervention in Brazil's political system in 1964, the extinction of the existing parties in 1965, and the design for the party wanted by the Executive. An analysis of the previous careers of the politicians that formed ARENA reveals the contrast between the rejection of the name "ARENA", especially after détente, and the same individuals' representativeness at the time.

In the third chapter I show how the early years of ARENA, from 1966 to 1968, were marked by uncertainty as to the nature of the regime and thus of the party itself. Various liberal *Arenista* leaders such as Afonso Arinos, Milton Campos, Adauto Lúcio Cardoso, and Daniel Krieger endeavoured to point certain directions for both the regime and the party that differed from those proposed by the Executive. Institutional Act No. 5 (AI-5) marked the defeat of these attempts.

In the fourth chapter I draw a profile of ARENA organized according to rulings issued by the Executive from 1969 to 1973. This period witnessed important heterogeneity among the *Arenistas*: on one side were the leaders authorized by the dictatorship, such as Filinto Muller and Rondon Pacheco, on the other the dissident voices of Daniel Krieger, Aliomar Baleeiro, and Herbert Levy. This shows that ARENA did not always defend the same ideals, that there were clashes among its members over the definition of what the party was supposed to represent.

In the fifth chapter I present the *Arenistas*' views of their defeat in the 1974 elections and the dictatorship's gradual loosening. From 1974 to 1979, some politicians in ARENA favoured speeding up détente, while others stood firmly by the AI-5. What is interesting to note is the *Arenistas*' perspective, alert to the shifting winds in Brazil's political field, the marginal position to which they were reduced, and the return to electoral competition.

The sixth chapter analyses the history of ARENA based on depictions of the party in political cartoons published in Brazil's mainstream press, which proved important for understanding the ways the party was grasped by Brazilian society, both during the dictatorship and later starting in the 1980s with the return to democracy. An analysis of the various portrayals of ARENA since its founding, throughout its political activity, and after its demise clearly shows that this image did not always exist, nor is it the only possible representation.

I basically drew on four types of primary sources for this purpose. The first, the study's central documental *corpus*, consisted of the documents in the archives of the ARENA National Committee. This is not a private collection, but institutional archives donated in 1980 to the Centre for Research and Documentation in Contemporary History of the Getúlio Vargas Foundation (CPDOC/FGV) by the party's last chairman, José Sarney. The ARENA archives feature a widely varying set of sources: transcriptions and recordings of meetings, official documents, party publications, and correspondence printed and sent to the National Committee. The documents reveal a sharp contrast between the time of ARENA's political activity and the silence of its heirs on the organization in recent decades. The archives contain records of initiatives and projects by the ARENA membership to build the party, highlighting its dimension as a political project. We thus discover ARENA as another political party seeking collaboration by intellectuals, endeavouring to forge a symbol, organizing courses for its new leaders, and working to create departments to approach its target publics (e.g., the women's, labour, and youth departments).

The second type of sources consisted of congressional debates. The Brazilian National Congress was so degraded during the dictatorship that little is known about what was said in those years. The legislative records (*Anais da Câmara dos Deputados*, *Anais do Senado*, and *Anais da Constituição de 1967*) can be considered regime-approved official sources, but their importance should not be underestimated. We often fail to pay proper attention to official sources, especially under dictatorships, but they have rich potential, like all sources. As always, it is crucial to know which questions can be posed for such a set of documents.

The congressional records, as the name indicates, seek to lay out an organized history or narrative year by year and can consist of a record of historical or personal facts.[2] In this case, the publications of the Brazilian National Congress are of prime historical importance, since they are intended to record the activity by the Legislative branch in great detail. An analysis of the congressional sessions shows the politicians in activity, where we can observe the issues discussed and voted on, the homages and exposés, the ever-present ceremonies and rituals, the pro-regime members of Congress in relation to the Executive, the absences in key votes, and interaction with representatives of the MDB. By searching the congressional record, we find both previously drafted and impromptu speeches. In most cases there are asides from other members of Congress, producing the debates where we can observe the relations between the various leaders.

The third type of sources consisted of the press, which I used extensively as a primary source. Research in newspapers allows an analysis of the facts as news and public statements over the course of political processes as they unfold, when the politicians show the existing alternatives, the string of stances, and their own analyses of the situations (often pointing to elements previously unknown to the researcher). Media repercussions are political facts, and the stances expressed in political cartoons, editorials, and specialized columns are often important parts of political processes.

These three types of sources, contemporary with the party's activities, were especially interesting for studying ARENA because they are not informed by the future. They thus constitute sources for examining circumstances and identities prior to the deeper effects of many facts, indicating the ideas, identities, and political cultures of those actors.

Finally, I consulted memoirs, biographies, autobiographies, and oral testimony gathered by other researchers, published or accessible in other archival centres. These narratives were incorporated to complement the other sets of documents, considering the specificities of retrospective testimony.

In broad strokes, the history of a party is the history of the struggle to define what the party is supposed to represent. In different conjunctures, a wide range of political actors assigned certain meanings to the ARENA, which can be revealed through different facets: the social memory of the party built in the 1980s and 90s, the academic literature produced on the subject, the Executive's plans and designs for the party when it was founded, the bills and projects defended by members of Congress and sympathizers during its existence, and its portrayal by the press at the time, both in articles and images. From these various angles, ARENA can be a clue for perceiving the complexity of Brazilian society and its relations with the dictatorship.

CHAPTER

1

Political Memories of ARENA

"— Anything can be political, my lady. A joke, a saying, any little thing can mean a lot".[1]

Machado de Assis

"ARENA is the wayward daughter of UDN that took to streetwalking".[2]

Villas-Boas Corrêa

Following the demise of Brazil's dictatorship, the recorded political memory of ARENA was marked by scorn. In the history of the 1964 movement, we find either silence on the pro-regime civilians or ridicule personified in the party. While I was conducting this research, many people looked at me with some alarm, asking if I had family members in the party or repeating clichés on ARENA as the "largest political party in the West", as claimed by *Arenista* Congressman Francelino Pereira. I also heard numerous times, "Oh, you're going to study the *Teatro de Arena*!", alluding to the *avant garde* theatre-in-the-round in São Paulo, known for staging oppositionist plays during the "leaden years" of ruthless repression. This is in fact a memory based on left-wing references common to a narrow segment of Brazilian society, which shows that memory is not neutral; on the contrary, it takes a side. Each time I heard such ironic remarks, I became more certain that ridicule was not the best approach for understanding the party.

Such recurrent attitudes apparently show that this object of study caused some alarm and discomfort in Brazilian society in the late 1990s and early 21st century. In an article on the concept of history of the present, French historian Henry Rousso highlights the importance of deconstructing a kind of mental blockade in relation to certain historical periods, considering observations of the relations they invoke in the present. According to Rousso, to understand a historical epoch or noteworthy fact, the historian should study its various representations, not only in historiography but also in society.[3]

A political party is not a thing, as common sense and academic and media analyses would lead us to believe.[4] Even party members and their opponents refer to party organizations as concrete objects. This way of dealing with parties, this reification, is so common that it even constitutes party identity. In other words, besides studying relations between party members and with members of other parties, government representatives, voters, and the press, it is essential to study the elaboration of political parties' memory and identity.[5]

In the case of ARENA, it is the party's derisory image that calls attention, since it was heavily incorporated by Brazilians' common sense. I thus found this image to be a promising point of departure for investigating the construction of a memory and history of ARENA. The analysis of these portrayals will be based on the observation of some modalities and contents that Henry Rousso calls "vectors of memory", i.e., indicators that explicitly or implicitly offer unique portrayals, dated in time and well-situated in space.[6]

Especially in the case of studies on political parties, political scientist Michel Offerlé identified a recurrent vocabulary on parties in academic and media analyses.[7] He lists the following topics: use of metaphors, normativism, reification of collective bodies, and reutilization of political scientists' production. Given this horizon, the author proposes a sociological approach aimed at deconstructing these issues.

From Offerlé's perspective, political parties are groups founded to intervene in the political market, prone to produce differentiated effects and to be the objects of diversified social investments and uses.[8] One of the fundamental points for investigation when working with parties is to verify how the stakeholders serve the parties and are served by them. A party is also a "collective brand", a collective undertaking on the order of political representation.

The author identifies and critiques the common anthropomorphic approaches in studies of political parties. But he also criticizes the extreme of understanding them merely as isolated acts by some of their more visible spokespersons. Rather, he contends that a party functions through agents that temporarily have the attribution and right to use the collective resources capitalized in the name of a "partisan moral person".

1 Political memories of ARENA in the 1990s

In the 1990s, a certain memory of the ARENA came to light in Brazilian newspapers. ARENA had rarely been mentioned at all in newspapers in those years. Some references were published when the leadership of the Party of the Liberal Front (PFL) announced plans to implement a process of modernization. Taking an extremely critical approach, this memory was triggered to show the desire of former ARENA members, now in other parties, to avoid being identified as the party's heirs. This was because the PFL was founded in 1985 by dissidents of the Social Democratic Party (PDS), the name adopted by ARENA after the party closed down in 1979.

In May 1995, the newspaper *Folha de S. Paulo* published a brief note entitled "Denying its Roots", saying, "PFL advisors are on a campaign with journalists to avoid further spreading the nickname '*Arenão*' [big ARENA], already popular in Congress, attached to the plans for party renewal".[9] This shows that nobody wanted (or wants to this day) to identify with ARENA or to be identified with it publicly, because its memory is full of negative connotations, especially "*adesismo*" (strict bandwagon or rubber-stamp subordination to the military). This image of ARENA, already consolidated in Brazil by the 1990s, is premised on the generalization that the *Arenista* politicians were grovelling latecomers, totally subservient to the Executive. Such bandwagon subservience is a phenomenon studied by political scientists, characterized by the rapid growth of political parties after they reach government power, when politicians elected on other party tickets switch parties after the elections. This mainly occurs due to patronage practices between politicians and their constituencies, which requires politicians' proximity to government in order to meet the demands of their political clientele. This type of practice is ancient and widespread (not only in Brazil), but the new fact in the case of ARENA was the image of subordination and subservience to the military in the dictatorship. That was the prime disqualifying element for ARENA's representativeness as an organization coalescing various conservative political forces. The term *adesista* also has a highly pejorative connotation of participation after the success of the 1964 movement rather than actual participation in the events leading up to the coup d'état. This is important because actual participation included both the risks in undertaking such political activities and support for and belief in that movement.

According to Villas-Boas Corrêa, in a definition that became ontological, "ARENA is the wayward daughter of UDN that took to streetwalking".[10] During the dictatorship, this well-known journalist and political analyst wrote numerous articles in mainstream Brazilian newspapers such as O *Estado de S. Paulo* and *Jornal do Brasil*. Yet the most common quote in academic publications is his picturesque, jocular remark during an interview with *Pasquim*, an alternative weekly lampoon. The definition by Villas-Boas carries an implicit view of the National Democratic Union (UDN) as a putschist but "decent" party, to insist on the terrain of moralism so dear to the UDN, and the characterization of ARENA as a party that failed even to do justice to the dubious UDN legacy of "correctness" and fell by the moral wayside. This example clearly illustrates how the comparisons between party identities forged by the politicians themselves, by militants, or attributed to them by journalists are recurrent themes in ARENA's history. As in the history of all partisan organizations, there are disputes for ARENA's memory, seeking to assign it a certain identity. In this sense ARENA's history involves a dispute for the memory of both the UDN and the PSD.

Throughout the dictatorship, ARENA was always associated with the UDN, and MDB with the PSD. Tancredo Neves, in an interview, referred to the regime as the "*Estado Novo* of the UDN".[11] But this image reproduced by former PSD members who now belonged to MDB says nothing of the PSD members that supported the 1964 movement and later joined ARENA. Throughout ARENA's lifespan, there was a broiling dispute been members of the old UDN, now in ARENA, and members of the extinct PSD, now in MDB. However, ARENA actually consisted of both *Udenistas* and *Pessedistas*. The presence of high-ranking officials from the *Estado Novo* such as Filinto Müller, Chief of Police of the Federal District during the *Estado Novo*, Gustavo Capanema, Minister of Education and Health, Benedito Valladares, intervenor in the State of Minas Gerais, and Marshall Eurico Gaspar Dutra, Minister of War, all leaders historically linked to Getúlio Vargas, leads one to view that image through a different prism. And in addition to the national leaders coming from the PSD, ARENA was formed by an extensive network of politicians organized in each municipality, originating from both the UDN and PSD memberships, and whose nationwide organization was one of the party's most valuable forms of political capital. The view of ARENA as heir to the PSD reaffirms its condition as a party connected to the state and to government and shows that ARENA was a party of continuity, of those who had been connected to government for decades.

Another widely cited reference to ARENA, this one tongue-in-cheek, was the quote by National Deputy Francelino Pereira, who labelled it "the largest party of the West". The quip became part of Brazil's political folklore, and it is difficult to determine when it was coined, although it was likely in the late 1970s. The phrase was even parodied in a political cartoon depicting ARENA as a grand ... schism. Of course, there were constant disputes in ARENA's local and state committees, and one of the trickiest issues for the *Arenistas* was to enable cohabitation, in a single party, of leaders from various extinct tickets, especially UDN and PSD, who had been traditional political adversaries since 1945. But perhaps ARENA really was one of the West's largest parties, since it combined most of the active politicians when it was founded in 1965. At the time, ARENA set up municipal committees throughout Brazil, demonstrating a huge organizational effort. In addition, after the party became defunct in 1979, it gave rise to two of the largest conservative parties in Brazil's democratic period inaugurated in 1984: PDS and later PFL.

In 1995, the party was also the butt of a political joke by Luís Fernando Veríssimo, who proclaimed: "The Brazilian PRI – who would have thought it! – ended up being ARENA".[12] The writer was referring to the Institutional Revolutionary Party of Mexico, founded in 1929 with the aim of convening the spectrum of political groups that had supported the Mexican Revolution.[13] PRI maintained its hegemony in the ballot boxes and in the Mexican government until the 1990s. The comparison of ARENA and PRI also appeared in a political cartoon by Ziraldo, where a Mexican explains: "*En Méjico, desde mucho más de cincuenta años, desembrujamos nuestro pacuete. Entre otras cosas encontramos dos partidos: uno que no pierde nunca ... y el otro*"[14] ["In Mexico, far more than fifty years ago we 'unwrapped our package'. Among other things in the package, we found two parties: the one that never loses... and the other one."] Although that may have been amusing in the 1980s and 1990s, ARENA was actually a political project in the 1960s. According to Brazilian journalist Carlos Castello Branco, Mexico's PRI really was viewed by many members of the 1964 movement as a model for the government's party.[15]

All these images invoke background issues pertaining to ARENA's history, as we will see throughout the book. When such portrayals of the party were picked up again by the Brazilian press in 1990s, all that was left were the jokes, while the understanding of the historical process that spawned them had been completely lost. Taking a critical stance, far from reiterating this ridiculous image, I contend that only an understanding of the social construction of these images will enable knowing the party and acknowledging it as an integral part of Brazil's political system and Brazilian society.

2 The historiography of ARENA

ARENA was not just the object of attacks by humourists and journalists; it was also cursed and ignored by social scientists. This relates again to the issue of the relationship between memory and social demand as a vector in the history of the present, since oftentimes the sources are even available, but there is a lack of interest in studying them. Not rarely, social demand directs the research. In the case of research on the Brazilian dictatorship, for years the studies concentrated on different forms of opposition to the regime. No one was interested in studying the organizations that supported a dictatorship that lasted for twenty long years.

There are many studies on the Brazilian military in power, particularly focused on the decision-making processes and the dictatorship's politics of repression. Meanwhile, the political parties drew scanty interest as objects of research, due to the widespread notion in Brazil that the parties were devoid of authenticity as such. As political scientist Otávio Dulci summarized, the consensus was that such organizations failed to meet the criteria for political parties and were thus considered irrelevant for interpreting the political process[16]. Since ARENA is an extreme case in which the shortcomings of Brazil's political parties are viewed as increased to the tenth power, the widespread notion that it was nothing but a party of grovelling, bandwagon subservience to the dictatorship weighed heavily on it.

Following the victory by MDB in the 1974 Senate elections, many studies were done on electoral competition in the two-party system. But the main tone of these analyses was to show the growth of MDB. Of course, in 1974 the MDB won a resounding victory in the Senate, gaining 16 out of 22 seats. But the elections to the Chamber of Deputies were always hotly contested, as shown in the table below. During the dictatorship, Brazilian society appeared to be divided, with a large share supporting the regime. Still, there are no studies seeking to really explain these numbers. The votes for ARENA are always interpreted as the result of fraud or "halter votes" (*votos de cabresto*).

The election results from 1970, when ARENA defeated MDB by a wide margin, are the most heavily contested. According to Bolívar Lamounier, there is even an "abnormal" feeling to those statistics due to the political circumstances, with the depletion of party life and elections at the peak of crackdown by the dictatorship.[17] Still, one can argue that voting for ARENA really was a conscious choice, underscoring the fact that there was a strong campaign for blank and null votes that year, with considerably high percentages.

Table 1.1 Results of at-large elections to the Brazilian Chamber of Deputies (1966–1978)

Year	ARENA	MDB	Blank/Null	Total
1966	50.5%	28.4%	21.0%	17,285,556
1970	48.4%	21.3%	30.3%	22,435,521
1974	40.9%	37.8%	21.3%	28,981,015
1978	40.0%	39.3%	20.7%	37,629,180

Source: Alzira A. Abreu, et al. ed. *Dicionário Histórico Biográfico Brasileiro Pós-30*. Accessed February 7, 2019. https://cpdoc.fgv.br/acervo/dhbb.

Other analyses, conducted still during the dictatorship, highlight the injustice of the legislation that allowed candidacies in multiple tickets (Portuguese: *sublegendas*), jeopardizing MDB. In 1972, Francisco Weffort wrote an article entitled *A vitória inchada da ARENA* [ARENA's bloated victory] that discussed the municipal elections.[18] The author lists the cases in which the party was victorious. In many municipalities, Weffort contends that there had not been an election *per se*, but a plebiscite, because there was only an ARENA candidate with no competitors from MDB. In other municipalities there was no contest between the two parties, but "only" multiple tickets under ARENA. Such situations were interpreted as illegitimate victories on grounds that they were the consequence of local political groups' dependence on the state governments, all controlled by ARENA.

Generally speaking, such analyses of election results fail to acknowledge the votes for ARENA as indicative of representativeness, demonstrating part of society's support for the regime. Only the votes for MDB are considered legitimate manifestations against the regime. But besides acknowledging the number of votes for ARENA, it is essential to know who the people were who ran for office and received these votes, since the vote is not oriented only to the party, but largely by the voter's recognition of the candidate. In other words, it is important that ARENA candidates not only represented the 1964 movement and the new regime, but also had ties to their constituencies that dated far prior to 1964 and represented much more.

The lack of studies on ARENA is thus worthy of note, but understandable. The historiography of the political parties created under Brazil's dictatorship incorporates into its discourse (acritically) the critiques and slogans used by ARENA's political opponents. One example was labelling ARENA as the "Yes Sir! Party" during confrontations with members of the MDB caucus in the National Congress. According to historian Rodrigo Patto de Sá Motta, MDB was known as the "Yes! Party" and the ARENA as the "Yes Sir! Party", meaning that both "yielded to power, but that ARENA did so much more subserviently and less shamefacedly" (Motta, 1999, p. 118).

Some of the well-known political authors even question whether ARENA could actually be considered a political party. The pioneering study by Maria do Carmo Campello de Souza makes some references to ARENA, using the notion of "pseudo-party" coined by Juan Linz. This is because one of the characteristics of dictatorships is purportedly the inability of parties to participate in formulating national alternatives, thus losing one of their fundamental attributions.[19] But other elements add to this view of a "pseudo-party". According to Maria Dalva Gil Kinzo, for example, the principal characteristic of ARENA and MDB was the diversity of its members' party origins, which was not merely "a natural consequence of the artificial way in which the two-party system was created, but also reflected the lack of clarity in the ideological and representative character of the old political parties" (Kinzo, 1988, p. 32). In another study, Lúcia Klein identifies ARENA as "a gigantic, shapeless, and unstructured machine, [since] rather than a political party, ARENA was actually an aggregate of political currents" (Klein, 1978, p. 82). According to Philippe Schmitter, Brazil's pre-1964 party system was destroyed and replaced by "artificial entities with no roots identified by the people" (Schmitter, 1973, pp. 211–212). Bolívar Lamounier and Raquel Meneguello, in the 1980s, stated that "ARENA was as recent and artificial and especially as powerless as MDB" (Lamounier, 1986, p. 67). Such analyses are marked by the idea of the party's artificiality, whether due to its limited influence on government or the diversity of its members' party origins. That is, ARENA's proposals are always characterized via absence, of what it was not, of what it lacked, and of what it failed to do. The question of what ARENA was and how it acted remains to be answered. The assumption is that ARENA did not act and did not exist, because it never really became a party.

However, we should understand that this literature tends to observe the post-1965 parties through a macroscopic or nominal approach, in the sense that the party names and acronyms really underwent changes. Altering the focus of analysis and understanding the parties as groups consisting of individuals socialized under previous political organizations opens up a new avenue for study.[20] While the acronym ARENA was recent and may not have echoed in the people's minds, the leaders that formed the party represented the cream of the country's politicians at the time. Therefore, if ARENA was invented by the regime, its members were not, and the majority boasted long careers in party politics, both before and during the years from 1945 to 1964. Many of them had served successive terms of various elected offices, so one cannot fail to acknowledge their visibility and representativeness in the population.

This negative image produced and consolidated by pundits (both journalists and academics) became part of the history of ARENA itself and the dictatorship. However, one cannot understand the party except from the perspective of preservation of the representative system and as one of the characteristics of the dictatorship that helped maintain the country's institutional continuity. As Bolívar Lamounier suggests, the representative system was preserved "within institutional parameters that not even the military could allow themselves to completely ignore or distort" (Lamounier, 1987, p. 56). And according to Maria Dalva Gil Kinzo, the characteristic of the Brazilian dictatorship that made it a unique case was precisely the fact that the military *dissolved* the old party system and *created* a new one in its place.[21]

Along this line of thought, the literature on the Brazilian dictatorship focuses mainly on the years 1964, 1968, and 1974. It mostly emphasizes certain themes in the 1964 movement, highlighting the ousting of President João Goulart, Institutional Act No. 5 (AI-5), the armed resistance, détente (*abertura*), and the role of the Brazilian Democratic Movement (MDB) under the dictatorship. MDB stands out due to its electoral victory in 1974 and its action in the 1980s, by this time under the new name PMDB, contemporary with the expectations for re-democratization. The memory that surfaces in this historiography is that of the facts that marked the violent enforcement of authoritarian rule and the opposition to it. The regime's daily routine and its attempts at gaining legitimacy have received little attention. Stripped of a major part of their political power and subordinated to the military, the pro-regime civilians have also scarcely been seen in terms of their participation in the dictatorship.

The more recent historiography on this period includes studies that seek to demystify a "simplified architecture" of the dictatorship, to use an expression by Daniel Aarão Reis Filho. In most of these studies, one of the fundamental points is the notion that the understanding of this period has been informed directly by the social memory that was consolidated later, under democracy. Generally speaking, Daniel Aarão Reis Filho identifies in the memory constructed on the dictatorship the thesis that "Brazilian society experienced the dictatorship as a nightmare that needs to be exorcized, that is, society has never had anything to do with the dictatorship" (Aarão Reis Filho, 2000, p. 9). He states:

[Brazilian] society repositioned itself as if it had always massively opposed the dictatorship. Society reframed its relations with the dictatorship, which appeared as the object of permanent hostility. Erased from memory was the broad mass movement which, through the Marches of Family with God and for Freedom, lent social legitimacy for installing the dictatorship. Vanished were the bridges and complicities between society and the dictatorship throughout the 1970s which, at the limit, constituted the foundations for the process of détente itself: slow, secure, and gradual.[22]

Analysing the press coverage on the occasion of the 30th anniversary celebration of 1968, the author thus shows that "the rebellion played an outstanding role in hiding the how's and why's of the visceral relations established between Brazilian society and the dictatorship. Remembering the rebellion against the dictatorship is a convenient formula for hiding what was reconciled with it" (Aarão Reis Filho, 1998, p. 4).

Along the same line that aims to complexify the relations between Brazilian society and the dictatorship, the myth of an oppositionist press was also discussed by Beatriz Kushnir. In her thesis, she shows the ambiguities present in the newsrooms of Brazil's mainstream newspapers, demonstrating how studies on censorship have focused solely on the issue of resistance to the dictatorship, creating

A duel in which the censor is either a tyrant, an executioner, or else an incompetent – intellectually unprepared for the task. Meanwhile, the journalist is described as performing heroic acts both large and small, defying the oppressor. Not everything is explained by this Manichean game.[23]

Meanwhile, the view of the dictatorship that Brazil's military attempt to defend and depict appears on the one hand as a competing point of view with this construction, while simultaneously corroborating the thesis that Brazilian society does not want to admit any compromise with the regime. This is shown in books by Maria Celina D'Araújo, Gláucio Ary Dillon Soares, and Celso Castro, which conducted a broad set of interviews with Ministers of the Army, the Superior Military Tribunal (STM), and the National Intelligence Service (SNI), cabinet chiefs, presidential advisors, and strategic individuals in assembling and acting in the intelligence system from 1964 to 1984.[24] Maria Celina D'Araújo recalls that "they all viewed the act of speaking with professional researchers as a possibility for revisiting the meaning of their past and for reassessing, in the present, the role of the Armed Forces in power" (D'Araújo, 1994, p. 151). In this study, one of the most pressing questions was the perception, among these members of the military, of a feeling of defeat in relation to the type of memory that society built concerning them. That is, in the work of the military's memory concerning the 1964 movement, they "attempt to overlook the partnership they had with society, a partnership that was quickly forgotten as soon as they left power" (D'Araújo, 1994, p. 158).

In the case of ARENA, the first sources pointing to a derisory picture of its political representativeness date to the authoritarian period, when the party was still in activity. More precisely, this started in the 1970s after the enactment of the so-called Party Loyalty Law, when ARENA began to be known as the "Yes Sir! Party". As often happens with such issues, one cannot say for certain who actually coined this label, but it is certain that members of the MDB congressional caucus used the expression often and persistently against their political opponents in ARENA. In the National Congress, in the verbal standoffs between leaders of the two parties, there are recurrent references to the "Yes Sir! Party" and some variations on the theme: "ARENA men always say yes",[25] the "I Agree Party",[26] and others. This was even a recurrent issue in the speeches by *Arenista* members of Congress, who attempted to respond to the criticism by the *Emedebistas* using the same terms.

Members of Congress from the MDB also referred to ARENA as the "government party", not simply in the sense of a party aligned with the regime, but in the sense of a party controlled by the government and with no autonomy whatsoever. This characterization was even the object of numerous debates, both in the National Congress and in national conventions of ARENA itself. Some members of ARENA admitted that they were not a "party in government", that they had no decision-making power in the Executive, which was an issue that needed to be resolved. But these same members of Congress in no way accepted the epithet of "government party", as a party devoid of autonomy.

For entirely different reasons from those of MDB and other areas of the opposition, the military also proffered many speeches deriding ARENA. The party was considered flawed and weak, as in speeches by Presidents Arthur da Costa e Silva and Ernesto Geisel. In certain situations, the military attacked ARENA violently, as in 1968, when the party failed to collaborate as expected in the episode of the vote to authorize purging Deputy Márcio Moreira Alves.[27] At the time, General Costa e Silva simply derided the party, rather than admitting that *Arenista* members of Congress had voted against instructions from the

Executive. The military's view of ARENA was also the object of a masterly chronicle by playwright and journalist Nelson Rodrigues in his daily column in O Globo on October 14, 1968, two months before Institutional Act No. 5 was decreed. The chronicle's main character is an Army colonel who explains pedagogically to a friend (the narrator) the country's prevailing political situation:

> He insisted that never, ever, have the Armed Forces had so little influence. And he gave a real-life example: "Just take ARENA. What do you say, my friend? ARENA is nothing. You can blow out ARENA like you blow out a little birthday candle. Am I wrong? My friend, you want to do a test? Go to Congress. Go out on the floor while they're in session, and shout, 'The cops are coming!' You know what would happen?" And he took a long, dramatic pause . . . Now the colonel was beside himself, hopping up and down: "You'll see the *Arenistas* rushing out, jumping out the windows, never to be seen again." As if regretting his histrionic overstatement, and panting from his false rage, he lowered his tone and added: "And we believe in ARENA. The Armed Forces believe in ARENA. The government believes in ARENA. ARENA is listened to. And if they listen to ARENA, anything is possible." He takes a deep breath and concludes, "And nobody suspects that you can't make a Brazil out of ARENAs".[28]

The story contains a mixture of scorn and threat: "You can blow out ARENA like you blow out a little birthday candle." Yet the military's purported singlemindedness did not stand up, and the military did not "blow out" the ARENA even after Institutional Act No. 5. In this case, the political scorn for ARENA is permeated again by moral derision, evidenced by the association with a band of thieves running from the police: "You'll see the *Arenistas* rushing out, jumping out the windows." There is also tremendous irony in the relationship built between the military and ARENA: "If they listen to ARENA, anything is possible."

Curiously, it was *Movimento,* one of the most prestigious alternative newspapers, with ties to MDB, that published one of the cleverest analyses of this process of deriding ARENA as a political party:

> Poor ARENA, it's tied to the whipping post. If détente is doing poorly, it's ARENA's fault. If the government can't count on many votes, it's ARENA's fault, because the party failed to communicate the official line. ARENA (the ruthless harangue proceeds) has no competent leaders. It's divided. It failed to renew its membership. It failed to attract

students and workers to its ranks. Having failed to reflect the people's aspirations and not always properly interpreting the government's thinking, it became a useless and impracticable party.

One cannot deny that some of these accusations are true. But is ARENA the only one to blame?[29]

The article "Party or Scapegoat" by journalist Sérgio Buarque (namesake of the renowned Brazilian historian) raises a series of questions that will be addressed in this book. These include the operation by the military to lock ARENA "in the pillory" during the dictatorship and to construct a memory (by now after re-democratization) that leaves ARENA in limbo.

Thus, the most recent studies on the civilian-military dictatorship point to the importance of a memory consolidated during Brazil's re-democratization and transition out of authoritarian rule. This was the construction of a memory with a view towards the return to democratic rule. Thus, one of the central aspects of this memory is Brazilian society's relationship with democracy. As highlighted, the predominant idea in this construction is that Brazilian society has always been democratic. What follows from this is a major difficulty in acknowledging the support by part of Brazilian society for the 1964 movement and the civilian-military dictatorship that prevailed in the country for twenty years. The image of ARENA as a joke is being understood here as one of the elements in the above-mentioned "simplified architecture" in the memory of the dictatorship in Brazil, to the extent that, through ridicule, the attempt is to demoralize one of the links between state and society. To take the "joke" more seriously means to help achieve a better understanding of the relations between state and society in Brazil's contemporary history.

3 Political party or scapegoat?

The history of political parties in Brazil is a history of successive interventions by authoritarian governments of various stripes. These include the Revolution of 1930, that of the *Estado Novo* in 1937, that of the dictatorship through Institutional Act No. 2 (AI-2) in 1965, and on November 29, 1979, with the last extinction of parties at the initiative of the National Executive, passed by the National Congress. Bolívar Lamounier and Raquel Meneguello postulate that there can be no doubt that the interventions in successive party systems in activity in the country, since the first formation in the Brazilian Empire (1822–1889), are one of the causes (although they can also be a consequence) of the party instability[30] prevailing in Brazil's political experiences.

According to Serge Berstein,[31] the conditions for the elaboration of a country's political culture are the result of a long historical process, so time and the events experienced in it are elements in the modification or affirmation of a given political culture. The successive extinctions of political parties in Brazil certainly hinder the consolidation of a positive image of the party institution in Brazilian society. In addition, the interpretations – academic and otherwise – of the political parties' history has reinforced the instability factor for these organizations, far more than the fact that they were extinguished by authoritarian decrees. This highlights more the parties' weakness than the arbitrariness of the regimes that eliminated them by decree. Notably, for example, many researchers referred to the parties extinguished in 1965 as "traditional" parties, since this label implies a negative judgment, thereby failing to emphasize that the AI-2 eliminated the existing parties while understating the violence of the destruction of those organizations.

The issue of political representation's authenticity transcends the sphere of any particular party and always occupies a large share of the discussion on representative systems in Brazil. This issue has always been present, in the reflections by the politicians of the Empire (1822–1889) and the Republic (since 1889), in the authoritarian ideologues of the 1930s, and in the discourse of the intellectuals in the 1950s and 60s. It is an issue that frequently traverses the entire Brazilian political spectrum.

This discourse is generally mobilized at moments of uncertainty or moments of attack on political representation, as a way of delegitimizing the prevailing institutional solutions. The argument of artificiality is related to a greater or lesser intelligibility and legitimacy that is intended to be assigned to the parties or forms of political representation. The authoritarians of 1937 and 1965 mobilized, at both moments, the argument of representation's authenticity in order to conduct party reforms. In 1937, after the coup d'état, all the existing political parties were extinguished and the National Congress was closed. But under such reforms, the political parties' status changes, from "an artificial faction, disaggregating the national interest" in 1937 to guarantee the "representative system's authenticity"[32] in 1965.

One possible solution for studying political parties in Brazil, given this political culture that reiterates the parties' lack of representativeness, is to historicize the debates in order to avoid falling into the common-sense interpretation of the inadequacy or impossibility of consolidating democratic institutions in the country. This may even be an advantage over studies by political scientists, who often generalize and compare party systems from different epochs.

The development of liberal political institutions is a classic theme in Brazilian political thinking. Both liberal and authoritarian thinkers from the 1920s to the 1940s and historians and social scientists from the 1940s to the 1970s questioned the possibility of incorporating liberal values into Brazil's political practices.[33] In the First Republic, the oligarchies monopolized the parliamentary political space, and the political parties only became broader organizational instruments starting in 1945, so they are thus a recent historical phenomenon in Brazil.[34] Therefore, the generation of politicians that founded the UDN, PSD, PTB, and other parties during that period can be considered the first generation of Brazilian politicians to participate in a more significant representative system. However, it was not unusual for those leaders and the entire political spectrum to turn to the military in order to conduct specific interventions. To a major extent, this is the source of the Armed Forces' so-called "tutorship power", tested at various moments in Brazil's history.

Many studies on the political parties in activity from 1945 to 1965 have attempted in one way or another to understand the process that led to the dictatorship. Such studies generally emphasize a series of factors such as the lack of institutionalization of the political party system, the absence of voters' party identification, and electoral fragmentation, ultimately suggesting a party system that was already falling apart in the early 1960s. An initial reference for this tendency is the thesis by Maria do Carmo Campello de Souza, dated to the 1970s, whose understanding of the regime inaugurated in 1946 and its crisis assumes a consistent diagnosis of the party system's lack of institutionalization. According to the author, this fundamental political fact can only be understood in the framework of the relations between state and political parties in Brazil.[35]

In her study of the PSD, Lúcia Hippólito also contends that the party system was already in a process of disaggregation. According to the author, when the PSD oligarchy opted to destroy its Youth Wing (Ala Moça), it moved away from the centre of the party system, which was not occupied by any other party or coalition. Having abandoned the centre, a centrifugal tendency took hold of the system; the extremes became irresistible poles of attraction, and "thus, starting in the late 1950s, the party system's disaggregation began. The PSD was fragmented internally, with dissidents on the left and the right; the party lost the minimum conditions of internal cohesion to lead the political process" (Hippólito, 1985, p. 255). Thus, for Lúcia Hippólito, the extinction of the political parties by the AI-2 meant the end of the agony for a party system whose death had already been predicted.

In the more recent production in the social sciences, some authors have questioned this interpretation that the democratic regime crumbled due to the crisis in the party system of 1945–1964. Antônio Lavareda, for example, takes an opposite position through an analysis of the stability of the formats in the electoral contests and a high level of party identification among voters, contending that Brazil's party system was undergoing a process of consolidation.[36] According to Argelina Figueiredo, there was an institutional break due to the political actors' radicalization and disregard for negotiation via Congress, signs of an instrumental concept of democracy shared then by the parties.[37] Such interpretations thus suggest a new dimension for understanding the post-1945 party system and the process that culminated in the elimination of the parties in 1965, with the creation of the two-party system.

The interpretation of the AI-2 as the interruption of a process of consolidation of the post-1945 party system opens a new direction for understanding the difficulties of the parties created under the dictatorship, as well as for evaluating the tensions between ARENA and the government. Maria Helena Moreira Alves highlights that the extinction of the parties in 1965 dismantled the opposition[38], but not only the opposition, since the AI-2 also dismantled the politicians' own organization as interlocutors of the 1964 movement. By extinguishing the parties, the AI-2 created new conflicts, since it strengthened the Executive and created an imbalance among groups that supported the movement.

Analyses of the post-1965 political system, mainly those performed prior to 1974, provided sketches of what was to be a new authoritarian political model, in which the liberal mechanisms of representation were completely marginalized. An article illustrating this perspective is *The Portugalization of Brazil*[39], by Philippe Schmitter. In the early 1970s, the author observes that participants in the 1964 movement, self-proclaimed defenders of the West and its forms of representation, were abandoning democratic liberalization to adopt permanent institutionalization of the dictatorship.

In the late 1970s, Francisco Weffort, Bolívar Lamounier, and Wanderley Guilherme dos Santos drafted proposals for studies on political liberalism taking political actors and authors into account. The aim was to take political action itself as the point of departure, understood as ideas translated into behaviours and ideas as political ideas that orient political action.[40] These authors triggered debates on political liberalism and authoritarianism, addressing the dictatorship and considering the broader framework of Brazilian political thinking.

Francisco Weffort, in his analysis of the 1946–1964 regime, endeavoured to value the institutional mechanisms of democracy and show the contrast between this regime and that of the First Republic, which was openly oligarchical.[41] When discussing the strategies of the Brazilian Communist Party (PCB) during the 1946–1964 period, Weffort criticized the instrumentalization of the concept of democracy and the lack of questioning of the regime's undemocratic aspects, besides pointing to the regime's preference for seeking support through direct mobilization of the population rather than by the latter's participation through institutional channels.

On the tendency toward instrumental conceptions of democracy, Weffort stated that therein lies:

> the 'grand misunderstanding' of freedom and democracy, which are never defined in and of themselves, but always as a direct and immediate function of the social or economic interests they express. Hence also our democratic imagination's peculiar difficulty in concretely considering the relevance of democracy's institutional mechanisms.[42]

Bolívar Lamounier noted that for a long time, Brazil's historiography and social sciences considered institutional issues as mere formalisms.[43] In the studies on the dictatorship, Lamounier showed that most of the analyses developed in *Authoritarian Brazil*[44] underestimated the importance of the liberal-representative antecedents for electoral processes and the formation of parties.[45]

Starting with the impact of the 1974 elections, the analyses of the regime began to devote more attention to the party organizations and elections, since the outcome of the Senate race indicated that it could mean a path to political détente. In 1980s, in light of the expectations on re-democratization, political scientists especially continued the studies on elections and the party system prevailing since 1965, emphasizing MDB's electoral possibilities.[46]

According to Lamounier, an in-depth analysis of the factors that enabled détente

> Should begin with the Brazilian ideological and institutional legacy, whose authoritarian nature has often been highlighted, but which also harbours important liberal components, so for that us a lasting authoritarian system is inconceivable, much less a repressive autocracy like that of the Médici era.[47]

Other political scientists such as Sebastião Velasco e Cruz and Carlos Estevam Martins showed that in 1970 and 1971, some pro-regime politicians such as Milton Campos, Herbert Levy, Petrônio Portella, and Magalhães Pinto were calling for adequate treatment of the institutional political issue given the political system's high degree of unpredictability.[48]

In her thesis on MDB, Maria Dalva Gil Kinzo identified specificities of the Brazilian dictatorship in contrast with various experiences in other Latin American dictatorships, including the fact that the Brazilian military never completely banned partisan political activities and even created a new party system. But Kinzo contends that "the military failed in their attempt to create a political organization capable of serving as the basis for sustaining the regime" (Kinzo, 1988, p. 224). In my study of the ARENA, Kinzo's reflection will unfold in various directions. First, not all the military and politicians that supported the 1964 movement wanted the same party model. Second, not all the successive military governments sought to strengthen their party.

The studies thus far have analysed the dictatorship from the perspective of the military and the opposition. This study proposes to analyse the regime and its party system from the perspective of the ARENA politicians. This approach stems from the understanding that a representative democracy is consolidated through a historical process, and that part of this process is the incorporation of its rules by the political actors. In this sense, the activity of the politicians themselves and the disputes for the exercise of political activity, observing those involved in each conjuncture, becomes an excellent object of study. What are the pro-government politicians' expectations and frustrations in relation to this political undertaking, assessed from the onset as high-risk? What are the affinities and clashes with the military? What action does the party take in this context?

In the development of relations between members of ARENA and the Executive, perceptible in debates and speeches, the issue of professional politics was always in the focus. Both the politicians and the military drew on various categories such as the *political class* and the *political field* to refer to *Arenista* city councilmen, deputies, and senators. There was thus a marked distinction between pro-government civilians and the military, on both sides, based on the different insertion of political activity in the lives of these groups. The military were extending their political activity beyond the military institutions, but they basically continued to pursue their military careers. In recent interviews one realizes that even when acting in the civilian sphere of the public administration, the relations among the military were based on typically military hierarchies. Meanwhile, the pro-regime civilians were mostly men with longstanding political careers.

Max Weber is one of the founding references for the study of politics as a profession. In this project I will prioritize this reference based on conceptual discussions by Pierre Bourdieu and Michel Offerlé, who further developed premises that are present in Weber's work. Importantly, this perspective gives autonomy and contends that it is

> A mistake to underestimate the autonomy and specific efficacy of everything that takes place in the *political field* and to reduce political history to a sort of epiphenomenal manifestation of the economic and social forces of which the political actors are purportedly the puppets, in a sense.[49]

The politicians are thus viewed not as puppets, but as men dedicated to political representation, conceived as a specific object of study that cannot be reduced to economic interests. The concept of *field* assumes that every social production has a particular *language* or logic, created by groups with a particular social insertion, certain functions, and specific interests.[50]

Pierre Bourdieu and Michel Offerlé resume the key idea based on which Max Weber studies politicians: "one can live for politics or from politics". Or, as Bourdieu prefers, "one can live from politics with the condition of living for politics" (Bourdieu, 1989, pp. 176–177). Weber showed that politics as a profession does not appear spontaneously.[51] For a long time, those who occupied public offices considered themselves enlightened amateurs, practicing a cultivated activity. The inherited notoriety and the network of clientele founded the social authority of noteworthy figures who were economically independent and available and could dedicate themselves to representation as an activity.

Politics has not always been as we know it today. There was a historical process of specialization through which a properly political field was formed as a space for action by professionals who have politics as a life project and a source of income. The *professional politician* is a product of the 20th century, intrinsically linked to the concept of modern political parties. In the current study, the politician is seen as someone who has a political career or intends to follow one; he belongs to a political party and participates in its organizational work and/or as an advisor; and he is available to fill political positions in the governments elected by his party. Politicians are political entrepreneurs of a particular type, i.e., they are distinct from warriors and administrators.[52] Politicians act in the *political field* and participate in the process of building this same field. According to Michel Offerlé, the analysis of the consolidation of democracy assumes first that representative democracy should be viewed as a regime in which representation is conducted through political parties, regardless (at this level of analysis) of whether they are substantively representative of society: a sort of institutional premise. Second, representative democracy is not necessarily a logical consequence of individuals' mobilization, but the result of the work of mobilization performed by *professional politicians*.

Thus, the study of representative democracy includes the analysis of the process of legitimation by which politicians have claimed the monopoly over access to political competition and have been granted it, but never entirely.[53] Over the course of this historical process, these men became professional politicians. From this theoretical perspective, the legitimation of democracy is not inevitable. On the contrary, it is a process of constant convincing and mobilization, tasks in which professional politicians play a prime role.

Meanwhile, politicians act through parties. For Offerlé, conceiving of history is to think of persons' action in the world, and "to think of party action is to think of the encounter between individuals endowed with social and political properties and a collective that they help make exist and make act" (Offerlé, 1987, p. 88). In this approach, the relations between party members are the central object of the analysis, since a party is not a thing. It should be analysed as a *field of forces*, that is, as a set of objective relations imposed on everyone who enters it and participates in it. Life in society involves a permanent interrelationship between fields. Professional politicians are in permanent competition for political authority, for intending to legislate on the limits of political action and on the legitimate way of resolving problems. Professional politicians are also in confrontation with other entrepreneurs in the political field: enlightened amateurs, political journalists, commentators, and political scientists.

The concept of *political field* has its origins in the historical experience of representative democracy. The concept thus refers to a given configuration of this same field. Bourdieu points to one of the foundations of this configuration, "except for periods of crisis, the production of forms of perception and politically active and legitimate expression is the monopoly of professionals and is thus subject to the inherent constraints and limitations to the functioning of the political field" (Bourdieu, 1989, p. 166). Thus, moments of crisis are precisely those in which the legitimacy of professional politicians' monopoly is at stake. Thus, historically, challenges to this monopoly can take the form of apolitical or anti-congressional movements, among others.

Positions and attitudes by politicians depend on the *political problematics*, on the field of strategic possibilities offered up for individuals' choice, on the positions actually occupied, and on the positions actually proposed in the field. In the political field, "nothing, not even in the institutions or agents, nor in the acts or speeches they produce, makes sense except relationally, through the play of oppositions and distinctions" (Bourdieu, 1989, p. 179).

The topic of the consolidation of representative democracy thus refers to the study of the political career's legitimation. In Brazil, the years 1964 to 1979 were times of widespread disputes and distrust in relation to the professional politicians' action: distrust by participants in the 1964 movement towards the opposition politicians, by the military in relation to most politicians, and by most of society towards both the *Arenistas* and the *Emedebistas*.

The years 1964 to 1979 will be seen as a time of crisis whose main characteristic was the loss of the monopoly over representation by professional politicians and ostensive action by the military in the political field. This was a historical configuration in which the field suffered major limitations by agents that were external to it. The proposal here is precisely to investigate how part of the professional politicians at a given moment in the internal dispute agreed to encourage the intervention in the political field, placing their monopoly in jeopardy on a basis never previously tested, that is, risking the legitimacy of the political career in a very broad and profound sense.

In the relations between politicians and the military, members of Congress also have a properly political culture that remains inaccessible to agents external to this field. This is due mainly to the complexity of social relations constituting the political field and the tendency of politicians to associate mainly with other professionals. Meanwhile, the military do not share this properly political culture, rather obeying a set of rules proper to the military corporations. But within the study's scope, there were also cases of military figures that entered the professional political career, joined parties, and ran for elective office.

Some of these issues correspond largely to the approaches proposed by micro-history. Italian historian Giovanni Levi emphasizes that "individuals constantly create their own identities, and the groups define themselves according to conflicts and solidarities which nevertheless cannot be presumed *a priori*, but result from the dynamics that are the object of analysis" (Levi, 1992, p. 152). From this point of view, fundamental importance is assigned to the activities, to the forms of behaviour, and to the institutions providing the framework within which their specific logics can be adequately understood.

This approach suggests a new dimension in the study of institutions, different from that of traditional political history, since it is not about the history of institutions *per se*, but about understanding individuals' participation as a constitutive part of institutions. In the case of political institutions, as Tocqueville recalled, "although the '*moeurs et habitudes*' constitute the most profound repository of democracy, what is immediately accessible to human intervention are the laws and institutions".[54] With this conceptual backing, one can address the theme of democracy through its more formal face, namely the representative system, seeking to also endow it with an individual dimension. This procedure thus implies the existence of personal choices based on individuals' trajectories.

Studies on political parties have revealed how their members' behaviour was diversified according to the type of relations maintained with the institution. These relations showed that the greater the political capital accumulated by individuals before joining the party (along with other types of capital from other fields, such as the intellectual field), the greater the person's autonomy in relation to the party. Inversely, as noted by Bourdieu, "their dependence is all the more complete, the weaker the economic and cultural capital they possess before they join the party" (Bourdieu, 1989, p. 198). Thus, one should distinguish politicians from their careers, measuring their personal trajectory and their relations with the political party as fundamental variables.

Politicians participate in various institutions that form their values and practices and are characterized by socialization in different institutions such as the parties, the Chamber of Deputies, and the Federal Senate, as well as in the public administration in general. This is in addition to their previous or specific background in certain political groups such as churches, schools, and even regionalisms. Based on this background, these individuals perceived the events that modified the *political field* during Brazil's dictatorship, such as the extinction of parties, the founding of new party organizations, and relations with an Executive consisting mainly of military officers.

The historiography of Brazil's dictatorship has heavily emphasized the arbitrary nature of the electoral and party legislation, the objective of which was purportedly to favour the government party, ARENA. However, the field of electoral and party legislation can be viewed as a field of disputes, not only between government and opposition, but in which diverse interests were vying with each other: the National Executive, the military, senators, deputies, and ARENA and MDB party representatives. The enforcement of a series of dictatorial decrees modifying the country's political institutions not only impacted citizens' lives, but directly affected the politicians. These interventions produced different and very specific meanings in people's lives. References to the careers of ARENA politicians may be tedious and repetitive for readers, but a fundamental part of the thesis is to show that those individuals' participation in the party was the result of their previous experience in other party organizations. This is central to the perspective that those who constitute and shape political institutions are the persons that participate in them directly.

Importantly, some military officers and jurists that drafted various electoral and party laws under the dictatorship attempted to turn Brazil's political past into *tabula rasa*. On the one hand, conceiving the extinction of party organizations and stripping popular leaders of their rights and/or declaring them ineligible, and on the other, fomenting the creation of new party organizations that assimilated individuals that were previously alien to the political field. The idea of extinguishing the political parties with Institutional Act No. 2 was to begin from scratch, to make *tabula rasa* of the country's partisan past. However, the Archives of the ARENA National Committee reveal a recurrent line of argument based on membership in the extinct parties.

Limiting the analysis only to the arbitrary measures would prevent a more exact idea of the politicians' reaction to such measures. In other words, the idea is to assess not only whether there was support for such measures, but what they meant for the persons involved directly in the institutions under intervention. By seeking to identify the politicians' view concerning the impacts of the 1964 movement on the political field, one realizes the diversity of shades in the various interests involved, indicating that ARENA and the government did not form a monolithic bloc.

CHAPTER
2

A Time of Conspiracy and Misgivings (1964–1966)

"— Your Excellencies have a mandate whose authenticity is contested".[1]

Adauto Lúcio Cardoso

The authenticity of Brazil's liberal representative political institutions has been contested numerous times in the country's history, both in speeches by government officials and in studies by sociologists, political scientists, and historians. There have been recurrent allegations of the parties' political bankruptcy or lack of authenticity, especially when they serve to legitimize interventions in the party system. However, from 1964 to 1968 these institutions were directly impacted by authoritarian measures: the deposing of the country's democratically elected president, the elimination of political rights and resulting loss of office for members of Congress, the extinguishing of the existing political parties, "indirect" elections, the municipalities' loss of autonomy, and even the forced recess of the National Congress. Institutional Act No. 5 became such an important turning point in the dictatorship's timeline that certain previous measures have been largely overlooked in studies on the dictatorship and its memory. Yet from the deposing of President João Goulart to the AI-5 on December 13, 1968, the intervention in the country's liberal representative institutions did not go unnoticed by the members of Congress and leaders that had participated in the 1964 movement. When it became clear that the military intervention would not be limited to ousting João Goulart and that the foundations were being laid for consolidating a new regime, various politicians that had supported the coup d'état began to debate the new juridical measures created by the Executive. Many continued in their political careers, some retired of their own accord, and others were stripped of their political rights and prevented from continuing in public life.

1 Opposition to the João Goulart government

Throughout the dictatorship, various politicians were jettisoned from the decision-making centre after having in participated activities in the conspiracies running up to the 1964 movement. From 1946 to 1964, politicians and the military maintained close relations all across the political spectrum. From the most conservative parties to the Communist Party of Brazil (PCB),[2] underground since 1947, they all had military members among their ranks and sympathizers. Some officers even ran for president, like Brigadier Eduardo Gomes, nominated twice by the UDN, in 1945 and 1950, Marshall Eurico Dutra, who was elected in 1945 by the PSD/PTB coalition, and Marshall Henrique Lott, who ran for president on the PSD ticket in 1959. His candidacy was strengthened by his role in 1955, when he guaranteed that Juscelino Kubitschek took office through a "legalist coup", besides his work in the Ministry of War in the Kubitschek government, guaranteeing the democratic order against the military rebellions in Jacareacanga and Aragarças in 1958. The appeals to the barracks were not limited to the UDN, but also came from PSD and PTB.[3]

Beginning in 1963, contact became more intense between UDN leaders and the top brass, with more active participation by Admiral Heck and Generals Castello Branco, Olímpio Mourão, Ademar de Queiróz, Odilo Denys, Cordeiro de Farias, and Arthur da Costa e Silva, as well as by *Udenistas* like Pedro Aleixo, Bilac Pinto, Paulo Sarazate, and Magalhães Pinto.[4] The conspiracy between *Udenistas* and high-ranking military officers from the Superior War College (ESG) involved not only "hardliners" from the UDN, but also the "liberals" or "historical legal experts", like Afonso Arinos, Adauto Cardoso, Aliomar Baleeiro, and Daniel Krieger.[5] In interviews in the 1990s, military men like Octávio Costa, a lieutenant-colonel in 1964, recalled the power of fascination these leaders exerted over them.[6] As President of Brazil, Castello Branco named several *Udenistas* to work in his government. He was a self-proclaimed "died-in-the-wool *Udenista*" and admirer of Carlos Lacerda and Adauto Cardoso, with whom he maintained friendly relations.[7]

One of the arguments by the participants in the 1964 movement for deposing João Goulart was the defence of legality. In 1964, Adauto Cardoso highlighted his "35 years in the courts of law after 10 years on the floor of Congress"[8] to alert his fellow deputies that the Goulart government was challenging the authenticity of their mandates. On the eve of the coup, on March 30, 1964, in the Chamber of Deputies, Adauto Cardoso unleashed his zeal against President Goulart: "In the history of Brazil there have never been presidents that have held rallies, a presidential experience that makes contact with the people on the streets or city squares,"[9] except during the *Estado Novo* (Getúlio Vargas' dictatorship). Since 1963, Adauto Cardoso had been attacking President João Goulart's policy of mobilizing the population in mass rallies organized by the PTB. For Cardoso, the issue was a veritable war with the objective "of sustaining the superior authenticity of His Excellency the President's representation, the people's representation, as opposed to our [congressional] representation".[10] The chosen alternative in this war was to abandon democratic principles in the name of the liberal institutions themselves. This wager resulted in less-than-ideal consequences even for some of the politicians that supported deposing João Goulart.

2 Brazilian politicians stripped of their political rights in 1964

Already in the first days of April 1964, one of the main issues debated in the National Congress was the purging of various members of Congress. Many politicians that supported the 1964 movement participated in the purges. An analysis of the press coverage and the debates in the Chamber of Deputies and Senate reveals the existence of various positions on the matter. Some openly defended the purges and organized lists of fellow deputies and senators that they felt should be expelled from Congress.

Deputy Herbert Levy (UDN – SP) proposed revoking political rights as part of the movement to "reclaim" democracy, and he was seconded by other deputies. Yet the majority of the UDN caucus in the Chamber of Deputies was against Herbert Levy's proposal to purge members of Congress or to organize a petition to expel certain members.[11] Deputy José Sarney (UDN – MA) opposed the position, claiming to be a liberal democrat, the reason he had originally joined the UDN.[12] Deputy Adauto Cardoso (UDN – GB) stated in an interview with *Jornal do Brasil*, concerning a purported list of 40 members of Congress to be expelled, that this was "so ridiculous and such an affront to the dignity of Congress that it can only be a provocation".[13]

The same news story stated that the *Clube Militar* (Military Club) intended to propose that certain members of Congress who were considered "leftists" be removed from office. Likewise, São Paulo Governor Adhemar de Barros (PSP) reportedly claimed that it was indispensable to remove the "leftists" from office in order or the "revolution" to achieve its goal. Citing the members of the Nationalist Congressional Front (*Frente Parlamentar Nacionalista*), which had supported the deposed government, he said they should be tried for crimes against national security.[14]

In the Chamber of Deputies, Amaral Neto (UDN – GB) and Gil Veloso (UDN – ES) gathered signatures for a petition to the *Mesa Diretora* [equivalent to "Presiding Officers" of the Chamber, headed by that body's president] requesting the purging of members of Congress that had been cabinet members in the Goulart government, like Abelardo Jurema, Oliveira Brito, Expedito Machado, Oswaldo Lima Filho, Wilson Fadul, General Jair Dantas Ribeiro, Santiago Dantas, José Ermírio de Moraes, and Pedro Calmon.[15] According to the newspapers, Deputy Amaral Neto received requests from 50 deputies to add names of politicians to the list of purges he had organized.[16] Meanwhile, Deputy Oscar Dias Corrêa (UDN – MG) proclaimed on the Chamber floor that it was up to the new government "to restore a house in ruins, clean it, sweep it out, and purge those infecting it".[17]

The press published the rumour that the decision by the UDN caucus to repudiate such attempts to remove deputies from office, according to the proposal presented by Herbert Levy, could result in the closing of Congress.[18] Other members of Congress were debating about drafting a bill to regulate the matter.[19] In some states the purges were decided by vote in the state legislatures.[20] As denounced by Senators Aloísio de Carvalho (PL – BA) and Josaphat Marinho (no party affiliation – BA), the mayors of many towns in Bahia were being purged violently and without due process.[21]

Meanwhile, representatives of the PTB in Congress attempted to reveal the contradictions in the positions by the *Udenistas*, sometimes heralds of political freedoms, other times defenders of ousting the "leftists" from office. Deputy Doutel de Andrade (PTB – SC) claimed to find it rather strange that part of UDN would remain silent, given the "atrocities" that were being perpetrated:

> The party leaders that were committed to all the hullabaloo are beginning to show signs of panic given the threat of a dictatorship [...] they're livid [...] with a heavy conscience, shamelessly proclaiming the need to restore the country to legality. . . . May they have the courage to face the tiger they created and that threatens to devour them![22]

Deputy Milton Dutra (PTB – RS) proposed that deputies should leave the Chamber floor to avoid being forced to submit to the military officers that were demanding the suspension of congressional immunities.[23]

Nevertheless, the first list of purges was published on April 10, with 102 names. Under orders from the *Comando Revolucionário* (Revolutionary Command), the president of the Chamber of Deputies purged these members and called up their alternates. According to the press, during that session the deputies from the PTB protested, and president Lenoir Vargas (PSD – SC) was nearly attacked, while the UDN caucus looked on in silence, with the exception of Aliomar Baleeiro (UDN – BA), who said he sensed "a scent of the *Estado Novo* in the Institutional Act".[24]

According to one news source, the first purges in the Chamber of Deputies sparked an uproar, with protests, tears, shouts, and gunshots. A deputy from the PTB was reported to have fired shorts in the Chamber halls during an argument with Deputy Milton Dutra (PTB – RS),[25] one of the signs of revolt in the face of the violence perpetrated against the dignity of Congress.

Deputy Milton Dutra appealed his case to the Presiding Officers of the Chamber of Deputies and announced that in order to reclaim his mandate he would appeal to all levels of government and even to the United Nations, where he would demand respect for the Universal Declaration of the Rights of Man, since he had been purged "with no grounds and without due process".[26] The members of Congress that had been purged intended to await the decision by the Committee on Constitution and Justice, appealing to the Human Rights Council.[27] However, in the committee, Deputy Djalma Marinho (UDN – RN) was consulted on the suspension of political rights and argued that the committee lacked the authority to speak on this ruling that had been handed down by the Executive.[28]

The debate on the first wave of purges created a controversy on the legality of removing members of Congress from office and the implications of the loss of their political rights. There were questions about whether the public offices and mandates would be suspended automatically, revealing the level of uncertainty in the direction taken by the new regime. The politicians were still debating under the terms of the rule of law, a perspective that was only to be lost gradually. For some time, the only possibility for confronting the purges would be through political solutions, but later not even this. To the extent that the regime consolidated its power, first the legal safeguards fell and then the possibilities for political negotiation.

In addition to the major institutional issues, there was another order of issues. The purges impacted the personal lives of deputies and their families. Many deputies from the PSD contended that the recently created Social Security Institute for Members of Congress should begin to pay pensions to the families of purged deputies.[29]

In late May 1964, after a veritable witch hunt in which many Brazilian politicians and trade unionists had been stripped of their political rights and dozens of members of Congress had been removed from office, an inventory began of the "abuses and violence" committed since April.[30] The President of Brazil himself and the General Inquiries Commission (CGI), nearly two months after the purges began, issued declarations that evidence was needed in order to revoke mandates.[31] Both the Chief of Staff, Luís Vianna Filho (UDN – BA), and the Minister of Justice, Milton Campos (UDN – MG), declared that purges were extreme measures that should be based on solid and irrefutable evidence.[32]

An extreme case in this wave of purges was that of Juscelino Kubitschek ("JK"), former President of Brazil and then-Senator from the state of Goiás. During the first rumours that "JK" might be purged, political journalists and PSD leaders showed that such an act would impact the PSD itself, with repercussions on the entire political system. Deputy Gustavo Capanema (PSD – MG) admitted that the party's position was extremely difficult, since purging JK would leave the PSD in "a state of national humiliation" (Castello Branco, 1977, p. 68). For Capanema, the PSD had never faced such a difficult situation, which he found all the more serious since the fate of the regime itself would be involved.

Meanwhile, Juracy Magalhães (UDN – BA), according to the headlines, considered purging JK as "necessary as breaking eggs to make an omelette". Juracy argued that it was just one more measure to save the country from the "forces of evil". He also admitted that the new government had practiced "some acts of annulling political rights without due process, but in the country's best interests and with no intention of personal persecution".[33] In the view of journalist Carlos Castello Branco, the suspension of JK's political rights opened prospects for new political measures such as postponing elections and altering the rules of the electoral game.

3 The extension of Castello Branco's term

One of the institutional changes proposed at this juncture was to extend the President's term. While the Executive that emerged from the 1964 movement had removed members of Congress from office and stripped many Brazilian politicians of their political rights, it also intended to govern by negotiating with the Legislative and not only via discretionary acts. According to then-Chief of Staff Luís Vianna Filho, support was expected from Congress, especially to pass constitutional amendments for political and agrarian reforms. The Executive was working to gain a broad congressional base consisting of ten parties, where only the PTB was left out of the pro-government bloc, and even so there were the so-called *"bigorrilhos"* ("nobodies" or "wimps"), PTB deputies that broke party lines and supported the government individually. The picture changed when JK was ousted from the Senate, with the ranks of the PSD oscillating between bewildered and annoyed and disillusioned, as Congress witnessed the meltdown of a caucus numbering more than 250 deputies.[34]

The idea of extending Castello Branco's presidential term enjoyed great support from UDN leaders that were dissatisfied with the likely candidacy of Carlos Lacerda to President. Then governor of Guanabara, Lacerda was close to the anti-Castello "hard line" and began to face opposition from the more liberal sectors within the UDN itself, such as Afonso Arinos, João Agripino, Milton Campos, and Daniel Krieger.[35] During a visit to the couple Anah and Afonso Arinos, Senators João Agripino and Daniel Krieger talked again about extending Castello's term. None of them was friendly to the idea of a victory for Lacerda, and they even believed that he would become a dictator if he reached the presidency. They thus favoured extending President Castello Branco's term for another year, giving him more time for the reforms and postponing the presidential election.[36]

Journalist Carlos Castello Branco reported in his column on the negotiations to pass an amendment to extend the President's term, with a strategy consisting of government leader Pedro Aleixo deliberately leaving the Senate floor in order for the debate to proceed without coordination.[37] Meanwhile, Senators Daniel Krieger and Filinto Müller, who favoured the proposal, were working to have the amendment passed in the National Congress. According to various witnesses, Senator Krieger was the "kingpin" in Castello's strategy in Congress. The negotiations to extend the President's term were one of Krieger's most important achievements, consolidating his position as the main character in the Executive's political scheme vis-à-vis Congress. The senator had become one of the most important leaders in that conjuncture, and it was already expected that if the extension passed, Krieger would come out extremely strong.

On July 22, 1964, the National Congress passed Constitutional Amendment No. 9, extending the terms of the President and Vice-president of Brazil until March 1967. After Juscelino Kubitschek was stripped of his political rights, the majority of the PSD positioned itself in favour of extending Castello Branco's term, with a view towards postponing the matter of presidential succession, since their candidate Kubitschek had been knocked out of the race. UDN's national convention in November 1964 confirmed Carlos Lacerda's candidacy to the succession. But by that time Lacerda had already distanced himself from the main leaders of the 1964 movement, and a new discussion occupied the national agenda: party reform.

4 Political party reform

August 1964 marked the exact moment in which the rumours began about extinguishing the existing political parties. Many leaders of the UDN, PSD, and PTB were against it. Marshall Castello Branco, Governor Magalhães Pinto (MG), and some electoral judges were in favour.[38] Yet during the year 1964 the government refrained from enacting any law pertaining to the functioning of the political parties that would have changed the prevailing party system.

In was not until July 15, 1965, more than a year after the military took power, and with a view towards the elections scheduled for October 3, the government issued a new Organic Law on Political Parties. The law suggested that the plan was to maintain the party system, but with a crucial change. The new legislation basically differed by increasing the barrier clause for parties' functioning to 3% of the electorate that had voted in the last general election for the Chamber of Deputies. Importantly, the law's initial objective was thus to *decrease* the number of parties, and not to *eliminate* the existing system as a whole.

However, the results of the elections in October 1965 precipitated a far deeper party reform. That year, in the gubernatorial elections, the UDN lost in 9 of the 11 states that were up for election, since in the remaining states the elections were only scheduled for 1966. The result went down in history as a victory of the *opposition* to the 1964 movement and thus a defeat for the *government.* Yet election results are open to a wide range of interpretations which are often produced by groups involved in the political dispute itself. At the time, the defeat of the UDN was interpreted as a defeat for the 1964 movement, mainly by members of the military that were interested in radicalizing the political process.[39] Over time, this reading was steadily consolidated and could be found in studies produced retrospectively, probably influenced by the parties' subsequent organization along the lines of for-versus-against the 1964 movement.

We can find various different analyses within the ranks of UDN, the main party affected by the election results. In a letter to Juracy

Magalhães, Aliomar Baleeiro (UDN – BA) emphasized: "Nobody is performing an indispensable self-criticism, since in my view everyone has their share of the responsibility for the disaster".[40] Years later, in 1977, Juracy Magalhães was even more blunt:

> It was a matter of political expediency. If the PSD and PTB had survived, those two parties together would have won all the elections. As the pragmatic man I had always been, I reached the conclusion that for the Revolution to enjoy any chance of an electoral victory, it had to start from something entirely new. If it had allowed the old parties to continue with their ties, the *'entente'* between the PSD and the PTB would have continued, and the UDN would have lost every time.[41]

In other words, those election results were also interpreted as the continuation of experiences from the previous twenty years, a record of successive defeats for the UDN at the hands of candidates in the coalition formed by the PSD and PTB, something totally distinct from the facts associated with the new regime. From this perspective, through the AI-2, once again the UDN used authoritarian ploys to fight electoral victories by the PSD and PTB, attempting to block democratically elected Presidents from taking office, whether by challenging the outcome on grounds of the lack of an absolute majority – which had no constitutional basis (the Vargas case in 1950) — or by plotting to encourage the military conspiracy (the JK case in 1955).

Yet not all the members of the UDN that belonged to the Executive at that juncture agreed with the measures imposed by the AI-2. To this point, the negotiations behind issuing the AI-2 involved a crucial change in the Ministry of Justice, with Juracy Magalhães replacing Senator Milton Campos (UDN – MG), who did not approve of the direction the regime was taking. According to Milton Campos, when he took office as Minister of Justice, he identified with the principles of the "revolution" and saw his role as working in the search for constitutional normalcy.[42] He was thus accused by the more radical or more "zealous" sectors,[43] as he called them, of insisting on legal formalities. In 1965, the Executive submitted constitutional amendments to the National Congress with which Campos disagreed, since he felt they facilitated excessive federal intervention and overextended the military courts' jurisdiction. Given these circumstances, he preferred to resign as Minister of Justice, arguing that his background prevented him from enforcing certain measures.[44]

Therefore, it was only after these amendments had been voted down by Congress and the election results had been announced that President

Castello Branco decided to issue a new institutional act. Juracy Magalhães took office as Minister of Justice and helped Senator Daniel Krieger draft the AI-2. Finally, on October 27, following a meeting with the military judges and the new Minister of Justice, Castello Branco decreed the AI-2, which radicalized the punitive measures already in force, increased the presidential powers, assigned to the Military Justice system the responsibility for trying civilians involved in crimes against the national security, increased the number of sitting judges in the Supreme Court from 11 to 16, extinguished the existing political parties, and established indirect presidential elections.

In the days following the AI-2, journalists searched out leaders and members of Congress from the various parties to obtain official statements. Meanwhile, the politicians needed to communicate to their constituencies and also to their peers with messages on the meaning of the extinction of their party organizations. In the immediate wake of the AI-2, PSD, PTB, PSB, and PDC distributed official press notes repudiating the concentration of powers in the Executive and the extinction of the parties. The newspaper headlines read: "UDN was the only major party to remain silent on the extinction".[45]

However, in all the parties there were agreements and disagreements on various aspects of the measure. The UDN membership featured support for AI-2 through declarations of "contentment" and "understanding" with the government. Senator Eurico Resende expressed his "'contentment with the heroic Institutional Act No. 2", noting that "it had been expected of the President [Castello Branco] for many months".[46] Meanwhile, Deputy Ernani Sátiro, the last chairman of the UDN National Committee, had drafted a critical note to the government that was ultimately not disclosed, since other UDN deputies purportedly argued that even if the party had been extinguished, Sátiro was not authorized to take positions that did not represent all the members of the now-defunct UDN.[47] Deputy Sátiro stated in his note that he was "shocked by the dissolution of the parties by the AI-2, a heavy-handed measure that deserves serious criticism".[48] Deputy Hamilton Nogueira was one of the few members of the UDN who spoke out openly against the AI-2 in the Chamber of Deputies, contending that "democracy can only be made through exercising the vote, with many elections. Democracy is made with love, not with various brainwashing techniques".[49]

One of the most controversial points in this debate was precisely the disappearance of the respective parties' names. PSD and PTB leaders were "devastated by the liquidation of the party acronyms".[50] A political reporter wrote that the dominant thinking among the PTB and

PSD leaders in meetings at the homes of Ivete Vargas and Amaral Peixoto, respectively, emphasized the importance of survival of the parties' acronyms and names.[51] Deputy Amaral Peixoto claimed categorically that his party did not want to change its name, considered "a legacy formed in 20 years of struggle for democracy in Brazil".[52]

The UDN membership did not appear to be equally attached to their party name. Given the impending party reorganization, they agreed that the new ticket should have a male gender in Portuguese, suggesting in the comments that an acronym in the female gender was not appropriate for a political party. The statement by Senator José Cândido Ferraz is illustrative: "My name is undersigned on the [new] party's founding minutes. I want it now, but with a masculine name".[53] However, among the leaders and rank-and-file, there were declarations that, beyond the acronym, the *Udenista* "political legacy" and "spirit" should be preserved. Deputy Oscar Dias Corrêa claimed that the political legacy "is ensured by itself, because although it is formally extinct, the UDN's existence is preserved in the very spirit of the men that belong to it".[54] In other words, the party would survive on the basis of its membership's political capital.

In a certain sense, therefore, the notes and declarations by leaders of the various parties were quite similar, especially regarding their assessment of the loss resulting from the extinction of their respective party acronyms. Their assessments used a vocabulary with very similar categories to express this sentiment: history, endowment, legacy, banner. The leaders of the defunct parties were expressing a common concern over the loss of their party organizations' material and symbolic endowment.

There was thus a major convergence, although by inverse routes, between the value assigned to the parties by the dictatorship and that attributed to them by the party members themselves. This became clear in the notes and declarations featuring the above-mentioned categories, showing that the AI-2 was achieving its objective. The leaders of the extinct parties were thus attempting to reaffirm their history, their ideals, and their struggles, demarcating their territory beyond the acronym that had brought them together. They were expressing the need to develop strategies to preserve their party identities, which they knew to be the channel by which they had communicated with their constituencies since 1945.

It is interesting to compare the perceptions of these historical actors (abundantly clear in all the documents) to the persistent reading produced by academic studies, which insisted on a situation of artificiality and dismantlement of the party system in the early 1960s. When we examine the circumstances of the parties' extinction, we find the effort by various politicians to preserve their parties' characteristics in the new organizations that were about to be created, which obviously highlights the latter's importance. The dissolution of the party system that existed from 1945 to 1965 did not result from a "natural" trend stemming from the system's weakening, but from an authoritarian, arbitrary intervention that met with considerable resistance. The intervention was conducted immediately after the 1965 elections, when the parties and the electorate showed that the 1964 movement had not erased the parties' autonomy and force among the citizenry and that Brazilian politics could have taken a different direction if the "old" parties had not been destroyed as they were.

5 The formation of a new party system

Brazilians awoke on November 20, 1965, to the announcement of Complementary Act No. 4 (AC-4), regulating the creation of provisional organizations with the attributions of political parties. AC-4 defined the new party system's profile. The government's objective was to prevent the restructuring of the extinct parties. The new parties would have to be organized at the initiative of members of the National Congress, with no fewer than 20 deputies and 20 senators. This meant a very limited number of parties, where the aim was neither a one-party system nor a broadly multipartisan system. That is, the Executive actually intended to have a system with just two parties, one to back the government and the other an opposition party.

Even among the politicians that supported the regime inaugurated by the 1964 movement, this new decree caused some bewilderment. After all, the country's main political leaders were attempting to imagine the consequences of a decision that broke with the experiences in partisan organization that had prevailed for some twenty years. Some leaders of both the PSD and the UDN came out publicly against the creation of a two-party system. PSD Senator Amaral Peixoto, for example, said to the newspapers that he considered it a mistake for the government to form just two parties, one a pro-government party and the other as an opposition party, setting the country back thirty years.[55] And UDN Deputy Ernani Sátiro criticized the new law in a conversation with journalists, calling it a foregone conclusion that the two-party system would be untenable in nearly all the states of Brazil.[56] He wagered on the strength of the "political reality" and found a mismatch between the two-party system and the diversity of political and ideological positions existing in

Brazil. UDN Senator Daniel Krieger, one of President Castello Branco's most trusted politicians, favoured "the creation of state-level parties that would authentically reflect the regional political struggles, with the founding, at the national level, of federations of parties".[57] The idea was that the creation of state-level parties would allow the parties' ongoing autonomy, at least in each state. Thus, at the state level (with the state and national deputies, senators, and governors), he imagined that the electoral competition would remain similar to that of a multi-party system.

It is thus crucial to note that the first references to the two-party system were debating institutional formulas that allowed dissidence and even state parties.[58] Therefore, and given the difficulties in shoehorning the politicians into a two-party system, electoral legislation was decreed that allow the parties to present candidates on multiple tickets. In other words, in the majoritarian elections, each party could present up to 3 candidates: sub-ticket 1, sub-ticket 2, and sub-ticket 3. This legislation allowed the leaders of the old parties like UDN and PSD, now in ARENA, to compete for votes from voters in each municipality, especially in the mayoral elections, since the AI-2 had eliminated direct elections for state governors and President. Scarcely a week after the AC-4 was decreed, on 29 November 1965, the government announced Complementary Act 26 (AC-26), consisting of the most visible result of the problems with adjusting a two-party system to the extinct parties' networks of relations and resistance.

Following the enactment of AC-4, the politicians held new meetings. Since it was now impossible for the old parties to continue, the negotiations to form new parties took a different direction. At this juncture, the party structure of the defunct UDN became the base for the government party, while most of the politicians from PTB that had not been stripped of their political rights organized MDB, the opposition party. These decisions corresponded clearly to their respective parties' images and to their members' stances vis-à-vis the 1964 movement. Thus, the main debate in the face of the new party rules occurred precisely in the PSD, the centrist party and moderator of the party system prevailing from 1945 to 1965, and now split.

Brazil's newspapers were publishing suggestive interpretations of this fact. According to the press, the formation of the new parties was related directly to the failure to form an "independent party" based on the PSD.[59] A reporter from *O Estado de S. Paulo* noted that "the government's quick action controlled the growing movement to form an independent party based on the PSD".[60] The government's position in relation to the party leaders revealed the intervention needed to shape the party system according to the regime's plans, i.e., with a two-party design. This effort also showed the government's concern over preventing the resurgence of PSD or any party like it, highlighting the value of the party's organizational structure and the government's determination to destroy it and to win over part of the PSD as its ally. This effort by the regime shows how the PSD structure – consisting of men and local committees all across Brazil – was still indispensable political capital for the government even after the coup d'état.

In studies on the two-party system, some authors have cited the fact that members of all the defunct parties joined ARENA and MDB as evidence of "the lack of clarity in the old parties' ideological and representative nature" (Kinzo, 1988, p. 32). Yet a closer look at that political moment leads to a different conclusion: when Filinto Müller explained his decision to distance himself from part of the PSD, laying out his differences in the party's conduct during the João Goulart government, he was touching on the principal political issue of those years. Thus, when the new parties were organized, there were choices based on internal political and ideological differences in the former parties themselves and that corresponded largely to the rearrangement for-versus-against the 1964 movement. PSD was the largest party in the previous system, but it had been experiencing significant internal differences, a process that was radicalized in 1965, leading to a split in its membership between the two parties that were being created.

This shows how the regime intended to form a grand party via the incorporation of UDN and a large share of PSD. However, a widespread fear among the PSD ranks that were willing to join the government party was "the risk that even in the majority, we would lose control of the new party to the forces that the government would identify more closely with its revolutionary objectives".[61] The reporter that raised the issue went on to cite examples of disputes between *Pessedistas* and *Udenistas* in various states. The *Pessedistas* wanted to know whether the government would acknowledge the party's political and electoral weight, or prefer the *Udenistas*, even if they had been defeated in the last elections.

The results of the October 1965 elections for state governments was viewed as one of the criteria for assessing the political forces in each state. Both the government and the politicians considered this a key point for party reorganization. The government pressured the elected governors to join its party, while the political forces that had been defeated in the states resisted joining the government party, even if they supported the 1964 movement, since the governor-elect was expected to join it. In other words, by joining the government party, many

Pessedistas feared having their historical identity jeopardized among their constituents, besides risking their subordination within a party formed mainly by *Udenistas*.

This widespread expectation within PSD was shared and reinforced by the *Udenistas*, since they truly expected to command the government party. A columnist from *Jornal do Commércio* identified the tone of the backstage negotiations in the office of Deputy Pedro Aleixo, a former *Udenista*, leader of the government in the Chamber and one of the coordinators of the new party's organization. Deputies Adauto Cardoso, a traditional *Udenista*, and Britto Velho, elected by a coalition between PL and UDN, witnessed joyfully as members of Congress from different stripes turned to them for information on the organization of the government party.[62]

Still, some *Udenistas* believed that the new parties would not necessarily become definitive political parties after the 1966 elections. They were thus planning the future creation of another political party. According to the press, one of the ideas behind the negotiations to form the government party was the temporary nature of the new party organizations.[63] The newspapers published that when President Castello Branco invited members of Congress to join the government, he claimed that after 1966 each one could go his own way as he saw fit.[64]

While many *Udenistas* and other *Pessedistas* were vying for control of the government party, even after the new party rules, some political groups were drafting plans for party organizations that did not fit the two-party system. In addition to the political leaders that had been stripped of their political rights and/or removed from office, others were resisting being shoehorned into two parties. Carlos Lacerda advised his closest allies not to join any party.[65] According to *Jornal do Brasil*, Rafael de Almeida Magalhães was working to create a national movement, encouraging Lacerda's supporters to oppose the two-party system. He was organizing a national front in favour of a constitutional congress and direct elections, with participation open to politicians connected to Juscelino Kubitschek and other purged leaders.[66] Among the politicians, the imposition of forming just two parties was surrounded by controversy. As mentioned, the politicians' logic in relation to party reorganization, which they saw as including elections, candidacies, and votes, was heavily oriented by the existing political competition and was not taken for granted. Crucially, the politicians' calculations were guided by a horizon by which they obviously expected electoral competition to prevail both in the short and medium term.

6 The creation of ARENA

In this context, the negotiation to form ARENA resulted in a draft document signed by members of Congress (as required by the AC-4) and the establishment of a National Committee and an Executive Board. On November 30, 1965, some members of Congress undersigned the Founding Bylaws of the National Renewal Alliance with the objective of "supporting the government of the Revolution".[67] The objectives of ARENA were first and foremost to struggle "for all measures aimed at the consolidation of the sanitizing and progressive ideals that inspired the March 1964 Revolution".[68] Secondly, the document underscored the commitment to seek "the improvement of representative democracy, and consequently against fraud, the influence of economic power in elections, and abuses of political power".[69]

The bylaws go on to list the following general objectives:

1. Democratization of opportunities;
2. Administrative reform, with strict observance of the merit system;
3. Economic and financial strengthening of the states and municipalities and elimination of regional imbalances;
4. Planned and self-sustainable development, without inflation and with strengthening of economic infrastructures;
5. Expansion of education at all levels, especially mandatory elementary education and technical-vocational training;
6. The fight against endemic diseases and poverty;
7. A fair tax system, as an instrument for economic development and redistribution of the social income, through growing use of progressive personal and direct taxes and observance of the criterion of essentiality in the choice of products subject to indirect taxation;
8. Growing improvement of the social security system and trade union organization as an instrument of social equilibrium and defence of the workers' legitimate interests;
9. Incentives for private initiative as a basic element of economic development and an indispensable factor for a fully democratic regime;
10. Implementation of a foreign policy that seeks to achieve the national objectives of development, security, and well-being for the Brazilian people;
11. Adoption of a constant and fertile endeavour in favour of international peace and understanding, rapprochement, and cooperation and support for the United Nations Charter;

12. Growing linkage between global trade and the economic development of the peoples, with the adoption of measures that correct the effects of deterioration in the terms of trade;
13. Maintenance and consolidation of a policy for Brazil's effective participation in the life system and values of Western civilization and in the mechanism of continental security, including full compliance with its international commitments and above all with strengthening of the Latin American economic integration.

Under the circumstances, these objectives served as the party organization's platform. Some points appear quite generic, revealing little of the new party's political hues. Yet one of the characteristics of the way ARENA was structured was precisely the absence of strong colours and the maintenance of traditional approaches to Brazil's problems. In other words, ARENA was affirming its commitment to the "1964 revolution", but none of its objectives was actually revolutionary.

As determined by the AC-4, both ARENA and MDB were organized by signing up national deputies and senators who were members of the parties extinguished by the AI-2. It is especially interesting that in ARENA, the difference between former members of UDN (86) and PSD (78) was quite small, only 8 members of Congress.

ARENA was headed by a National Executive Board and in each state (or territory) by state executive boards, whose members could be members of Congress or not. The duties of the state executive boards included "convening state conventions to nominate candidates to state governor and deputy governor"[70] and "nominating candidates to senator, national deputies, and state deputies".[71] In the municipalities, there were municipal executive boards in charge of nominating candidates to mayor, deputy mayor, city council members, and justices of the peace. Participation in the national conventions included senators, national deputies, and three representatives from each of the state executive boards. That is, the entire planning of ARENA's structure aimed to serve fundamental aspects of the country's political tradition, namely the importance of the states and municipalities.

The bylaws' section on "multiple tickets" (sub-legendas) confirms this characteristic. The electoral legislation allowing candidacies in multiple tickets was so crucial to the organization of ARENA that its founding bylaws already included articles on the matter. The document listed the requirements for establishing multiple tickets for each election: by way of a vote by at least one-third of each state executive board; by a vote of the candidates that had received at least 10% of the valid votes in the previous election for the office they intended to run for. More than

Table 2.1 The formation of ARENA and MDB according to the party affiliations of representatives from the extinct parties in the Brazilian Chamber of Deputies (1966)

Extinct parties	ARENA	MDB	Total
UDN	86	9	95
PSD	78	43	121
PTB	38	78	116
PSP	18	2	20
PDC	13	6	19
PTN	8	4	12
PRP	5	—	5
PR	4	—	4
PL	3	—	3
PST	2	—	2
PRT	2	2	4
MTR	—	3	3
PSB	—	2	2

Source: Kinzo, Oposição, 32.

an expedient to defeat the MDB, multiple tickets were a way to ensure the candidacies of ARENA members who had opposed each other for many long years in election campaigns. The multiple tickets were a guarantee of altering as little as possible the power relations in Brazil's municipalities, maintaining the disputes between the local groups through elections.

ARENA's bylaws end with the composition of the National Executive Board, formed at the invitation of President Castello Branco.[72] From 1965 to 1968 it consisted of a chairman, Senator Daniel Krieger (former UDN/RS); three assistant chairmen: Senator Filinto Müller (former PSD/MT), Deputy Teódulo de Albuquerque (former PTB/BA), and Senator Wilson Gonçalves (former PSD/CE); the secretary-general was Deputy Rondon Pacheco (former UDN/MG); and the treasurer was Deputy Antônio Feliciano (former PSD/SP). The National Executive Board also included five other voting members, Deputies Raimundo Padilha (former UDN/RJ), Paulo Sarazate (former UDN/CE), and Leopoldo Perez (former PSD/AM), Senator Miguel Couto Filho (former PSP/RJ), and Colonel Jarbas Passarinho.

The bylaws go on to list the names of the party's founders. The list begins with several military officers: Marshall Eurico Gaspar Dutra, former President of Brazil, elected by the PSD in 1945, followed by one representative from each of the Armed Forces, namely Admiral Edmundo Jordão Amorim do Valle, Brigadier General Antônio

Fernandes Barbosa, and Army General/R1 João Punaro Bley, chief of staff to the Intervenor of Espírito Santo from 1930 to 1943, all names that had traversed Brazilian politics since the Revolution of 1930. The list also included Flávio Suplicy Lacerda, Minister of Education under Castello Branco, and General Edmundo Macedo Soares, Minister of Transportation and Public Works in the Dutra government and Minister of Industry and Commerce under Castello Branco. The presence of these names among the party's founders aimed to grant representation to the Armed Forces, but this was really a formality, since the National Committee consisted mostly of members of Congress. This was confirmed in the meetings held in subsequent years, in which the participation was limited to deputies, senators, and governors from the party.

The composition of the National Executive Board and National Committee reveals the basis on which the party was organized, with names from UDN, PSD, PDC, PSP, and even PTB. As shown in the chart below, the selection of politicians in the membership of the National Committee represented all the states of Brazil, and in each state the various extinct parties that formed ARENA.

Rather than observing just the acronym ARENA, it is interesting to examine the names that formed the party, since they include a major share of the cream of Brazilian politics that had built UDN and PSD.[73] Nearly all of them were professional politicians who from 1945 to 1964 had been elected successively to various terms in Congress or executive offices, and some had started their political careers in the 1930s, whether as members of Congress until 1937 or having been named to high-ranking positions in the *Estado Novo* dictatorship. The members of the ARENA National Committee in 1966 included 2 former intervenors, 3 former governors of territories named by the President of Brazil, 9 former governors elected by direct vote, 18 senators, and 38 national deputies. The National Committee consisted of experienced politicians that were representative in their states, most of whom had been elected to consecutive terms from 1946 to 1964, including various state governors, senators, national deputies, and state deputies.

In some states, like Minas Gerais, the composition only included leaders that were extremely well known at the national level. Members of the extinct PSD included Benedito Valadares (intervenor in Minas Gerais during the *Estado Novo*) and Gustavo Capanema (intervenor in Minas Gerais and Minister of Education from 1934 to 1945), while members of the extinct UDN included Milton Campos (elected governor in 1947) and Magalhães Pinto (elected governor in 1960), besides Arthur Bernardes Filho (son of one of the Presidents of Brazil during the First Republic), member of the defunct Republican Party (PR).

Table 2.2 Political background of members of the ARENA National Committee, 1966

State	Name	Party	Background
AM	Leopoldo Peres Sobrinho	PSD	uncle (member of Constitutitional Congress, 1946, national deputy 1946-1948) national deputy (1962)
AC	José Guiomard	PSD	military officernamed governor (1946–1950) national deputy (1950, 1954, 1958) senator (1962)
AC	Jorge Lavocat	PSD	named mayor of Rio Branco
RR	Francisco Elesbão	UDN	named governor
RO	Hegel Morhy	PSP	candidate to national deputy (1962) alternate to national deputy (1962) director of General Administrative Services, Rondônia, chief of staff to the governor of the territory (1963)
AP	Janary Nunes	PSP	military officer named governor (1944–1956) CEO of Petrobrás (1956–1958) Ambassador to Turkey (1960) national deputy (1962)
PA	Catete Pinheiro	PTN	mayor of Monte Alegre (1939–1943) (1948–1950) alternate, national deputy (1950) state deputy (1954, 1958) Minister of Health (1961) senator (1962)
MA	Eugênio Barros	PSD	governor (1950) senator (1958)

Table 2.2 Continued

State	Name	Party	Background
MA	Alexandre Costa	PSP	mayor of São Luís (1951) Secretary of the Interior and Justice (1951–1956) deputy governor (1955) alternate, national deputy (1962)
MA	Clodomir Millet	PSP	deputy (1950)
PI	Joaquim Santos Parente	UDN	senator (1958)
PI	Gaioso de Almendra	PSD	father (judge, national deputy 1900–1914) military officer member of the Constitutional Congress (1934) governor (1955) national deputy (1962)
CE	Wilson Gonçalves	PSD	state deputy, Constitutional Congress (1946) state deputy (1950, 1954) deputy governor (1958) senator (1962)
CE	Paulo Sarazate	UDN	member of the Constitutional Congress (1946) national deputy (1946) governor (1955) national deputy (1958)
RN	Jessé Freire	PSD	city councilman (1950)
RN	Dinarte Mariz	UDN	revolutionary (1930, 1932) senator (1954) governor (1955–1961) senator (1962)

Table 2.2 *Continued*

State	Name	Party	Background
AL	Segismundo Andrade	UDN	state deputy, Constitutional Congress (1946) state deputy (1950)
PB	Plínio Lemos	UDN	national deputy (1954, 1958, 1962) member of the Constitutional Congress (1946) alternate, national deputy (1950) mayor of Campina Grande (1951–1954) national deputy (1954) alternate, national deputy (1958) national deputy (1962)
PB	Ernani Sátiro	UDN	member of the Constitutional Congress (1946) national deputy (1950, 1954, 1958, 1962)
PE	Nilo Coelho	PSD	state deputy (1946) national deputy (1950, 1954, 1958, 1962)
PE	João Cleofas	UDN	deputy (1935) member of the Constitutional Congress (1946) Minister of Agriculture (1951) national deputy (1954, 1958)
SE	José Rollemberg Leite	PSD	governor (1947) alternate, senator (1962)
SE	Lourival Batista	UDN	national deputy (1947) mayor of São Cristovão (1950) national deputy (1958, 1962)
BA	Rui Santos	UDN	member of the Constitutional Congress (1946) national deputy (1950, 1954, 1958, 1962)

Table 2.2 Continued

State	Name	Party	Background
BA	Theódulo Lins de Albuquerque	PTB	member of the Constitutional Congress (1946) national deputy (1947, 1950, 1958)
MG	Benedito Valadares	PSD	intervenor (1933–1935) governor (1935–1937) intervenor (1937–1945) member of the Constitutional Congress (1946) national deputy (1947, 1950) senator (1954)
MG	Gustavo Capanema	PSD	revolutionary (1930) intervenor (1933) Minister of Education (1934–1945) member of the Constitutional Congress (1946) national deputy (1947, 1950, 1954, 1958, 1966)
MG	Magalhães Pinto	UDN	member of the Constitutional Congress (1946) national deputy (1947, 1950) governor (1961)
MG	Milton Campos	UDN	member of the Constitutional Congress (1946) governor (1947) deputy (1955) senator (1959) Minister of Justice (1964)
MG	Arthur Bernardes Filho	PR	national deputy (1935) member of the Constitutional Congress (1946) senator (1950) Minister of Industry and Commerce (1961)

Table 2.2 Continued

State	Name	Party	Background
ES	Eurico Resende	UDN	national deputy (1950, 1954, 1958) senator (1962)
ES	Oswaldo Zanelo	PRP	revolutionary 1938 state deputy (1950, 1954) national deputy (1958, 1962)
GB	Gilberto Marinho	PSD	military officer, revolutionary 1930, Deputy Chief of the Military Cabinet (1945–1946) alternate, senator (1947, 1950) senator (1954, 1962)
GB	Adauto Lúcio Cardoso	UDN	city councilman (DF) national deputy (1954, 1958, 1962)
GB	Hélio Beltrão	UDN	father (national deputy DF 1950) Secretary of the Interior and Planning under Governor Carlos Lacerda (1960–1965)
RJ	Raimundo Padilha	PRP	*Integralista* movement, revolutionary 1938, alternate, national deputy (1950) national deputy (1954, 1958, 1962)
RJ	Miguel Couto Filho	PSP	state deputy (1935–1937) member of the Constitutional Congress (1946) national deputy (1950) governor (1954) senator (1958)
SP	Antonio Feliciano	PSD	city councilman (1926) national deputy (1946, 1950, 1958)
SP	Auro de Moura Andrade	PSD	deputy, member of the State Constitutional Congress, SP (1947); national deputy (1950) senator (1954, 1962)

Table 2.2 Continued

State	Name	Party	Background
SP	Herbert Levi	UDN	revolutionary 1932, national deputy (1947, 1950, 1954, 1958, 1962)
SP	Hamilton Prado	UDN	revolutionary 1932 alternate, national deputy (1954) national deputy (1958, 1962)
SP	Batista Ramos	PTB	national deputy (1954, 1958) Minister of Labour (1960–1961) national deputy (1962)
SP	Plínio Salgado	PRP	*Integralista* movement national deputy (1958, 1962)
MT	Filinto Müller	PSD	military officer, revolutionary 1922, 1924, 1930 chief of police, DF (1933–1942) senator (1947, 1954, 1962)
MT	Ytrio Correa da Costa	UDN	family of Governor Fernando Corrêa da Costa member of the Constitutional Congress (1934) national deputy (1954, 1958, 1962)
GO	Benedito Vaz	PSD	state deputy (1947) national deputy (1950, 1954, 1958, 1962)
GO	Emival Caiado	UDN	traditional family of politicians state deputy (1950) national deputy (1954, 1958, 1962)
PR	Adolpho de Oliveira Franco	UDN	governor (1955) senator (1962)
PR	Emílio Hoffman Gomes	PDC	national deputy (1962)

Table 2.2 Continued

State	Name	Party	Background
SC	Celso Ramos	PSD	brother of Nereu Ramos (intervenor, governor, senator) governor (1960)
SC	Osmar Cunha	PSD	city councilman (1950) mayor of Florianópolis national deputy (1962)
SC	Irineu Bornhausen	UDN	city councilman (1923, 1927) governor (1950) senator (1958)
SC	Britto Velho	PL	state deputy (1947) national deputy (1962)
RS	Tarso Dutra	PSD	state deputy (1947) national deputy (1950, 1954, 1958, 1962)
RS	Daniel Krieger	UDN	member of the Constitutional Congress (1947) senator (1954, 1962)
RS	Euclides Triches	PDC	mayor of Caxias do Sul (1951) national deputy (1962)

Sources: Documento Constitutivo da Aliança Renovadora Nacional (ARENA 65.11.30 op/co), and Abreu, *Dicionário*. Accessed February 7, 2019. https://cpdoc.fgv.br/acervo/dhbb.

Table 2.3 Party origins of members of the ARENA National Committee, 1966

UDN	PSD	PSP	PRP	PDC	PTB	PL	PR	PTN	Total
22	19	5	3	2	2	1	1	1	56

Sources: Documento Constitutivo da Aliança Renovadora Nacional (ARENA 65.11.30 op/co), and Abreu, *Dicionário*. Accessed February 7, 2019. https://cpdoc.fgv.br/acervo/dhbb.

In this change of scale, we find both the names of the members of the ARENA National Committee and the candidates to the main offices up for election. Most of the candidates from ARENA to the Chamber of Deputies and Senate were highly experienced politicians. In the first elections after the creation of ARENA and MDB, Deputy Rondon Pacheco, secretary-general of ARENA, issued a resolution to the Executive Cabinet that considered "as automatic candidates to elective offices the sitting national deputies that are duly registered with the Presiding Officers of the Chamber of Deputies as members of the ARENA caucus".[74] The next day, Daniel Krieger, chairman of the National Committee, sent telegrams to the party's state committees announcing this decision.[75]

Among the members of the National Committee and candidates from ARENA to the Senate, the predominant profile was that of a party consisting of professional politicians that had made their political careers from the 1930s to the 1960s, belonging to the leading parties in activity from 1945 to 1965, having in common decades of experience in national political life. Each of the political leaders chosen to occupy these honorary positions, like the National Committee, or each name with sufficient political weight to win the nomination to candidate to the Senate can be considered evidence of a network of political relations in each state. Far from being a caricature, as is claimed so often, the leaders of ARENA attempted to build a new organization based on incontestable political forces in each state and municipality.

An analysis of the candidacies in 1970 reveals the type of social and political representativeness in those elections. In Minas Gerais, ARENA's candidates were Gustavo Capanema and Magalhães Pinto, two leaders with long political careers, with extensive action in Brazil's national political scenario, each from one of the main conservative parties from the previous regime, PSD and UDN, respectively.

The majority of the ARENA caucus consisted of politicians whose careers covered several consecutive terms in the Chamber of Deputies, and many belonged to traditional political clans in their respective states.

Table 2.4 Political background of ARENA candidates to the National Senate in the 1966 elections

State	Senator/Alternate	Original party	Political background
AC	Edgard Pedreira Cerqueira Filho		military officer governor (1964)
AM	Evilásio de Araújo Maia		
	Álvaro Botelho Maia	PSD	intervenor (1930) member of the Constitutional Congress (1934) governor (1935) intervenor (1937) member of the Constitutional Congress (1946) senator (1946)
AM	Flávio Costa Brito		
	Vivaldo Lima Filho*	PTB	
	Ney Rayol		
PA	Jarbas Passarinho	UDN*	military officer
	Milton Trindade		
AL	Teotônio Vilela	UDN	state deputy (1954) deputy governor (1960)
BA	Arnaldo Pinto Guedes de Paiva		
	Aloísio de Carvalho Filho*	UDN	member of the Constitutional Congress (1934) deputy (1935)
	Antonio Silva Fernandes	PSD	member of the Constitutional Congress (1946) senator (1946)
CE	Paulo Sarazate	UDN	member of the Constitutional Congress (1946) deputy (1946) governor (1955)
MA	Valdemar de Alcântara	PSD	deputy (1958)
	Clodomir Millet	PSP	deputy (1950)
	Achiles de Almeida Cruz		

Table 2.4 *Continued*

State	Senator/Alternate	Original party	Political background
MA	Eugênio Barros*	PST/PSD	
	José S. Machado		
PB	Aluísio Afonso Campos		state deputy (1934)
	Américo Maia		state deputy (1951)
PE	João Cleofas	UDN	deputy (1935)
			member of the Constitutional Congress (1946)
			deputy (1946)
			Minister of Agriculture (1951)
PI	José do Rego Maciel	PSD	deputy (1954, 1958)
	Petrônio Portela	UDN	state deputy (1954)
			mayor (1958)
			governor (1962)
RN	Benoni Portela Leal		
	Francisco Duarte Filho	UDN/PDC	
	Luiz Gonzaga de Barros	UDN/PST	
SE	Leandro Maciel	UDN	member of the Constitutional Congress (1935)
			senator (1935)
	Gonçalo Rollemberg da Cruz Prado		member of the Constitutional Congress (1946)
			deputy (1946, 1950)
			governor (1955)
GO	José Fleury	UDN	deputy (1950)
	José Cruciano	PSD	

Table 2.4 *Continued*

State	Senator/Alternate	Original party	Political background
MT	Fernando Corrêa da Costa*	UDN	father (governor, senator in the First Republic) mayor of Campo Grande (1947) governor (1950); senator (1958) governor (1961)
MT	Paulino Lemos da Costa	UDN	
	João Ponce de Arruda	PSD	
	Paulo Tostes de Souza		
ES	Carlos Fernando Monteiro Lindemberg	PSD	revolutionary 1930, member of the Constitutional Congress (1934); deputy (1935) member of the Constitutional Congress (1946) deputy (1947) senator (1951); governor (1958)
ES	Henrique Del Caro		
	Jefferson de Aguiar*	PSD	
	Justiniano de Melo e Silva		
GB	Venâncio Igrejas	UDN	alternate, senator (1961)
	Aguinaldo Silva		
MG	Milton Campos*	UDN	member of the Constitutional Congress (1946) governor (1947) deputy (1955) senator (1958)
	José Ferreira Filho	PSD	
RJ	Paulo Torres		Minister of Justice (1964) Military officer revolutionary (1922) governor of Acre (1955) military commander, Amazonia (1963) governor (1964)
	Cordolino Ambrósio		

Table 2.4 Continued

State	Senator/Alternate	Original party	Political background
SP	Carvalho Pinto	UDN	governor (1959) Minister of Finance (1963)
PR	Virgílio Lopes da Silva Ney Braga	PDC	military officer deputy (1958) governor (1961) Minister of Agriculture (1965)
RS	Octávio Pereira Júnior Guido Mondim*	PRP	state deputy (1950) national deputy (1955) deputy mayor (1957) senator (1958)
RS	Naziazeno de Almeida Mário Mondino Lucy Monteiro	PL/PDC	
SC	Celso Ramos	PSD	brother of Nereu Ramos (intervenor, governor, senator) governor (1960)
	Álvaro Bocayuva Catão	UDN	

Sources: TSE and Abreu, Dicionário, Accessed February 7, 2019. https://cpdoc.fgv.br/acervo/dhbb.

*Candidates to re-election

For example, leaders such as Juracy Magalhães (ARENA – BA) and Luís Vianna Filho (ARENA – BA), who were cabinet members under Castello Branco not only belonged to clans with intense participation in Brazilian political power since the Empire, but they themselves already had long political careers by the 1960s.

Comparing only the families of members of the ARENA National Committee and candidates to the Senate in 1966 with a study by Sérgio Miceli on Brazil's post-1930 political elite,[76] one finds numerous contact points. In Minas Gerais, entrants to ARENA featured heirs to important oligarchical clans such as Israel Pinheiro, José Francisco Bias Fortes, and Levindo Ozanam Coelho. In Espírito Santo, Carlos Fernando Monteiro Lindenberg. In Santa Catarina, both the National Committee and the candidates from ARENA to the Senate included names from various traditional clans in the state's politics, like the Konder, Bornhausen, and Ramos families.

According to Sérgio Miceli, in the states of Sergipe and Paraíba, the majority of the UDN members of Congress belonged to clans that dominated the main economic activities, like Walter Prado Franco (SE), Leandro Maynard Maciel (SE), Ernani Sátiro (PB), and Plínio Lemos (PB). The latter two were part of the National Committee in 1966. Leandro Maciel was candidate to the Senate, and Walter Prado Franco's brother (Augusto do Prado Franco) ran for the Chamber of Deputies in 1966 and the Senate in 1970 and was named senator in 1978.

Such oligarchical origins have often been analysed as a negative aspect of many Brazilian political parties. This is one of the reasons that they are only considered organizations based on family feuds and not as markedly ideological parties. However, various authors such as Max Weber, Pierre Bourdieu, and Michel Offerlé show that political representation is classically an extension of social authority. Yet, over time and especially during the 20th century, other social sectors organized themselves politically and began to adopt politics as a profession.

In addition, ARENA's political disputes have always been interpreted as regional disputes. That is, once again they have not been interpreted as ideological disputes,[77] but as personal power struggles. Focusing again on the history of ARENA's formation, based on the extinction of the parties in activity since 1945, it is perfectly understandable that there be regional political clashes within the new party. This showed the consequences of the prior experiences of the actors involved in ARENA.

Equally important is that oligarchical party origins do not rule out an ideological brand or the creation of a well-defined political project. In addition, the fact that a party is not predominantly ideological does not mean that it has no ideology at all. In many cases it is even more appropriate to work with the concept of political culture. Not coincidentally, men from families and parties that had been political opponents for so many years agreed to unite in a new party organization. This could only have happened for extremely strong reasons. In the 1940s and 1950, *Udenistas* and *Pessedistas* would never have imagined forming a single party. PSD and UDN managed to build electoral coalitions in some states of Brazil, especially in the Northeast, but also in the southernmost state of Rio Grande do Sul (where the PTB was very strong). But it seemed impossible to set aside the rivalries marked by *Getulismo* (the political legacy of Getúlio Vargas).

It is crucial to realize that this oligarchical base in nearly all the states of Brazil reveals the ample social backing for a government party under the dictatorship. This shows us how different factors were at play in the composition of ARENA. The negotiation between members of the extinct parties (where the multiple tickets played a fundamental role at the local level) allowed winning broad social backing. That is, the institutional arrangements established during the dictatorship included important negotiations with the regional elites. Considering the history of the formation of UDN and PSD, and that most of these groups joined together in ARENA, we are looking at a virtual consensus of the Brazilian elites.

There are numerous monographs on ARENA in the various states of Brazil produced during its 15 years in activity, featuring analyses of the election returns.[78] This literature repeatedly characterizes ARENA as a party organization made of UDN and PSD leaders, besides emphasizing the oligarchical origins of many leaders. By observing ARENA on this scale, there were apparently not many changes. This is suggested by both academic articles and contemporary press stories. In 1971, in "*Informe JB*", a short newspaper commentary referred humorously to voters' resistance to abandoning their traditional political identities:

> On a trip through the hinterlands of Pernambuco, Governor Eraldo Gueiros needed some eyedrops, so he stopped at a pharmacy.
> 'I need some neutral eyedrops,' he said.
> The reply was quick:
> 'Nothing is neutral around these parts, mister. It's either UDN or PSD'.[79]

Throughout the 1970s there was still this widespread view about the population's resistance to identify with the new parties. The jokes and tales about the UDN and PSD, especially, found in a wide variety of sources reporting on ARENA's history, showed precisely that generation's partisan political culture, the for-versus-against *Getulismo* watershed. This was a profound mark of the party system that was eliminated in 1965, a brand that the politicians and population gradually replaced with a for-versus-against 1964 divide. Political scientist Bolívar Lamounier, in his research conducted at the time, attempted to show the existence of a dynamic in the two-party system's meaning, suggesting that the ARENA-versus-MDB watershed, although created by decree, began to make real sense to the electorate. In the introduction to his *Voto de desconfiança (No confidence vote)*, an anthology published in 1980, Lamounier defended the idea that:

> The behaviour of the majority of the population at the ballot boxes can be understood as a choice between the two acronyms, ARENA and MDB. In the eyes of the 'elites' – of the political militants, the journalists, and the intellectuals – this claim often sounds like an unforgiveable heresy, since they are accustomed to witnessing the internal disagreements in both parties.[80]

Meanwhile, political scientist Maria Manuela Renha de Novis Neves, in a case study on ARENA in the state of Mato Grosso, contends that:

> The moment of the party break appears to have been the climax of the cohesion between these groups as the dominant elite, and it is reasonable to assume that their party reshuffling led to a channelling of votes, and the realignment of pre-existing political cadres and municipal structures, defining the directions and the profile of the new parties. The force of this channelling would have the power to turn ARENA into the majority party and guarantee it hegemony, firmly planted in the web of patronage-based relations and the maintenance of traditional *coronelista* mechanisms in a state with markedly rural and *cartorial* features". [*coronelista* refers to the "colonels" or large landowners/political bosses in rural Brazil; *cartorial*, literally "notarial", refers to the "*cartórios*", the notary public offices with cradle-to-grave influence and power over the population – Translator's note].[81]

These studies essentially develop approaches oriented to the analysis of institutional variables: the party ruptures, the party elites' resulting realignment, and the reorientation of votes. However, by focusing on the institutional angle, they largely overlook the ideological and sociological factors.[82] In order to understand the organization of ARENA, the majority party for many years under the dictatorship, it is essential to incorporate the ideological and sociological factors that allow a broader understanding of the Brazilian political system itself. This diversity of meaning is indicative of ARENA's rootedness in Brazilian society. Although it might appear paradoxical, an organization harbouring the family and partisan rivalries between *Pessedistas* and *Udenistas*, besides member of the PL, PR, and PSP, is a party that harbours a major share of the universe of conservative politicians and voters in that society.

In other words, crucially, the negotiations behind the organization of ARENA involved a great concern regarding Brazilian society's support for the new regime. Chief of Staff Luís Vianna Filho, in his notes on the creation of ARENA, reveals the difficulties involved in forming ARENA in Minas Gerais and São Paulo, for example, two of Brazil's most important states and cradles of great political leaders. In a meeting, General Golbery do Couto e Silva is reported to have remarked to Castello Branco that it was impossible "to take the largest electoral state and throw it out, simply to leave it with Adhemar",[83] referring to São Paulo Governor Adhemar de Barrros.

It is true that one of the difficulties in organizing ARENA was the party's size. Many political leaders at the time wanted and/or needed to support the government, while the MDB was facing the opposite problem. It lacked the required number of names to officially register as a party. However, the academic studies do not view this as a positive sign, in the sense of supporting the 1964 movement, but merely as a negative sign, of *"adesismo"* (bandwagon opportunism). Of course, there was opportunism, but to reduce this process of party affiliation to opportunism is to ignore its political implications and limit the participation of conservatives to a patronage game, which is to underestimate them.

Support for the regime was on the mind of General Golbery do Couto e Silva, who warned Castello Branco: "Mr. President, in addition to electing the next President of Brazil, you have to guarantee support for him in order for him not to depend on support from the Armed Forces".[84] In other words, in the Castello Branco government, leaders like Golbery were busy engaging in dialogue with the political leaders of the different parties that had supported the 1964 movement and negotiating the possibility of uniting them in a single party. This did not happen by chance or due solely to the politicians' interests, but certainly also due to the interests of the military.

Accommodation with the party structures was extremely important because it organized the local and state political disputes. Thus, while the military leaders were preparing an accommodation among the politicians originating from the various extinct parties, they guaranteed the representation of the traditional oligarchies in the states and municipalities, ensuring extensive civilian support for the new regime. One cannot lose sight of the fact that the party structures included both their members' inclusion in society and (just as importantly) their inclusion in the political field, where their careers guaranteed experience and the incorporation of political values. In a word, the political learning or "wisdom", materialized in the knowledge and recognition of the divisions between the groups, the rules, etc.

In Brazil, the legislative political field during the First Republic (1889–1930) and for decades was limited to the oligarchies. Still, the parties were not devoid of representativeness, as is often argued to deride them politically. They represented a few, that is, the few that participated in party politics, which only became a mass-based activity after 1945.[85] Experience with political party organization, a social activity, part of Brazil's political culture and considered a guarantee of prestige in certain social circles, cannot be underestimated, because it indicates the recognition of a party and the institutionalization of inherent practices in representative democracy.

This was doubtless one of the reasons why an extensive organizational structure was preserved and elections were maintained throughout the dictatorship. This organizational investment cannot be underestimated, even admitting that the elections took place under harsh repression, with an exclusionary party system, etc. This network of men organized in all the country's municipalities functioned throughout the dictatorship. Thanks to the politicians of both ARENA and MDB, the elections, one of the most important sources of the regime's legitimacy, were held uninterruptedly. And the military did not participate very directly in this gearwork. This job remained in the hands of the politicians, and the elections were held in all of Brazil's municipalities, based primarily on the extinct parties' organizational structure.

Both in politicians' memoirs and testimony and according to observations by sociologists and political scientists, various politicians that joined ARENA, like Afonso Arinos de Mello Franco, Adauto Lúcio Cardoso, Daniel Krieger, Mem de Sá, Milton Campos, and Pedro Aleixo are identified as historical liberals from the UDN. Most of the academic studies on the dictatorship display a certain effort to identify such liberals as isolated men who participated momentarily in the 1964 movement and later diverged from it as the dictatorship radicalized. Meanwhile, there are very few records of participation by former PSD leaders in ARENA, like Benedito Valadares, Gustavo Capanema, and Filinto Müller, to cite just leaders with national stature. This involves a complex operation that implicitly attempts to separate these respectable

UDN and PSD leaders from the ARENA, a party increasingly loathed in Brazil's memory.

7 Archives of the ARENA National Committee

The central importance of the experience of senators, deputies, city councilmen, and sympathizers from ARENA can be appreciated through extensive research in the Archives of the ARENA National Committee. The archives reveal a different memory of the organization, unlike the derisory view of ARENA that circulated in the Brazilian press, built mainly by its political opponents. The documents produced by the National Committee and distributed to the party's leaders over the years point to different dimensions in the organization, allowing a new reading of the social memory that became hegemonic in recent decades.

The ARENA National Committee's archives do not contain any earth-shaking news. There is no journalistic scoop. But reading the documents allows studying them from a highly original perspective. The papers filed at the National Committee were produced when the party was founded and throughout its activities. Since they are contemporaneous with the political facts, they reveal a sensitivity that is distinct from that of the memory of ARENA built after the fact. French historian Henry Rousso refers to a process of recontextualization, "which implies the need to examine more or less complete series in order to understand the logic, in time and in space, of the actor or institution that produced this or that document" (Rousso, 1996, p. 89).

In the case at hand, the ARENA archives allow us to know the perspective of the politicians that formed the party, highlighting the constant reference to membership in the parties that were extinguished in 1965 (UDN, PSD, PTB, PSP, and PL, among others); the difficulty of highly experienced congressional leaders in dealing with the power assigned to the governors named directly by the military to the ARENA state committees; and the organizational effort to keep the municipal, state, and national committees functioning.

As with every political party, ARENA was formed by a set of persons that established differential relations with the organization: professional politicians, militants, and sympathizers. Not to mention the voters. The documents in the ARENA National Committee's archives reveal various signs of people's participation in the party, in many municipalities both in the Brazilian countryside and in the metropolises. An overview of the ARENA National Committee's papers allows us to assess the inner workings of its bureaucracy in the organizational effort needed to keep a party functioning nationwide. Even the various series created by the archivists to organize the collection reveal a large share of the political party's routine: correspondence, elections, party organization, and constitutional affairs.

The "Correspondence" series consists of subseries: general correspondence, requests, invitations. The correspondence mainly involved exchanges between chairmen of the National Committee and directors of the state and municipal committees, in addition to various associations, ministries, labour unions, and politicians. The correspondence sent to the National Committee allows tracing a profile of the people identified with the organization. In 1966, letters came addressed to the chairman of the National Committee from politicians from every corner of Brazil who either intended to join ARENA or had just joined.

The letters show that the senders – ARENA militants and sympathizers – occupied a very wide range of positions in Brazilian society. Semi-illiterate workers, doctors, and lawyers wrote to the National Committee. A physician, resident of the upscale Lagoa neighbourhood in Rio de Janeiro, introduced himself as "an ARENA voter" and wrote suggestions to the National Committee. Others reported their reasons for joining the party:

> A revolutionary in 1964, I joined ARENA not only because it is the party of the revolution, but because I've always been against communism, anarchy, and corruption, which is why I consented to my wife going out in the company of my sisters-in-law in the march that started the revolution of 1964, "WITH GOD, FATHERLAND, AND FAMILY".[86]

Sent both from capitals like Rio de Janeiro, São Paulo, Belo Horizonte, Goiânia, Manaus, Recife, and Porto Alegre and from smaller cities from all regions of Brazil and addressed to the party's National Committee, the letters in the archives express the political culture of the *Arenistas*, their hopes for building a new country, and their hate for their opponents. In most of the messages, the senders introduce themselves by reporting a little of their political background in the Brazilian right-wing. They endeavour to show that they are not political newcomers, but legitimate representatives of the extinct political parties.

"Speaking to you here is a heart-and-soul *Arenista* that does not want to see the party defeated, an *Udenista* by family tradition who also loves our Glorious Revolution of 31 March 1964,"[87] says one of the letters, referring to the National Democratic Union (UDN), founded in 1945 and the principal opposition party to Getúlio Vargas. By recalling this common past, the intent is to seek complicity among the national leaders that originated in the old parties: "I come before Your Excellency as a citizen belonging to ARENA ever since it was founded and a former militant of the extinct PSD."[88] Another presents himself as an heir to the Democratic Social Party, also founded in 1945 and also closed down in 1965.

The senders often boast of their own anti-communist past. One report from Londrina, Paraná State, tells proudly of a clash in 1955: "It was a Saturday, on the eve of those rallies, it was Prestes' birthday [Luis Carlos Prestes, leader of the Brazilian Communist Party], and in the dead of the night they strung up a huge Russian flag right in the middle of town, on the mast of the Altar to the Fatherland, where the Sacred [Brazilian] Flag is hoisted. Right then and there I burned that disgusting Red Rag."[89] During election years, letters came informing on the opponents from MDB. An *Arenista* from Guarulhos, São Paulo, accuses the opposition party of being a "communist hat rack",[90] while another from Cruz Alta, Rio Grande do Sul, denounces "communist infiltration in the MDB".[91]

Others openly defend the dictatorship's most authoritarian intervention, the AI-5, which closed the National Congress in December 1968 and granted exceptional powers to the President of Brazil. "May the AI-5 never be repealed!"[92] From Araçatuba, São Paulo, in November 1977, an *Arenista* wrote: "So the Army holds a Revolution forced by the people, to just leave everything the way it was before?! Help President Geisel not to commit the crime of losing another REVOLUTION that the people wanted and support."[93]

According to the militants themselves, an *Arenista* was "first and foremost a revolutionary"[94] or "a civilian revolutionary of March 1964".[95] For them, the 1964 movement was not an exclusive feat of the military: rather, the Armed Forces had served as an instrument of the people's will against communism.

From São Joaquim do Monte, Pernambuco, came recollections of the fights against Miguel Arraes and Francisco Julião at the head of the *Ligas Camponesas* (Peasant Leagues): "The Brazilian Armed Forces interpreted our people's patriotic sentiment by conducting the March 1964 Revolution. From the anonymity of the hinterlands there echoed brave voices against the subversion that was attempting to take root in the midst of the working class, and these anonymous voices witnessed and fought against communist infiltration in the countryside."[96] From Belo Horizonte, Minas Gerais, the memory of the Marches of the Family with God for Freedom sounded like a crusade: "They came to the March of the Family with God! Rosaries in trusting hands, against the communist atheists, in downtown Belo Horizonte. The glorious Armed Forces united with the people and proclaimed: 'Enough!'"[97] The political discourse of these militants reveals both how they value representation and the Brazilian party tradition prior to the AI-2.

Some of the letters are typewritten, others with the fine penmanship of one who has the habit of writing, and still others are scribbled in clumsy block lettering, revealing huge effort by the authors. Many were written on letterhead stationery from the ARENA municipal committees and the town and city councils, as well as from trade unions, neighbourhood associations, and law firms.

Of course, the letters also include the traditional requests for job placements, scholarships, letters of introduction, and public service promotions. Mayors make all manner of requests, from ambulances to funds for building bridges, sidewalks, and sports courts. Yet there are also veritable political speeches, reiterating their undying support for the dictatorship. In these, the militants express their opinions and proposals, demonstrating their wish to participate in the party and collaborate with the government: "Moved by utter joy and with my sentiment focused on our Fatherland . . . ",[98] "I beg for your indulgence to offer some suggestions . . . ",[99] "Read this entire letter. Truly, read it."[100]

In the mid-1970s, some of these letters sent to the National Committee were rubber-stamped with the following messages prepared by the party: "Brazil is made by us"[101] or "For a stronger ARENA!"[102] Viewed from this other perspective, the context of the time becomes more complex, and it is possible to learn a little about what ARENA voters and militants thought, their references, and their political opinions.

The "Elections" series consists of subseries: election proceedings, electoral legislation, and election campaigns. The election proceedings feature appeals to the National Committee pertaining to the party's candidacies and committees, dealing with intervention in the committees, party loyalty, and election campaigns. The subseries on election campaigns consists of various types of documents: reports on voter polls and election results and a candidate's manual prepared by the National Committee.

The "Party Organization" series is made up of subseries: minutes and proceedings (from the meetings of various ARENA committees, including voting minutes, tallies, and party conventions), the ARENA Youth Department, party composition (documents pertaining to the composition of the state executive boards and their respective executive offices, founding documents: charter, bylaws, letter of principles, internal rules of the national office, norms for organizing the municipal executive boards; documents on the ARENA platform in various conjunctures), various documents on the party's conventions (speeches and others), committees (membership of the national, state, and municipal committees and the executive boards; transcriptions of the National Committee's meetings dealing with appeals from the state and municipal committees), meetings of the ARENA caucuses in the Chamber of Deputies and Senate (transcriptions of meetings on various topics).

Finally, the "Constitutional Affairs" series is subdivided into documents pertaining to the Constitutional Reform of 1967 and documents on the campaign led by MDB to convene a Constitutional Congress (1976).

This body of documents suggests participation in the party by large numbers of people. This should be interpreted as an important decision by the party and not as a trivial matter, since it reflects a choice within a culture of political participation that should not be underestimated. Many of the documents reveal the background and thus the experience of those involved in Brazil's partisan political activities.

The various ways of participating in the party organization, more or less engaged, running for office or merely writing to the party, can only be understood from the perspective of political participation. What appears evident is that these attitudes, which have been recorded in Brazil's history as mere opportunism, are also a form of conservative political participation. Whether in the small towns or the large metropolises, a large share of Brazilian society were engaged in organizing ARENA, its committees, and its candidacies, allowing nationwide elections to be held. In our view, the maintenance of this structure to hold electoral disputes for local power was one of the pillars in the social backing that allowed the dictatorship to last for so long. Local politics was thus a fundamental part of national politics, and it is impossible to consider it a minor issue.

One reflection resulting from this perspective is that elections are not events that can be interpreted merely as processes to build legitimacy for the dictatorship. Elections are complex facts that involve numerically relevant participation in the parties' organization, in the candidacies, and in voting itself. Thus, it was not merely a matter of lending legitimacy to the regime in the eyes of the international community. This was certainly an important argument for keeping elections, but through them the regime also allowed political participation to continue by a large share of Brazilian society, regardless of their positions for or against the 1964 movement.

CHAPTER

3

A Time of Uncertainty and Division (1966–1968)

"Far from being a road to the abyss of illegality, this indirect election will be the path by which we reach the port of complete constitutional normalcy."[1]

Ernani Sátiro

ARENA was founded to guarantee congressional support for successive governments stemming from the 1964 movement. Yet this support was not won without setbacks, a fact that often goes unnoticed, for a variety of reasons, including Brazilian society's memory and experience of both ARENA and MDB. The dictatorship initially decreed its discretionary measures with no major difficulties, but the politicians of ARENA gradually began to voice critical positions, and some ventured as far as outright confrontation or political negotiation. On this point, ARENA and MDB were closer to each other than has hitherto been recognized. Other *Arenistas* defended the government from all sorts of criticism.

Political parties are founded with certain objectives. Their members assign a meaning to their organization by defending the representation of certain ideas or classes, according to a certain political culture, and this constitutes an important part of their identity. Yet party organizations are in a constant process of elaborating their identity, above all because the different groups that form the parties are constantly vying for the definition of what the organization should represent. From this perspective, the relations between party members and their action are prime research objects.

At first, in the 1970s, the historiography of the dictatorship attempted to make clear that the political process of 1964 was not a revolution but a coup d'état, the result of a conspiracy between civilians and the military.[2] Since the 2000s, the literature emphasizes that the movement of civilians and the military enjoyed widespread support from

Brazilians,[3] which is key for understanding the process that took place. Thus recent research on ARENA brings to the fore the question of the revolution as a way of learning about the perspective of the politicians that supported ousting João Goulart and installing the dictatorship, i.e., the self-proclaimed "revolutionaries". In reading the sources produced by party members in meetings and congressional debates, noteworthy is how consistently the 1964 movement is referred to as a revolution with members defining themselves as revolutionaries. From this perspective, the "1964 revolution" is a founding event of a political identity. ARENA, its partisan expression, was created by decree, of course, but the party had ideological ballast. However, the derisory image of ARENA became so strong in Brazil that it went down in history as the "government party", totally over-looking the existence of a project for ARENA as the party of the "1964 revolution".

Throughout the dictatorship, various ARENA leaders distanced themselves from the government at different times in the face of attacks on Brazil's institutions of political representation. Among the original conspirators of 1964, some ended up disagreeing with the political persecutions and repudiating the extinction of the political parties and the extension of the President's term. Some even refused to join either of the two recently created parties. In other words, there was great diversity in the leaders' commitment to the institutions and to the directions taken in leading them. Yet in all cases they did not fail to call themselves "revolutionaries". It was this diversified set of "revolutionaries" that made ARENA.

1 Founding ARENA

On 31 March 1966, the second anniversary of the "1964 revolution", an official inaugural session was held for ARENA. On the occasion, Deputy Último de Carvalho retold the history of the party's project in which he acknowledged the formation of ARENA as part of the 1964 movement. From 1963 to 1966, the deputy was serving another of his terms representing the state of Minas Gerais on the PSD ticket, the party that he helped organize and by which he had been elected mayor and state deputy for two terms. During the João Goulart government, the deputy had participated actively in the opposition to the Executive, and after the AI-2 he was one of the first members of the PSD to speak out for forming a government party rather than reorganizing the PSD.

His speech during the inauguration of ARENA highlights the population's support for the 1964 movement: "On the streets, in the rallies, on the floor of the National Congress, in the state legislatures, in the city councils, in the trade unions, in the student unions, in the comfort of people's homes, in the Marches for Family and Freedom".[4] For this deputy, the creation of ARENA was the acknowledgement of a *de facto* state and a path for collaboration among members of the old parties, since "members of the UDN of the time, PSD of the time, PTB in the government, PSP, PDC, PR, and PRP from all over Brazil thronged to the city squares decrying, many of them, their former parties".[5] Members of UDN, PSD, and other parties had in fact formed successive congressional alliances to block the passage of reform bills by President João Goulart prior to March 1964.

At the first ARENA convention, held on the floor of the Chamber of Deputies in May 1966, delegates' speeches were based on a certain order of affairs: the 1964 movement, extinction of the political parties in 1965, "indirect" elections, and civilians' relations with the military. Their speeches illustrated the types of issues that the founding members of that party itself were posing for themselves.

From the convention delegates' point of view, the creation of ARENA appears mainly as part of the process of extinguishing the former parties. Geraldo Freire, former chairman of the Catholic Agrarian League, former vice-leader of the UDN in the Chamber of Deputies, and then-chairman of the ARENA state committee in Minas Gerais, was named to represent the latter's members at the convention. According to tradition, Freire began his speech by saluting the party's chairmen, the presidents of the Chamber of Deputies and Senate, ministers, and governors. According to the deputy, it was with "immense sadness"[6] that they had seen their parties fragmented little by little and that "more than a dozen party tickets had led Brazil to understand itself less and less".[7] He thus equated the multiplicity of parties with confusion and misunderstanding, which jeopardized governability and raised an argument frequently used by politicians interested in restricting the country's electoral competition.[8]

Even so, when justifying the government's intervention in the party system, he explicitly acknowledged it as an attitude of restricting freedom of political organization. Geraldo Freire predicted: "It will not be possible to keep men within just one or two acronyms. In the future they will have the opportunity to organize around ideas according to each one's preference."[9] In this sense, as with other party members, Freire actually believed that ARENA would be a temporary organization aimed at replacing the old parties until a new party order could be established. Thus, throughout his speech he referred repeatedly to the *Arenistas* as "we men united by the same tendencies, who yesterday belonged to UDN, PSD, PTB, PDC, PSP, and so many other parties acting in this country".[10] For all the politicians, this perspective clearly indicates the importance of previous party affiliations rather than identification with the new division of parties as a *de facto* partisan order. The new parties were thus seen as tendencies/possibilities that would eventually reorganize into new parties in the future.

Likewise, Senator Daniel Krieger (ARENA – RS), chairman of the National Committee, reaffirmed the need for extinction of the political parties and the creation of a "new formula" that would allow holding elections in 1966.[11] But he failed to present a single argument to back eliminating the old parties. The senator felt that ARENA was a temporary organization, but he believed it could become a definitive party. Krieger further emphasized that the main tasks for ARENA were to ensure congressional support for the Castello Branco government and to present candidates for the general elections in 1966.

On the occasion of the first ARENA convention, for the first time the *Arenistas* seconded the candidacy of a military officer to an indirect election for President of Brazil. Deputy Ernani Sátiro (ARENA – PB), the last chairman of UDN, saw two possible developments resulting from that compromise between ARENA and the military: "a road to the abyss of illegality"[12] or a path "to the port of complete constitutional normalcy".[13] ARENA and that first indirect election were consolidating the concentration of powers in the Executive, combined with the maintenance of the representative system. Thus, Ernani Sátiro shows how the pro-government politicians were fully aware of the risk of seconding a military candidacy to an indirect election. A little later, even while exalting Costa e Silva's candidacy, the deputy revealed this alternative's ambiguities:

> Without ever having practiced politics, at least in the sense that politics is partisan activism, disputes, exercise of elective office, without having been a politician, but rather a soldier, without having been deputy or senator, but rather a general, Minister Costa e Silva felt no embarrassment in conversing with the politicians when it was necessary to hear them and to speak to them.[14]

Ernani Sátiro already had a long political career by 1966. He had been elected to his first term in Congress in 1934 and had been one of the founders of UDN in 1945, the party by which he was elected to national deputy for five consecutive terms. How would these men relate to each other, coming from such different backgrounds? On the one side, professional politicians with solid political careers, and on the other, military officers with entirely distinct resumés, although also with political implications. The ambiguity of these positions suggests how the pro-government politicians both wagered on and feared temporarily abandoning liberal democratic principles. This issue was present throughout the dictatorship, at some moments very intensely.

It was thus no coincidence that Deputy Pedro Aleixo, picked as the candidate to Vice-President of Brazil, delivered a long speech precisely on political representation in which he attempted to demonstrate the legitimacy of the indirect elections. He began by emphasizing the authentic representativeness of the convention delegates themselves: "Holders of mandates freely awarded in other legislatures, mandates that turn your opinions and votes into overseers, in order for the convention not to continue being subject to challenges and impugnation."[15] Next, he stated that there were three types of critiques of the indirect electoral system. In the field of the far left, there were those who

> wish to install in this country, under the guise of a popular democracy, a soviet republican regime. (applause) However, wherever the Soviet State has triumphed, we all know that to various degrees the highest agencies of the public power are chosen by indirect election, when there is an election at all.[16]

At the other extreme, there were those who

> striking out against the formula of the Institutional Acts, they acknowledge the impossibility of changing the course of the events in favour of their designs. Such opponents are never interested in making direct elections an instrument to defend the manifestation of the people's will. In the course of their rocky careers, we often find them as extreme defenders of the extension of terms or deceptive creators of exotic electoral colleges.[17]

Finally, he acknowledged that there was also a category "worthy of respect due to the sincerity with which they present themselves and maintain that direct elections are the most democratic process for choosing the people's representatives".[18] His speech was addressed to them.

In Cold War times, Pedro Aleixo argued that the indirect electoral system was nothing new for either the Soviets or the Americans. He then reviewed the history of electoral laws in Brazil since the Empire, highlighting that the indirect election process was the preferred modality during the First Reign and in most of the Second. He also recalled that indirect elections had been the system chosen by most of the drafters of the preliminary versions of Brazil's republican constitutions and concluded by extolling their legitimacy for the people's representation when choosing the country's President or Vice-President. Deputy Pedro Aleixo even cited the Constitution of 1937 as an argument, as one of the symbols of the *Estado Novo* that mobilized the opposition in the 1940s to draft the *Manifesto dos Mineiros*, of which Aleixo himself had been one of the signers.

At the time, Luís Vianna Filho referred in his notes to the municipal "intervenors",[19] showing that for that generation it was all about intervention. But the term "intervenor" was deeply associated with the *Estado Novo* and could not be used in the 1960s, when the model of representative democracy was highly valued, especially as opposed to the prevailing regimes in the Soviet Union and China.

2 The purges of 1966

Like many politicians of his generation, Adauto Lúcio Cardoso had a legal training and background. He became one of the *"bacharéis"* (legal experts) of the UDN, leaders known for valuing legal formalisms and for their taste for rhetoric. He had been one of the founders of UDN, had served several elective terms, and had been city councilman in the Distrito Federal and later national deputy for three consecutive terms, the first two from the state of Rio de Janeiro and the third from the state of Guanabara, created after the national capital was transferred to Brasília in 1960, always on the UDN ticket. In the Castello Branco government he headed the Revolutionary Congressional Bloc (*Frente Parlamentar Revolucionária*) that supported the regime. Following the AI-2, he joined ARENA. Adauto Lúcio Cardoso was one of the personifications of UDN. He became invisible in ARENA. It was not for lack of spectacular acts, on the contrary, but because his action was always dissociated from ARENA's image.

Interviewed by *Jornal do Brasil* in 1964, Adauto Lúcio Cardoso claimed that it was an overstatement to call the investigations in Brazilian universities and the imprisonment of intellectuals an expression of a "primary McCarthyism".[20] He contended that democracy was prevailing in Brazil and argued that there was freedom of the press and that the news concerning torture in the country's prisons was false according to the official inquiries.

In 1965, Adauto Lúcio Cardoso supported the principal measures contained in the AI-2. Adauto and Aliomar Baleeiro joined the ranks of the Congressional bloc that backed the Castello Branco government, including on the matter of extending his term until 1967 and the resulting suspension of elections in 1965.[21] As for his views on the extinction of the parties by the AI-2, there is little information available. But there is material on his role in the negotiations to organize ARENA. Therefore, until 1966 everything appeared to be running smoothly in the eyes of *Arenista* politicians like Adauto Lúcio Cardoso. That year, during an interview to *Realidade* magazine, he was asked if there was freedom in Brazil and he replied that the country was in "a transition regime, in which the democratic institutions survived, maintaining the essence: freedom of opinion, of transmitting thinking, and temporary mandates".[22] Following the indirect election of Costa e Silva to President, Daniel Krieger and Adauto Cardoso reportedly saluted the result as a victory, a stage in consolidation of the democratic regime. According to Adauto, "a difficult stage, but certainly a decisive one for all of us".[23]

However, before the year 1966 ended, Adauto Lúcio Cardoso led one of the first clashes between members of Congress and the military. President Castello Branco used precisely one of the regime's prerogatives that Adauto and Auro de Moura Andrade, president of the Senate, wished to revoke. In October 1966, Castello Branco issued a decree stripping six national deputies of their political rights, resulting in the loss of their mandates. Adauto Lúcio Cardoso, then president of the Chamber of Deputies, did not officially acknowledge the purges and allowed the six deputies to continue in office. He issued a press release in which he reaffirmed his support for the 1964 movement, as well as his disposition to guarantee the prerogatives of Congress to rule on the national deputies and revoke their mandates and political rights. He stated at the time:

> I made the Revolution and am the first to defend Congress. I conspired to depose a President who was threatening not only the independence and dignity but even the security of the institution I swore to serve. Corrupt and subversive men are deplorable. A free Congress is thus more important than they are.[24]

This attitude isolated the deputy from the rest of ARENA. During the session to vote on the purging of the six deputies, ARENA supported the government via a strategy of emptying the Congress floor, with only four *Arenista* deputies in attendance. In the end, the National Congress was surrounded by Army troops to force Adauto Lúcio Cardoso to enforce the decree revoking the terms of the six deputies. That very same day,

President Castello Branco decreed a Legislative recess. In November, Adauto resigned as president of the Chamber.

This was the first episode in which arguments were raised on the inviolability of congressional mandates and in defence of the independence and autonomy of Congress, together with the hierarchical definition of the 1964 movement's political objectives. As Adauto stated in his resignation speech, "our first and highest duty in the investiture of our mandates by the people's sovereign will, lies in preserving our mandates' inviolability and the independence and autonomy of Congress",[25] whereby "revolutions" were temporary in contrast to the legislative institution to be preserved.

In the midst of this standoff, both the government and the ARENA leadership chose to keep a low profile. Newspaper commentators acknowledged that "although censuring the 'flagrantly contradictory' conduct of those who challenged the revolutionary legislation, the statement by the party leaders does not mention Mr. Adauto Cardoso by name".[26] The crisis in Congress was unfolding in the midst of the election campaign in which Adauto was running for re-election to national deputy. His critics included those who saw the confrontation as a risky electoral strategy. Others claimed that no sanctions would be taken against the deputy, "not even expelling him from ARENA, since the party's position has improved in the state of Guanabara with his name on the ticket, much less including his name on the list of new purges".[27]

Meanwhile, Adauto attempted to reaffirm his position, denying that he was part of the so-called *Frente Ampla* (Broad Front): "Goulart, Brizola, and Kubitschek can have that side to themselves. We're all the same revolutionaries of 1964."[28] Because of this stance by Adauto, a deputy from MDB reportedly compared him to "a candidate in orbit",[29] claiming that with his attitude in Congress he was not only in trouble with President Castello Branco and his own party, but that he had failed to convince the opposition. According to the press, Adauto felt that his low vote in the election suggested that his constituency was expressing support for revoking congressional mandates, which he had opposed.[30]

The political lore on Adauto features a gem attributed to Marshall Castello Branco, who supposedly said that just as there are problem children, there are also problem men.[31] However, Castello did not punish the deputy directly, but he did manage to remove him from Congress. The solution was to name him to a seat on the Supreme Court (STF). According to the newspapers, Adauto's nomination sparked widespread resentment in ARENA. The presiding officers of the Chamber of Deputies "believe they have been treated unfairly, since they were the ones that exposed themselves to public criticism when, out of loyalty to the government, they overruled Adauto Cardoso's resistance to the purges".[32]

Adauto Cardoso was an attorney, politician, and Justice of the Supreme Court. His career is a prime example of the contradictions experienced by the "historical legal experts" of UDN that joined ARENA. In a sense, the support for a government made up mainly of military officers was an autophagic process for the Brazilian politicians. In this process, they undermined their own foundations: direct elections, inviolability of elective mandates, and political freedoms. All these so-called formalisms were the object of debates and delicate political decisions. An irrelevant clash when compared to their commitment to the regime, some might say. But this is the world of the liberals: the world of principles and juridical formalism. And in the liberal perspective there are no mere formalisms,[33] as realized by the authoritarian thinkers that left profound marks on Brazilian political culture.

3 Drafting the 1967 Constitution

Since April 1964, Brazil's Executive, consisting mainly of military officers, had continued to rule through laws, even though these were institutional acts and decrees. The year 1966 marked the beginning of negotiations to draft a new constitution, another indication of the government's preoccupation with juridical formalisms. President Castello Branco felt that starting in March 1967 the country should conclude the "revolutionary" period and return to a constitutional regime. However, the expectations concerning a new constitution and the degree of scepticism towards a democratic future varied considerably.

The return to a constitutional regime was not a new issue. Afonso Arinos and Milton Campos, at least, had already attempted to steer the "revolution" in this direction. According to Afonso Arinos, soon after 1 April 1964, he drafted a resolution by which Congress would grant full powers to the revolutionary command. But the proposal by Francisco Campos won out in the end, taking exactly the opposite perspective, claiming that it was "the revolution that 'legalized' Congress" (Arinos, 1968, p. 264).

In 1966, Castello Branco initially invited jurists Levi Carneiro, Seabra Fagundes, Orozimbo Nonato, and Temístocles Cavalcanti to prepare a draft constitution, illustrating his concern for consulting highly qualified experts, acknowledged in the legal field. Yet Castello Branco ended up sweeping this draft aside and decided to name Carlos Medeiros Silva, known for his anti-liberalism, to Minister of Justice.

The announcement of the Executive's proposal to draft a new constitution met with widespread criticism over its drafting procedures. The press featured the view of the constitutional drafting process as "an operation by the Executive".[34] Some also wondered whether it would not be more appropriate to wait for the new members of Congress to take office in March 1967. Senator Eurico Resende (ARENA – ES) felt that the constitutional draft should be voted by members of Congress elected to the next legislature, since he did not acknowledge the legitimacy of a constitution passed by a lame duck Congress.[35]

Yet the greatest difficulty for legitimating any work by Congress to draft a new constitution was the threat of further political purges. Since October 1966, Adauto Lúcio Cardoso and Auro de Moura Andrade, then president of the Chamber of Deputies and president of the Senate, respectively, had been appealing to Castello Branco to revoke articles 14 and 15 of Institutional Act No. 2; they contended it was necessary to restore the Legislative's autonomy and inviolability. Adauto and Auro argued that this was an indispensable condition for the legitimacy of the constitution to be voted on by Congress.[36] Meanwhile, Senator Daniel Krieger approached Castello Branco with the same concerns. Castello Branco even wrote to Krieger promising not to revoke the terms of deputies or senators while the constitution was being drafted.[37] In fact, Castello Branco knew what the threat of purges meant, and said that "the atmosphere caused by the purges was 'worse than the Inquisition'",[38] but he did not waive the power granted to him by Institutional Act No. 2.

In late October, Adauto Cardoso and Auro de Moura Andrade took the position that it was useless for President Castello Branco to seek collaboration from the National Congress to draft a new constitution without first restoring the Legislative's autonomy and inviolability. Speaking on the Executive's proposal, Adauto argued didactically:

> Any constitution coming from Congress under the current conditions will be tantamount to a constitution issued directly by the head of the Executive. To lend the new constitutional charter legitimacy and durability would require the set of factors that normally characterize the Legislative branch as the source of this same legitimacy. Among such factors, the essence is the inviolability of the elective mandate, which has become non-existent since the President attributed to himself the power to decree purges, regardless of review by the Judiciary branch itself.[39]

However, in December the presidents of the Chamber of Deputies and Senate gave in and decided to collaborate with the Executive in passing a constitution. Senator Daniel Krieger was among the first to receive the new proposal. Based on correspondence, the draft proposal was sent next to "experts from ARENA",[40] according to Castello Branco. ARENA organized a Joint Committee in the National Congress to analyse the draft, consisting of some of its own members of Congress with legal backgrounds, historical cadres from among the "legal scholars" of UDN and PSD. The Joint Committee on Constitutional Reform consisted of the following representatives of ARENA: Pedro Aleixo, Adauto Lúcio Cardoso, Djalma Marinho, Antônio Feliciano, Accioly Filho, Oliveira Brito, Tabosa de Almeida, Antônio Carlos Konder Reis, Eurico Resende, Heribaldo Vieira, Wilson Gonçalves, Manuel Vilaça, Rui Palmeira, and Vasconcelos Torres.

Deputy Adauto Cardoso, when accepting the invitation to participate in the committee, was reported to have said that he would try to "salvage something", emphasizing that abstaining would lead nowhere.[41] Senator Auro de Moura Andrade took the same line, noting that "even the most radical or most conservative members should debate and present their ideas".[42] This was one of the possible dialogues between the politicians and the military from the 1964 movement.

The debates in the National Congress and the press coverage revealed disagreements between the presidents of the Senate and Chamber of Deputies on one side and the Executive on the other, indicating the existence of divergent understandings and relative autonomy for members of Congress. Over the course of the constitutional drafting processes some names from ARENA stood out, such as Afonso Arinos (ARENA – GB), Britto Velho (ARENA – RS), and Flores Soares (ARENA – RS). Since they opposed various items in the government's proposal, they took the floor on numerous occasions. The leaders of the government in the Chamber and Senate defended the proposal submitted to Congress, while the silent majority of ARENA passed the Executive's measures.

One of the most important debates in the 1967 constitutional drafting process concerned the chapter on individual rights and guarantees, because the draft proposal sent to Congress only listed the rights, but failed to include the respective guarantees, leaving it up to ordinary legislation to set the terms by which individual rights and guarantees would be exercised. For Afonso Arinos, the proposal "left Brazilians' freedom up to the decision of a legislative majority that is subject to manipulation by the Executive, paralyzed the Judiciary, and in short, suffocated public freedoms in Brazil".[43]

The senator voiced his concern to Daniel Krieger and Pedro Aleixo, who proposed that he draft an amendment. Amendment No. 326, signed by Senator Eurico Resende, was one of the few proposals passed by Congress. However, Afonso Arinos did not sign the amendment because it maintained the clause on the suspension of political rights.

In Congress, the leader of the MDB in the Chamber of Deputies, Martins Rodrigues, declared that it was the only amendment that changed the government's proposal for the better.[44] On the floor, Afonso Arinos made an issue of highlighting more than once that the Chamber's Proceedings (*Anais*) should record the efforts that were made for the Executive to accept the amendment:

> The acceptance of article 150 . . . involves a negotiation in the positive sense, a political negotiation. The group in charge of examining this matter was mobilized to obtain from the government the other part, the general part. Two reasons led us to consider the convenience of such a transaction – I use these words 'transaction' and 'negotiation' in the loftiest political sense, the sense of conciliation, to defend the Brazilian state from authoritarian tyranny, from military regimes, from the threat of dictatorship. Indeed, we should not forget that whoever may say that Congress should be toppled, that whoever declares publicly, on television or in the newspapers, that a military dictatorship should be installed, will be subject to the sanctions, to the punishments, to the warnings provided in that article.[45]

Yet Deputy Martins Rodrigues noted that he, unfortunately, did not share the same optimism as Afonso Arinos. The senator later reiterated that "there was pressure on our part and concessions on the government's part".[46] The political negotiation he was referring to had been spearheaded mainly by Daniel Krieger, with Marshall Castello Branco.

Another polemical point in the Executive's proposal was indirect elections for President of Brazil. Senator Josaphat Marinho (MDB – BA) proposed to alter this article through Amendment No. 463, arguing that direct elections for President were consistent with the ideals of the 1964 movement. In his allegations, the senator stated that he intended to restore the wording of Constitutional Amendment No. 9 of 1964, thus voted "under the revolutionary government".[47] He further cited a speech by Castello Branco proclaiming the timeliness of "calling on the people for the noble dispute in the ballot boxes, inseparable from an authentic democracy".[48]

In the Joint Committee on Constitutional Reform, assistant rapporteur Deputy Accioly Filho (ARENA – PR) drafted an opinion in favour

82 | A Time of Uncertainty and Division (1966–1968)

of the amendment for direct elections. The deputy acknowledged that the matter was the object of "the most heated positions in the houses of Congress",[49] such that "it was up to the legislator to choose, between the two solutions, that which best reflects our people's character and aspirations and the most appropriate for Brazil's reality".[50] He went on to list a history of the indirect presidential elections in the country: 1891, 1934, 1964, and 1966. He showed that "these [indirect] elections did not result from the mere development of a revolutionary episode ... but served as an interesting political solution to crises".[51] He concluded that they should not become a principle of the country's Republic.

At the time, Accioly Filho was serving his sixth term of elective office. He had been elected state deputy in 1947, re-elected in 1950 and 1954, when he had served as the speaker of the Paraná state legislature. He had been elected national deputy in 1958, again on the PSD ticket, the party he left in 1959 due to disagreements with Governor Moisés Lupion, also a member of the PSD. He had been re-elected in 1962, this time on the PDC ticket, and in 1963 he re-joined the PSD, where he was elected chairman of the party's Paraná state committee.

He was thus a deputy who had made his career in the PSD of Getúlio Vargas and Juscelino Kubitschek, having conducted major successful election campaigns in the 1950s. In his view, indirect elections "lack the gift of linking the people to the heads of government, they do not produce solidarity between the people and government. People do not feel bound by the public power, they do not contribute their warm enthusiasm or criticism to achieving the public tasks."[52] And he argued:

> No campaign sparks more enthusiasm, elicits greater devotion, and obtains more solidarity than the election to President of the Republic. To deprive citizens of the right to choose the nation's leaders directly after having done so for so many generations may end up deepening the divorce between the governors and the governed. Why fear that the people do not know how to choose?[53]

Meanwhile, the Joint Committee's rapporteur-general, Senator Antônio Carlos Konder Reis (ARENA – SC), submitted an opinion against the amendment for direct elections. In a few words, he contended that "there is nothing antidemocratic about an indirect election",[54] while failing to advance a single argument. At the same time, some deputies from the ARENA like Afonso Arinos declared their votes in favour of direct elections: "Mr. President, I belong to ARENA, and on many of these brackets I will vote with the MDB, because my leader gave me the right to vote according to the commitments that I made to myself. On the matter of the direct election . . . I will vote with the MDB."[55]

Since there was no party loyalty law at the time, congressmen were free not to vote the party leader's line. It was precisely the leader of the government in the Chamber of Deputies, Raymundo Padilha (ARENA – RJ) (who had also risen through the ranks in the UDN), who defended the Executive's proposal by questioning the inconsistency between an indirect election and the requirements of a democratic system. Unlike Deputy Accioly Filho, he derided Brazil's experience with campaigns for direct elections:

> The prognostication of a direct election to President of the Republic was synonymous with civil war, at least a latent one. The nation did not take positions according to principles and was placed in a tragic dilemma, where it had to opt for this or that more or less charismatic leader.[56]

Like many opponents of Getúlio Vargas (and of his successful heirs in the ballot boxes), Raimundo Padilha was deriding the massive popular mobilizations and the population's choices.

The amendment was finally rejected by 178 votes to 143, with 13 abstentions.

The proposal for the 1967 Constitution sent to the National Congress was thus characterized by the pre-eminence of the Executive over the other branches of government. One of the points most criticized by members of Congress was article 170, which provided for exemption from judiciary review for acts by the Executive. Deputy Oswaldo Lima Filho (MDB – PE) suggested eliminating this article via Amendment No. 356, alleging that judiciary oversight of Executive acts constituted a key pillar of democracy.[57] A member of Congress from ARENA, also against this provision, referred to it as "general amnesty for the revolution" (Castello Branco, 1977, p. 635). Deputy Último de Carvalho (ARENA – MG) was one of the few to defend article 170 on the Chamber floor.

The amendment eliminating article 170 received support not only from members of Congress from MDB, but also from some figures in ARENA. Deputy Britto Velho (ARENA – RS), in declaring his vote for the amendment, stated that article 170 was unworthy of inclusion in the Constitution since it violated the most fundamental ethical principles, "approving acts that are unknown to Congress, that have not been reviewed by us, and worse still, future measures enacted from now until 15 March".[58] But the amendment suppressing article 170 ended up being rejected in the Chamber of Deputies, with 118 ayes, 176 nays, and 11 abstentions.[59] Among the 118 ayes, there were only 36 from ARENA.

Two other amendments with this same sense of restoring the balance of powers that had been disfigured in the Executive's draft constitution sparked huge controversy in the National Congress. Amendment No. 359, submitted by Deputy Humberto Lucena (MDB – CE), was intended to restore the provisions of the 1946 Constitution related to declaring state of siege, which had required congressional approval.[60] The Special Joint Committee's assistant rapporteur, Senator Wilson Gonçalves (ARENA – CE), drafted an opinion in favour of the amendment. Based on a historical perspective, he alleged that to submit the Executive's decision to Congressional review followed Brazil's political tradition: "The nation's experience shows that in cases of real necessity, Congress has always collaborated with the President of the Republic when decreeing a state of siege".[61]

Rapporteur-general Antônio Carlos Konder Reis disagreed. In his brief, he stated that "in the face of Brazil's reality"[62] the changes pertaining to the state of siege did not seem appropriate, which missed the merit of the matter. In the end the amendment was rejected. In the Chamber of Deputies there were 9 ayes, 206 nays, and 6 abstentions.[63] Deputy Flores Soares (ARENA – RS) submitted the formal allegations of his vote to the Presiding Officers:

> At the eleventh hour I must insist that I have witnessed and participated, with the greatest and deepest sorrow, in the vote on the Constitution, helter-skelter, confusingly, overwhelming pressed by time. Everything moving in fits and starts, under the government's iron fist. . . . What do they want? What are they planning? May God have pity on Brazil![64]

Another extremely important and unacceptable point for various members of Congress was the establishment of the so-called "decree-law" (*decreto-lei*). Deputy Britto Velho (ARENA – RS) drafted an amendment intended to eliminate section V of article 47, which included the decree-law as one of the admissible legislative procedures. In another amendment, the same deputy attempted to exclude article 57, which allowed the President of Brazil to issue decree-laws. Deputy Britto Velho argued that such procedures were unacceptable in the presidential system, since in such a system "we, the members of the Legislative branch, are left in the hands or in the clutches of the Executive".[65] In his view, the decree-law represented "an exaggeration, . . . an inconvenience and a danger".[66] His position was complemented by Deputy Oscar Dias

Corrêa (no party affiliation – MG), one of the traditional legal experts of UDN, and one of the few politicians that refused to choose between ARENA and MDB, remaining party-less until the end of his term, when he retired from public life:

> I find it odd that this National Congress would pass measures that incredibly curtail its own jurisdiction. It is as if this Congress had arrested itself, as if it had cut away its own prerogatives. I cannot believe that the men that defended the democratic regime here will agree to the unspeakable absurdity that is afoot.[67]

The rapporteur-general of the proposed Constitution, Antônio Carlos Konder Reis, claimed: "If Your Excellency asked me if I am in favour of the decree-law provision, I would answer without hesitation: 'No'. But I had the duty to examine it."[68] Deputy Britto Velho even compared the position of the President of the Republic in the Executive's proposal to "a virtually all-powerful entity, as in the time of the pre-constitutional monarchies",[69] that is, the absolute monarchies. Britto Velho replied to Konder Reis quite bluntly: "The objections raised [to the decree-law provision] by the distinguished deputy-rapporteur sound weak to me, with all due respect."[70]

One of the strongest objections by members of Congress from ARENA to the draft constitution targeted these two points. Deputy Herbert Levy took to Congress a written declaration of vote signed by him and 105 *Arenistas*, and announced:

> I wish to say, Mr. President, that we are authentic revolutionaries of the first hour, and that we wish to give the Revolution the means to consolidate its principles, and after all, to also correct its mistakes. It has indeed made some, but we do not wish to commit excessive concessions that would lead to a clear deviation in the path we have laid out through dozens of years of public life, of the struggle for freedom and democracy and the fight against corruption in this country.[71]

Next, the deputy read the following statement concerning the vote:

> We regret that the circumstances created around the voting on the constitutional amendments have prevented us from reviewing two points contained in the government's proposal and that cannot merit our support, despite our integration in the National Renewal Alliance, the political organization that was created to fulfil the ideals of the March 31 Revolution.

> The matter is the authorization granted by the proposal to President of the Republic to issue decree-laws and to declare a state of siege without first hearing Congress. Many of us have struggled for democracy and freedom in Brazil for dozens of years, while also fighting decidedly against corruption. We have always found that many of the ills we face have been the consequence of excessive powers granted to the President of the Republic.
>
> Whenever the latter has strayed from his duties, the consequences have been tragic and impossible to correct by peaceful means. How is it possible then, to further strengthen such powers? Who can guarantee that in the future we will not have presidents that fail to fulfil their duty? In these circumstances, can we in clean conscience vote to reinforce powers that may prove ruinous to the nation, in light of the experience suffered in our long journey?
>
> Therefore, we stand decidedly against such provisions and trust that the party heads and leaders will quickly take the necessary measures to expunge them from the Charter, thus easing the minds of those who defend the betterment of Brazil's democratic institutions.[72]

The headline in the newspaper *Jornal do Brasil* announced: "Congress Surprised as 106 *Arenistas* Repudiate Proposed Constitution".[73] The reaction by Raimundo Padilha, leader of the government in the Chamber of Deputies, was simply to ridicule the manifesto as "a rhetorical outburst" by some "romantic deputies" (Castello Branco, 1977, p. 644).

An analysis of the proposal for the 1967 Constitution shows that, in fact, the majority of ARENA members only voted for the amendments which the party leaders had negotiated with the Executive, such as individual rights and safeguards. Other amendments sparked debate and divisions in the party. However, although the amendments were supported by many *Arenistas*, they were voted down, according to the wishes of the ARENA leadership and the Executive.

Some episodes help understand the conundrum faced by many of these *Arenistas* in Congress. In his memoirs, Deputy Afonso Arinos tells how he left the Chamber to return to his university department chair in Constitutional Law: "How could I stand before my students without taking a position to resist that assault?" (Arinos, 1968, p. 275). He thus prepared a series of speeches criticizing the proposed constitution, as a kind of farewell to his congressional mandate. At the initiative of the president of the Senate, Auro de Moura Andrade (ARENA – SP), the speeches were printed and distributed to the members of Congress as they were being delivered.

On the eve of the passage of the final text of the 1967 Constitution, the National Congress appeared to be gripped by a melancholic air. Some speeches by Afonso Arinos attempting to clear the air, and record many contradictory impressions of those days:

> Mr. President, distinguished congressmen, whoever watched the Congress floor on the last day of discussion of the Constitutional reform proposal, as it is today, would tend to agree with the pessimistic forecasts of those who think Congress has been following helter-skelter the drafting process, crucial to the country's fate, in a state of capitulation and despondence. It is not proper to give in to pessimism, to tedium, to discredit, to the feeling of helplessness and abandonment that appears to transpire from much of the commentary on the constitutional drafting process we are experiencing.[74]

The deputy was emphasizing his displeasure with the 1967 Constitution, against which he had spoken on several occasions. But even so, he was attempting to show that he believed in the future of the National Congress. After all, he saw a victory in the passage of certain amendments to the Executive's proposal.

In the early morning hours of 24 January, the Constitution was passed by the National Congress. According to the newspapers, Senator Auro de Moura Andrade ordered all the clocks on the floor to be stopped in order for the new national charter to be passed within the established deadline.[75] He was thus complying with the legal requirements, but Moura Andrade reportedly remarked to another Congressman: "The only thing you'll remember about this Constitution is remorse" (Castello Branco, 1977, p. 654).

Even during the constitutional drafting work there had already been a movement proposing to revise the text. According to Herbert Levy, the document signed by many *Arenistas* gave an accurate idea of the party's direction. The sentiment was for reopening the debate and correcting certain aspects of the regime, which, according to some *Arenistas*, were unnecessary for consolidating the principles of the March 31 Revolution.[76] Thus, soon after the bill's passage this movement's echoes could already be heard in the press. Even Senator Daniel Krieger was reportedly convinced that a revision was inevitable in the next legislature, believing that it would find support in both ARENA and MDB.[77]

The constitutional drafting process and the legislature were drawing to a close, and several members of Congress paid homage to Afonso Arinos, who had decided not to run for any office in the 1966 elections. Adauto Lúcio Cardoso was also leaving Congress, but to join the

Supreme Court. In that context, ARENA was losing these two prestigious figures from the UDN, conspirators in 1964 but who disagreed with the direction the regime was taking. Other liberal congressmen were distancing themselves from the military government. Senator Mem de Sá from the state of Rio Grande do Sul, purged as Minister of Justice to make room for Carlos Medeiros e Silva, wrote to Daniel Krieger and Filinto Müller about his absence from the vote on constitutional reform. He began by stating his disagreement with the AI-4 that had convened the National Congress to vote on a constitutional reform proposal submitted by the President of the Republic. He went on to explain the differences between the terms of the constitutional proposal and his convictions: "With my background and nearly 45 years of public life, it is impossible for me to vote for ideas that are the antithesis of my thinking and convictions" (Krieger, 1976, p. 250). Since the "hyper-presidentialist" government system was consolidating itself, he concluded by referring to his first political identity:

> I came of age and opened my eyes to public life in a collective body that called itself 'liberator'. I joined it when I was 17 years old and I practiced politics in it. I owe everything I am and have been to the Liberator Party and to the liberators.[78]

The vote on the 1967 Constitution was a harsh test for the *Arenista* politicians, laying bare the degree of compromise, distancing, and ambiguity in relation to the direction taken by the 1964 movement. Yet the most polemical points in the debates made the main issue very clear in this diverse group of professional politicians: the possibility of a political détente and the role Congress should play in this process. In this sense, the year 1968 would be very elucidative.

4 Revoking local government autonomy: ARENA and government in discussion

In 1968, under the new Constitution, a new debate was launched between the Executive and ARENA. A decree by the Executive in May turned 68 municipalities into national security areas. The municipalities covered by the decree would not have direct elections for mayors, who would thenceforth be named by the governors. In this context, some ARENA Congressman who were against depriving the municipalities of their autonomy presented similar arguments to those of their MDB peers on the Chamber floor.

Deputy Flores Soares (ARENA – RS) said that he had repudiated this measure ever since the "pseudo-Constitutional Congress",[79] as he called the passage of the 1967 Constitution, when he had spoken out against the constitutional provision authorizing the President of the Republic to declare municipalities national security areas. Flores Soares identified two controversial points. First, he disagreed "that a mayor chosen by the people should automatically be considered incompetent and dishonest, while a mayor, solely by virtue of being named [by the Executive], should automatically be considered honest and competent".[80] Secondly, he contended that national security was the responsibility of the Armed Forces: "Distinguished deputy, I fail to understand why national security should require naming mayors while sacrificing democracy, depriving the people of the right to vote in these municipalities."[81]

Deputy Osmar Cunha (ARENA – SC), in an aside, agreed with the argument by a deputy from the MDB. The deputy had been elected to his first term as city councilman in 1950 on the PTB ticket; he had been mayor of Florianópolis and national deputy under the PSD. In 1963 he had resumed his position as chairman of the Brazilian Association of Municipalities, and in 1966 he was elected again to national deputy, now under ARENA. He realized that the decree should not be challenged only by the opposition:

> The bill affects all the deputies in this House. Rejecting it is a civic duty for the Chamber of Deputies at this moment, in order for us not to slip once and for all into a dictatorship, which will have its first foot in the door if this bill to strip Brazilian municipalities of their autonomy is passed by this House.[82]

He later added:

> After a hundred years with named mayors, why are [the territory of] Acre and its municipalities still as backward as they are today? It's likely, it's possible, that if the mayors were elected by the people, they would spend the budget funds properly.[83]

Other national deputies from ARENA, like Saldanha Derzi and Weimar Torres, both from the state of Mato Grosso, spoke against stripping the municipalities of their autonomy.

Although the bill was under review in the Chamber of Deputies, the Senate was also debating the matter. Eurico Resende, leader of the government in Senate, argued in favour of the decree to include municipalities in the national security area, thus revealing the disagreements inside ARENA itself. According to the leader of the government the criterion had not been political, since most of the targeted municipalities were under ARENA's control. The criteria were assumed to be the international border and the coastline. Therefore, he claimed that a matter of national security should not be subject to the principle of municipal autonomy, and that said principle was observed through the city councils.[84]

Around the same time journalist Carlos Castello Branco noted that despite instructions by the President of the Republic to make the vote for the bill mandatory for government party members, many ARENA figures refused to contradict their local constituencies. Hence the decision by Ernani Sátiro to avoid letting the bill come up for vote, in order not to be surprised by votes from ARENA against the government's instructions.[85]

Among the Congressmen from ARENA that opposed the bill, the main argument was that the municipalities could not be stripped of their autonomy, or that the people could not lose their right to elect mayors. These congressmen contended that there was no relationship between direct elections and naming mayors, and guarantees (or lack thereof) of national security, and there was also no relationship between this interpretation and the enforcement of the National Security Doctrine. In fact, the deputies repudiated this new measure on grounds that it undermined the practices by local political groups, since traditionally they were the ones that organized in parties and competed in municipal elections.

One of the numerous obstacles to the institutionalization of democracy identified by political scientists and historians is precisely what has been called "localism". In this case, however, the pressure against including municipalities in the national security area indicates the incorporation of mechanisms of electoral competition by the local oligarchies, sustaining their interest in maintaining the electoral practices of representative democracy. That is, it was the municipal politicians, numerous and diverse, a social group with partisan organizational experience, that was confronting the government. Thus, perhaps paradoxically, for many it was from municipal politics that strong resistance emerged to the suppression of procedures that guaranteed broader electoral practices.

This conclusion helps rethink a recurrent interpretation of Brazil's political regime from 1945 to 1964, illustrated here by the observations by Maria Dalva Gil Kinzo. She emphasizes that during this period, one of the characteristics of competition between parties at the federal and state levels was the dispute for distribution of "bureaucratic power": "In other words, a system based on patronage rather than on ties of political representation was reinforced" (Kinzo, 1988, p. 21). This clear distinction between a system based on patronage standards rather than on ties of political representation should be analysed with caution, especially in extreme situations, when the maintenance of political activity itself is in jeopardy. The question can thus be phrased in less dichotomous terms, where the goal is to determine whether this "patronage" pattern belongs to one of the possibilities for the relations established between politicians and voters, while also serving as a form of representation.[86] Thus, regardless of the type of relationship a political group establishes with its constituency, the group's primary interest is maintenance of the representative system, a perspective common to members of both ARENA and MDB. That is, interest in maintenance of the electoral system can act as an element of resistance and struggle for practices that sustain representative democracy itself.

5 Daniel Krieger resigns: ARENA and government in transaction

> The two-party system, government, and the government party form a single political unit. They share the responsibility for building a common political destiny. There can be no relations of subordination between them.[87]

During the Costa e Silva government, Senator Daniel Krieger served as both leader of the government and ARENA chairman. But the possibilities for negotiations with the Executive were not the same as during the Castello Branco government. In Krieger's own words, he and President Costa e Silva did not share the same affinity.[88] The senator had also been one of the renowned legal scholars in the UDN,[89] and until the debates on constitutional drafting process, when he defended the government's interests, he stayed in a sort of delicate balance between his commitments to the 1964 movement and ARENA and the path of Congressmen acting in the Legislative branch.

In May 1968, the vote was scheduled in the Chamber of Deputies on one of the most important bills reviewed that year, namely the rules governing the so-called "*sub-legendas*" (multiple tickets). However, since congressmen from the MDB who opposed the bill had decided not to discuss it or vote on it,[90] and since several deputies from ARENA also failed to appear on the floor for the same reason, the vote was suspended for lack of a quorum. Given this impasse, which revealed ARENA's internal divisions again, Senator Daniel Krieger resigned as party chairman. What might have been merely an internal crisis in the party took on a much bigger meaning, shaping up as rejection of the government. According to journalist Carlos Castello Branco, the incident revealed the existence of a growing abyss between government and the politicians.[91]

For this very reason, Krieger's resignation was the object of debates among senators of both ARENA and MDB. Senator Argemiro de Figueiredo (MDB – PB) requested that "for your party's security and greater tranquillity for my party",[92] he should continue as chairman of ARENA, as an element of trust in the country's democratic institutions. At the time, Senator José Guiomard (ARENA – AC) already raised the possibility of Daniel Krieger remaining as party chairman, stating the members wanted him to stay.[93]

In the end there was a negotiation between Krieger and Costa e Silva in which the senator presented a document drafted together with Senators Mem de Sá and Filinto Müller, listing measures they considered necessary for an understanding between ARENA and the Executive.[94] In the document, Krieger attributed his resignation to difficulties in the relations between party and government, which again emphasizes that the fact that ARENA was made up of professional politicians established certain minimum parameters for possible relations with the government. The three senators argued that the party should be the main channel for communication between the government and the population, and this required that the party should share in the major government decisions. The leaders also demanded places in the administration, and that the politicians in the states where those positions were to be filled should have prior knowledge of the persons to be named. After all, in their opinion,

> between one citizen with no active participation in political life and another citizen, affiliated with the majority party that supports the government... preference should be given to the latter, or else the state will be seen to encourage alienation from public service, discouraging those who often have long careers of services and sacrifices, struggling for the common good in the ranks of a party organization.[95]

Referring specifically to the relations between government and the ARENA congressmen, the senators demanded that the bills of law, especially those with political consequences or that were open to controversy, be reported in advance to the leaders in the Chamber of Deputies and Senate, since it was untenable for them to continue to be surprised by certain measures from the Executive. Thus, based on these broad strokes, the ARENA leaders hoped to ensure some participation in the government.

In this same context, the party attempted to approach the Executive through joint committees, like the Special Committee chaired by Minister Hélio Beltrão with the precise aim of promoting integration between the party and government, according to Senator Carvalho Pinto (ARENA – SP).[96] That is, the politicians from ARENA attempted in various ways to actually participate in the government. Thus, in June 1968, Daniel Krieger was re-elected to party chairman in the ARENA National Convention.

Interestingly, the matters discussed at this convention featured recurrent suggestions and analyses on party–government relations. The party's conventions were occasions when the messages on relations between ARENA and the Executive were made public. There, the Presidents of the Republic gave speeches to the party members and were saluted by them. These speeches are evidence of the internal party discussions in the different conjunctures.

The 2nd ARENA National Convention took place in Brasília on June 26–27, 1968. Senator Filinto Müller (ARENA – MT), acting party chairman, opened the proceedings by emphasizing that ARENA should consolidate itself as "the civilian force that the Revolution needs for backing, especially in the scenario of the National Congress".[97] Deputy Raymundo Padilha (ARENA – RJ) spoke on behalf of the National Executive Board and acknowledged the presence of the President of Brazil and the other convention members.[98] His speech provided an overview of the most important political struggles of the time, reaffirming what ARENA should be. He began by recalling the "March 1964 Revolution" as a reaction to the lack of discipline: "civilians played against the military, workers against bosses, young against old – everyone against authority".[99] Next, he attempted to downplay the political dimension of the purges by referring to them as "unemployment", in addition to deriding the demonstrations against revoking political rights, calling them grumbling and whining: "for some, political *chômage* is an unbearable drama. They complain less in Brazil today about the unemployment of millions upon millions of Brazilians than the unemployment of a handful of washed-up politicians".[100] The deputy also attempted to downplay the purges by referring to those affected by them as "has-beens":

> Here we have the past flowing again. . . . It is all over the place, spreading out, begging to return, begging to go back to the days before 1964, for the return to all that chaos, to dole out favours, and for a

display of chronic incompetence ['*Hear! Hear!*' – long applause], for the protection of demagoguery, for the spurious alliances, and to call '*democracy*' that which is the essence of anti-democracy.[101]

Deputy Raymundo Padilha concluded by exhorting to party unity and turned the floor over to President Arthur da Costa e Silva, who insisted along the same line. Finally, he raised the issue of Daniel Krieger's return to the ARENA chairmanship, requesting party unity. A motion was read next, requesting Krieger's reinstatement. After the motion was read, Senator Filinto Müller invited him to resume as chairman of both ARENA and the convention.

From another perspective, the speeches by Arnaldo Cerdeira (ARENA – SP) and then-Governor of Bahia Luís Viana Filho (ARENA – BA) also questioned the kind of relations established between ARENA and government. Deputy Arnaldo Cerdeira complained of the "lack of a political and administrative connection between the federal government... and the party forces that elected it and support it in the National Congress" and proclaimed that "the time has come for us to achieve integration between the government and its party".[102]

Governor Luís Viana Filho argued that the "revolution" could only consolidate itself through the politicians and collaboration between government and the party bases. He felt that it was normal for every party member with power responsibilities to feel part of the government, no matter how small. He further emphasized that nothing was "more pernicious than the prejudices that lead to attempts to weaken politics or politicians, who are sometimes criticized, but without whom nothing lasting can be done".[103]

The reaction to the speech among senators from MDB was immediate. Senator Aurélio Viana (MDB – AL) was an experienced congressman, elected national deputy on the UDN ticket in 1945 and 1950; beginning in 1954, he was elected national deputy under the PSB and served two more terms; in 1962 he was elected senator. In 1966 he was leader of the MDB in the Senate. In those circumstances, Aurélio Vianna highlighted the defence of a constitutional reform by Luís Vianna Filho, in his opinion a position espoused by the country's most serious politicians, "including politicians among our adversaries' ranks. But never has anyone dared to defend it in a party convention".[104] Senator Josaphat Marinho (MDB – BA) underscored Luís Viana Filho's words on the "need to value politics and politicians",[105] to which Aurélio Vianna replied: "What I don't understand is how our opponents' party doesn't close ranks to support these positions, these principles."[106]

Reading the Congressional sessions allows mapping the diversity of congressmen from ARENA. On one side were the guidelines from the ARENA leadership in the Chamber and Senate, members of Congress chosen in agreement with the President of the Republic, considered official party spokesmen. On the other side were discordant voices. One of the central ideas of the two-party system was to place the two parties' members in opposite poles: ARENA with the government at one end and MDB at the other. Still, an examination of the congressional debates reveals some possibilities for interaction between members of MDB and ARENA, especially during moments of disagreement between the Executive and its congressional base. Some MDB congressmen thus attempted to encourage their ARENA peers to review their positions and vote against the government, besides supporting speeches by ARENA congressmen against some of the government's objectives. In these cases the *Arenistas* added arguments to the speeches by the *Emedebistas* and congratulated them in asides.

The National Congress experienced a period of friction in May 1968 in relations between some ARENA congressmen and the Executive, leading MDB Senator Aurélio Viana to remark that for the first time they were witnessing the spectacle of an internal struggle: "ARENA is divided, and in a certain sense this division is good for the country, since it can serve as a warning to the government to take a stance, for a reanalysis of its attitudes."[107] However, contrary to what members of Congress from MDB and some from ARENA expected, the government did not change its positions. On the contrary, they radicalized its authoritarianism, with a fatal outcome in late 1968.

6 The Márcio Moreira Alves affair and Institutional Act No. 5: ARENA and government on a crash course

In September 1968, National Deputy Márcio Moreira Alves (MDB – GB) spoke in the Chamber of Deputies criticizing the invasion of the University of Brasília by the Military Police.[108] His speeches were not reported by the press, except for a single note published in *Folha de S. Paulo*, demonstrating that some facts can lead to unimaginable consequences. In this case, General Garrastazu Médici, then-director of the National Intelligence Service (SNI), distributed copies of the deputy's speeches to all of the country's Army units,[109] and Army Minister Aurélio de Lira Tavares sent a memorandum to President Costa e Silva calling for urgent measures.

Bowing to the military pressure, the Executive decided to request authorization from the Chamber of Deputies to try Márcio Moreira Alves. Senator Daniel Krieger, who just a few months previously had been re-elected as ARENA chairman, made some attempts to dissuade Costa e Silva, reiterating the principle of congressional inviolability, which the government was planning to ignore by punishing the deputy. In a letter to the President, Krieger announced that the party would not require members to support the measure, since it did not have the right to coerce its representatives to vote against an explicit constitutional safeguard.[110]

Thus, Minister of Justice Luís Antonio da Gama e Silva took the lead in the negotiations on the vote to authorize trying the deputy.[111] The leader of ARENA in the Chamber, Deputy Geraldo Freire, working with Gama e Silva, replaced in the Committee on Constitution and Justice the nine deputies who were against the authorization to try Deputy Márcio Moreira Alves. Senator Daniel Krieger recorded in his memoirs that Geraldo Freire and the Minister of Justice were breaking traditional rules of order in the Congress, since the committees had always been respected: "The political decision is up to the plenary. That's the tradition in Congress."[112] From his point of view the acts by Deputy Geraldo Freire and the Minister of Justice were inconsistent with the institution. Besides, in late October, President Costa e Silva had criticized Congressmen from ARENA who were against punishing Márcio Moreira Alves, saying that regardless of their position, the deputy would be purged.

Starting with such measures as the substitution of members of the Committee on Constitution and Justice (CCJ), the members of Congress began to realize the nature of the change in relations between government and Congress. In November, Daniel Krieger decided to step down as leader of the government in the Senate. After the substitutions, the CCJ approved the authorization to try Deputy Márcio Moreira Alves. Deputy Djalma Marinho (ARENA – RN) then resigned as chairman of the committee, claiming that he did not wish to be acquitted while others were being convicted.[113] His attitude appears to have brought some relief for deputies from ARENA who, in growing numbers, were hesitating to support the government.[114]

The negotiations lasted until 12 December, when the vote was held. In the pressroom of the National Congress some 40 journalists, 20 deputies (15 from MDB and 5 from ARENA) and Chamber staff members organized a bet on the outcome.[115] The unusual fact of a bet reminds one of the true range of possibilities involved in a vote, subject to widely diverse factors. In principle, the process is characterized by uncertainty. An office boy won the bet: 216 deputies voted against the authorization to try Márcio Moreira Alves, 141 in favour of the authorization, and 12 abstentions. Among the votes against purging Moreira Alves, 122 were from MDB and 94 from ARENA.[116] In addition, 35 deputies from ARENA and four deputies from MDB did not appear for the vote, as reported by *Jornal do Brasil*, listing the names of all those absent from the vote and noting that only one of the *Arenistas* failed to appear because he was hospitalized,[117] thus insinuating that those *Arenistas* had chosen omission as their strategy.

The outcome of the vote in the Chamber of Deputies was celebrated on the floor to the sound of the Brazilian National Anthem. According to the newspaper coverage, that demonstration sparked great enthusiasm.[118] At that moment the fact that the majority of Congress had denied authorization to try Márcio Moreira Alves was viewed as a reaction, as a possibility for glimpsing a different *Horizon*, as it was called in the editorial in the newspaper *Correio da Manhã*.[119]

But Institutional Act No. 5 was decreed on the same day as the celebration of the reaction by Congress. Thus, in addition to signalling the closing of the National Congress and state legislatures, in ARENA's history the AI-5 represented the apogee of a long crisis between the party and government. A year later, in November 1969, Deputy Pedro Vidigal (ARENA – MG), in an aside to ARENA leader Cantídio Sampaio (ARENA – SP), voiced his interpretation of the story:

> The genesis, the origin of the AI-5, was the victory by Mr. Márcio Moreira Alves in this House on 12 December 1968. And who gave him that victory? ARENA, with 94 of its representatives, whose names were saluted in the press all across Brazil. Some people even had the hidden desire to denounce, for public execration, the names that were not on that list.[120]

The deputy underscored a fundamental point that appears to have been forgotten over time: the impact of this vote on society. The vote had these effects both for the names that voted against and those that voted for the Executive; they were all either "celebrated" or "execrated" by public opinion. In other words, Vidigal even suggested that the votes by deputies from ARENA in favour of the Executive should not be taken for granted, as they appeared later, which is why they received widespread publicity. In this sense, Deputy Vidigal inverts the version later consolidated on the relations of Congress's subordination to the Executive in that conjuncture: "His Excellency the President of the Republic had begged the House to grant the authorization. This verb 'to beg' is not synonymous with the verb 'to ask for'. To ask for is a request made between equals. To beg is a plea from a believer to a divine power. It is not even from an underling to a superior."[121]

The deputy certainly overstated the metaphor of divinity. But overstatements aside, what interests us here is the acknowledgement of the existence of tense negotiations between the Executive and its Congressional base, and the proper recognition for the attitude by 94 Congressmen from ARENA that voted with the MDB, denying authorization for the regime to purge Márcio Moreira Alves.

One of the most frequent accusations made by MDB against ARENA was that of its "complacency, for behaving in Congress as a silent, passive voice" (Kinzo, 1988, p. 115). In fact, a strategy by the *Arenistas* was to fail to appear on the Congress floor in case of conflicting interests with the Executive, which happened in 1966 and again in 1968, in the vote on the bill to include municipalities in the national security area and in the regulation of the "multiple tickets". In other words, in the Márcio Moreira Alves affair the fact that *Arenistas* appeared on the floor and voted against the request for authorization was truly an unprecedented stance on their part.

Many years later, Jarbas Passarinho stated that there was no leader that could "compete with Krieger, a man who was highly respected by all of us. The government leadership was aggravated by the presence of the most radical Minister of all, Gama e Silva. He and Krieger did not get along at all. And Krieger refused to accept that position".[122] There was even a standoff between the government leadership, represented by Daniel Krieger in the Senate, and the Executive, made up of military men and jurists, like Gama e Silva, with no political finesse whatsoever. Besides, according to Passarinho, they had told President Costa e Silva that the case against Márcio Moreira Alves was going to pass in the Chamber. Several times they said, "We're going to win. It's going to be close, but we're going to win" (Dines, 2000, p. 337).

On another occasion, Jarbas Passarinho acknowledged as a complicating factor the "terrible relationship between the Minister of Justice and the leader of the government, or rather, between the Minister of Justice and the politicians" (Viana, 1982, p.11), which may have prevented a compromise solution like drawing on the prerogatives in the Chamber's internal rules for the Presiding Officers in the Chamber to punish Deputy Moreira Alves, rather than the Executive requesting authorization to try him.[123] Based on this testimony, it becomes very clear that there were alternatives to the radicalization, and that they could have been very successful. But the Minister of Justice and the President brushed them off, which definitely led to the government's defeat.

Against this backdrop, a comparison of the purges of 1964 and 1968–69 suggests a substantial change. In 1964, the government-line deputies consented, because at the beginning of the movement the purges mainly affected members of the PTB. The elimination of the increasingly competitive PTB opponents had been welcomed by most members of Congress. However, by 1968 the intervention by the military in the institutions had already taken on a different dimension from that intended by the politicians that had supported the 1964 movement, and there was now a clear threat to the Legislative branch. In other words, the purges could no longer be interpreted as an electoral advantage by means of knocking the wind out of a party or of political groups whose power was growing. They clearly showed that they were an anti-partisan and anti-Congressional expedient that affected the politicians indiscriminately, that hurt Congress as a whole.

There was thus a change in the reaction by the government-line politicians to the revoking of mandates and the suspension of political rights, where the purging of Deputy Márcio Moreira Alves was seen as a threat to the principle of inviolability of congressional mandates, thus assuming a distinct symbolic dimension.

From December 1968 to January 1969, the ARENA senators and President Costa e Silva exchanged correspondence. On the day after the AI-5, senators from ARENA met in the Monroe Palace, the former seat of the Senate in Rio de Janeiro, and sent a telegram to President Costa e Silva stating that since it was impossible to speak from the floor of Congress, they were manifesting their disagreement with the government's solution.[124] Costa e Silva replied that he had resorted to the AI-5 due to the lack of partisan political support, due to "the party's veritable hostility".[125] On the evening of 31 December 1968, Costa e Silva broadcast a message on the government's act through the National News Agency (Agência Nacional), on radio and television, largely holding the Congressmen of ARENA accountable for the decreeing of the AI-5: " . . . due to the irresponsibility with which a group of congressmen decided to humiliate, disrespect, and challenge the Armed Forces, with an apparently insignificant crisis precipitating a bleak outcome".[126] The President claimed that the government's partisan political base in the National Congress had failed, proving inconsistent and fragmented.[127] However, what had happened was not a failure on ARENA's part, but a demonstration of organization and confrontation with the Executive through the prime instrument available to members of Congress: the vote.

President Arthur da Costa e Silva claimed that he had initially issued warnings, interpreted as threats and heard as an expression of disregard for the so-called political class. In this speech, the President argued that it was impossible to rule the country through the institutions, since the party was not following his orientation. But according to various sources, the reality was the absence of negotiations. At this moment of clashes, the government and the ARENA congressmen introduced the category "political class" into the debate, where it appeared in many congressional meetings and in the press. Its use points to one of the conflicts that played out over the course of the dictatorship.

When analysing these episodes, various authors have identified a liberal moral reserve in the historical members of the UDN, among the politicians of the time. This group that was taking a distance from the government can be expanded by examining the careers of various members of Congress that had come from different parties and now belonged to ARENA. Surveying the careers of these politicians shows that some had served successive elective terms for some 20 years as city councilmen, deputies, or mayors. In addition to the moral reserve of these historical *Udenistas*, who were nationally known and respected, there was also interest among a number of politicians without major national prestige or renown, but who had long careers in administrative or legislative public life. When they had their prerogatives curtailed they launched a struggle to defend their work's legitimacy, motivated by maintenance of the monopoly over political representation by the professionals.

The Márcio Moreira Alves affair may even have been a pretext for decreeing the AI-5, as many studies claim. But the emphasis on the metaphor of a "sham" or "farce" to refer to the political negotiations has been employed by those who lack commitments to a constitutional order. For them, the AI-5 was greeted as an instrument that represented the possibility of interventions in the economy, such as then-Minister of Finance Delfim Netto[128]. Importantly, it was the second time since April 1964 that the President of Brazil had declared a congressional recess. In both 1966 and 1968, the problem was disagreement between members of Congress and the Executive. Thus, the idea of a "farce" should be taken with a grain of salt. After all, why would the government expose itself to such great attrition by closing the National Congress? The AI-5 marked the end of the farce, if by farce we understand the attempts at negotiations and the efforts to restore the rule of law, which would only happen years later, beginning in 1974.

Among the various civilian conspirators of 1964, there appears to have been a series of bewilderments and capitulations in response to the measures taken by the government, such as the endless purges and the resulting concentration of powers in the Executive. Yet while they disagreed with the direction taken by the regime, the *Arenistas* were always quick to reiterate their support for (or belief in) the principles of the "1964 revolution". Some ARENA leaders even emphasized the fact that although they disagreed, they did not consider themselves oppositionists and did not intend to join the MDB.

In a presidential system, when the President of the Republic lacks his party's support, there are usually internal crises, negotiations over policy orientation, a search for support from other parties, or even sanctions against some of the party's own members. In parliamentary systems, if the Prime Minister lacks Parliament's confidence, he (or she) falls. In a dictatorship, concerned with maintaining the representative system, when the party did not support the President of the Republic, it fell. This was definitely the fact that led the Executive to reorganize ARENA in 1969, substantially modifying the profile of the leaders authorized by the party.

CHAPTER
4

A Time of Silence and Reorganization (1969–1973)

"The origin of the AI-5 lies in the challenge by 94 deputies from ARENA to the Armed Forces, in the challenge with which they affronted His Excellency the President of the Republic".[1]

Pedro Vidigal

The outcome of the vote on the authorization to try Deputy Márcio Moreira Alves and the AI-5 placed the matter of relations between ARENA and government squarely on the order of the day again. A strong indication of this fact was the redefinition of the prevailing vocabulary that incorporated the terms "political class" or "politicians" on one side and "the military" or "the Armed Forces" on the other. Thus, beginning with the AI-5, there were many questions concerning the lack of interest in the political career and the expectations concerning the politicians, more clearly separated from and even opposed to the military. Increasingly, even among the government-line politicians, professional political activity was becoming limited by and subordinated to the Executive. From 1969 to 1973, the politicians from ARENA vied with the government, consisting mainly of military officers, for a possible margin of autonomy to exercise party activities in the elections and in the National Congress. Many of the rifts appear in the debates waged by different actors concerning the party and electoral legislation following the AI-5. This was one of the few areas in which some debate was still possible.

Starting with the AI-5, the press was more heavily censored, including with prior censorship. The organizations engaged in armed resistance to the dictatorship stepped up their activities and were harshly repressed. Most of the deaths of political prisoners under state custody in Brazil occurred during this same period. Given this confrontation, some representatives of the Catholic Church approached representatives of the

Armed Forces in search of dialogue for solution to the policy of torture practiced by the state.[2] At that juncture, even for representatives of the top echelons of the state and the Church, only "dialogues in the shadows" were possible. At the same time, Brazil was living the so-called "economic miracle". It is true that this economic development generated social and regional inequalities, but it also benefited various sectors of the middles classes, such as public servants, especially those in the state-owned companies, as well as self-employed workers and skilled blue-collar workers.

1 The alternatives for ARENA

Immediately after the AI-5, ARENA either did not produce many documents, they were not filed in the National Committee's archives, or they were removed later, but the fact is that the best sources found to analyse the prevailing expectations in the political milieu are the articles published in the Brazilian press. Political cartoons, stories, and press notes continued in the newspapers, indicating that everything appeared to be suspended temporarily and attesting to the political leaders' disorientation in the wake of 13 December 1968. In the moments of greatest uncertainty throughout the dictatorship, journalists and politicians worked with very little information, but they did not fail to imagine possible outcomes even for the most difficult situations. The result is a series of news based on a few facts and much speculation. No one knew what to expect of the regime.

In fact, only one thing was certain: ARENA would not be the same. It might be shut down or reorganized, or react to the Executive's instructions. National Committee Chairman Daniel Krieger and other senators approached President Costa e Silva to protest the AI-5.[3] Under those circumstances, Krieger and João Roma, executive secretary of the National Committee, resigned their positions. Krieger argued that he already differed from the government on policy orientation, a situation exacerbated by the Márcio Moreira Alves affair. Besides, he did not accept the President's criticism of the party's action, or the official version, repeated on several occasions, that the AI-5 had resulted from ARENA's irresponsibility.[4] Meanwhile, other *Arenista* leaders such as Rondon Pacheco, Geraldo Freire, and Filinto Müller openly shared the government's position that the vote backing Deputy Márcio Moreira Alves meant a betrayal of the government by ARENA. The party's rifts, which had always existed, became more evident than ever before. Many politicians were thus wondering whether the government would create a new party or allow ARENA to continue to exist. That is, shutting down ARENA was considered a possibility given the party's "treason" and the need to establish new relations with the government.

In statements to the press, the leader of ARENA in the Chamber of Deputies, Geraldo Freire, contended that it was indispensable to create a new party to serve as political backing for the government, because ARENA had "failed and was condemned to the grave".[5] For the deputy, the extinction of ARENA was the most feasible formula for forming another revolutionary party, oriented to defending the principles of March 1964.[6] The basic difference between ARENA and a future party should be unlimited loyalty to the Executive, eliminating forever the notion of any "rebellion" such as the one that had occurred in December 1968.

Journalists attempted to survey the leaders' positions by mapping the political situation in the states. In Belo Horizonte, Minas Gerais, in the circles of the *Palácio da Liberdade* under Governor Israel Pinheiro, a PSD old-timer and friend of Juscelino Kubitschek, dissolving ARENA and thus forming a new pro-government party was considered the best solution.[7] Deputy Carvalho Neto, leader of the ARENA caucus in the Guanabara State Legislature, also favoured the creation of a new political party to replace ARENA, claiming that the latter would never achieve the ideal homogeneity to ensure support for the government.[8] Geremias Fontes, chairman of the Rio de Janeiro State Committee, resigned his post arguing that ARENA, as the "party of Revolution", had failed to meet its commitments when the government most needed it.[9] As we can see, for quite different reasons, many ARENA members favoured the party's extinction.

Such statements sparked a series of contrary reactions from other members of Congress. The chairman of the São Paulo State Committee, Deputy Arnaldo Cerdeira, former State Secretary of Agriculture under Governor Adhemar de Barros, opposed eliminating the party. In his view, ARENA "immobilized gives the impression that it failed. And that's not true, because the majority of ARENA supported and continue to support President Costa e Silva. Only a few betrayed him".[10] In the same sense, Clóvis Stenzel, considered a spokesman for the military, was also against the idea of extinguishing the party, because it would not be possible to build solid foundations for a regime with repeated measures to extinguish political parties.[11]

In general, most *Arenista* congressmen were against the idea of eliminating the party, although this did not mean the defence of more autonomous positions such as those defended by many prior to AI-5.

On the contrary. For that very reasons, some *Arenistas* publicly acknowledged the need to expel certain party members. Arnaldo Cerdeira himself defended a cleansing of the organization, "purging those that act hypocritically against the revolution's objectives".[12] From Minas Gerais came support from old *Udenistas* for the proposal to promote the party leaders' resignation. For them, ARENA should reorganize itself based on self-criticism.[13]

The political leadership and specialized journalists were asking themselves how long the congressional recess would last and when ARENA would mobilize again. Some members of Congress launched a movement to convene a meeting of the National Committee's Executive Board. However, Filinto Müller, acting chairman of ARENA since Krieger's resignation, disagreed.[14] The senator considered any proposal from the politicians a mistake, acknowledging the Executive's pre-eminence and awaiting its initiative.[15]

Finally, in March, Filinto Müller and Arnaldo Prieto were officially designated to serve as chairman and secretary of ARENA, respectively.[16] But the party remained inert, and the new chairman's prevailing stance was to await the government's decisions. According to Müller, it was "up to the government to shape things more in its favour, besides imposing, and increasingly so, the rules of the political game".[17] With these statements, the senator was pointing to an impasse in the relations between party and government, as well as its obvious consequences: the need for a new institutional arrangement.

In this conjuncture, journalists, politicians, and the military increasingly underscored the distinctions between the civilian and military leaders. The difficulties experienced by the politicians after the AI-5 was decreed were widely reported in Brazil's mainstream press. In this context, January 1969, coordinated by the Minister of Justice, the General Commission for Investigations (*Comissão Geral de Investigações* – CGI) began its inquiries into alleged cases of illicit enrichment, mainly targeting political party leaders.[18]

Early that same month, the newspaper *Correio da Manhã* published a revealing note on the situation. It was a report on an encounter at a party between an Army commander and a national deputy from ARENA in São Paulo, soon after AI-5. Since the deputy had voted "against the government in the Márcio Moreira Alves affair, the general refused to greet him, thus revealing the true rift that exists between military and the politicians of ARENA who one day thought that they could act independently".[19] This note illustrates the new relations between the military and the ARENA congressmen, while also showing that even in the press, the vote against the authorization to try Márcio

Moreira Alves was reported as a vote against the government, reaffirming the certainty of the impossibility of ARENA acting with autonomy.

In the midst of speculations on ARENA's future, one journalist remarked that "to speak of government-line politicians nowadays is somewhat of an overstatement. The truth is that a handful of them still maintain contacts through the branch with some spheres of power, and from there, through comments and opinions, they filter information out to the journalists".[20] Through notes like these, many politicians got their message out, and there was a sort of bewilderment over the conditions in relations between politicians and the military, with fear of ridicule and humiliation.

According to *Informe JB*, Deputy Lopo Coelho, chairman of the ARENA State Committee for Guanabara, felt that the demand by many politicians to reopen Congress exposed them to ridicule. The deputy reiterated his support for the 1964 movement by explaining his view that the "revolution" should dictate the rules for Congress to function. But at the same time, he concluded: "Whoever is able to accept the rules with dignity as a democratic imposition, may he survive. I do not wish to survive politically on the basis of favours",[21] indicating the contradictions plaguing the government-line politicians, between the "revolution" and their own dignity.

Another highlight was the fact that any overly prolonged congressional recess could create difficulties for the political institutions themselves. Even Senator Filinto Müller, who was waiting for an initiative from the Executive, feared that a prolonged and forced recess in political activity might generate a vacuum, and that when the government decided to call on the politicians, "it would only find newcomers, because the more experienced politicians would refuse to participate in adventures".[22] Thus, the government-line politicians pointed to various spinoffs from the congressional recess for the representative system's functioning in the medium run. Their concerns included both the politicians' dignity or credibility, impacted by attitudes that represented total subservience to the Executive, as well as disinterest itself in professional political activity.

Finally, on 20 May 1969, Complementary Act No. 54 (AC-54) was decreed, setting new dates for elections to the political parties' municipal, state, and national committees. The Brazilian press reported a mixture of relief and scepticism among members of Congress.[23] From the politicians' perspective, the AC-54 signalled the reopening of Congress at any moment and the continuity of the two existing political parties.

Despite the disagreements between ARENA and the Executive, the government did not extinguish the party. In the press, Rondon Pacheco, then Cabinet Chief, denied that he was making contacts to form a new party.[24] The issue was seen as both a problem and a solution, because according to press notes, General Costa e Silva felt that it was preferable to maintain ARENA because it had a nationwide party structure. However, ARENA needed an exemplary reorganization.[25] The government was thus planning a new orientation for ARENA in the National Congress, but it acknowledged its organizational structure's value and did not intend to dismiss it.

The new legislation brought some changes, such as ignoring the law on "multiple tickets". According to the Minister, the multiple tickets were a "fiction aimed at reconciling the unreconcilable".[26] However, Filinto Müller convened the *Arenista* congressmen to examine the provisions and the practical consequences of the AC-54, where various suggestions were made, then submitted to the Superior Electoral Court (TSE).[27] The *Arenistas*' main concern was the contradiction between the AC-54 and the multiple-tickets law. Several days later, the TSE ruled in favour of the party's claim to maintain the multiple tickets, contrary to orientation from the Minister of Justice.

The government's intent with the AC-54 was to eliminate the multiple tickets from the electoral legislation, but the ARENA leadership resisted this change. This episode reinforces again the importance of the multiple tickets for the ARENA politicians: they were a form of expression of the extinct parties and of ARENA's own viability. The multiple tickets allowed the political leaders, many of whom had been political adversaries in the 1945–1964 regime, but joined in a single party since 1965, to continue competing with each other for electoral offices. Once again, the government gave in to ARENA's structural conformation, which had allowed and continued to allow the party to consolidate itself all across Brazil.

2 Reorganization of ARENA

2.1 Career politics discredited: Alienation and purges

The five years that transpired between the AC-54 and the presidential inauguration of General Ernesto Geisel in March 1974 were marked by ARENA's reorganization. The backdrop was the military's distrust towards its party, and the aim was to control it rigorously. On 24 May 1969, "National Infantry Day", President Costa e Silva spoke at a commemoration at the *Vila Militar* in Rio de Janeiro, making the news in various dailies. He expressed the tone of the relations between the government and the government-line politicians at that moment, announcing that he was reopening the doors to the politicians, but warning that "as I have counselled on other occasions, if we stray along the wrong paths, we will hold a new revolution within the revolution".[28]

According to the press, Filinto Müller considered the AC-54 "a test for the parties",[29] because if the new rules were not followed "out of carelessness, oversight, disillusionment, or disinterest by the politicians", the parties would be extinguished and "we will fall into a total dictatorship by our own hands".[30] Along the same line, days later, Rondon Pacheco revealed that the reopening process represented "one more challenge for the political class"[31] and stated that Costa e Silva wanted "to achieve a united ARENA that can truly play the role of government party and give political backing to the government's decisions. And ARENA will be called on to fulfil its mission and will have its role in guiding the revolution".[32]

At no point was there any discussion of disagreements between ARENA and government as a legitimate issue, and there was even the suggestion that ARENA would be responsible if the regime had to crack down again. Meanwhile, Minister Gama e Silva found a lack of identification between "the so-called government party" and "the revolutionary ideology".[33] Yet the *Arenistas* that voted against the authorization to try Márcio Moreira Alves had also supported the 1964 movement. However, they believed in another "revolutionary" direction, different from the path chosen by the members of the Executive.

After the AC-54, the government attempted to patch up these differences, significantly modifying the composition of ARENA's Executive Board, now chaired by the above-mentioned Rondon Pacheco. The newspapers hinted as possible chairmen Gama e Silva, Rondon Pacheco, and Jarbas Passarinho, but these hints appear to have been hearsay.[34] As Filinto Müller had noted, the government was attempting to shape the party in its favour, after suffering defeat in the Márcio Moreira Alves affair, even the rumours only mentioned names that were tightly bound to the military.

Minister of Justice Gama e Silva was a jurist from São Paulo with no previous legislative experience, viewed in a poor light by deputies and senators. Colonel Jarbas Passarinho had only taken up political activity in 1964, when Castello Branco named him Governor of Pará. Rondon Pacheco was one of the UDN legal experts from Minas Gerais. Starting in 1947, he had served one term as state deputy and four terms as national deputy, always on the UDN ticket. In 1966 he was elected again to national deputy under ARENA and was named Cabinet Chief.

He ended up being chosen as party chairman, but a few months after he took office to head the National Committee, journalists identified increasing resistance to him among members of Congress, who saw him as a placeman of the Executive.[35]

On the same occasion, in the National Executive Board, secretary-general João Roma resigned and was replaced by Arnaldo Prieto. João Roma, during the proceedings to request authorization to try Márcio Moreira Alves, had resigned his seat in the Committee of Constitution and Justice (CCJ) of the Chamber after the replacement of various full committee members from ARENA who were leaning towards denying the authorization.[36] On the other hand, Deputy Arnaldo Prieto was described in the same news story as a young politician with ample transit among the military and uncontested loyalty to the government's political line, and who would be able to survive any reformulation of the party.

At that stage, these measures were viewed as a necessary reorganization for reopening the National Congress. In this process, the government launched the work to revise the 1967 Constitution, convening Minister Gama e Silva, Pedro Aleixo, Rondon Pacheco, and jurists Carlos Medeiros e Silva, Themístocles Cavalcanti, and Miguel Reale. However, the constitutional revision would not be negotiated as expected, due to Costa e Silva's illness and death.

At this moment, the clash between the politicians and the pro-government military reached its peak, when Vice-President Pedro Aleixo was prevented from taking office as President. In late August 1969, Costa e Silva suffered a stroke and was rushed to Rio de Janeiro, accompanied by family, physicians, and advisors, and was confined to the *Palácio das Laranjeiras*. As his condition worsened, the Armed Forces High Command decided that he should be removed from office. In September, the military ministers officially took over the government, vetoing Pedro Aleixo from stepping up as President.

Deputy Rondon Pacheco was considered trustworthy by the military but was kept in the dark for weeks about the severity of Costa e Silva's condition. General Portella recalls that although Rondon Pacheco was trusted, as a politician he was closely connected to Pedro Aleixo, whom the military commanders had distrusted since the AI-5.[37] The view of a "betrayal" by the politicians and ARENA in the Márcio Moreira Alves affair was the crux of the argument by the military to prevent Pedro Aleixo from rising to the Presidency. General Jayme Portella presents this argument repeatedly in his memoirs on the Costa e Silva government. Portella felt that the Vice-President had fallen into disfavour with the Armed Forces when he voted against the AI-5 in the National Security Council (Conselho de Segurança Nacional), because for the military, Márcio Moreira Alves had insulted them, and AI-5 was the response to the Chamber of Deputies for refusing to authorize revoking Moreira Alves' mandate.

From the perspective of these military men, the congressional recess was a punishment for the politicians and a redress for the Armed Forces. The idea of the forced congressional recess as punishment for the politicians also appears in several contemporary newspaper articles: "The six-months recess is primarily a punishment meted out by the President of the Republic and the military leaders against the politicians, as the main culprit in the challenge to the Armed Forces".[38]

It was precisely during the congressional recess that ARENA members became increasingly identified as "politicians" or "the political class", according to various sources. This perception appeared among ARENA members themselves, influential military men, and journalists, who all used these terms extensively. The case of the governors is quite illustrative. Since they were mostly not career politicians, they were treated by everyone as a separate group, distinct from the "political class".

2.2 The purges following AI-5

On 30 December 1968, the first list was announced with purges from political offices and suspension of political rights based on the AI-5 that struck various members of Congress. From January to September 1969, on the eve of the reopening of the National Congress, the Executive purged successive waves of full members of Congress and alternates from both ARENA and MDB. On 16 January, the National Security Council purged and suspended the political rights of two senators, 35 national deputies, 38 state deputies, and one city councilman. That same month, the government discussed the criteria for new purges. It hesitated to adopt the criterion of party infidelity to revoke terms, since such a device, at the limit, would lead to the dissolution of ARENA itself.[39]

The Archives of the ARENA National Committee contain a list of the names of the *Arenista* Congressmen that were purged following AI-5. The list was organized state-by-state, recording whether the deputy was a full member of Congress or an alternate, and totalling the number of purges. The São Paulo caucus was the most heavily hit, with eight members stripped of their mandates, and the state was especially punished by the purging of Arnaldo Cerdeira, chairman of the ARENA State Committee. This was just one such list, but it illustrates the party's need to survey its losses. The government was shaping a new ARENA.

Table 4.1 ARENA deputies purged in 1969

State	Name	Date mandate and political rights revoked	Observations
Alagoas	Oséas Cardoso	29/4/1969	
Bahia	Oliveira Brito	11/9/1969	
Goiás	Jayme Câmara	13/3/1969	Alternate
Minas Gerais	Paulo Freire	7/2/1969	
	Antônio Luciano	29/4/1969	Alternate
	Marcial do Lago	7/2/1969	Alternate
Pará	Gilberto Azevedo	30/9/1969	
	Montenegro Duarte	7/2/1969	
	Epílogo de Campos	7/2/1969	Alternate
Paraíba	Pedro Gondim	7/2/1969	
	Vital do Rêgo	16/1/1969	
Paraná	Jorge Curi	16/1/1969	
Pernambuco	José Carlos Guerra	30/12/1969	
	Mouri Fernandes	7/2/1969	
	Ney Maranhão	7/2/1969	
	Souto Maior	29/4/1969	
	Bezerra Leite	29/4/1969	Alternate
Rio Grande do Norte	Aluízio Alves	7/2/196	
	Erivan França	97/2/1969	Alternate
Rio Grande do Sul	Flores Soares	16/1/1969	
Roraima	Atlas Cantanhede	7/2/1969	
Santa Catarina	Osmar Cunha	16/1/1969	
	Osmar Dutra	16/1/1969	
São Paulo	Arnaldo Cerdeira	30/9/1969	
	Cardoso Alves	16/1/1969	
	Celso Amaral	7/2/1969	
	Cunha Bueno	16/1/1969	
	Harry Normaton	16/1/1969	
	Israel Novaes	16/1/1969	
	Marcos Kertzmann	16/1/1969	
	Yukishigue Tamura	16/1/1969	
Sergipe	Machado Rollemberg	29/4/1969	

Full deputies purged	26
Alternates purged	6
Total	32

Source: ARENA 69.10.20 el/ce.

112 | *A Time of Silence and Reorganization (1969–1973)*

Table 4.2 National Executive Board of ARENA, 1969

Position	Name	Former party affiliation
Chairman:	Deputy Rondon Pacheco	UDN (MG)
1st vice-chairman	Deputy Batista Ramos	PTB (SP)
2° vice-chairman	Senator Wilson Gonçalves	PSD (CE)
3° vice-chairman	Deputy João Calmon	PSP (ES)
Secretary-general	Deputy Arnaldo Prieto	PDC (RS)
1st secretary	Deputy Raymundo Padilha	UDN (RJ)
2nd secretary	Deputy Virgílio Távora	UDN (CE)
1st treasurer	Senator João Cleofas	UDN (PE)
2nd treasurer	Senator Dinarte Mariz	UDN (RN)
Attorneys	Deputy Gustavo Capanema	PSD (MG)
	Deputy Rui Santos	UDN (BA)

Source: ARENA 68.06.25 op/cp and Abreu, *Dicionário*, Accessed February 7, 2019. https://cpdoc.fgv.br/acervo/dhbb.

Table 4.3 National Committee of ARENA, 1969

	PSD	UDN	PSP	PTN	PTB	PRP	PR	PDC
AM	José Lindoso							
AC	José Guiomard dos Santos							
RR		Francisco Elesbão						
RO					Paulo Nunes Leal			
AP				Janary Nunes				
PA					Cattete Pinheiro			
MA	Victorino Freire		Clodomir Millet					
PI		Petrônio Portella						
CE	Wilson Gonçalves	Virgílio Távora						
RN		Dinarte Mariz						
AL		Oceano Carleial						
PB	Aderbal Jurema	Plínio Lemos						
PE		João Cleofas						

A Time of Silence and Reorganization (1969–1973) | 113

Table 4.3   *Continued*

	PSD	UDN	PSP	PTN	PTB	PRP	PR	PDC
SE	Arnaldo Garcez							
BA		Ruy Santos Manuel Novais (UDN/PR)			Theódulo de Albuquerque			
MT								
GO		Emival Caiado						
MG	Gustavo Capanema	Rondon Pacheco José Bonifácio					Arthur Bernardes Filho	
ES	João Calmon					Oswaldo Zanelo		
GB	Mendes de Morais	Hélio Beltrão						
RJ	Gilberto Marinho	Raimundo Padilha						
SP	Antonio Feliciano	Herbert Levy			Batista Ramos	Plínio Salgado		
PR	Accioli Filho							Ney Braga
SC	Celso Ramos	Irineu Bornhausen						
RS	Daniel Faraco Ary Alcântara							Arnaldo Prieto

Source: "Estatuto da Aliança Renovadora Nacional, 1969." Documento no. 5 BN IV–221, 3, 6 n° 3.

3   Reopening of the National Congress

> ARENA and government – i.e., the Revolution and its Party – are not merely allied here or signing a pact of coexistence, but proclaiming that the two form an inseparable whole with two parts in close solidarity, neither of which can live fully without the other.[40] Rondon Pacheco

In the 3rd National Convention of ARENA, General Médici and Deputy Rondon Pacheco made speeches that exemplified the National Committee's political reorientation.[41] In the July 1968 convention, Daniel Krieger and Luís Viana Filho had demanded more participation by ARENA in the government, seeking to show the specificities of the relations between the Executive and the party that supported it. In this 1969 convention, Rondon Pacheco, far from attempting to underscore party autonomy, appeared to blame ARENA outright for the government's possible difficulties: "For us of the National Renewal Alliance, the time for responsibility has come".[42] As chairman of the National Committee, Rondon Pacheco attempted to reaffirm a unity often belied by the events. In this same sense, the motions passed at the meeting featured one defending party loyalty and party support for the government, submitted by Deputy Geraldo Freire and Senator Petrônio Portela.[43]

The National Congress was not reopened until 22 October 1969, after eleven months in recess and dozens of purges. The return to legislative activity was marked by speeches on Constitutional Amendment No. 1 of 17 October 1969. The new legislation made the intervention in the political field even harsher, especially with the elimination of Congressional inviolability and the imposition of party loyalty. The political reforms launched by Gama e Silva during the Costa e Silva government followed the same path under the command of Alfredo Buzaid, Médici's Minister of Justice. Both were considered extremely radical by many politicians and military.

When Congress was reopened, Deputy Benedito Ferreira (ARENA – GO) asked, "Mr. President, distinguished deputies, a pressing question is hanging over the nation: What good is the National Congress, given the new Constitution?"[44] For the deputy, it was necessary to show society the importance of the Legislative branch under such circumstances. After all, he noted:

> With shame and especially with great sadness for us, that substantial segments of the population are displaying an undisguisable satisfaction over the recess inflicted upon us, and among the more exalted, and definitely the least informed, a desire, not just for a recess, but for an outright shutdown, since they see our institution as idle and useless.[45]

When Congress was reopened, the Chamber of Deputies resumed functioning with 321 deputies (there had been 406 at the start of the 1967 legislature) and the Senate resumed with 59 senators (as opposed to 66 previously). Eighty-eight deputies and 5 senators had been purged.[46] According to Governor Luís Viana Filho, Cabinet Chief in the Castello Branco government and one who had demanded greater participation by the politicians in the government during the party's convention in 1968, what was left of Congress after the purges in 1969 sufficed "to keep face and help save the institutions, while time passes and with it the remaining resentments and animosities".[47]

Among ARENA's leadership in the National Congress, Filinto Müller replaced Daniel Krieger as leader in the Senate and Geraldo Freire stayed on in the Chamber of Deputies. Yet over the course of the Médici government, Deputies Cantídio Sampaio (ARENA – SP) and Daniel Faraco (ARENA – RS) also acted as leaders in the Chamber.[48] Under those circumstances, the leader of MDB took the floor numerous times to analyse the positions by the government party members. Often ironic, the oppositionists focused on the difficulties created by the Executive for the politicians in general, affecting ARENA just as much as MDB. Deputy Nelson Carneiro (MDB – GB) was unforgiving:

> The negotiators of the [constitutional] revision forgot, however, that one thing is ARENA and another thing is the *Arenistas*. And that the fickle winds and furious hurricanes, despite the feminine names that fear assigns to them, mainly destroy the poor man's shack, it's true, but also sweep away the rich man's pompous mansion.[49]

Among the consequences of the hurricanes' fury, Nelson Carneiro was hinting at the change in the ARENA leadership's profile, which no longer included the likes of Senators Daniel Krieger, Milton Campos, and Carvalho Pinto, considered liberal leaders.

National Deputy Petrônio Figueiredo (MDB – PB) insisted on the same point, seeking to show the reorientation implemented by the government, since even compared to the other legislation created since 1964, Constitutional Amendment No. 1 was radical: "[Congressional] inviolability was impacted by alarming restrictions".[50] Along the same line, the deputy pointed to the lack of consensus among the *Arenistas* as an argument for the need to reformulate the law. After all, the Constitution had been widely criticized because of the constraints on congressional immunities, in speeches by Senators Milton Campos, Carvalho Pinto, and Aloísio de Carvalho.[51]

There was also major controversy over the legislation on the criteria for ineligibility.[52] The legislation originally determined that whoever had ever served as mayor or governor and their relatives were ineligible.[53] The given the opposition from the *Arenistas*, the Executive reconsidered.[54]

The principal case of ineligibility was the former governors, most of whom were important politicians capable of mobilizing other national, state, and local party leaders and large constituencies, because the state governments were – and still are – a strategic position in the Brazilian political system. The decree thus limited state gubernatorial candidacies to members of Congress or novices in party politics, certainly owners of scanty political capital compared to the former governors, or of political capital that was associated exclusively with the military themselves. In either case they were people with little potential autonomy.

The main target of expanding the criteria for ineligibility was apparently the politicians of ARENA themselves, since the governors were now chosen by the military and elected by the state legislatures, mostly controlled by the *Arenistas*. Therefore, the ARENA Congressmen felt that the ineligibilities decree was "unjust and monstrous as a rule for limiting political careers" (Castello Branco, vol. 3, 1979, p. 464).

In the Senate, Milton Campos gave a speech, cited numerous times as an authoritative argument, making his position very clear: he opposed the AI-5 and opposed the impediment to Pedro Aleixo, making a point of not appearing for either the ceremonial approval of the candidacies or the election of Médici and Radmaker. After a long career in which he served as deputy and governor of Minas Gerais, always under the UDN, the Senator did not fail to admit that in these most recent events, ARENA had done nothing but second the decisions by the Armed Forces High Command.

Based on this observation, Campos analysed the most extensively commented issue of that period: the marginalization of the "political class". First, the senator pointed to the impropriety of the category in use, citing its origins in Gaetano Mosca and Vilfredo Pareto. Second, he explained that there is always turnover among political leaders, who can have diverse backgrounds, referring directly to the military and the technical experts. The fundamental point, he warned, was the way political representation was built: "it is dangerous to promote it from the top down, because then the people fail to participate in it, and the democratic inspiration is forgotten, turning the political elite into a politically irresponsible bureaucracy" (Campos, 1972, p. 289). He thus clearly highlighted one of the representative system's fundamental principles: hearing the people and the resulting turnover in power.

In his conclusions, Milton Campos defended his project for the party and, referring to ARENA, recalled "my commitments to freedom, and on this basis, to be able to serve the democratic regime and the revolution that was made to guarantee it" (Campos, 1972, p. 290). He thus attempted to remember a certain "revolutionary" orientation, always very complex and ambiguous, especially in that conjuncture. After all, what could people expect from a time in which one of the main party leaders, Filinto Müller, defended curtailing election advertising on radio and television, arguing that "too much campaigning ends up turning into a weapon against the parties and against the elections themselves"?[55]

4 Membership and party loyalty in ARENA

Certainly not everyone thought like Milton Campos, and among those who did, not everyone dared criticize the government on the floor of the Chamber or Senate. But neither was Filinto Müller a consensus among the *Arenistas*. In the ARENA caucuses, various controversial issues were raised for debate.

ARENA, like MDB, did not have its own national headquarters, so its meetings were held mainly in the Congress offices. In many of such meetings, the speeches by members of Congress were recorded directly on the house microphones by staffers. The speeches' spelling and grammar were corrected by the speakers themselves. However, some original excerpts were redacted, probably intending to prevent future reading. But wherever it is possible to make out the redacted phrases, one discovers little ironies and signs of friction between members of Congress.

The caucuses were coordinated by the chairman of the National Committee, who usually opened the meetings with a speech outlining the business of the day and adjourned the meeting with another speech. During the meetings the Congressmen expounded on their issues and debated with each other and the party chairman.

In July 1970, Rondon Pacheco chaired a meeting of the ARENA caucus on the party conventions and the elections for deputies, senators, and governors.[56] The ARENA congressmen knew that the situation was not particularly favourable for partisan and electoral activities, since it increasingly kept the politicians away from the activities involved in mobilizing their local constituencies. Therefore, Deputy Daniel Faraco, who had served five consecutive terms in the Chamber of Deputies, always on the PSD ticket, emphasized the need to restore the floor of Congress as the stage for grand debate. Meanwhile, Deputy Hamilton Prado (ARENA – SP), then serving his fourth term, announced that he planned to base his campaign on the grand feats of the 1964 movement "in order for us to integrate our party with the achievements of the revolutionary process".[57]

There was also evident concern over the effect of the string of purges on the politicians' credibility. As a means to reconcile the interests of ARENA and government, Senator Clodomir Millet (ARENA – MA) proposed that the party should organize a dossier of candidates to analyse their individual situations, claiming that

> It is very annoying for us that a party should organize its convention – especially the government party – and for one reason or another, after

having picked the candidate, the party can't register his candidacy because it has been discovered too late that he lacked the qualities required by the internal rules and that of course the revolution also requires.[58]

These ARENA congressmen were organizing to continue their activities. They acknowledged the need for (and even proposed) their own submission to the government intelligence agencies for the selection of candidates, paradoxically, as a means to safeguard their legitimacy with the electorate.

Among the measures to control ARENA, the most notorious was the party loyalty law, decreed as part of Constitutional Amendment No. 1. Article 152, sole paragraph, ruling on the matter, determined the loss of mandates for members of Congress who "by attitude or by the vote, oppose the guidelines legitimately established by the party leadership or abandons the party by which he was elected". In the political field, this was one of the main consequences of the vote by some ARENA deputies against the government line in 1968. The law aimed to control the congressional party caucuses through the party legislation, without the need to resort to authoritarian measures alien to the institutions' functioning and without paying the political price of closing down Congress, as had occurred in 1968.

The party loyalty decree was not regulated until 1971, with the passage of a new Organic Law for Political Parties. Concerning the latter's provisions, the ARENA Archives contain transcriptions of caucus meetings on the new Organic Law, all held in May and June 1971. A certain irony permeates the references to Congress's scanty participation in drafting the bill. Reading these transcriptions is highly revealing, as illustrated by the dialogue below. Note that some passages appear in brackets in the typewritten transcription filed in the ARENA Archives. These comments were redacted, crossed out with a ballpoint pen, but they can be read easily and we have retrieved and quoted them here.

These caucus meetings were chaired by Deputy João Batista Ramos. In 1971, Rondon Pacheco was named governor of Minas Gerais, and Batista Ramos took over as ARENA chairman. At that stage he already had a long political career. He had been secretary-in-chief of the Ministry of Justice in the Dutra government, and beginning in 1954 he had served three consecutive terms as national deputy under the PTB. He had also been Minister of Labour, Industry, and Commerce under the Kubitschek government. He was thus a rare case of a member of the PTB who had subsequently risen within the ARENA ranks.

The matter of party loyalty had also been heavily debated by Deputy Antônio Mariz, who was also no newcomer to politics. On the contrary, he had a family tradition, his father having been state deputy from 1928 to 1930 and federal intervenor in the state of Paraíba from 1934 to 1935. In 1962, Antônio Mariz served as deputy cabinet chief to the governor. He was elected mayor of Sousa, Paraíba state, in 1963, and in 1970 he was elected national deputy. From the pinnacle of this experience, the deputy asked:

> I wish to know whether the purpose of this meeting is to inform the ARENA caucuses of the decisions taken in *'petit comitê'*, as Deputy José Carlos Fonseca described it, that is, by delegates of the Executive Board and by congressional leaders and representatives of the Executive, or rather, if the meeting was intended to guarantee party discipline in the vote on the matter currently under review by Congress.
> The Chairman – . . . I would say that it is for both purposes. We are here exchanging ideas with our colleagues, and this exchange results in reciprocal clarifications.
> [A Deputy – We're letting off steam.]
> [The Chairman – You are correct, letting off steam is so good.]
> [A Deputy – That is all we are doing. (laughter).]
> [The Chairman – That is not all.] I feel some colleagues are being rather unfair. I will explain why. Suffice it to compare the original bill with the substitute version, and now with the version with the last changes. I mean, considering all the constraints that still exist for the political world, we have been as liberal as possible. We have come here to exchange ideas with our colleagues. We can still receive some suggestions, because we will still discuss the matter with the rapporteur.
> [A Deputy – Is anyone taking notes?]
> [The Chairman – The suggestions are being recorded. Any other questions?]
> [The Deputy – Very well, thank you.]
> The Chairman – Everything we're doing here is in the liberalizing spirit of our leaders, who after all have confirmed this spirit in the solutions they have handed down. The senators and deputies have witnessed all this. And the leaders defended their proposals enthusiastically, as the object of amendments. That is why we were able to [soften] improve the original bill.[59]

In the meeting on 27 May 1971, Chairman Batista Ramos explained in his opening remarks that he had initially considered drafting an electoral bill that would replace the AC-54. But over the course of the discussions, suggestions were made, accepted by the government, to also include party loyalty in the Organic Law. A meeting began haphazardly with speeches on a wide range of matters until Senator José Lindoso[60] summarized the debate with its two main points, party membership and party loyalty. According to Lindoso, this put the relationship the government was imposing on its party back on the order of the day again: "This is going to require well thought-out collaboration and deep reflection on the desire to find a balance whereby the party can survive as a unit of party thinking and expression while not annihilating its members".[61]

According to various members of Congress, the party was now fenced in, subject to a series of constraints on its autonomy. One of the main criticisms for the bill was its inclusion of certain matters as juridically binding rather than being governed by the party's own internal bylaws, a provision that deprived the party members of decision-making power over their own organization. Deputy Antonio Mariz argued that party caucus discipline should be determined by the party's bylaws rather than by laws, since each party would be free to have its own way of dealing with political action and of determining what it would require of its members.[62]

Further discussing the matter of party discipline, Mariz argued that the caucuses had a dual responsibility, as party representatives and as Legislative representatives, regardless of which party they belonged to. Thus, he argued, a deputy could not submit exclusively the party,

> Except in the extreme parties, with severe discipline, as with the Communist Party or the Fascist Party. Except in such cases, a deputy preserves a margin, albeit minimal, in which he attempts to reconcile the interests of his party, which is factious by definition, with the national interest, to which he is committed by virtue of his popular mandate.[63]

Considering the horizon of the discussion in the 1970s, the comparison with Communist Party discipline was a telling argument. The deputy was making a distinction between ARENA and the model of a Communist or Fascist revolutionary party in order to defend relative autonomy for members of the Brazilian Congress vis-à-vis their own parties, based on the argument of representing the people. The deputy was thus defending the idea of a government party that preserve some autonomy. The argument of popular representation, of holding an elective office, clearly indicated the tension in the forms of representation in the regime: the congressional form, backed by citizens' votes, alongside representation of the federal Executive, enforced by a power grab.

Further on the party loyalty issue, several members of Congress questioned the fact that the article only ruled on deputies and senators, so they demanded that it be extended to mayors and governors. One of the most important speeches on the matter was by Senator Nei Braga, who not only had military training and had served as Chief of Police in the Paraná state government from 1952 to 1954, but was also an experienced politician.[64] Nei Braga, in the June caucus meeting, also complained that the Executive had not been included in the party loyalty legislation.[65]

Filinto Müller agreed that members of the executive branches should also be included, but that the Constitution only mentioned senators and deputies, so that governors and mayors could not be included.[66] Even after this observation, Deputy Rui Bacelar insisted: "If Your Excellency recalls, and if this house recalls as well, why not extend the loyalty principle to holders of executives offices?"[67] Deputy Rui Bacelar argued that as things stood, whoever occupied an executive office could even be expelled from the party, but without losing his mandate. After all, the senators and national deputies of ARENA refused to accept a statutory difference in the party between themselves, as members of Congress, and the governors. This was one of the main points in the debate on regulation of party loyalty.

The law theoretically served as a factor for party cohesion, but in that context, it reinforced the difference between members of Congress and governors in the party. It is thus crucial to analyse the law's meaning and effects on a government party in a dictatorship, and whose National Committee was controlled by the Executive. Under those circumstances, the law was criticized because it obviously eliminated any pretence at autonomy for members of Congress from ARENA, which they were debating precisely because they contended that legislation pertaining to party loyalty should be up to the party itself to decide. Each party organization should rule on its members according to its own bylaws. These were the *Arenistas*' concerns and expectations when they debated the proposal for the Organic Law, clearly expressing a strategy that aimed to reinforce the party and its internal power.

Political scientist Timothy Power emphasizes that the party loyalty law and the ban on switching parties was exactly the sort of institutional innovation that many had been recommending for some time to reverse the purported Brazilian tradition of weak and undisciplined parties.[68] However, this law was seen as clear meddling by the Executive in Congress's jurisdiction, with exactly the opposite objective as that intended by those who had originally recommended such a measure. The law aimed to weaken ARENA by further limiting its autonomy.

Although the *Arenistas* could not voice such a view so emphatically in public, many of them shared it and even expressed it behind closed caucus doors, and it could be stated publicly by a member of the opposition to the regime, such as Ernani do Amaral Peixoto. On the occasion, the senator stated to the press that according to the bill, party loyalty was to become a veritable permanent delegation of powers that the National Congress would yield to the President of the Republic. After all, as Amaral Peixoto imagined the effects of party loyalty, "ARENA gives the orders to Congress, and the government gives the orders to ARENA".[69] Which reminds us of the famous *sorites* speech by Nabuco de Araújo on 17 July 1868:

> Is this not a veritable absolutism, given the current state of elections in our country? Consider this fatal sorites. This sorites eliminates the representative system: the Moderating Power can call on whomever it wants to organize cabinet ministries; this person holds the election, because he is supposed to do so; this election makes the majority. There you have our country's representative system![70]

Here is another breach of the principle of separation of powers, using the metaphor of the President or Executive as the Moderating Power. This was also true in the political negotiations led by President Campos Salles in Brazil's First Republic, with the so-called "politics of the governors".[71]

5 The "politics of the governors": Indirect elections and leadership in the state committees

Beginning in 1969, one facet of the dispute between Congress and government involved the leadership of the state party committees, since one of the manoeuvres by the Executive to better control ARENA was to maintain "indirect" elections for the state governments while delegating authority to the governors to command the state party committees. According to the draft bill for the Organic Law, in practice the governors would now control the regional committees, and through them the respective members of Congress, although with certain limitations. This was tantamount to a kind of "politics of the governors" transposed historically to 1970, the last year of the term for those elected directly in 1965. Under the new law, from 1970 all the governors would be persons connected directly to the federal Executive.

Such circumstances have led to interpretations such as those of David Fleischer and Robert Wesson, who view ARENA to a certain extent as a party of the state governors.[72] This was true because the party controlled the state legislatures, which elected the governors, who were nominated by the military Presidents. But it should be said that this governors' party model was the Executive's idea, and that it only materialized under protests from several ARENA deputies and senators.

According to political scientist Margaret Jenks, the recruitment of new governors became the principal form of control of the states' politics, and via them, control of the ARENA federal caucus.[73] The governorship was probably the most coveted position, not only because it was strategic for one's political career in Brazil, but also because civilians had been excluded from running for President.

In 1970, ARENA chairman Rondon Pacheco travelled to the states to negotiate the candidacies to the state governments. The press saw the so-called "Rondon Pacheco mission" as politically complementing the work by the intelligence agencies. Through this process, Médici would scrutinize the list of pretenders to office as governors, senators, and national deputies. According to newspaper columnist Carlos Castello Branco, the mission consisted in preparing the party ranks to receive the governors handpicked by the President, suggesting that the politicians would have to wait a little longer before hoping to have a say in the government's decisions.[74]

The negotiations involved in this "politics of the governors" and the diversity of leaders with various party origins forming ARENA sparked many reactions among *Arenista* deputies and senators. In this sense, indirect elections to state governments was one of the main bones of contention at the time. Senator Clodomir Millet appealed to the members of Congress in a caucus meeting:

> I will begin by calling attention and asking for everyone's understanding. For there to be true understanding when organizing the election tickets, when it comes time for the committee to meet to choose the candidates for governor, to avoid having discordant voices, with people dissatisfied, dissatisfied deputies, deputies that haven't been heard and who may voice their protests by voting against the decisions at the committee meeting, for governors, which in the final analysis would mean discredit for the candidate chosen in the manner that we're all aware of.[75]

The senator is arguing that it was an exceptional situation. He does not defend the new mechanisms for party functioning, but he recognizes them and justifies them as the only possible alternative, which had to be handled with a minimum of attrition.

At a meeting of members of Congress from ARENA and Minister of Justice Alfredo Buzaid, National Deputy Edilson Távora (ARENA – CE) suggested to the minister that a meeting be convened on issues pertaining to the Legislative, and particularly to the bill for the Organic Law on Political Parties drafted by the Executive.[76] The deputy referred to the bill as "yielding the power to judge a deputy's acts to the parties' Executive Boards", focusing on the controversy over congressional prerogatives:

> I have served four terms as deputy, 16 years as deputy, and I have never been invited to participate in a party committee or executive board. Therefore, I will not allow a boy who has lost the election to judge my attitudes as deputy, since I have struggled for long, my victory having been won with effort and with my people's trust, the people of my state.[77]

In a debate between members of Congress and the party chairman on the article pertaining to the party conventions' schedule, several deputies and senators defended holding municipal and state conventions during the congressional recess. On the other hand, the governors opposed holding party elections during the recess, when deputies and senators would have more time and would be in a better position to influence the formation of the municipal and state committees.[78]

Deputy Jairo Magalhães insisted in the caucus meetings, "Mr. chairman, Congress is not in recess in August and September,"[79] in a speech met by applause. Other deputies, such as Maurício Toledo, argued that all the congressmen attending the meeting backed the proposal to postpone the elections until the recess, because they experienced the difficulties of party recruitment, and they thus deserved to be heard. Deputy Siqueira Campos reiterated: "Our participation in these elections to the municipal committees would be excellent for honouring the municipal and state leaders,"[80] while Luiz Braga insisted:

> We are aware that in August and September, in the President's words and under his instructions, we will have the regimentation for the elections to the municipal committees. We will thus elect the delegates who will, in turn, elect the state committee. A month later, these delegates will also be elected to the national convention. Our mission, therefore, is of the utmost importance, since it involves the party's organization. Without it, our presence in the Chamber would be meaningless. Through our parties, we represent the trends in our regions. Through

these contacts, the guidance is decided for the state deputies, mayors, and city councilmen, as to the party's organization.[81]

The issue was raised again at the meeting on 24 June. Batista Ramos reported that the change in the calendar had been accepted, so that the municipal conventions were now scheduled for January, the state conventions for March, and the national convention for April. The debates on the party membership process, the dispute between governors and members of Congress over the election schedule, refer to the organizational practices that are necessary to keep a political party functioning. This reveals the need for mobilization of the membership, even for a government party under a dictatorship.

The debate continued to mobilize members of Congress even after the new Organic Law was passed. Some deputies in ARENA caucus meetings sustained the discussion on the party's organization. National Deputy Élcio Álvares (ARENA – ES) noted in one of these meetings:

> There is a dominant feeling among the deputies – a desire already expressed by some governors – that the committees would obey the governor directly in their composition, with the political class represented by us, the national deputies, somewhat distant from our home territories, and the state deputies only receiving orientation which would be an eminently decisive criterion from the governor. The national deputies and, allow me, the senators, are now the most vulnerable class in terms of political discredit, because being far away from our states, we suffer the attrition of the future candidates and are also far from that common political decision-making centre, which is our committee.[82]

In a reply to Álvares, Batista Ramos identified a mismatch between the governors and the "political classes", acknowledging major differences between the party members according to their positions in the political field, i.e., deputies and senators versus state governors.

The following year, Batista Ramos submitted a report whose main theme was party integration. The chairman felt it was necessary to promote better relations between the Executive and the "political community", as he referred to the members of Congress. Among the causes of the difficulties, he identified the indirect election of governors, by definition disconnected from the political community, and the choices for the party secretariat, mostly technical. The commentary by Batista Ramos suggests that political representation via indirect gubernatorial elections placed a distance between the "political community" and the leaders named to the important position of state governor. In his report, Batista Ramos describes the relations between the ARENA membership and the Executive based on the view of the AI-5 as a "punitive recess", addressing its consequences very revealingly:

> The AI-5 was a punitive recess that created a distance between the government and the members of Congress and politicians, who came to be viewed (and who even viewed themselves) as unwanted by the administration. It was thus urgent to find new paths to restore good relations between the state governors and the members of Congress, consistent with the revolutionary principles. This has already been happening, since the majority of the governors, who are sensitive to the problem, are testing criteria with this objective.[83]

The political report by Deputy Theódulo de Albuquerque (ARENA – BA) emphasized the effort by Batista Ramos, who had visited all the states to make contacts and meet with all wings of the party, attempting to smooth over the discontentment.[84]

ARENA held its municipal, state, and national conventions from January to April de 1972. The incoming executive boards and committees were sworn in at these meetings. The 4th National Convention was held on 22–23 April 1972 in Brasília and approved the party's new bylaws, code of ethics, and letter of principles.[85] Filinto Müller was sworn in as chairman of the National Committee at this convention. A few days later, in a meeting with the party's Chamber and Senate caucuses, he opened the session introducing himself as the mediator between the party and the government, having as their common goal "to strengthen our institutions and respect for the Legislative branch".[86] He remarked, however, that

> The only thing I can offer my distinguished colleagues is a contact, a two-way street between the Legislative and the Executive. I am not going to just bring the suggestions referred to me by the Executive to submit to the Legislative for its approval or review. Above all, I want to take the suggestions and demands from the Legislative for them to be examined and later for us to be able to discuss them and implement them, here, in our common endeavour . . . that we may join efforts to achieve this common goal of consolidating and expanding our congressional prerogatives (Applause).[87]

Over the course of the meeting, several members of Congress submitted proposals to expand the politicians' activities in mobilizing elections.

Deputy Maurício Toledo (ARENA – SP) drafted a bill for a constitutional amendment to restore the July recess in order to allow deputies to have more contact with their constituencies.[88] Deputy Tourinho Dantas (ARENA – BA), who had served three terms as state deputy beginning in 1950 and one as national deputy in 1962, always under UDN, introduced himself as a spokesman for the Bahia State Union of Mayors, proposing to restore the coinciding years for municipal, state, and federal elections,[89] starting in 1974, arguing that staggering the elections undermined administrative continuity. He also argued that coinciding election years would result in a major political fact in which the deputies would be the main protagonists. He defended the issue energetically before the chairman of the National Committee, contending that the very fact that he had shown the "audacity" of submitting a document signed by 367 mayors from his state should not be grounds for threatening to revoke his mandate for reasons of party infidelity.

In the end, however, Filinto Müller, who had just been sworn in as party chairman promising to expand Congress's prerogatives, commented on some speeches and now recommended precisely the opposite:

> I would ask that you not collect any more signatures for constitutional amendments, especially by us, ARENA, who did not guarantee the quorum for a constitutional amendment proposed by the other party. This is essential, because otherwise, if we were to guarantee the quorum for a constitutional amendment proposed by MDB, there would be a flood of amendments. But to Deputy Maurício Toledo, who has already begun collecting signatures for a certain amendment, pertaining to the July recess, I ask you to cease your work until I advise you that you may continue.[90]

Filinto Müller thus showed that he was aware of the expectations by members of Congress to expand their activities, but at the same time he was instructing them to curtail such initiatives. During the same meeting, Filinto Müller made several recommendations on the vote for Constitutional Amendment No. 2, which reinstituted indirect elections for state governors. The new chairman of ARENA argued that it was still too early to promote changes and told the deputies and senators that if there were no quorum for the vote on the constitutional amendment, he would be stripped of his position: "I appeal to all the colleagues from the Chamber and the Senate to show up and vote. We have 223 deputies. I would like to have 223 ayes. We have 59 senators. I would like to have 59 voting for the amendment".[91]

128 | A Time of Silence and Reorganization (1969–1973)

The debate in Congress on the matter of establishment of representation in the state governments turned into a broader debate on the country's institutional political model. Throughout the dictatorship, the government had used various arguments to defend the lack of direct elections to governors. The regime's frequent arguments referred to the "threats" from "populists", initially to defend against "demagoguery", and later the "terrorists", after the AI-5.

Meanwhile, the *Emedebistas* argued that the "indirect" elections directly jeopardized the *Arenistas* themselves. Deputy Daniel Faraco, as leader of ARENA, replied that MDB was a taking selfish view of political activity, whose ultimate goal was "the common good". Faraco challenged the interpretation by MDB of the *Arenistas*' expectations:

> The situation would be such that it would be impossible to exercise political activity satisfactorily, and those devoted to it would feel frustrated, and rightfully so, by the practical uselessness of the role left to them. The constitutional amendment, according to our distinguished colleagues from the opposition in this House, is purportedly an example of this state of things, since it impacted the political structure heavily, annihilating the leaders that were legitimately proposing to run for to state governors.[92]

ARENA leader Daniel Faraco argued further that the election campaigns were threats to economic development due to the "psychological mobilization of thwarted interests, inevitable in heated and impassioned campaigns such as those for state governors".[93] Meanwhile, Deputy Cantídio Sampaio acknowledged that support for indirect elections was not a consensus among the ARENA Congressman.[94] Deputy Élcio Álvares, when explaining his understanding of the process, showed that there were different readings of the indirect elections:

> Today, as before, we believe that indirect elections were not a punishment, and that they were not meant to downgrade the political class. Indirect elections represent – and this is our way of thinking and that of the ARENA chairman – an opportunity by which the political classes can renew their ideas and renew their conduct, and will be able, in the future, to fully exercise all their duties and obligations pertaining to seriously serving a congressional mandate.[95]

In an aside, Deputy Juarez Bernardes (MDB – CE) offered some ironic comments on the speech by the leader of ARENA, showing "surprise" and "disenchantment" with the argument that direct elections might hurt the economy: "As for their highly touted 'Brazilian miracle', they try to exclude the people, who want a voice, to give their verdict on the veracity (or lack thereof) of the [economic] miracle. Either the saint no longer believes in his own 'miracle', or he fears losing his robes".[96]

In the end, the vote in favour of Constitutional Amendment No. 2 by the members of Congress from ARENA was the object of congratulations by members of the party itself. Deputy Amaral de Souza (ARENA – RS),[97] who defended the indirect elections, thought they should be incorporated permanently into the Constitution rather than temporarily, as provided by the amendment. On the occasion, the deputy called everyone's attention to the passage of the amendment:

> Mr. president, distinguished deputies, the overwhelming vote by ARENA in favour of the constitutional amendment . . . is particularly significant in our political life. There were no blank votes. There were no desertions, by means of strategically failing to appear [on the floor] or for lack of interest. What the press reported actually happened: of the 223 *Arenistas* in Congress, only 3 failed to appear for the sessions, two of whom were justified by reason of illness. And 220 in attendance voiced their 'ayes' to the constitutional amendment.[98]

In the same tone, Deputy Etelvino Lins (ARENA – PE)[99] highlighted that vote as a milestone,

> Due to the meeting's special significance, for the first time since December 1968, between two powers, the revolutionary power and the constitutional power of Congress. Therefore, may we be capable of reaping from this episode the optimistic perspective that opens up for the necessary compatibility between the revolutionary spirit and the democratic institutions.[100]

Deputy Airon Rios (ARENA – PE) was one of the few in ARENA to clearly oppose the indirect elections for state governors:

> Mr. president, distinguished deputies, experience has shown that it is not a proper political and administrative solution to choose governors that are disconnected from their states' party systems. In most cases they appear as if persons hired for for services, as if communities were like raw materials like large construction projects. They are often men with no spirit, no soul, no pulse, nothing but greenhorns.[101]

And he concluded: "Politics is a valid, respectable, and indispensable activity. The state is a political expression".[102]

This "politics of the governors" produced several consequences as an intervention in a political field with complex results. Even if the governors were handpicked by the President of the Republic, who often chose a party leader, this choice failed to solve the conflicts between party members, since the diversity of leaders forming ARENA in each state hindered the acceptance of any single choice via indirect elections for state governors.

Bolívar Lamounier called attention to the importance of formalisms in representative democracy, where electoral systems are crucial because they authorize the elected officials in a general sense, as a vote of confidence, a process which thus involves some degree of uncertainty. On the other hand, "nomination pure and simple, that is, turning over total control of communities to specifically designated individuals or factions would be tantamount to authorizing the chosen faction to totally exclude all the others" (Lamounier, 1981, p. 240).

Brazilians were already quite familiar with the argument that dictatorships were necessary to ensure the future consolidation of democratic regimes, thus affirming the transient status of authoritarianism.[103] An analysis of the debates in meetings of ARENA congressmen shows that the argument was also used within the party itself, as a way of lending legitimacy to the breach of the democratic regime, while simultaneously affirming the exceptional nature of the moment and the need to glimpse other scenarios for the pro-government politicians themselves.

The *Arenista* politicians envisaged a regime based on strong control of whoever participated in the electoral contests, but based on the rules of a representative democracy, a system that most of these men had experienced for twenty years. From 1945 to 1965, they had organized municipal and state committees and had run for elective offices, living under institutional rules such as those typically governing a political party, with which they were familiar and did not intend to change so completely. The dictatorship altered many of these rules profoundly but did not totally eliminate the institutions' functioning. ARENA's relative autonomy in relation to the government points to the existence of specific interests among these politicians, independently of the military's interests, and such interests were tied closely to the representative system.

It may actually be better to describe the break with the 1945–64 regime by observing how the ties were maintained between the two regimes at certain levels of political competition. Mainly, as I seek to show, there was no suppression of the politicians' expectations as to the permanence of certain liberal procedures. The debates that waged in the ARENA meetings both on electoral and party legislation and on the politicians' own participation in the elections show that various classic representative mechanisms had never been deactivated. Since one of the most important mechanisms for a representative system to function is the existence of individuals interested in participating in these institutions, one cannot understand Brazil's dictatorship without accompanying the continuity of political activity by these representatives, organized in a political party during the authoritarian period, even at the peak of repression.

6 The ARENA leadership

Since ARENA was founded in 1965, its leaders had considered the "revolution" a solution for the defence of liberal institutions. Following the AI-5, the authorized leaders of ARENA began to argue that due to the communist threat, represented by the organizations in the armed resistance to the regime, it was necessary to reconsider the liberal political model.

Minister of Justice Gama e Silva was one of the greatest enthusiasts in deriding liberalism, as he demonstrated during a speech in May 1969 at the Superior War College (Escola Superior de Guerra/ESG). Newspaper columnist Maurício Lacerda of *Jornal do Commércio* noted that the only thing missing from Gama e Silva's speech was "to declare liberalism dead and buried in relation to party politics. Even the special sessions of Congress, the Minister said, will be controlled by the Executive".[104] Deputy Clóvis Stenzel, in a lecture to hundreds of Brazilian Air Force cadets on "the perils of communist infiltration in democracies"[105], also endeavoured to show that liberals were one of the greatest "dangers" of democracy. In his view, "liberal democracy" was "the best path to the development of the totalitarian left".[106]

ARENA's project for itself as the party of the "revolution" clearly gained force especially starting in 1969. This conjuncture also featured recurrent recourse to the argument of the "revolution" as the justification for the end of the rule of law, as symbolized by the AI-5. Paradoxically, but precisely for this reason, ARENA under Filinto Müller's leadership was marked by initiatives to strengthen the party. Yet these initiatives now revealed a project to strengthen the party that was very different from the attempts prior to the AI-5, which had aimed to ensure autonomy for the National Congress and its members (a party model consistent with liberalism).

Even before Filinto Müller was sworn in as chairman of the ARENA National Committee, he attempted to link the party to the Superior War College (ESG). This was a strategy to bolster the party's prestige, since a close link between ARENA and ESG was seen as a way to "wipe the party's record clean" and eliminate "the wall of obstacles accumulated over the years".[107] However, the attempt to include ARENA among the institutions that were considered worthy of prestige by the government actually failed, since the Superior War College had no interest whatsoever in collaborating with ARENA. The newspapers reported that there was "an irritated refusal by the ESG"[108] to the overture by the future chairman of ARENA. On another occasion, the reports were that studies by the War College might even provide backing for ARENA to draft a platform, but the actual drafting would be up to the party itself.[109]

Meanwhile, the initiative by Filinto Müller met with resistance among members of his own party. According to the press, Müller's moves sparked in ARENA "a stubborn, irritated movement of discomfort and reaction to the decision to take inspiration from the Superior War College's doctrine of [economic] development subordinated to national security".[110] Such conflicts reveal the differences between the groups comprising the network sustaining the regime, as well as the independence between the institutions that supported it.

In this reorganization process, party leaders even asked for suggestions for its platform and letter of principles from intellectuals such as sociologist Gilberto Freyre and jurist Miguel Reale, both known for their authoritarian sympathies.[111] In his reply, Miguel Reale, then-rector of the University of São Paulo (USP), proved to be extremely attuned to the government and the ARENA leadership. His main contribution was the suggestion for creating a topic entitled:

> THE ARMED FORCES AND NATIONAL SECURITY, emphasizing what they represent as a pole for development through their multiple action in community services (National Air Mail Service, roadbuilding, ports, literacy training, etc.), in addition to their decisive contribution to Brazil's national technology through Institutes of the highest scientific calibre.[112]

The reply by Gilberto Freyre, then-director of the Joaquim Nabuco Institute for Social Research, was also quite consistent with pro-regime guidelines. In his suggestions for the ARENA platform, Gilberto Freyre stated that the party could help with the search for "Brazilian solutions to Brazilian problems",[113] a proposal by President Médici. Freyre emphasized the need to find solutions that were appropriate for Brazil's unique national reality, responding directly to the main denunciations against the Brazilian state at the time, namely the breach of liberal principles, considered universal (political representation and human dignity).

From Freyre's perspective, the interventions in institutions of political representation were indicative that Brazil was seeking

> To develop its own forms (including political forms) of social organization, independently of any copy or semblance of foreign organizations. The latter organizations cite absolute or perfect models, and through their press or by other means, they claim to view as aberrations vis-à-vis 'democratic' regimes or 'respect for human rights' the daring deviations from such models and the original approaches currently under way in Brazil.[114]

With this reasoning, Gilberto Freyre resorted to a traditional diagnosis in Brazilian social thinking on the impossibility or difficulty of implementing liberalism in the country in order to elaborate a clear defence of the Médici government, even in the face of accusations of torture. In his suggestions, Freyre is extremely critical of liberal principles, defending the development of "typically Brazilian democratic institutions"[115]: "stripped of puffed-up liberal ideas, but rather based on respect for that sentiment of freedom, that love of diversity, that tendency to tolerance, so typical of our traditions and our mores".[116]

This description of a new meaning for institutions is highly vague, but it is clear enough in relation to the critique of juridical formalisms that are the basis of political representation in democratic regimes. In order to highlight his own project, Freyre raises the argument of democracy's demagoguery and inability to solve the bigger social issues: "Democratic institutions that do not serve the demagoguery of ferment for merely transplanted ideologies, but rather aim first and foremost at Brazilians' socioeconomic well-being".[117] Later, he derides the importance of constituting political representation through elections, comparing the prevailing regimes in the 1970s: "In Brazil today, as in other democracies around the world, elections are no longer the definitive way of making the democratic system work".[118]

However, beginning in 1969 the *Arenista* ideologues and leaders considered liberalism insufficient, due to the threats of "subversion" in the country. In the National Congress, during the Médici government, the ARENA leadership outdid themselves in their condemnation of liberal institutions, arguing generally in defence of the AI-5 and the dictatorship, and that the threat of the "revolutionary war" and "terrorism" required exceptional measures. From this perspective, in the struggle against "terrorism", democratic regimes would have to arm themselves with "defensive frameworks" such as those adopted by Brazil in order not to be "reduced to chaos".

The lack of freedom was defended as prevention against "subversion". At other moments, the ARENA leadership harshly criticized the *Emedebistas* for so persistently questioning the regime's institutional aspects: "It's as if Brazil has not grown, has not reorganized, has not achieved the goals proposed by the Revolution in this seven-year period, which the distinguished colleague [from MDB] appears to assess exclusively on the basis of institutional appearances".[119] Along the same line, Deputy Clóvis Stenzel pondered that MDB was imitating "the strategy of the old *marching band* of the defunct UDN, by worrying only about democracy's formal aspects".[120]

Deputy Cantídio Sampaio was one of the foremost defenders of the AI-5 in the National Congress, arguing countless times that there had been a "revolution":

> It would do no good, distinguished deputies, spilling out disagreement, to analyse facts occurred over the course of a regime of exception. A revolution really does practice acts that cannot always be appreciated according to the purest structures of our law. Every revolution leaves a trail of injustices – and why not say it? – due precisely to the heat of the moment in which it acts.[121]

The threat of "subversion" was one of the most frequent arguments in defence of the AI-5. According to Deputy Cantídio Sampaio,

> To refuse to acknowledge the exception of the moment and the need for these remedies is to turn one's back on Brazil's reality, to turn one's back on Mariguela and his lackeys, to turn one's back on the subversion in the Church itself, to the traffic to Uruguay, protected by the monasteries, by religious orders, to the risk we all run – have no doubt! – because the nation is under threat of awaking to bloodshed if there we do not have a government with adequate legal resources to wage this war, exported to us by nations that are enemies of democracy in the attempt to destroy the more unwitting Brazilian groups.[122]

National Deputy Nazir Miguel (ARENA – SP) agreed with Cantídio Sampaio and acknowledged his colleague's efforts in defence of the Institutional Acts "with civic zeal",[123] recalling that Cantídio Sampaio had been Secretary of Public Security in São Paulo, "the centre today of the revolutionary war that is propagating to mire the nation in chaos".[124]

In the 1970s, the restrictions on political freedoms and freedom of the press and reports of torture were the hottest topics among members of Congress from both ARENA and MDB. In response to the denunciations of torture suffered by political prisoners, various ARENA leaders counter-argued by denying its existence or down-playing the issue as "excesses", "diversions", or "isolated cases". At the beginning of the 1964 movement, its civilian leaders denied torture, turning it into a partisan political phenomenon: to deny torture was synonymous with defending the regime, and to denounce or confirm it meant to attack the regime.

In the Chamber of Deputies, Pedroso Horta (MDB – SP) stated that a documentary was being shown in the United States with testimony by Brazilian exiles denouncing the torture perpetrated in Brazil's prisons. For the leader of ARENA, Cantídio Sampaio, that claim was one more battle in the "psychological war":

> To criticize, to lie, to twist the truth in every way and repeatedly, to demoralize, to revile, is part of the game, distinguished Deputy Pedroso Horta. This is also how the revolutionary war achieves one of its goals, by demoralizing the established authorities of nations that are opposed to the red ideology.[125]

The documentary was being shown in the United States of America, the world's prime opponent of the communist countries, but Deputy Cantídio Sampaio was drawing on the mobilizing force of the anticommunist fearmongering shared by part of Brazilian society and by many *Arenistas*. After all, every year in National Congress, members of Congress from ARENA paid tribute to those who died in the episode known as the *Intentona Comunista* ("Communist Putsch") of 1935.

According to Deputy Nina Ribeiro (ARENA – GB), the publications that denounced torture aimed to vilify Brazil as the "country of torture",[126] the country that disrespected human dignity. Nina Ribeiro was worried about Brazil's image and the dignity of the Armed Forces. He contended that the attitude of "the military commanders is above suspicion. They are honourable men, dignified men, who defended our external and internal sovereignty by risking their own lives".[127]

In defending the regime, there was major concern over replying to the reports coming from abroad. One way of downplaying such reports was to generalize the existence of torture. Thus, Deputy Nina Ribeiro argued that "there have always been isolated cases, episodes all over the world, in every corner".[128] Taking the same line, Deputy Élcio Álvares, as party leader, indirectly acknowledged the existence of torture but considered it a "distortion" or "deviation in the police apparatus". This was justified through a generalization riddled with a sense of inevitability: "This has always happened and will always happen throughout time, both in Brazil and in other countries".[129] In an aside, Deputy Alceu Collares (MDB – RS) questioned this government stance in the face of reports of torture and disappearances: "The government chooses to remain silent, failing to deal with these irregularities, to give the population the explanation it deserves, not even giving an explanation to the Congress that represents it".[130]

The tireless *Emedebista* congressmen also denounced (on countless occasions) the censorship practiced against the country's mass media. On one occasion, Deputy Aldo Fagundes (MDB – RS) criticized what could be considered the height of censorship, where even speeches by ARENA congressmen were being cut. The deputy cited from the Chamber floor a telex message from journalist Júlio de Mesquita Filho of *O Estado de S. Paulo* on the following case: "Speeches by leader Petrônio Portella and Senator Ruy Santos (in a tribute to Ruy Barbosa) and by Deputy Alencar Furtado were censored".[131] It was no coincidence that references to Ruy Barbosa were censored. Members of Congress from MDB and even from ARENA, like Senator Rui Santos (also from Bahia and a namesake of the great early twentieth-century Brazilian jurist and diplomat) often quoted Ruy Barbosa to defend various liberal institutions. The *Arenistas* in Congress also frequently denied or downplayed censorship. Deputy Cantídio Sampaio claimed that interference was minimal in the newspapers, television, and radio (indirectly suggesting that all the media channels were affected). And Deputy Daniel Faraco asked:

> When the [censorship] authority interferes to prevent certain information from being published or broadcast in a certain way at a certain time, does he do this to conceal the information? No! He does so to avoid creating an environment of turmoil, a hostile environment, to avoid producing a certain mentality [sic].[132]

In other words, this was an attempt to avoid mobilization by the population. From the regime's authoritarian perspective, it was to prevent "an environment of turmoil" or opposition in the form of "a hostile environment". But not all the *Arenistas* agreed. The extension of censorship to certain media channels worried some members of Congress, such as Cardoso de Almeira:

> As a deputy from ARENA, I consider this censorship, which has been applied with increasing intensity, as a danger to the entire country. I consider the newspaper *O Estado de S. Paulo* the principal bulwark of the 1964 revolution. Such censorship is actually producing insecurity for the government, not security. (Hear! Hear!).[133]

The government leader in the Chamber of Deputies frequently defended policies that violated the principles of freedom of the press, equality, and balance of powers with the simple argument that Brazil's prevailing laws allowed it. It was the argument of *fait accompli*. On one occasion, Deputy Daniel Faraco contended that traditional legal instruments were insufficient.[134] Among the ARENA leadership, Geraldo Freire was also quite blunt:

> Mr. President, Your Excellency, the leadership of MDB speaks of disrespect for the Brazilian Constitution. However, they forget the Institutional Act No. 5. Do Your Excellencies doubt its existence? Well, I have a copy in hand for whoever wants to read it. Institutional Act No. 5 says the following: "The President of the Republic may issue complementary acts for the execution of this Institutional Act, and may adopt, if necessary, in defence of the Revolution, the measures provided for under items a and d, paragraph 2, Article 152 of Constitution".
>
> These measures include suppression of freedom of assembly and association, as well as censorship of correspondence, the press, telecommunications, and public entertainment. There has been a revolution in this country. This revolution is in full sway. What exists is surveillance and, let us admit it, censorship itself, to avoid jeopardizing the public order. (Hear! Hear!).[135]

The leader of ARENA quoted the press in Argentina, where "terrorists" had declared war on the same government that had released them from prison. Deputy Geraldo Freire was attempting once again to convince his audience that the principles of liberal democracy had failed in the face of the reality of "subversion" and the communist regimes:

> Why don't they show freedom of the press in Russia, in Cuba, in China? Why don't they cry for freedom in Russia, in the name of democracy? We will never sit back and see the Brazilian people's freedom destroyed in the name of so-called freedoms for those who do not know how to take advantage of them for the benefit of the Fatherland. (Hear! Hear! Applause. Congratulations).[136]

At that stage of the economic miracle, according to Deputy Daniel Faraco, the challenge was "to rethink the problem of freedom of the press in Brazilian terms",[137] which meant guaranteeing "progress, order, and our future as a nation".[138]

Such arguments were not new or "original" as Gilberto Freyre contended. The most constant arguments featured many ideas that were dear to anti-communism, an extremely active movement in the 1930s and 1960.[139] On the other hand, one of the most frequently cited thinkers by members of Congress from MDB and ARENA to defend the balance of powers, amnesty, and *habeas corpus* was Ruy Barbosa. These disputes between party projects that transformed ARENA include traces from different traditions in Brazil's social thinking. On the one hand, defence of the importance of legal formalisms, and on the other, defence of the pre-eminence of national specificities – considered an argument for abandon principles such as popular representation. This shows that ARENA was not actually an "aberration", but a project comprised of many facets of Brazilian political culture formed from these traditions.

7 The jurists, the "third party" proposal, the "hooded ones"

During the Médici government, the defenders of formalisms reached a historical low. Yet many political leaders affiliated with ARENA still wondered whether a liberal exit strategy for the dictatorship might be possible. The critics included active members of Congress such as Daniel Krieger, Milton Campos, and Herbert Levy, personalities that had left party life, such as Adauto Lúcio Cardoso and Aliomar Baleeiro, who were occupying court positions, and others like Pedro Aleixo, who left the party after being prevented from taking office as President of Brazil in 1969.

Adauto Lúcio Cardoso was named Supreme Court justice by Marshall Castello Branco in 1967. He resigned in 1971, creating a major political situation. In response to Decree-Law No. 1.077, which established prior censorship for books and periodicals, MDB filed an unconstitutionality suit with the Office of the Attorney General. The attorney general refused to refer the party's suit to the Supreme Court. In response, MDB filed a complaint against the attorney general's ruling. During the session on the case, Adauto Cardoso contended that the complaint was valid, and that the Supreme Court had the jurisdiction to review and rule on the issue of the decree's unconstitutionality. When the other justices voted against him, Adauto Cardoso resigned his office:

I believe that with today's ruling, the petition to declare [the decree's] unconstitutionality is defunct. In the country's current condition, no private citizen will dare challenge the constitutionality of public laws. Citizens could only do so by petitioning the Attorney General. And he has become the lord and judge of such petitions, even overriding the Supreme Court and excluding it. This is tantamount to making the Executive branch the judge of laws' unconstitutionality.[140]

The newspapers reported on the commotion that had seized the Supreme Court: in a secret session, the other justices convened in Adauto Cardoso's chambers, hoping to convince him to change his mind. The newspaper *O Estado de S. Paulo* described Adauto Cardoso's startling gesture: "He stood up, pulled his shirt sleeves out from his suitcoat, and flipped his robe up over his head, symbolically consummating his resignation".[141] A recurrent topic in the press was the analysis of his gesture's high load of drama. At the same time, both journalists and politicians lauded Adauto's excellent career in Congress and in the Supreme Court. Several *Arenista* leaders closest to the Executive, like the deputy leader of the government in the Senate, Eurico Resende, claimed that the Supreme Court had definitely lost with Adauto's "spectacular gesture".[142] According to the same senator, Adauto Cardoso's resignations were "a matter of temperament, forged or valued by deeply rooted convictions that give this clear-thinking public man a unique angle, unprecedented in the nation's life".[143]

The members of Congress emphasized the political dimension of Adauto's gesture. Eurico Resende reportedly stated that he would not have been able reconcile his positions as "combative congressman" and "eminent judge" when there were political matters up for vote.[144] MDB Deputy Adolfo de Oliveira saw in his attitude "a gesture of rare beauty, very consistent with his life and his past as a public man".[145] In the Supreme Court, Justice Luiz Gallotti, when declaring his vote, described Adauto's perspective as one of "unbridled pessimism" that under those political conditions no one would dare challenge the government's unconstitutional acts.[146] But a harsher analysis of his resignation appeared in an editorial in the newspaper *O Estado de S. Paulo*, comparing his resignation to a pebble dropped into a pond, causing ripples that soon fade away.[147]

The political folklore on Adauto Cardoso highlights his brilliant performance in the UDN "Marching Band" and his resignations as president of the Chamber of Deputies in 1966 and from the Supreme Court in 1971. One journalist summarized Adauto's style as "affirmation by resignation".[148] Yet his gestures were not gratuitous. All of his resignations were motivated by the defence of political and civil freedoms. Adauto returned to private legal practice after stepping down from the Supreme Court. In 1973 he had the courage to defend the publishing house *Editora Inúbia*, responsible for publishing the alternative newspaper *Opinião,* arguing precisely on grounds of the unconstitutionality of prior censorship. He passed away shortly afterwards, on July 20, 1974, in Rio de Janeiro.

On the occasion of his resignation from the Supreme Court, there was no lack of speculation on his gesture's true meaning. The press spoke of Adauto's likely affiliation with the Democratic Republican Party (PDR), Pedro Aleixo's political brainchild. In 1970, after being prevented from taking office as President of Brazil, Aleixo left ARENA, turned down the invitation to join MDB, and devoted his energies to plans for organizing a third party. Some *Arenistas* condemned Pedro Aleixo for endeavouring to organize a third party. Others believed the project was doomed to failure, either because the government was against it, or because of difficulties in recruiting members.[149] Deputy Francelino Pereira argued in the Chamber that it was not politically expedient for the PDR to divide the government's congressional base.[150] Along the same line, Senator Filinto Müller saw in the creation of PDR a strategy aimed at weakening ARENA.[151]

Pedro Aleixo's initiative and the comments by *Arenistas* such as Francelino Pereira and Filinto Müller pointed once again to the existence of different political shades even among the defenders of the "March 31 revolution". Pedro Aleixo guaranteed that the first and foremost principles of PDR were precisely:

> Commitments taken on by the 1964 revolution, i.e., the practice of a representative democratic regime in its purest form. To that end, our point of departure can be respect and the guarantee of human rights. Next, a position defended by former Senator Milton Campos, namely, reestablishment of the country's legal order.[152]

The government ultimately refused to allow the creation of the third party.

Under those conditions, the criticisms by ARENA congressmen were not always public, but veiled. The newspapers published occasional notes on the "redeemed ones"[153] and the "hooded ones",[154] terms used for ARENA Congressmen that favoured greater participation by Congress in the regime. The "redeemed ones" referred to junior members of Congress and the "hooded ones" were experienced senators.

In September 1972, Herbert Levy and Daniel Krieger made declarations that sent ripples through the press and Congress. On the Senate floor, Daniel Krieger defended the simple right for Senators from ARENA to disagree, with the understanding that disagreement did not constitute a breach of party loyalty. The press nicknamed these dissident leaders of ARENA the "hooded ones", because they had been so discreet with their criticisms for so long.[155] At that stage, however, given the persistent "tactic of immobilism" by the ARENA leadership, the solution was to "take off the hood and speak clearly and directly".[156] The journalist highlighted quite correctly that the critics were also "front-line revolutionaries, with resumés listing services to the March 31 movement that in some cases were superior to those of Filinto Müller and Geraldo Freire", leaders of ARENA in the Senate and Chamber of Deputies, respectively. But unlike the latter leaders, the "hooded ones" wanted a more active party.

The emphatic denials of disagreements and the insistent reaffirmation of party unity were interpreted as an obvious sign that the government was worried. As for how representative the dissatisfied members were, the widespread perception was that Daniel Krieger was speaking on behalf of a large share of the ARENA caucus:

> Every *Arenista* senator must have his own reasons for complaining against a state of things that leaves them notoriously marginalized and surrounded by disdainful distrust. There are many reasons for their discontent. The most obvious and frequent reason is the ransacking of Congress and political activity as a whole.[157]

In an interview with *Jornal do Brasil*, Herbert Levy signalled precisely the marginalization of Brazil's politicians, who were not participating in the government's decisions.[158] One of the regime's main problems was the Executive's pre-eminence through party loyalty, which under those circumstances meant unconditional support for the government by members of Congress from ARENA and even the total absence of discussion on the bills sent to Congress.

At the time, when *Arenista* congressmen or personalities that had participated in the party raised objections to the regime's procedures, the ARENA leadership was quick to point out that such initiatives had not come from legitimate party voices. In the Chamber of Deputies, Cantídio Sampaio, as leader of ARENA, commenting on the declarations by Herbert Levy, guaranteed that not all the caucus agreed with the deputy, precisely because everyone knew that the party's influence was increasing. In the same tone of denial, Cantídio Sampaio claimed that no *Arenista* felt frustrated: "On the contrary, we all feel enthused".[159]

These debates gained further impetus in December 1972 with the declarations by Aliomar Baleeiro, then chief justice of the Supreme Court who had served consecutive terms as national deputy from 1946 to 1965, always under the UDN. Having been named to the Supreme Court by Castello Branco, he gave an interview in 1972 condemning the AI-5, denouncing the restrictions it imposed on the Judiciary and comparing the act to a Damocles sword hanging over Brazil's justice system: "Judges can be fired or forced into early retirement with no defence, appeal, or explicit grounds. Little does it matter if this Damocles sword has not been wielded yet under the current government. It exists in is potential state".[160]

Meanwhile, the members of Congress from MDB attacked the regime by emphasizing the existence of criticism coming from the *Arenistas*, citing Adauto Cardoso, Aliomar Baleeiro, Aloísio de Carvalho, Daniel Krieger, Carvalho Pinto, Milton Campos, and Pedro Aleixo. This list even included some military officers like Marshall Cordeiro de Farias and General Moniz de Aragão, who had spoken out publicly against the military's prolonged intervention in politics.[161]

Among the MDB leadership, Deputy Laerte Vieira attempted to show that a consensus existed between the two parties, since several *Arenista* representatives were particularly criticizing the government for the difficulties Congress was experiencing. According to Laerte Vieira, the interview by Herbert Levy was a veritable denunciation of the regime and reproduced the thinking among the MDB membership, that it was not "possible to further delay the promised democratic détente or to continue to block the reestablishment of National Congress's deliberative power, that is to say the prestige of the political class".[162] In their defence of Congressional prerogatives, various deputies from both MDB and ARENA argued in the politicians' favour by citing jurists (Ruy Barbosa, Aliomar Baleeiro, Nelson Hungria, Adauto Cardoso). At times they quoted the work of Ruy Barbosa and at other times the speeches by Baleeiro and Adauto Cardoso in the Supreme Court. But the idea was apparently the same: an attempt to back the legitimacy of their demands based on legal arguments, since Brazil's political culture views the legal field as neutral, with widely acknowledged authority. They thus played down the issue of prerogatives as an essentially political and partisan dispute, presenting it rather as a juridical issue for which there was only one correct solution, and not political solutions. The debates on the complex relations between the three branches of government under the dictatorship point to the expectations of some *Arenistas* in restoring the rule of law.

8 The issue of congressional immunity

> It's an old topic. If we peruse the pages of history, both ancient and modern, we see that the first act by revolutions is to close Congress.[163]

Over the course of 1973, the debate on the case of Deputy Florim Coutinho (MDB – GB) raised questions concerning the political regime, principally regarding the prerogatives of the National Congress. In May, Deputy Ildélio Martins (ARENA – SP) filed a petition for *habeas corpus* for Deputy Florim Coutinho, who was on trial in the Supreme Court for slander due to a speech he had delivered on the Chamber floor.[164] According to Article 32 of Constitutional Amendment No. 2, deputies and senators, while serving their terms of office, were unimpugnable on grounds of their opinions, words, and votes, except in cases of slander, libel, or defamation or as provided in the National Security Law. Ildélio Martins argued that the second part had not been regulated in organic law and thus the deputy had not committed any crime.[165]

When presenting his arguments to defend Florim Coutinho's immunity, Ildélio Martins made various critiques of the control of the Legislative by the Executive. These included the power of the president of the Chamber of Deputies (at the time named by the President of the Republic) to censor speeches by members of Congress, preventing their publication in the *Anais do Congresso Nacional*.[166] Several members of Congress from MDB publicly congratulated Martins for his defence of Florim Coutinho. Deputy J.G. de Araújo Jorge made a point of it: "Your Excellency is sustaining the constitutional principle of harmony and independence between the Executive, Legislative, and Judiciary branches and even more, the guarantee of our very political survival: congressional immunity".[167] In his long speech, Martins stated that he was particularly worried by "the institution's irremediable decline, its melancholic twilight".[168] The Supreme Court ultimately denied the *habeas corpus* for Florim Coutinho. In October that same year, Ildélio Martins drafted a bill for a constitutional amendment modifying the article on the inviolability of members of Congress.

On the other hand, ARENA leader Geraldo Freire defended the government by shrugging off the issue of balance of powers: "It's *passé*,"[169] the deputy claimed. The leader resorted to the same arguments on numerous occasions, the main one being that every revolution determines its own law. Various ideas derive from this perspective that attempt to justify the AI-5, the key issue in the institutional debate. One of the basic ideas was that the AI-5 had to be decreed, out of necessity. The deputy was attempting to attenuate the magnitude of the AI-5 by contending that the discretionary legislation had been created for certain targets, and not for Brazilian society as a whole. In his words: "The provisions of the AI-5 are not targeted typically against Congress or against the nation's sovereign powers, but essentially against those who, by corruption or terror, threaten the Republic's very existence".[170] He also recalled that the AI-5 had not been used to curtail freedom of speech by members of Congress or to revoke mandates. As for the lack of safeguards for exercising judiciary office and congressional office, he stated: "If there are punishments, if there are restrictions, they are imposed exclusively on those who intend to do harm to Brazil. The honest judges, the good civil servants, and the decent politicians have nothing to fear".[171]

A fatality changed ARENA's direction. On July 11, 1973, Filinto Müller, chairman of the party's National Committee, died in an airline crash in Paris. The following month, Senator Petrônio Portella was sworn in as chairman of ARENA and leader of the government in the Senate. Several months later, Portella set up a committee to draft a constitutional reform bill. In Congress, some deputies glimpsed the possibility of rediscussing the congressional prerogatives.[172] The press published notes on the *Arenista* caucus, which "is no longer as docile as before. Discordant voices are making themselves heard in informal conversations and in many cases on the floor of Congress".[173]

Even under new leadership, the measures were to be very slow. In November, the president of the Chamber of Deputies, Flávio Marcílio, named to the position by Médici, intended to reform the Chamber's internal rules, restoring autonomy to Congress. However, the reform was passed according to the government's objectives, rejecting the extinction of the leader's vote and the leader's election by a secret vote of the caucus, maintaining the process of naming the leader by the President of the Republic.[174] In that context of presidential succession, the politicians had growing expectations towards the new government, and in the press Flávio Marcílio reiterated the politicians' desire to collaborate with the future administration, especially to increase political activity and pave the way for reclaiming certain prerogatives.[175]

The debates continued in the National Congress on restoring congressional prerogatives and the rule of law, even under the Médici government. This indicates that the proposal for détente developed during the government of Ernesto Geisel enjoyed backing from part of the government's base and was not disconnected from the other political actors, as if Geisel were an enlightened sovereign or more representative of MDB's positions (as was speculated) than those of ARENA. These debates also illustrate the diversity of political projects in ARENA.

A Time of Silence and Reorganization (1969–1973)

The fluid boundaries in the possibilities for action by the pro-government politicians and the differences among the *Arenistas* concerning the creation of these possibilities persisted throughout one of the periods with the harshest repression in Brazil, from 1969 to 1973. Concerning this period, the Archives of the ARENA National Committee include transcriptions of congressional caucus meetings concerning the debates on a series of matters, such as party loyalty, autonomy of the caucuses, voter recruitment, calendar of party conventions, election campaigns, and party membership, among others.

As we have seen, the analysis of this material shows how even at the time of the heaviest crackdown by the dictatorship, a large share of the pro-government politicians continued working for the party's organization and vying for its control, with a view towards holding the elections for the state legislatures, the Chamber of Deputies, and the Senate (in 1970), as well as for mayors and city councils (in 1972). As regards the new electoral and party legislation, the deputies and senators from ARENA attempted to defend some control of the political resources for themselves, notwithstanding all the constraints.

An analysis of those dissensions indicates the existence of a struggle for political space between politicians and the military, as much as among members of the party itself. This allows reconsidering the interpretation by which the *Arenistas* were purportedly shirking or even renouncing the attempt to restore the political debate. In other words, given the restrictions on the party's political activity, that ARENA was attempting to turn itself into an agency with merely technical functions.[176] On the contrary, the documents show that the discussion was profoundly political, addressing various principles of the representative system such as the balance of powers and the alternatives for constituting political representation.

The debate among *Arenistas* on party and electoral legislation indicates how they were attempting to maintain control of their activities, at least in the states and in the National Congress. This points to the attempts to ensure congressional prerogatives and the political power for members of Congress in the party. In this sense, these members of Congress were attempting to preserve the conditions for the continuity of their political careers, and by so doing, they were defending the continuity and expansion of the conditions for exercising congressional politics itself.

CHAPTER 5

The Time of Political Détente (1974–1979)

> "We paid the price for negligence in the last election, because the people, always alert to examining legitimacies, do not forgive those who renounce or shirk their duty to preserve their own authority".[1]
>
> Aluísio Campos

In the wake of the defeat in the 1974 elections, the issue of legitimacy struck the politicians of ARENA full force. It was necessary to react to the population's pressure, expressed through the vote (the basis for their political representation), and at the same time continue to act in partnership with the military. During the governments of Ernesto Geisel and João Figueiredo, the military and the politicians from ARENA and MDB dealt with the changes in the rules of the game, with a view towards liberalizing the dictatorship. During this period, the leaders of ARENA in the Chamber of Deputies and Senate became interlocutors for the Executive again. The project for "easement" ("*distensão*") included the congressional debate in the process of transformation of legislation created by the institutional acts since 1964. In the National Congress, the *Arenista* leaders played their role of defending the government from criticism by MDB, but in the ARENA caucus there were also voices that disagreed with the party leadership. In the process of transition from Brazil's military regime, the National Congress voted on bills to revoke the AI-5, the National Security Law, amnesty, and party reorganization. In most cases there was no room to alter the bills handed down by the government via congressional amendments, even if drafted by members of ARENA.

Brazil's political détente in the 1970s has been studied mainly from the points of view of the military, MDB, and organized civil society. However, the political impasses shaped during détente included some clashes between the military and the politicians of ARENA, highlighting the specificities of these actors. In this game of contrasts, it is quite interesting to note the picture painted for the military by some members of ARENA. In an interview in the 1990s, Deputy Célio Borja (ARENA – RJ) summarized the peculiarities of the military's view of political problems:

> The military Presidents were highly sensitive to the slightest ripple in their base, in their constituency. They could feel things we did not even perceive. It was like they had a magnifying glass or binoculars. And looking through a magnifying glass, any little fly became a monster.[2]

The images of the "monster" and phantoms were recurrent during the years of détente, spectres created to scare others and to leave themselves undisturbed. It was about a menacing discourse, more or less veiled, depending on who it was addressed to, because it insinuated that any pressure to hasten the regime's liberalization could result in setbacks. At various moments, politicians from ARENA itself, like Luís Vianna Filho and Augusto Lins e Silva Neto (ARENA – PE) referred to this strategy by the military and by *Arenistas* interested in continuing the regime. On the eve of the closing of Congress in 1977, Senator Luís Vianna Filho criticized groups in the government that "make things difficult, create terrible phantoms, terrifying dangers, with the aim of preventing détente".[3] According to the senator, they were "deliberately overblown obstacles",[4] hardly ingenuous.

Senator Daniel Krieger, in turn, criticized the position of the Armed Forces by drawing a distinction between the détente or the "return to the barracks" and Brazil's previous experiences with military interventions in politics: "I have the utmost respect for my country's Armed Forces, and in all the circumstances they have behaved with impartiality and bravery and restored order and turned the country over to civilian power".[5] In these analyses, produced in the context of détente, one notes a critique of the predominant military discourse that pressure from the opposition could lead to setbacks, while implying that for those leaders the détente could be much less slow.

If the military could sense the slightest signs from their base, the *Arenistas*' sensitivity also became particularly keen after the elections in 1974. From that election defeat until the extinction of ARENA and MDB on 29 November 1979 marked the period of greatest electoral competition between the two parties. Both the growth of MDB and the détente policy impacted ARENA in its relations with the government and its expectations towards the political and party system. The regime's liberalization, the return to partisan and electoral activities, and a democratic framework oriented the positions and debates in ARENA. According to Lucia Klein, ARENA's difficulties led its candidates to adopt some of the positions defended by MDB.[6] Interestingly, however, the study of various proposals by politicians from ARENA shows that the two parties shared some goals even before 1974, reframing the process from then on.

1 The meanings of 1974

On the eve of the 1974 elections, the press reported the satisfaction on the part of the government, ARENA, and MDB with the atmosphere of relative freedom for holding the election campaign. For the first time under the regime, the candidates were using radio and television. MDB endeavoured to conduct a well-planned campaign with professional agencies preparing the party's radio and TV advertising and researchers from CEBRAP preparing its Campaign Handbook.[7] In ARENA, Deputy Célio Borja perceived the politicians' difficulties with the mass media: the candidates had no experience whatsoever speaking on radio and TV and had trouble communicating their ideas in just four minutes.[8] The *Arenistas* were also attempting to expand the spaces for campaigning. They petitioned the Superior Electoral Court (TSE) to reconsider the ban on newspapers publishing commentary or statements by members of Congress that were running for re-election.[9]

At the time of the elections, Geisel himself was making statements to the press proclaiming that an atmosphere of freedom was essential. According to the media community, for many years Brazil had not held elections in an environment with such favourable political expectations.[10] But the 1974 elections brought a huge surprise. That is, on the eve of the elections returns there were already inklings. The media had already perceived that ARENA was worried by the latest opinion polls and the low abstention rate.[11] Various studies have explained the low rate of blank and null votes precisely according to the access to information that was allowed that year under the détente policy.[12]

Finally, on 15 November 1974, ARENA won 233 seats in the Chamber of Deputies, compared to 187 for MDB, while in the Senate, MDB won 16 seats against only 6 for ARENA. These 16 victories in the Senate became an extremely important turning point in the regime's history. They pointed undeniably to an election race in a legitimate field and a feasible way of challenging the government.

After the election returns were announced, there was a major debate on its causes and meanings. The victory by MDB apparently stunned everyone in the *Palácio do Planalto*. The analysis of the election results, as published in the press, was the object of many conversations between Geisel and his leaders in the Senate and Chamber. The interpretations of MDB's electoral success occupied the agenda in the National Congress, the media, and the reports by the National Intelligence Service (SNI); the stark contrast between the meanings assigned to the election results reveals the different actors' views. The analyses on Brazil's national politics by journalist Carlos Castello Branco, published in *Jornal do Brasil*, were a reference for the principal political actors: members of Congress, military officers in the Executive, and the SNI.[13] The journalist's daily column featured chronicles on the institutional crises and policies that explained the operational logic of the politicians and military and affirmed a political sensitivity based on the representative system's formalisms. For Castello Branco, those elections were a turning point, representing a firm step in the return to politics as a matter for politicians.[14]

The other end of the political spectrum featured the analyses produced by the intelligence community. One of the attributions of the SNI, created in 1964, was to advise the President of the Republic in orienting and coordinating intelligence and counter-intelligence activities, particularly regarding national security.[15] The SNI staff, mostly military men, drafted the so-called "assessments" on the widest possible range of topics considered relevant to national security. These analyses were then passed on to certain authorities. The assessments by SNI after 15 November 1974 argued that the elections had not strengthened democracy, since the voting had not been "enlightened".[16] The analyst criticized the results and suggested that the situation could lead the regime to take "extreme measures to guarantee the continuity of the revolutionary process", clearly evidencing the threatening reaction by the SNI to the growth of MDB and the plans by the intelligence community for tightening the regime.

The politicians of ARENA were concerned with a whole other order of issues. Their stinging defeat in the elections opened room for members of Congress to discuss a number of inherent problems in the party's organization and functioning that had been simmering since 1965. The *Arenistas* pointed to the disputes between the governors and other leaders in their states as one of the party's serious problems. According to the newspapers, Deputy Airon Rios (ARENA – PE) pointed to "'the total disregard for the political class as 'government' without participating in the government, and above all the predatory action by various state governors on the authentic leadership"[17] as reasons for the electoral debacle. Journalist Carlos Castello Branco agreed with these interpretations, recalling that the governors had been handpicked by the *Palácio do Planalto*, nearly all imposed on the party, banned from holding conventions.[18] Meanwhile, Célio Borja, then-leader of ARENA in the Chamber of Deputies, was looking to the future and preferring to believe that there would be direct elections to choose the future governors.[19]

There were other readings besides these critical reflections. Senator Eurico Resende attempted to downplay the role of MDB as a challenge to the regime, shrugging off the significance of the opposition's victory. He emphasized that the MDB was a legally acknowledged party, unlike the "agents of unrest",[20] banned from public life, so even if the opposition had pulled off a surprise victory, that victory was not a challenge to the regime but a result of the democratic game.

Yet some *Arenistas* also glimpsed a deeper positive meaning in the election outcome. Petrônio Portela saluted MDB as a strong party, and Daniel Krieger recalled that in democratic regimes, the people's decision is the source of national sovereignty.[21] In the Senate, Orlando Zancaner (ARENA – SP) compared the 1974 elections to those of 1970: "the low rates of abstentions and blank and null votes and the large numbers of candidates on the party's ticket show that we had a rational, not passional election",[22] which he viewed as Brazilian public opinion's reconciliation with the politicians.

Senator Jarbas Passarinho, vice-leader of the government, made a quite comprehensive assessment of the issue: "Mr. president [of the Senate], distinguished senators, the series of Senate sessions have served to perform an exegesis of the victory or of the defeat".[23] According to Passarinho, there were several causes for the unfavourable outcome for ARENA, the main one being the population's dissatisfaction with the cost of living. The second major cause, in his opinion, was "the ARENA politicians' depletion": [24]

> As long as the government politician was the government's go-between with the ballot boxes, between the government and voters, he was a highly trained instrument to communicate with the constituency. Yet unfortunately in our revolutionary system, the government politician has lost this substance. And this was expressed drastically when he returned to his constituency again.[25]

In the third cause that he identified, Passarinho praised the capacity of MDB to capture the blank votes:

I believe, distinguished senators of the MDB, that it is a thousand times preferable for us men of the government that the resentments be channelled by the peaceful road in the struggle. Mr. President, distinguished senators, and here I further laud the MDB, I believe that what happened was the taming of the revengeful. They were tamed and placed on the proper path, the peaceful road.[26]

The senator further identified a fourth cause for the election defeat:

From now on it no longer suffices to win the party's nomination behind closed doors, with the fighting, sometimes via scarcely ethical processes, scarcely recommendable, for nominations in the conventions in certain select cases, because they were practically guaranteed in ARENA and as such, the mere approval by the convention was a guarantee of the nomination. This will mean that the men who truly enjoy prestige with the people will be authorized under the country's political process and within the government party, to represent their party.[27]

Some senators from MDB agreed promptly with Passarinho concerning the regime's disregard for the politicians. Senator Nelson Carneiro gave a short speech as an aside, noting that for several years, one of the characteristics of Brazil's national politics was to disregard Brazilian politicians, especially those from the government's party.[28] Senator Ernani do Amaral Peixoto concluded the session by saying that he expected measures to be taken on the major issue identified by Senator Jarbas Passarinho: the rehabilitation of Brazilian politicians.[29] However, the subordination of civilian politicians was an issue linked profoundly to the kind of regime installed in the country since 1964, which could only be changed very slowly.

2 Geisel, the politicians, and ARENA

Beginning in 1974, the debate on the politicians' role in the regime became essential for elaborating ARENA's identity. On the one hand, in the voters' eyes, because MDB was now attacking ARENA precisely by accusing it of being the "Yes Sir! Party". On the other, in the search for participation in a government whose Executive disrespected both the party and the members of Congress in general. In meetings with politicians, Geisel claimed that he wanted the "political class" to discuss and formulate new instruments.[30] Over the course of 1975, however, General Geisel made various declarations criticizing ARENA. In other words, while he asked for the party's help to promote détente, he derided the party by calling it timid and lacking initiative.[31] São Paulo Governor Paulo Edígio also drew on these same images, claiming that ARENA needed to overcome "the fear, the apathy, and the infighting".[32] But the governor still took it for granted that the government could purge members of Congress and intervene in local governments through the AI-5, as President Geisel did.

In practice, Geisel disrespected the politicians in numerous ways. First, he maintained the AI-5, tantamount to the absence of congressional immunity. Before the Geisel government, when members of MDB attacked the AI-5 in congressional debates, the more radical leaders of ARENA such as Cantídio Sampaio and Geraldo Freire argued that the decree was only a "security" measure, only to be used in exceptional cases. Second, the Geisel government prevented free debate via the party loyalty law, which forced members of Congress from ARENA to vote exclusively according to the regime's line. In addition, few *Arenista* leaders (such as Petrônio Portella) were invited to participate in the conversations on fundamental political issues.

Over the course of his government, Geisel turned various times to the prerogatives guaranteed by the AI-5 for the President of the Republic: he revoked the political rights of members of Congress, decreed an intervention in the municipal government of Rio Branco, and suspended the National Congress. During later interviews (in the 1990s), Geisel claimed that he had not exactly loved the AI-5, but justified it as an essential instrument for achieving his plans for détente.[33] However, in taped conversations between Geisel and Golbery in the 1970s, the general simply stated that he could not do without the AI-5.[34] For each political incident in which he enforced the AI-5, the general-president argued that he had acted in response to the sensitivities of the more radical military groups. The military repeatedly claimed that pressure from the opposition was interfering with détente, leading the government to reverse its steps, as in enforcement of the AI-5. In these interviews, the former President described the decree's use as an unavoidable procedure (an argument that does not justify any act in the political field). In the 1970s, the AI-5 became a watershed between members of ARENA and MDB. Still, as in every political party, there was a diversity of opinions in ARENA, and whenever the President of Brazil enforced the AI-5, the reactions ranged from ostensive support to silence. These reactions can be seen in both the congressional debates and the press, which always attempted to obtain comments from the *Arenistas* on such occasions, confronting them with the Executive's authoritarian measures.

The autonomy of the Legislative branch was affronted during the Geisel government through the purging of members of Congress on several occasions. The following national deputies were stripped of their political rights and congressional mandates: Francisco Pinto (MDB – BA), Marcelo Gato (MDB-SP), Nadyr Rosseti (MDB-RS), Amaury Müller (MDB-RS), Lysâneas Maciel (MDB-RJ), Ney Lopes de Souza (ARENA-RN), Wilson Campos (ARENA-AL), Marcos Tito (MDB – MG), and Alencar Furtado (MDB – PR). State deputy Nelson Fabiano Sobrinho (MDB-SP) and city councilmen Glênio Peres (MDB – RS) and Marcos Klassman (MDB-RS) were also purged, for a total of 10 *Emedebistas* and two *Arenistas*.

At the very beginning of the Geisel government in 1974, National Deputy Francisco Pinto (MDB – BA) gave a speech accusing General Augusto Pinochet, then on an official visit to Brazil, of torture. The Executive searched for a way to revoke the deputy's mandate via a judicial procedure, without enforcing the AI-5. On the occasion, Célio Borja, leader of the government in the Chamber of Deputies, argued that the government was correct in its decision to submit the matter to the Supreme Court. Later, during an interview in the 1990s, Borja claimed that he had been extremely alarmed when he saw the government trying a deputy for a speech given on the Chamber floor.[35] Deputy Francisco Pinto was tried in the Supreme Court and sentenced to six months in prison and fined nine *cruzeiros*.[36] The conviction suspended his political rights for the term of his sentence, and he lost his congressional mandate as a result.[37]

In 1975 it was the turn of an ARENA congressman. In his memories, even Senator and Colonel Jarbas Passarinho, known for being close to the hard-line Brazilian military, recalled the purging of Senator Wilson Campos (ARENA – PE) as an example of Geisel's "authoritarian personality":[38]

> Campos had been accused of corruption. *Jornal do Brasil* published the transcription of a tape in which a person claimed the senator had extorted money for his election campaign. Senator Krieger expressed his agreement with President Geisel's position in favour of revoking the political rights of the senator from Pernambuco, on grounds of misconduct. In the session voting on the matter, Luiz Cavalcanti made an impassioned defence of his colleague, whom we acquitted for lack of convincing evidence of his guilt. President [Geisel] did not hesitate. He enforced the AI-5 and revoked his rights, in reprisal.[39]

The press reported that General Geisel had not hidden his surprise from Senator Petrônio Portela over the outcome of the vote. One of the controversies concerning the incident was the existence (or lack thereof) of a "rebellion", to use the recurrent expression among members of Congress and the press at the time, by the ARENA caucus, which had voted against the government's instructions to purge the senator. While Senator Petrônio Portela avoided commenting on the possibility of further purges,[40] São Paulo Governor Paulo Edígio argued that if there was an internal rebellion in ARENA, it was unfortunate, a political mistake.[41] The standoff had thus come to a head. Senator Petrônio Portela held several meetings and consulted members of Congress from both parties in search of a solution to the crisis.[42] *Arenistas* attempted to convince Wilson Campos to resign.[43] The press awarded extensive coverage to the incident, attempting to show the reactions by *Arenistas* to the use of the AI-5 to strip the senator of his political rights.

On another occasion, in April 1975, the Acre State Legislature rejected the names recommended by the governor for mayor of the state capital, Rio Branco, again signalling resistance to the process of indirect elections. President Geisel responded by decreeing intervention in the state capital, defended by various *Arenista* leaders. São Paulo Governor Paulo Edígio Martins stated that enforcement of the AI-5 in Rio Branco had not been a surprise,[44] expressing agreement and support for the measure taken by Geisel. On the Senate floor, during the debate unfolding between the leaders of ARENA and MDB, Franco Montoro (MDB – SP) stated that according to the government, the AI-5 over-rid the Constitution, while Dinarte Mariz (ARENA – RN) claimed that President Geisel had acted constitutionally, on grounds that the AI-5 was part of the country's Constitution. Petrônio Portella, meanwhile, replied that the AI-5 was an emergency act but that it would eventually lead to the rule of law.[45]

If it was necessary to rehabilitate the politicians, many *Arenistas* felt that it was essential for the party to alter ARENA's subordination to the government. The party's ambiguities and the resulting electoral defeat in 1974 were also the main themes in the National Convention in 1975, held on 20–21 September in Brasília. Replying to recurrent criticism from *Emedebistas*, ARENA National Committee chairman Senator Petrônio Portela addressed the issue of subordination to the government, highlighting the inadmissibility of the opposition's derisory catch-phrases: "It is necessary to debunk the position by the opponents of ARENA and the government, that the government is daring and creative, while ARENA remains silent and inert".[46] Even such references ultimately expressed a positive assessment of the Executive and a negative one of ARENA. In other words, even the opponents of the 1964 movement admitted the existence of positive aspects in the government, while the more shameful aspects such as silence and inertia were associated mainly with the pro-regime party.

The chairman of the National Committee insisted, as Deputy Rondon Pacheco had done during his administration, that government and ARENA were one and the same. Petrônio Portela finally attempted in every possible way to reinforce the idea that it was "increasingly up to ARENA to influence the administration's policy guidelines in order to actually witness, once and for all, the identification between party and government".[47]

The senator resumed the dilemma of 1964 by reaffirming that all the *Arenistas* were "democrats and revolutionaries".[48] Based on this assertion, he analysed the crisis of 1968 as a breach of trust between "administrators" and politicians, which had created a deviation in the course of the revolutionary movement. In such a delicate political context, Senator Portella was referring vaguely to "administrators", when the breach had occurred mainly between politicians and the military. At that moment, Petrônio Portela identified the beginning of "the definitive renewal of ARENA, putting an end to the phase of transition and emergency originating in the political crisis of 1968",[49] which he referred to as the "mistakes of 1968",[50] further emphasizing the dimension of confrontation in the vote against granting authorization to purge Deputy Márcio Moreira Alves.

While the chairman of the National Committee was attempting to explain the party conflicts, some politicians from ARENA itself admitted these difficulties and searched for ways to deal with them, claiming greater decision-making power within the party through arguments based on the new political scenario. In the same convention, during a session on ARENA's platform, Aluísio Campos (ARENA – PB) submitted an amendment suggesting the inclusion of explicit recommendations for the party to preserve its prerogative of self-determination. Among the objectives, he proposed the inclusion not only of the free exercise of political activity, including support for governments elected under the party ticket, but also free and unfettered debate of political, economic, and social problems, relying on participation or stimulus from the party's representatives at all levels of representation.

Campos contended that the party's self-determination was the essential issue for ARENA, since

> When the parties stopped being the true source of political power, the party tasked with electing and supporting the President of the Republic began to face limitations on its exercising its autonomy. This is the

fundamental and grave problem of ARENA, which supports but does not participate, concedes but does not criticize, obeys without being heard, fails but does not correct itself. It is the negative, deteriorated, but predominant image, increasingly widespread, based on the conviction that we do not take independent decisions, since we lack the self-determination to choose.[51]

Campos was not arguing against the accusations by the opposition, which attaching an increasingly negative image to his party due to the type of relations established with the government. On the contrary, at least within the party's ranks, he acknowledged the problem's existence, as revealed by the documents we consulted. He believed that ARENA was suffering all the political consequences of the government's decisions and that the defeat in the recent elections indicated "the price of negligence, because the people, always alert to examining legitimacies, do not forgive those who renounce or shirk their duty to preserve their own authority".[52]

The motions submitted during the convention included a proposal to create a "Press Advisory Department for the National Committee", [53] with the aim of publicizing the government's achievements, which many considered ARENA's greatest political capital. The convention's various state delegates also submitted motions such as "applause and unrestricted support for His Excellency Mr. President Ernesto Geisel",[54] by the state caucus of Rio Grande do Sul, a motion of "confidence, applause, and loyalty"[55] by the state delegates from Espírito Santo, and a motion of "solidarity for His Excellency Mr. President Ernesto Geisel for the work his government has conducted in the political, economic, and social field",[56] by the state caucus from Amazonas. Senator Petrônio Portella also received motions of "recognition and applause" [57] for his work leading ARENA.

Senator Teotônio Vilella went down in the history of Brazil's détente as the "minstrel of Alagoas" (as immortalized in a song by popular composers Milton Nascimento and Fernando Brant) and a true oppositionist. Yet before he joined MDB in 1979, the senator had been active in ARENA, pursuing similar objectives. In April 1975, in the Senate, he showed that he believed in the possibility of détente as announced by Geisel: "We now have a President who is decidedly concerned with the political sector of which he is a part, not only by party affiliation, but mainly because the exercise of power is a political function, and those who practice politics are the politicians".[58] This was a constant demand by part of the members of Congress from ARENA, like Daniel Krieger, one of the few senators to congratulate Teotônio Vilela on that occasion (besides José Sarney and Luiz Cavalcanti). In this sense, at the National Convention in 1975, the senator attempted to give ARENA an identity that was very similar to that defended for the organization by Milton Campos in 1969. Since the 1974 elections had truly knocked the wind out of the *Arenistas*, Teotônio Vilela, when referring to that previous year, traced out a profile for what ARENA should be:

> If we had said that we acknowledge the state of exception but that ARENA's goal is the rule of law, we would not have suffered the embarrassments that we did. And we would not have handed our banner over to our opponents. The institutionalization of the democratic regime is ARENA's banner.[59]

At this convention, Deputy Francelino Pereira was sworn in as chairman of the National Committee, speaking precisely to the issue of relations between ARENA and government, touching especially on the issue of the politicians' place in the regime. While singing praise to the works achieved since 1964, he highlighted the importance of political support: "to ensure this backing, we, the politicians, are irreplaceable, nearly always misunderstood in our noble mission and treated unfairly when our acts are judged".[60] On the same occasion, Francelino Pereira acknowledged a difference between the Médici and Geisel governments due to the expansion of "relations between government and the party".[61] But he considered it urgent to establish closer collaboration, "without fears, without misgivings",[62] so that in participating in the government's acts, ARENA could share both the responsibilities and the successes.

This was a recurrent theme. On 22 October 1975, President Ernesto Geisel gave a speech with the suggestive title "ARENA is government"[63] to the members of the National Executive Board and chairmen of the party's state committees. The National Committee later sent copies of this speech to the municipal committees and the CEOs of the state-owned companies, attempting to get that message out. Many acknowledged having received the speech.

Still, the differences between the politicians and the military appeared to become increasingly complex. The year 1976 witnessed both arbitrary measures such as purges of MDB congressmen and concern over ARENA's electoral performance. In January 1976, General Geisel revoked the political rights of National Deputy Marcelo Gato and State Deputy Nelson Fabiano Sobrinho, both members of the MDB from São Paulo. Again, the purging of deputies using the AI-5 had huge repercussions in the press. MDB promptly condemned the measure. In ARENA, many considered it correct, while others expressed the contradictions between Geisel's inaugural speech and his actions, and still others openly opposed the purges. According to Senator Magalhães Pinto, President Geisel had used the powers of the AI-5 on legitimate grounds.[64] Deputy Paulino Cícero (ARENA – MG), on the other hand, recalled Geisel's inaugural speech, in which he depicted the AI-5 as a reserve measure, only wishing to use it after exhausting all the ordinary legal channels.[65]

Some *Arenistas* kept a low profile on the punishments, like Célio Borja, who declined to comment.[66] In an interview in the 1990s, Borja recalled that he had considered resigning at the time. Yet many deputies reportedly convinced him not to follow the experience of Adauto Lúcio Cardoso, who had resigned as president of the Chamber of Deputies in 1966.[67] President Geisel, in turn, had also avoided more radical measures, having recommended caution to Minister of Justice Armando Falcão in order to keep the case from "snowballing".[68]

Throughout 1976, the ARENA National Committee attempted to strengthen the party organization by focusing on the election campaign in various ways. Chairman Francelino Pereira encouraged the state committee chairmen to "urgently promote understandings with our local party leaders to prevent the marginalization of important party factions, which should necessarily participate in the electoral political effort through the multiple tickets".[69] The National Committee also sought to promote closer contact between ARENA and labour unions, sending correspondence to many organizations.[70]

Many *Arenistas* sent suggestions with strategies to proceed with the municipal elections. Senators, deputies, city councilmen, and sympathizers wrote to the National Committee. Some recommended identification between ARENA and the military governments' achievements as the best way to garner votes for the party, such as Senator Jorge Kalume (ARENA – AC). He recommended proclaiming

> The Revolution's grand feats all across Brazil, in all sectors, using the appropriate language for those receiving the MESSAGE. Order the preparation of CHAPBOOK LEAFLETS (in colour) for the Brazilian hinterlands and humble neighbourhoods of the state capitals.
>
> The RADIOS AND TVS in each state should broadcast and televise on a daily basis the slogans on the magnificent results achieved by the Revolution and recall how the country was YESTERDAY. The main scope of this part is to enlighten today's youth, who in 1963, when they were still children, KNEW NOTHING OF THAT BRAZIL of meagre harvests, and compare it to the giant's awakening since 1964.[71]

The senator went on to list various achievements by the "revolutionary governments"[72] that should be remembered during the election campaign: social security, FUNRURAL (the Rural Workers' Assistance Fund), increased school enrolment, meningitis vaccination, transportation, risk contracts ("so fiercely opposed by MDB" [73]), Brazil 200-mile territorial waters ("when it used to be only 12 miles"[74]), the nuclear agreement with Germany ("recalling that initiatives such as the latter two had to overcome major difficulties given the opposing interests of great nations, but overcome thanks to the bravery of President Geisel and his government"[75]), besides the economic development issue.

Meanwhile, the Executive prepared extremely arbitrary electoral rules attempting to benefit ARENA. On 14 June 1976, Congress passed the "Falcão Act", which reduced radio and TV election advertising to a minimum. Yet the issue was not a consensus, and some *Arenistas* spoke out against the new legislation. Some members of ARENA searched for an alternative to strengthen the party based on the political field's traditional principles, such as Senator Teotônio Villela, who became famous for his stances against the government's measures. Still, his was not the only dissonant voice in ARENA.

In the case of the Falcão Act, Teotônio Villela voted against the government's proposal: "Nothing is more discouraging for a politician than to have to vote against limitations on his own prerogatives" (Kinzo, 1988, p. 173). Along the same line, Deputy Lins e Silva (ARENA – PE) failed to understand how re-democratization could be achieved by measures that limited politicians' participation, as with the proposed Falcão Act. His report described the vote as a paradox: "We recently passed a bill, without major discussion, banning our own participation in political debates on the television stations, one of the most valid instruments for the Brazilian people's political awareness and maturity".[76] In the same vein, the following year, Deputy Jarbas Lima wrote from Porto Alegre to the National Committee: "We suggest making available to the political parties the unrestricted use of radio and television. We can only improve the democratic exercise of the popular vote by revoking the Falcão Act".[77]

There had been no demonstrations in Brasília since 1964. In 1976 there was a large mobilization on the city's streets. On 22 August 1976, Juscelino Kubitschek died from a motor vehicle crash on the Via Dutra (the main motorway connecting Rio de Janeiro and São Paulo). His body was flown to Brasília. President Geisel, after hours meeting behind closed doors, declared three days of official mourning for the former President. An estimated 20 thousand Brazilians joined in a nightlong vigil in the cemetery, in a demonstration never seen before in the country's capital. Five thousand vehicles followed the cortege from the airport to the cathedral, where a requiem mass was spoken. Schools suspended classes and government offices and businesses remained closed. According to the newspapers, the most touching homage was the cortege to the cemetery, a 15-kilometre procession made by more than 60 thousand Brazilians.[78] In the municipal elections of 15 November 1976, ARENA won throughout the country, with the notable exception of the large industrial centres. After the election returns were announced, many members of ARENA from cities and towns all across Brazil wrote to the chairman of the National Committee endeavouring to explain the unfavourable results in the large cities.[79]

3 Congressional recess and political reforms

President Geisel used the AI-5 several times from 1974 to 1976, causing revolt in the opposition and embarrassment among the more liberal pro-government politicians. Yet the enforcement of the AI-5 that revealed the regime's contradictions most clearly occurred on 1 April 1977, when Geisel declared the National Congress in recess.

The Geisel government attempted to shift the debate on the transition to the National Congress, by which it gradually replaced the legislation created since 1964 with more liberal provisions. In this sense, Geisel tasked Senator Petrônio Portella with negotiating with MDB to pass a constitutional amendment to introduce political reforms. However, the so-called "Portella mission" failed to make headway. The Executive appeared to be valuing the Legislative by sending its main proposals on political reforms for debate and voting on the Congress floor. Yet at the same time, when Congress showed signs of vitality, Geisel purged national deputies and did not hesitate to close Congress in April 1977. This was evidence of the Geisel government's inability to deal with Congress or even with its own party, leading to a new clash with the politicians.

In March 1977, Deputy José Bonifácio took to the Chamber a government bill proposing the end of party loyalty. The bill was heavily criticized because it allowed politicians to switch parties but maintained mandatory party loyalty on votes in Congress. On the one hand, the *Emedebistas* complained that in that context, the government was only interested in having some of their own members switch to ARENA and vote for an amendment regulating indirect elections for governors. On the other, some *Arenistas* such as Augusto Lins e Silva Neto (ARENA – PE) argued that the proposal to end party loyalty should be expanded so as to truly mean a step towards the country's re-democratization, allowing freedom of speech and action by members of Congress as a whole rather than through the party leaderships:

> Congress should have greater freedom of action during the important national debates and should not be hindered by decisions taken by the party's top echelons, merely ratifying isolated positions that often fail to represent even the party's own consensus. In this House, we should no longer have our consciences violated by absolutely isolated measures.[80]

In this same context, Senator Luís Vianna Filho gave a long speech on the political reforms bill prepared by the government and sent to the National Congress by Geisel. The senator was an important political leader with a long career. In 1945 he was elected deputy to the Constitutional Congress under the UDN, re-elected consecutively until 1966, when he ran for governor of the state of Bahia. In 1964 he was named Chief of Cabinet in the Castello Branco government. In 1965, when Milton Campos resigned as Minister of Justice while the dictatorship was cracking down, Luís Vianna Filho served as acting minister until Juracy Magalhães was sworn in. At the ARENA convention in 1968, he defended the renewed value of politicians. In 1974 he was among the few politicians invited to fill positions in the Geisel government.[81] He gave a long speech in the Senate, drawing on his years of experience. Luís Vianna began by making his position quite clear as a spectator of the President's initiatives: "In the month or two prior to the reopening of our sessions I have heard and read so much about the political reforms that have already been decided in the government's sphere that I decided to wait for them to come to light in order to learn of them and judge them".[82] Underscoring the lack of debates and negotiations, even with ARENA, he contended that "nothing is to be done, since they have been included on the list of things decided irreversibly".[83] But having heard news that General Geisel was expecting debates, he considered this a sign that "although the détente is not as verdant as we would have wished, and remains quite modest, it is nevertheless not dead, and it behoves us to cultivate it with care". [84] The senator was thus ready to serve the President "as Ruy [Barbosa] tells us he served Deodoro [da Fonseca, first President of Brazil, 1889–1891], resisting him, resisting while enlightening him".[85] With this purpose in mind, the senator from Bahia identified some of the crucial issues in that conjuncture, asking whether it was necessary to maintain the AI-5 and touching one of the regime's nerve points:

> It occurs to me to ask whether, as in many other countries, it is possible for us to maintain the democratic legal order, in which no power is above the laws and the courts, where force is not an expression of arbitrary rule, or if it is only possible to maintain the security that is indispensable for the country's tranquillity and development by postponing the law and the courts along with everything they represent for citizens' rights and guarantees.[86]

Luís Vianna Filho went on to give a long and quite didactic explanation on political parties' objectives:

> To govern the nation at the moment in which it wishes this to be done by the vote. That is why they exist, that is what they struggle for, that is why they preach ideas, defend platforms, recruit members. To win the government and to implement administrative programs is this very reason for their existence, which should not be confused with that of any other kind of organization.[87]

He concluded his speech by stating that neither ARENA nor MDB were in conditions to exercise all the activities of a political party, because ARENA had no voice and MDB was denied access to the government.

The leader of ARENA in the Senate, Eurico Resende, attempted to downplay Luís Vianna Filho's criticism of the partisan political system by praising the debate waging on the floor: "The reality is so beautiful, that Your Excellency has just been consecrated in this very House by applause from our noble Opposition".[88] Alert to the nuances, Senator Franco Montoro added: "And from the government party as well". [89] The episode reveals the conflicts and internal contradictions in ARENA, which included both the support for the government leader in the Senate, Eurico Resende, and applause by congressmen from MDB and ARENA for Senator Luís Vianna Filho. Just a few days later, General Geisel decreed a recess in the National Congress, confirming Senator Luís Vianna Filho's familiarity with the matter.

In October 1976, Geisel sent Congress a bill for a constitutional amendment providing for reforms in the Judiciary. However, the congressional debate grew and expanded more than the Executive intended, since certain processes, once launched, can take unpredictable directions. Senator Accioly Filho (ARENA – PE) was tasked with presenting the government's proposal, and he introduced several changes. These featured giving back to the Supreme Court (as provided in the Constitution of 1946) the power to rule on any case of *habeas corpus* involving the risk of violence being consummated before another judge or court could review the petition.[90] The Geisel government rejected such changes, and the substitute bill was criticized by its official rapporteur, Attorney General Henrique Fonseca de Araújo, and the Minister of Justice, Armando Falcão. Senator Accioly Filho stood his ground, arguing that he had conducted consultations throughout Brazil as the rapporteur selected by ARENA. Still, the government ordered the leaders of ARENA in Congress to draft a new substitute bill that would alter the fundamental points in Accioly Filho's proposal.[91]

The committee tasked with examining the Judiciary reform then approved the substitute bill submitted by the leader of the government in the Senate, Eurico Resende. Given this manoeuvre, Accioly Filho resigned as rapporteur, turning his position over to the leader, voting against the substitute bill, and refusing to present it as his own. Meanwhile, the members of Congress from MDB decided to insist on the amendments pertaining to *habeas corpus* and the judiciary safeguards. As a result, the government failed to pass the Judiciary reform bill in Congress, despite massive support from ARENA. The bill was rejected because the constitutional quorum was not reached during the votes, since the *Emedebistas* strategically exited the floor.[92]

This episode highlights how the legislative process has a provocative dimension by urging analysis and expression of opinions on bills under review. The process includes a democratic dimension in the sense that it confronts diverging opinions by seeking, through arguing, to win the approval of those who think differently from oneself. It is a difficult movement to control, but which can be dealt with in at least two ways: through extensive negotiation or by breaking the rules of the game. At such moments, the contradictions in the Brazilian dictatorship (which maintained the representative system) appeared quite clearly, contextualizing the role of the politicians in Congress, even those belonging to a party allied with the government.

Congress had not been shut down again since the AI-5 was decreed. According to various sources, Senate president Petrônio Portella attempted to solve the standoff, but failed. When he announced to Congress the President's decision to declare Congress in recess, the senator called it a profoundly regrettable fact[93] and said he was experiencing one of the saddest moments in his public life.[94]

In an interview to the press, Senator Daniel Krieger said that despite some disagreements, he hoped that President Geisel could find a model consistent with a worthy reconciliation of freedom and order.[95] Meanwhile, Senator Jarbas Passarinho justified the need to temporarily sacrifice some prerogatives.[96] According to the press, the senator believed that re-democratization was possible but wondered whether it was advisable.

In this transition, the Executive appeared to aim at approval for its bills and projects, but without any major input from the politicians, centralizing the decisions in the *Palácio do Planalto*, the Presidential Palace. According to several witnesses, after Congress was closed the constitutional amendments were written up by a committee behind closed doors at the *Riacho Fundo*, one of the President's official residences.[97] The issue of ARENA's alienation from the decision-making processes thus surfaced again in this episode. The newspaper headlines showed the difficulties in the government's own base, allowing its marginalization. On 4 April 1977, *Jornal do Brasil* splashed the headline "ARENA left out of reforms during recess".[98] Yet the following day the newspaper showed the other side of the issue: "José Bonifácio challenges Francelino and reports that ARENA will discuss reforms".[99] Soon afterwards, with Congress still in recess, Jarbas Passarinho wrote a letter to Francelino Pereira that revealed a little of the party's internal debate on these issues. Passarinho reported to the ARENA chairman in a meeting with journalists:

> They asked me about the "news".
> I replied: "I learn the news from you, by reading the newspapers."
> They asked me: "But you sir, the first vice-chairman of ARENA, know nothing, are not listened to?"
> I replied: "Indeed, I know nothing, I'm not listened to, and this is nothing new, since the leaders in the Chamber and Senate are not heard either, according to what I read in the newspapers."
> Another question: "Do you think that's proper?"
> I replied: "The way the reforms are being done in the Executive sphere, there's nothing unusual about it. Besides, the party chairman is connected directly to the studies. With continuous access to decisions".
> The rest was just joking on my part, quoting Chinese proverbs ("Be worried, but not too worried"), because a veritable debate was waging in the lobby: they were attacking and I was defending the Executive's conduct.[100]

The *Arenista* leaders defended the Executive while at the same time criticizing it, making it clear that they were not heard. In a sense, they were trying to shield themselves from the embarrassment caused by not participating in the government's decisions, while not confronting the government directly. In other words, several *Arenistas* had a very clear idea of the distortions taking place in the political field, and some were more critical than others, but they all attempted to negotiate with the military.

During the congressional recess, the Executive issued some decrees and Constitutional Amendments 7 and 8, the former pertaining to Judiciary reform and the latter to electoral legislation.[101] This set of measures came to be known as the "April package": the President's terms were increased to six years (even sitting President Geisel's term was increased, a sort of coup within the context of détente); governors continued to be elected indirectly by a college of state deputies and delegates from the city councils; one out of three senators would be elected indirectly; and the Falcão Act was extended to all the direct elections. Congress remained closed for 14 days and was reopened under the impact of this new situation.

In his memories, Jarbas Passarinho, deputy leader of the government in the Senate, admitted that Constitutional Amendment No. 8 was a precautionary measure, motivated by the outcome of the 1974 elections and that brutally changed the rules of the game.[102] In the Senate, Paulo Brossard repudiated the new measures vehemently. In the Chamber of Deputies, José Bonifácio took charge of responding to the opposition quite menacingly:

> While the regime's challengers proceed with their challenges and provoke crises, like the latest ones they spearheaded, the Revolution will not shirk the revolutionary mandate that the Nation granted to it and will not hesitate to use democratic resources in its self-defence, as spelled out in the AI-5, the enforcement of which is guaranteed in Article 182 of the Constitution. Brazil's democracy needs the AI-5 just as peace-loving citizens need arms to face the treasonous enemies.[103]

Some months later, in August 1977, Petrônio Portella resumed his "mission" of negotiating the political reforms, talking not only with MDB but with representatives of sectors of civil society (leaders of various professional societies, representatives of the Catholic Church, and leaders of business associations and trade unions).[104]

In December 1977, the issue of constitutional reforms returned to the national agenda. In a ceremony in the *Palácio da Alvorada*, General Geisel gave a speech announcing the end of the AI-5.[105] Many *Arenista* politicians filled the main hall of the Palace, and his speech was interrupted by applause when the President announced the end of the emergency decrees. Some also applauded his reference to the obstacles created by "sincere but radical revolutionaries"[106] and the irresponsibility of the "passional oppositionists".[107] Versions differ as to how the speech was received by the cabinet members, governors, and members of Congress from ARENA. Deputy Theódulo de Albuquerque (ARENA – BA), described in the press as "the leader of a rebel faction in the party",[108] claimed he had lost his wedding ring from clapping so long and hard, and Deputy Nelson Marquezan (ARENA – RS) called the speech *"prafrentex"* [roughly equivalent to "groovy" and connoting "forward-thinking" – T.N.], indicating that the *Arenistas* could now seize the reforms banner.[109] However, Senator Teotônio Villela criticized the cold shoulder the speech received in some areas.

Finally, in July 1978, President Geisel sent the National Congress Message No. 203, a constitutional amendment bill that provided for the repeal of the institutional and complementary decrees insofar as they clashed with the Constitution. These measures resulted in the restoration of *habeas corpus* and such other constitutional or legal guarantees as tenure, irremovability, and stability. They also revoked the discretionary power of the President of the Republic to declare the National Congress in recess, decree intervention in the states and municipalities, suspend the political rights of citizens or electoral mandates, declare or extend a state of siege without authorization by the National Congress, or ban Brazilians from the country.[110] Senator José Sarney was chosen by General Geisel to present this bill, which Congress passed in September 1978.

After the passage of Constitutional Amendment No. 11, various measures were taken with a view towards the moment in which the AI-5 would be repealed.[111] Among the most important, a bill was drafted for a new National Security Act under the care of Petrônio Portela. In the discussion on the repeal of the AI-5 and the drafting of a new national security law, some deputies from ARENA highlighted in their speeches that they had condemned this decree for some time, returning to the issue of rule of law. Deputy Célio Fernandes (ARENA – RS) presented himself as

> One of the few who, from this floor and in meetings with the President of the Republic, showed that no one could stand the AI-5 anymore, that in an election year we were heavily jeopardized by this act, which we could understand during the revolutionary period but which we could no longer accept.[112]

Deputy Jorge Arbage, one of the ARENA "hardliners", acknowledged the new conjuncture, addressing his comments to Deputy Célio Fernandes:

I, too, am witness to your pioneering words in combatting the emergency acts. Your Excellency has always been a democrat. So often have I taken opposing positions to those of Your Excellency, and I make no secret of this nor do I regret it, because I believe, as does the President of the Republic, that it was necessary to maintain in force in the country the discretionary instruments to guarantee order and security and, above all, the continuity of the revolutionary process.[113]

However, the new National Security Act was criticized by some members of Congress from ARENA, even after its passage, because it prevented the total restoration of congressional prerogatives. Deputy Nina Ribeiro argued that there were many mistakes in the bill with regards to the congressional mandate's inviolability. According to the bill, in the crimes specified in the National Security Act whose review dispensed with authorization by the respective house of Congress, and the case having been filed by the Attorney General with the Supreme Court, the deputy or senator would be suspended from office until the final ruling. This was inconsistent with exercise of the congressional mandate.[114]

According to Deputy Flávio Marcílio, the repeal of the AI-5 should be greeted with joy, as should the restoration of judges' prerogatives and the immunities of the Legislative branch. However, he criticized the maintenance of state of siege and the establishment of state of emergency. But he highlighted two points that were kept in the reform: the restoration of direct gubernatorial and senatorial elections.[115]

Since the AI-2, when indirect elections for state governors were first instituted, this measure had never been officially written into the Constitution and had been the object of debate at each successive election. There had never been a consensus among the *Arenistas* on the nomination of governors. Politicians from ARENA had opposed this system in various contexts. After the municipal elections of November 1976, the issue of electoral reforms hit the newspapers. Some ARENA leaders claimed that the next gubernatorial elections would be direct, while others remained silent, such as Deputy Francelino Pereira, who refused to make predictions on the elections in 1978.[116] During the Congressional recess in April 1977, some *Arenista* congressmen voiced support for the indirect elections,[117] while others expressed their disapproval.[118]

Some politicians in ARENA gradually attempted to reoccupy positions that the civilians had lost to the military since 1964. In 1978, in the National Congress, since the beginning of the legislature, deputies from ARENA such as Augusto Lins e Silva (ARENA – PE) and others from MDB such as Florim Coutinho (MDB – RJ) defended Magalhães Pinto's candidacy to President of Brazil. In March 1978, Lins e Silva read the candidate's platform in the Chamber of Deputies.[119] The main points were:

1. Direct elections to President of the Republic, as well as the defence of restoration of the Legislative and Judiciary prerogatives, "ceasing their current condition of subalternity".[120]
2. Repeal of the AI-5, Decree 477, and article 185 of the Constitution and the "law that prevents election advertising under the pretext of regulating it",[121] full restoration of *habeas corpus*, the "inviolability of the courts, the recognition that not even the law itself can exclude from judicial review any violation of rights, and the elimination of mechanisms that restrict freedom of thought and information".[122]
3. Freedom for trade unions and student unions.
4. Human rights.
5. Amnesty ("it is imperious to erase the marks of misunderstandings from memory"[123]).
6. The "democratizing reforms".[124]
7. A "plebiscite to legitimize indirect choices":[125] "a national consultation for the people to give their say on [the President's] permanence in the position, as well as that of the governors and senators that have been elected indirectly".[126]

The platform concluded with a list of economic policy points: income distribution and an end to indexation, agrarian reform, privatization, improvement of living conditions in the cities, exploration of new energy sources, and the defence of an independent foreign policy, because "we refuse to have international trade continue to be a means for exploiting developing countries",[127] resuming the criticism by economists from CEPAL/ECLAC such as Celso Furtado against unequal trade relations between developed and underdeveloped countries.

Shortly before the ARENA National Convention in April 1978, Senators Magalhães Pinto and Severo Gomes launched a document denouncing the convention as "a defrauding of ethical norms and national aspirations"[128] and reaffirming their decision to maintain their candidacies, "using all legitimate resources to defend the civil rights and will of the Brazilian people".[129] At that convention, the party confirmed the candidacies of General João Baptista Figueiredo and Aureliano Chaves to President and Vice-President of the Republic, respectively, indicating the lack of support by the majority of ARENA for an initiative such as that of Magalhães Pinto and Severo Gomes in defence of civilian candidates. In the midst of the convention's debate on political reforms, Senator Jarbas Passarinho proclaimed incisively that ARENA would not accept "any type of concession that would lead the country back to the country of 1963 that we knew, the country of fake democracy".[130] The motions featured one of "applause and solidarity" [131] for General Geisel in light of his "determination to improve the democratic system, maintaining the constitutional safeguards that prevent the weakening of democracy, its destruction, disruption of order, anti-patriotic agitation, and attempts by extremists".[132]

On the other hand, Ezequiel de Melo Campos Filho, chairman of the Belo Horizonte Municipal Committee, defended election of the governors with participation by ARENA, justifying this position as doubly important since it served the party members' interests and was a strategy to compete with MDB. Although he believed that the majority of the delegate would not find his proposal feasible, he suggested that the party should manifest to the President of the Republic that it was

> Public knowledge, although many would not say it, that there is quite widespread discredit in the party's bases as regards what will apparently happen, that is, each state will have one candidate for governor, without granting the ARENA state conventions the right to choose, between alternative names, the one who will first and foremost serve the Revolution's interests, while also serving our party's interests. What many say, namely, that a dispute on the convention floor would weaken the party, is absolutely not consistent with the facts, since we all know that every convention dispute, rather than weaken the party, will strengthen it, since its constituencies cannot disagree with something to which they alone have contributed.[133]

In February that same year, Ezequiel de Melo Campos Filho had already sent a letter to Francelino Pereira with similar demands.[134] This motion was intended to make the intent clear to grant the regional convention the right to choose between the candidates with sufficient party backing. As for the gubernatorial succession in 1978, according to Maria Dalva Gil Kinzo, the regime's plan was "to create the conditions for a future party reform: the chosen candidates would be the ones that not only showed loyalty to the central government, but also displayed their own prestige and were capable of creating a strong base for reorganizing ARENA" (Kinzo, 1988, p. 206). But as the speeches and debates show, this was not only the Executive's plan, but a recurrent demand by *Arenista* congressmen.

Indeed, the diversity of political leadership in ARENA – previously organized in parties rooted in Brazil's states and municipalities and later combined in a single party – led to constant tension with the party organization. At the state levels, the difficulties in cohabiting in the same party were apparently exacerbated when indirect elections stripped the party's leaders of decision-making power on gubernatorial succession.

Still, in October 1978, in the vote on the Franco Montoro amendment, which provided for the reestablishment of direct elections for governor, deputy governors, and all the senators, the majority of the *Arenistas* abstained. The ARENA leadership failed to show up on the floor, and Senators Petrônio Portela and Jarbas Passarinho and Deputy Francelino Pereira were booed when their names were called for the vote. Meanwhile, the *Arenista* members of Congress that broke ranks and voted for the amendment, especially Senators Magalhães Pinto, Accioly Filho, and Teotônio Vilela, were applauded enthusiastically.[135]

The reaction by *Arenista* politicians to MDB's competitiveness included both support for discretionary measures decreed by the Executive and the search for greater autonomy in relation to the Executive, defending important measures for the country's re-democratization such as the end of indirect elections, proposing civilian candidates, and the end of party loyalty.

The electoral legislation requiring indirect elections for governors and one-third of senators not only curtailed Brazilians' political rights but also interfered in ARENA's internal disputes. The party's candidates were no longer chosen according to the political field's traditional criteria, but were handpicked mainly by the successive Presidents of the Republic starting in 1965, all of whom were Army generals. After 1974, various *Arenistas* openly criticized different aspects of the electoral legislation, which they considered harmful to ARENA's organization and the party's electoral success, especially questioning the naming of governors by the President. In other words, while détente was on the horizon, ARENA suffered a major electoral defeat. Certainly because of the defeat, various *Arenistas* defended a return to party organization based on popularity, the prime political capital that materializes in votes.

Some *Arenistas* in Congress began to defend the return to the rule of law, highlighting the repeal of the AI-5, as well as direct elections for state governors, among other measures. These members of Congress attempted in various ways to expand the regime's liberalization by getting ahead of the steps dictated by the Executive. In that scenario, the *Arenistas* read the growth of votes for MDB as Brazil's public opinion lining up in favour of democratization and a reality they needed to react to, because their own representation would soon be based exclusively on the popular vote. Still, other *Arenistas* such as Jarbas Passarinho and Jorge Kalume were wary of détente.

Meanwhile, the demonstrations were growing in Brasília. In October 1978, the vote by the electoral college to choose Geisel's successor was accompanied by demonstrations and clashes between the population and the police. Two thousand participants in the Democratic Day for Free Elections were prevented from entering the National Congress until a deputy opened an entrance to his office. Finally, a glass panel was broken at the main entrance to Congress, and several demonstrators made it in. General João Batista de Figueiredo, soon after his confirmation as President, issued a famous remark that made history: "[my government] will be to open up [the regime], and whoever doesn't want it to open up, I'll arrest them and beat them".[136]

The elections were held on 15 November 1978. ARENA won 233 seats in the Chamber of Deputies compared to 187 for MDB, and 15 seats in Senate compared to 6 for MDB. According to David Fleischer, these results indicate that ARENA had failed to reverse the growth of MDB, but at least had not let it grow more.[137] The new electoral rules imposed by the "April package" guaranteed a Senate majority for ARENA, which probably would have been won by MDB if there had been direct elections.

4 Amnesty and party reform

On 1 January 1979, Constitutional Amendment No. 11 entered into force, repealing the AI-5. The Brazilian government was still far from a democratic regime, but several changes could already be felt. Architect Oscar Niemeyer, known for his activism in the Brazilian Communist Party, proceeded with his projects in Brasília. Niemeyer later reported that he finished the interiors in the Senate building with the support of Petrônio Portella, in the Chamber with that of Marco Maciel, in the Supreme Court with that of the Chief Justice, and the parks and theatre in Brasília with the mayor's support.[138]

During the first year of the João Figueiredo government, Petrônio Portella as Minister of Justice and Golbery do Couto e Silva as Chief of Staff proceeded with the policy of liberalization by submitting bills to Congress for amnesty and party reform. Early in the year, Senator Portella posed the following question on the order of the day: "Amnesty is a path to national reconciliation. And I am certain that the matter will be discussed exhaustively in General Figueiredo's government".[139]

Luís Vianna Filho opened the ninth legislature and his swearing-in as president of the Senate by saluting the repeal of the AI-5. The congressional debates on amnesty became frequent in 1979, and the time had come to address one of the key themes in processes of transition from a dictatorship to a democracy. The speeches on the matter by *Arenistas* are another example of the party's diversity.

The members of Congress from ARENA and MDB were split on the proposals to review sanctions and grant "wide, general, and unrestricted" amnesty, according to the slogan in the campaign led by the Brazilian Committee for Amnesty. Yet there were some that did not consider any such concessions, such as Deputy José Bonifácio, who guaranteed that the government was not planning to grant amnesty or reverse political sanctions.[140] This was a surprising position, since Petrônio Portella, one of the political leaders most respected by the government, had opened the debate.

For many *Arenistas*, amnesty meant national reconciliation. In March 1979, speaking on behalf of the party leadership, Deputy Claudino Salles (ARENA – CE) presented his view on the matter: "Amnesty should be preceded by a policy of national appeasement, reconciliation, and fraternity. One cannot speak of amnesty, which is pardon, if hate still prevails".[141] The *Arenistas*' concerns included the potential consequences of an amnesty law. The representative of ARENA was concerned about the future, considering the reference by a member of Congress from MDB to future judicial sanctions as a "threat" or "revenge, pure and simple".[142] The leader of ARENA in the Chamber of Deputies, Jorge Arbage, defended the government's proposal in several speeches that focused on a defence of the Armed Forces' honour:

> No one in this country except the leaders of recklessness have attempted to raise doubts concerning the civic faith devoted by the troops and officers of the Army, Navy, and Air Force to the sacred principle of the inviolability of human rights. The Armed Forces, as we know, have always struggled to train men forged in the most exemplary lessons administered in the barracks, and it has never been possible to detect among them any tendency towards the violence and sadism of torture. This does not mean to defend those who are purportedly accused, but to avoid the guilt associated with simple mistakes from exposing the military institutions to discredit in the public eye in Brazil.[143]

Jarbas Passarinho noted in his memoirs that the government could not give in, because it had a commitment to its "'internal constituency', to military men and civilians who had risked their lives in the fight against terrorism and did accept unlimited amnesty" (Passarinho, 1996, pp. 486–487). On the other hand, Senator Teotônio Vilela endeavoured to expand the bill through meetings with state amnesty committees to organize the public campaign.[144] Senator Luís Vianna Filho, during the debate on the amnesty bill, visited political prisoners in Rio de Janeiro who had been on a hunger strike for 30 days.

The demonstrations in Brasília increased over the course of the détente process. On the eve of the vote on the amnesty bill, on 21 August 1979, Brasília was stage to several incidents. A thousand people watched the congressional debates, packing the galleries in the Chamber of Deputies.[145] During a demonstration with a thousand people in front of Congress for wide, general, and unrestricted amnesty, two unidentified individuals on the entrance ramp to Congress tossed tear gas cannisters into the crowd, hitting congressmen and a journalist. A bus bringing family members of political prisoners to demonstrations in Brasília had one of its tyres shot out. The attackers were never identified.

The vote's result showed how divided the country was. The National Congress passed the amnesty law by just 206 votes to 201. On 28 August, the government declared amnesty. After this concession, several changes were added to related provisions such as simplifying requirements for documents by eliminating criminal background checks.[146] Amnesty was a key political element for détente. The other main proposal was party reform.

The contradictions in the party system created in 1965 deepened after ARENA's defeat in the 1974 elections. Unlike the extinction of the parties in 1965, the result of an unexpected decree, Brazil had waited years for the party reform in 1979. Throughout ARENA's existence, its members frequently debated the feasibility of a system with only two parties.

Beginning in 1974, the controversy over party reform became a central issue for the regime's legitimacy, since MDB had become competitive at the national level, so that the party system could really be considered bipartisan. The end of the two-party system, as most of the analyses have emphasized, was a strategy by the government to divide the politicians from MDB into several parties.[147] The Executive was thus scheming to restore a multi-party system capable of allowing it to maintain control of the electoral process and the majority in the National Congress. But in addition to serving as a strategic project for the government, party reform was a demand by a large share of the politicians from both ARENA and MDB.

Many *Arenistas* favoured liberalization of party organization. According to a survey in March 1979, 92% of the MDB and 85% of

ARENA favoured a return to the multi-party system.[148] Most *Arenistas* thus defended the creation of two or three more parties, not only to allow divisions in the MDB, but also as a way of solving internal dissent in ARENA. Studies by political scientist David Fleischer identified

> An ARENA that was more fragmented than MDB, since the government party had a higher proportion of deputies in 1979 that identified with the former parties, when compared to MDB: 82 versus 60%, respectively. This means that the odds were just as high (or perhaps higher) for ARENA to implode, when compared to the opposition party. This *Arenista* fragmentation, according to the cleavages of the former parties, was due mostly to state-level political disputes, so that a considerable number of *Arenista* deputies could be expected to adhere to the banner of the 'independent party', following an auxiliary line, to position themselves better in the struggle between political currents in their states, with an eye on the election contest in 1982— thus resisting pressure by the government to remain faithful to the party of João [Figueiredo], the so-called "Arenão" ["Big ARENA"].[149]

In the newspapers and in the ARENA convention itself, the issue was mobilizing the politicians. In 1975, according to columnists from *Jornal do Brasil*, although Petrônio Portela and other members of Congress had declared that the idea of extinguishing the two parties had been ruled out, the journalists claimed that the idea had not been ruled out entirely, but that some of its proponents believed that party reform was not appropriate in that conjuncture and were awaiting a new debate, possibly after the municipal elections the following year.[150] For Deputy Amaral Neto, party reformulation was a "latent" issue on the Congress floor, and there was a consensus that it was necessary to find a solution to the party system problem.[151]

The ARENA National Committee received letters from all corners offering suggestions on party reformulation: senators, deputies, city councilmen, and sympathizers all gave their input. Deputy Airon Rios (ARENA – PE) defended a return to the multi-party system, asking why UDN and PSD could not be restored. After all, in the deputy's opinion, even "after twelve years, the country's most traditional parties, UDN and PSD, have not disappeared, since they even found a legal mechanism to survive"[152] (i.e., the multiple tickets).

Some groups devoted great energy to the reform. In May 1977, the Goiânia City Council approved a document requesting that the ARENA and MDB chairmen issue statements in favour of creating several political parties, arguing that the two-party system had reached its critical point, and defending the multi-party system.[153] The chairman of the São Paulo State Committee, Cláudio Lembo, sent a letter in July 1977 to the chairman of the ARENA National Committee, Francelino Pereira, in which deputies from São Paulo requested a party reform. The discontented signatories made a clear diagnosis of the situation. They admitted that

> The Revolutionary Power of 1964, intending to discipline Brazil's chaotic political situation, established the existence of just two parties. That decision obviously clashed with Brazilians' political background, accustomed to seeing partisan plurality as the proper way to exercise their political rights. In fact, this [two-party] positioning never occurred, and today, thirteen years later, experience has shown that it is impossible for the political class to limit itself to such a precarious and constrained party environment.[154]

Most *Arenistas* felt that extinction of the parties aimed to interrupt the party system's dynamics, which had become increasingly competitive since the 1960s, and saw the two-party system as a temporary expedient, and a frustrated experience at that.

Party reform was discussed openly throughout 1978 and 1979. In a detailed review of contemporary press coverage, Maria Dalva Gil Kinzo identified one of the main traits in the proposals for the creation of new parties: the return to the defunct acronyms, since they were still the party system's principal reference.[155] Her observation was confirmed by the documents on file at the ARENA National Committee, in letters from party members and in negotiations among members of Congress.

In May 1979, the National Committee took the initiative of conducting an opinion poll on party reform among the party membership. Then-chairman of ARENA José Sarney sent a questionnaire to the *Arenista* members of Congress and governors, explaining that the party should take a stance on the party reformulation issue due to the changes in the chapter on political parties under constitutional amendment No. 11.[156] If the member of Congress chose reformulation, he was supposed to answer some questions about what he thought the new party and the new party system should be. One member of Congress wrote: "No one can stand this two-party system any longer, which is at its end, thank God".[157] Another deputy, concerning the parties' extinction, wrote: "May they be soon, GOD WILLING".[158]

For those who favoured dissolving ARENA, the questionnaire asked whether the party should "return with other names to the party framework basically similar to the period prior to 1966?"[159] In this case, they were asked, "Which of the old parties should this new party most resemble?"[160], with the following alternatives: PSD, PTB, UDN, or another. Most of the *Arenista* congressmen unfortunately failed to answer this question. However, among those who did, the vast majority identified the new party with the extinct PSD, seen as the prime model for a majority pro-government party in Brazil's political history. This choice was unexpected, compared to the memory that was built of ARENA as the heir to the UDN. The result indicates that the *Arenistas* themselves had widely varying views of what ARENA meant and should mean. That is what is suggested by some of the answers in the questionnaire on the topic pertaining to the "old party" that the new party should most resemble: "None; PSD or PDS, because they fight for new ideas, with perhaps the same operational philosophy".[161] Another suggested: "a little of PSD and a little of UDN",[162] but with the following caveat: "with direct elections for governor in 1982".[163] Among the *Arenistas*, the association between ARENA and PSD was more frequent than one might imagine.

Thus, in April 1979 the press announced that former PSD politician Gastão Müller defended in the Senate the restoration of the PSD, reporting that the senator would be resuming his negotiations for forming a grand party, joined mainly by members of the old PSD. However, it would not be just one more restructuring of the PSD, for two reasons: first, the political context was different; second, if the PSD were re-established, the future party would not be able to count on the support of the old UDN membership, although they shared the same convictions.[164] This was an interesting and realistic observation which, in the new context, highlighted again the importance of the party's acronym, vocabulary, and ultimately its history.

The letters on file with the National Committee reveal that the initiative by then-chairman of ARENA José Sarney to discuss party reform mirrored the concerns of many of his fellow *Arenistas*. Many members wrote to the party offering suggestions on the reformulation of ARENA and the party system in general. In several letters, the multi-party system extinguished in 1965 appears as a model to be avoided, since it was considered a threat to ARENA. An *Arenista* from Nova Lima, Minas Gerais, wrote to the chairman of the National Committee in March 1978 applauding the initiative to change the party's name, but suggesting not to allow the return to the old acronyms such as PSD, UDN, PR, PST, and PTB, abolished by the AI-2, because he believed that they were "dead and buried".[165] He imagined that if they re-emerged:

The confusion will return, and the government (by force of the circumstances) will have to dissolve everything and start all over again. Revenge is in the crosshairs of the Brizolas, the Arraes, etc., etc., with the communists of MDB already travelling to Europe with their leaders to meet with the exiles.[166]

In September 1979, an ARENA sympathizer from Mostardas, Rio Grande do Sul, sent a list of suggestions for the new party system, in which he believed that the main parties' acronyms would still be strong forces for attracting voters' preferences. He therefore suggested that the old parties remain banned,

> This would avoid the creation of the PL in Rio Grande do Sul and other parties like the PSD. The creation of these parties would weaken the government party. PTB would be included in the ban. Mr. Leonel Brizola would not be able to create the PTB, but he could create another acronym, who knows, perhaps the Socialist Party, but not the Brazilian Socialist Party, which was one of the old party names.[167]

In this sense, although remaining as a reference for party identity during the two-party system and despite the comparisons and even the aspirations provoked by the post-1945 multi-party system in the late 1970s, the participants in that old system did not consider it feasible to reedit those organizations. For the *Arenistas*, basically, to employ the acronyms banned by the AI-2, such as PSD and UDN, would mean to separate their members vis-à-vis their position in relation to "*Getulismo*" (the political and social legacy of Getúlio Vargas, 1883–1954). In that context, due to the electoral growth of MDB and its expanding legitimacy as an opposition party among various organized sectors of Brazilian society, the cleavage between ARENA and MDB gained wide social recognition.[168] *Getulismo* was thus no longer the fundamental political watershed in Brazilian society as it had been from 1945 to 1964.

In the late 1970s, what divided Brazilian society was the stance in relation to the civilian-military dictatorship, so that for the former members of the PSD who had joined MDB, it would not make sense to abandon the new party that had gained electoral legitimacy and force, precisely as opposition to the government of the dictatorship. The acronym MDB was thus a legacy formed in those years, whose dividends proved fruitful and lasting. As history would have it, the same was not true for ARENA.

5 The "Yes Sir! Party"

In the late 1970s, ARENA was known as the "Yes Sir! Party". A reading of the Proceedings of the Chamber of Deputies (*Anais da Câmara dos Deputados*) and the Proceedings of the Senate (*Anais do Senado*) reveals that this rubber-stamp image was first used in the congressional debates in the years following 1974, when Brazil's electoral competition became quite fierce and MDB began to threaten the dictatorship at the ballot boxes. Interestingly, the idea that MDB was the "Yes! Party" does not appear in the congressional debates, at least the numerous volumes I consulted. This suggests that the derogatory label originated in sectors of the opposition that were critical of MDB, but outside the party sphere itself.

The issue of subservience, the label of the "Yes Sir! Party", appears to have impacted the *Arenistas* profoundly. From 1974 to 1979, this issue was the object of heated speeches in various forums: in Congress, in the press, and inside ARENA itself. The fact that the issue appeared in internal proceedings, meetings, and documents is particularly revealing of its importance for party members. Such speeches were not addressed to the party's local constituencies or to defend the party from the MDB in public, but were truly internal forums with restricted access, for discussing party matters.

In 1975, State Deputy Martinho Herculano Guizzo (ARENA – SC) was accused of party infidelity and was declared guilty by the party's Santa Catarina State Committee, who ruled that he should be stripped of his office. The deputy appealed his case to the National Committee. The grounds for accusing him of party infidelity are indicative of how seriously ARENA took criticism from MDB. According to the proceedings:

> Mr. Martinho Guizzo says he agrees with statements by the MDB, according to which the members of Congress from ARENA merely approve decisions [already taken]. This public statement to the newspapers contains a blatant criticism of his own political party, ARENA, and constitutes a flagrant violation of Article 74, item II of Law No. 5682 of 21 July 1971.[169]

Beyond the verbal confrontation by which *Emedebistas* sought to demoralize ARENA by accusing it of being the "Yes Sir! Party", a broader perception was taking shape on the political harms from this situation. Congressmen from both MDB and ARENA itself realized that this stigma was just the tip of an iceberg. In April 1975, Senator Paulo Brossard, leader of the opposition in the Senate, denounced:

> Ten years of exclusive domination by the government caused grave harm to ARENA. Reduced to the 'government party', as an object belonging to the government, its lord and master, which has exercised domination and possession of it, the party has suffered inevitable harm from the condition to which it has been reduced. The government has been less an extension of the party, enjoying a wide majority, and more of an appendix at the former's service.
>
> As a Brazilian, I would prefer that ARENA were a party <u>in the government</u>, (Hear! Hear!) rather than an <u>avowedly government party</u>. It has been said, and has just been repeated by the distinguished deputy Mr. Nelson Marquesan, that his party 'is the government party, but it is not in the government'.[170] (*O Estado de S. Paulo*, April 16, 1975)

During the negotiations to pass the reforms in September 1978, Deputy Airton Soares (MDB – SP) denounced:

> It's the party that has given legislative backing to all the government's acts in these 14 years, the party that seconds this 'little reform', this change to the Constitution that changes nothing, the party of 'Yes, Sir' and of the members of Congress who unfortunately either cannot or prefer not to stand up, rather submitting to the decisions taken in the *Palácio do Planalto*, which sends here to poor ARENA, to this poor congressional caucus, the decision already taken, and receiving back, simply, "Yes Sir! I approve".[171]

The label of the "Yes Sir! Party" was so frequent in the congressional rhetoric that even the *Arenistas* often referred to it when attempting to defend their own organization. At the beginning of a speech, Santos Filho (ARENA – PR) highlighted:

> Mr. president, distinguished deputies, out of deference to the leader of my party, ARENA, I now take the floor in a demonstration to some distinguished colleagues from the Opposition who constantly claim that the men of ARENA only say "yes", or are members of the "Yes Sir!" Party.[172]

National Deputy Célio Marques Fernandes attempted to set himself apart, explaining that he was "part of a small but active group that attempts to popularize and democratize ARENA, because we are not resigned to an ARENA that only says 'amen', that only receives orders from above and never represents the demands from the bottom up".[173]

Some deputies such as Herbert Levy, a veteran congressman, re-elected consecutively from 1945 to 1962, always under the UDN and since 1966 under ARENA, acknowledged those contradictions:

> Your Excellency touched on a pertinent point in saying that ARENA is and is not government. This is a critical point, and we *Arenistas* complain of it. We are left with all the government's burdens – which are undeniable, and to which I have already referred – and with none of the advantages. And this is precisely because the governments are not *Arenista* governments, not markedly partisan. And they should be.[174]

One of the leaders of ARENA in the Chamber of Deputies, Cantídio Sampaio, defended the party passionately:

> Your Excellency intends to place us in a position of submission to the Executive, a shameful and humiliating position. You are sorely mistaken! We men of ARENA are as worthy and independent (Hear! Hear!) as our colleagues from MDB. We never suffer pressure that might besmirch our dignity.[175]

The label of the "Yes Sir! Party" struck ARENA's very legitimacy and dignity, issues profoundly related to authority, such that this image reinforced precisely the lack of party autonomy. Beginning in 1974, the *Arenistas* began to respond to these attacks. Those connected closely to the government such as Cantídio Sampaio and Jarbas Passarinho defended themselves by denying that such problems existed. In the 1978 convention, one of Passarinho's main concerns was to defend ARENA from MDB: "They offend us, my dear colleagues. They shout that we are a hesitant, spineless party, a party of underlings. They tell us we are a party of weak-necked, spineless flunkeys".[176]

On the other hand, the more liberal leaders admitted ARENA's relations of marginalization and subordination to the government, acknowledging the need for changes and often presenting proposals for this purpose, as in the case of Luís Vianna Filho, Célio Fernandes, Teotônio Vilela, Herbert Levy, Lins e Silva, and others. The phantom of subordination appeared to torment many *Arenistas*, and at the convention in 1975, the main speakers endeavoured to defend themselves from that onus, including Teotônio Vilela: "We acknowledge our limitations out of principle and not out of subjugation. We understand that it is impossible to obtain what we desire overnight, or even tomorrow".[177]

In 1978, Deputy Lins e Silva expressed his support countless times for the candidacy of Magalhães Pinto to President of the Republic:

> Mr. president, distinguished deputies, we should no longer passively accept the condition, albeit apparent, of spokesmen for arbitrary rule and defenders of the state of exception that has been installed in the country. Furthermore, conformism, resignation, submission, subservience, or servility will never mean patriotism. It behoves us, as politicians who legitimately represent more than a hundred million Brazilians without participation, to eradicate such a disease. And this will only be possible by taking a stance, an attitude at least consistent with basic democratic principles. Even if it displeases those who make nefarious and sickly radicalism a profession in our country.[178]

ARENA's marginalization from decision-making and participation in the government were summarized in its characterization as a "government party". In 1979, in response to the questionnaire sent by the National Committee, various *Arenistas* complained openly that they wanted "a party in the government and not a government party", as the phrase went at the time. On April 13, 1979, from the municipal committee in São João de Meriti (RJ), an *Arenista* wrote a letter to the chairman of the National Committee entitled *ARENA's Agony*. Based on his experience, he predicted that "ARENA will not survive even with all the candidates that attract the most votes in the world, because what is vital for the party is to change its essence, for ARENA to become more representative and a party in government rather than a government party".[179] Among the *Arenistas* in Congress, lack of participation in the government was the most frequent complaint at the end of the questionnaire on party reformulation, in a space reserved for open-ended observations. One deputy stated that it was indispensable "to provide the party that supports the government with real participation in the government team, where it will actually collaborate in the decisions and thus also share the responsibilities".[180]

The deputies ultimately argued, even literally, that the government should assign more prestige to ARENA. According to one of these *Arenistas* in Congress, "the dissociation between the deputies and the people has created in the constituency a veritable lack of appreciation among those who receive the benefits, as if everything were done without any role by the politicians".[181] He suggested that the government should acknowledge the politicians "by allowing them to submit bills that are popular with the people, which at the moment come mostly from Congress as initiatives by the Executive".[182]

Some deputies believed that the party's actual participation in the government was vital, otherwise the new party would be doomed to failure. There were observations that "despite the expansion of options for partisan political action, of 'supporting, without being the government, i.e., being of the government without being in the government', we will witness the disappointing failure of the new national political structure".[183] In the same vein, another congressman acknowledged that "ARENA has suffered all this attrition mainly because it has never been in the government at the federal level. Whatever party succeeds it without participating in the government will inevitably suffer the exact same fate".[184] In other words,

> It is important for the politicians that have backed the Executive to be brought into the government, to participate in it, influencing economic and financial policy-making. The new party legislation should bury party loyalty – as it is conceived today – as well as the nefarious multiple tickets.[185]

Furthermore:

> For those acting in the government party, for both to become stronger, suffice it to establish a true dialogue, broad collaboration, and absolute coordination between the two entities at all levels and in all areas. And then ARENA will be strong, as it is, and will remain in the majority for a long time.[186]

Another congressman appeared keenly aware of the changes in Brazil's political scenario, glimpsing the possibilities for new legitimacy based on votes: "The government should fear neither the ballot boxes nor the emergence of a large independent centrist party. That's what alliances are for, normal in any regime".[187] In this inventory of ARENA's experience, the members of Congress were again seeking to expand their room for action.

The suggestions and alternatives glimpsed by the more liberal politicians of ARENA to respond to the attacks against the party's subordination had the democratic transition as their horizon. According to many *Arenistas*, ARENA would only be able to build an image as a legitimate, independent party by adopting liberalizing measures. There were nuances even among the more liberal *Arenistas*, with some defending civilian candidates for President, the elimination of party loyalty on votes in Congress, and actual participation in the government. In other words, it may even have been impossible (because it was profoundly contradictory) for a strong, autonomous government party to exist under a dictatorship that maintained a system of political representation along liberal lines.

In fact, the professional politician's practice involves a formal legal structure that includes partisan and electoral systems. When we revisit the history of liberal political representation, we find a series of founding principles: popular sovereignty, peaceful transition of power, and balance of powers. Such principles are the basis of party and electoral legislation in a democratic regime. They constitute the regulation of a historical dispute for political participation. In the *Arenistas*' commentary, there was no defence of democracy as a universal value, but dissatisfaction with the constraints and de-characterization of the formal channels for participation and competition among the politicians.

The concept of political field features the importance of certain values such as recognition, credibility, and dignity in the establishment of political authority, which also implies perceiving their reverse, the fundamental dimension of attack through slander and libel. Reading the various sources revealed how many leaders of ARENA were aware of the changes in the political field in relation to the professional politicians' dignity. The recurrent losses of congressional prerogatives were notorious, as were the loss of prestige.

Meanwhile, the most bitter criticisms of ARENA were exactly those that attacked its dignity: "latecomer rubber-stamp" ("*adesista*"), the "Yes Sir! Party", and so on. The party's opponents used comical nicknames aimed precisely at the *Arenistas*' honour (one of the most important forms of capital for politicians). The attacks that were most remembered years after the party was extinguished were those against its credibility.

Over the course of ARENA's history, different values were assigned to the party's name. The survey of members of Congress in 1979 and the letters from *Arenistas* reveal part of a process for studying a change in the party's name. It was a consensus that the acronym, one of the most significant forms of party capital, should change to a new name bearing absolutely no similarity to the old one, because many deputies were aware that it was "stigmatized as the party of arbitrary rule and should thus disappear in order for us to be able support the government under a different mantle, without this stain",[188] as one congressman noted.

The party reform bill drafted by the Executive solved this issue by requiring that the names of new organizations begin with the word "party", which sparked major resistance from representatives of MDB. In September, José Sarney, then-chairman of ARENA, gave a lecture at the Superior War College (ESG) entitled *Political parties*, a text that the

ARENA National Committee later distributed to various individuals.[189] Just a few days before the vote on the new legislation, Sarney received congratulatory telegrams citing the negotiations he had spearheaded.[190] On 29 November 1979, Congress passed the new party reform law, extinguishing ARENA and MDB.

Some members of Congress sent suggestions for the new party's profile, such as Adhemar de Barros Filho, who emphasized the importance of certain underlying ideals: "representativeness, multiple parties, independence for the body politic".[191] Deputy Herbert Levy sent a telegram to the ARENA chairman: "If you want the name PDS, you'll have to pay royalties,"[192] suggesting the name's paternity. The new organization was ultimately called the Social Democratic Party, forming the acronym PDS, quite similar to the traditional name for the PSD.

Following extinction of the two parties, only 37 deputies left ARENA to join another party and 79 deputies from MDB switched parties.[193] PDS emerged as the party with the largest congressional base, since most of the *Arenistas* joined it. In the context in which PDS was founded, Minister Ibrahim Abi-Ackel, accompanied by Golbery, made statements attempting to mark the new party's identity: "The party is born as the government party, incorporating into its formation the contribution and shared responsibility of those holding positions in the government".[194] Thus, Abi-Ackel attempted to respond to the recurrent demand by *Arenistas* to actually occupy the government.

But while ARENA was extinguished, the names that made the party continued in activity and reorganized, taking with them to the new party organizations the political capital accumulated in those last fifteen years. The changes in the process of choosing state governors and the concentration of power in the respective state committees strengthened new leaders for whom the dictatorship had been an important time of ascension in their political careers and a moment of capitalizing power resources for a generation of politicians who had been relatively young in 1964.

CHAPTER 6

A History of ARENA in Cartoons

During my research, as I was reading *O Estado de S. Paulo*, the political cartoons stood out from the newspaper's pages. It was almost impossible not to look at them. Armed with powerful visual appeal, they caught my attention and slowed down the research that was intended to focus on political news coverage. But this involuntary detour was not in vain. There, for the first time, we find ARENA depicted as a woman in widely varying and unusual circumstances. The portrayals of ARENA in political cartoons published in Brazil's mainstream press show how an image of the party was built, and how that image was consolidated as a derogatory one. Through the analysis of these various portrayals of ARENA, elaborated since the party was founded, throughout its activity, and after it was extinguished, it becomes quite clear that this image did not always exist, nor was it the only possible version.

1 Press, memory, and political humour

The controversy over the social memory of Brazil's dictatorship is profoundly linked to the versions published in the newspapers. There is a plethora of special commemorative editions in the press on historical facts. These editions feature articles by journalists, politicians, historians, and other social scientists. The special editions themselves are interesting primary sources for studying the memory built on such facts in our societies.[1] The images produced and reproduced by the press appear recurrently in speeches on the regime by various social actors, demonstrating their outstanding role in this political dispute to shape public opinion.

Brazil's political journalism has a certain humorous tradition. The jokes and picturesque tales involving political leaders are part of a style forged in the newsrooms. During the dictatorship, this watershed of political commentary gained an anthology published by journalist and purged Deputy Sebastião Nery, entitled *Folclore político brasileiro* (*Brazilian Political Folklore*), a series of books with anecdotes on Brazilian politicians, mainly portraying the years of the liberal-democratic experience from 1945 to 1964.[2] Humourist Millôr Fernandes, in the introduction to one of the volumes, says:

> There is a moment in the midst of the crises – at the centre of the dramas, over the course of the fatigue in a struggle that is sometimes grandiose but is mostly mediocre and routine – when the politicians laugh. They laugh a lot at others. Sometimes they laugh at themselves. Brazilian politicians love to tell tales, many of which are original, that really happened, and many with remote origins, lost in the incommensurable time of folklore.[3]

Brazil's political humour is thus not always the object of repudiation by those depicted in it: quite to the contrary. Cartoonist Ziraldo Alves Pinto published a humorous magazine from 1964 to 1966 entitled *Fotopotocas* in which he created political cartoons based on photographs, basically produced by photojournalism. In each photograph he inserted balloons with lines or thoughts, as in comic strips. According to Ziraldo himself, the politicians liked *Fotopotocas* so well that some sent photographs to the newsroom. On one occasion, when Ziraldo was visiting José de Magalhães Pinto, a leader of the UDN who joined ARENA in 1965, the politician from Minas Gerais gave him several photographs and the two men spent several hours together creating jokes.[4] The experiences of Millôr Fernandes and Ziraldo thus point to a relationship of proximity established between humourists/journalists and politicians and to a position by the latter in Brazilian society in the 1950 and 60s, when the politicians encouraged (and had fun with) a kind of folklore about themselves and their peers.

But starting in 1964 and throughout the 1970s, political cartoons became an important vector for critique. In times of authoritarian rule and political crisis, given the censorship imposed on periodicals, Brazil's press developed alternative strategies to do its work through political humour and economic journalism.[5] In this context, cartoonists gained an important place because they were able to summarize extremely critical messages in their drawings. There is a rich debate on the repercussions of various strategies to denounce censorship in the Brazilian newspapers, questioning the understanding of publication of cake recipes or poems by Luís de Camões, a device used by the press to mark the place of the censored news articles. In the case of political cartoons, there was not exactly a new strategy; on the contrary, there was a tradition, a consolidated political learning process concerning the cartoons' meaning.

Brazilian periodicals had been famous for political cartoons since the nineteenth century, during Brazil's Imperial Period. During the First Republic and in the 1930s, illustrated magazines flourished, including *O Malho*, *Careta*, and *Fon-Fon*, which featured caricatures and political cartoons by artists such as Angelo Agostini, Storni, J. Carlos, and K. Lixto. In the 1950s, Carlos Lacerda would be branded forever as "the Crow", a historical caricature by Lan.

In the field of political humour, political cartoons became an important part of news coverage, and in most of Brazil's mainstream newspapers they have a privileged place in the layout, close to the editorial or next to signed opinion columns or even on the front page. As Sebastião Nery himself recorded, Millôr Fernandes, Ziraldo, Henfil, Jaguar, and Caulos could be considered political editorialists of Brazil in those years of the dictatorship and censorship.[6]

The introductions to the various anthologies of political cartoons published in the 1980s feature personal testimony like this, demonstrating the recognition enjoyed by Brazilian cartoonists' drawings and the partnerships formed between professional artistic and textual journalists. Journalist and writer Antônio Callado, in his preface to an anthology of illustrations by Fortuna, acknowledges the clear editorial vein of that period's political cartoons in the Brazilian press. His words are exemplary and doubtless apply not only to Brazil:

> In countries like ours, with relatively little freedom, cartoons tend to become a sort of background article. Brazil, generally occupied by a censorship with solid backing from powerful landowning interests, began to be surreptitiously occupied and colonized by caricatures. Cartoonists are our squatters. They occupy the forbidden land of the editorial, of political commentary, and plant themselves there with a blasé air, brush in hand as if it were a hoe.[7]

In *O pipoqueiro da esquina* (*The Corner Popcorn Vendor*), poet Carlos Drummond de Andrade demonstrated what he saw as the "eternal law of the caricature: to reveal, to demystify, to castigate, to feed, by its totally uncommitted critical view, man's fragile hope" (Andrade, 1981, p. 5). Darcy Ribeiro, in the essay *Aos trancos e barrancos: como o Brasil deu no que deu* ("*By Fits and Starts: how Brazil got the way it is*"), tells how he turned "unabashedly" to Fortuna and other cartoonists because of their capacity to capture "the exemplary figure, because of his admirable or detestable posture, but at any rate they always surprise him in a laughable way. My view nearly always coincides with theirs".[8] All these commentaries reveal the strategic place and respectability acquired by political humour in Brazil's newspapers. Their place was doubtless much larger than the cartoon production from the early twentieth century, viewed by other intellectuals and journalists at that time as minor, marginal artwork.[9] Studies on caricatures and humour generally show that in the late nineteenth century and throughout the 1930s, 40s, and 50s, humour was derided as a form of social expression; one of the recurrent arguments in this discourse was that of the "immediate and raw link between humour and the everyday facts. This explains why they were labelled as superficial, light, and minor".[10] However, historians increasingly understand that their everyday reality, rather than invoking superficiality, constitutes a promising field for studies on practices profoundly incorporated by societies. Political images and political humour in general have thus been considered original sources for studies on social practices.

On the other hand, political humour's status changed in the 1970s and 80s. Political cartoons in the press were celebrated by many intellectuals and were easily found reedited in books, conquering the status of works of art, high-quality journalistic production, and highly expressive political critique.

Various anthologies were published in the 1980s by cartoonists that were consecrated in the press, covering work done during the dictatorship. These projects were produced by publishing houses such as Codecri (publishers of the weekly lampoon *O Pasquim*), Circo Editorial, LPM, Record, and others. The publishing projects aimed to elaborate a memory of the authoritarian period. The anthologies generally organized the political cartoons in chronological order, building a narrative on the political regime that was drawing to a close. Some even made this meaning explicit in the title, such as *1964–1984: 20 anos de prontidão* (*1964–1984: 20 Years at Attention*) or *Aberto para balanço* (*Open for Inventory*) These political cartoons are a veritable treasure trove for recording the possible type of opposition raised to the regime through the press. The material was so highly prized that in 1994, thus ten years after a civilian had been sworn in as President of Brazil, the Brazilian Institute of Social and Economic Analyses (IBASE), a nongovernmental organization headed by sociologist Herbert de Souza, brother of cartoonist Henfil, published the anthology *Henfil nas eleições* (*Henfil in the Elections*) as part of the campaign *Citizens' Action against Poverty and in Defence of Life*.

The anthologies thus intended to make history, as the authors and prefacers indicated in several of them. In the opening pages to *20 Years at Attention,* Ziraldo noted:

> When most of these drawings were published, they were subjected to crude censorship, which scratched out and ripped up our originals. The author's hope is that the work presented here will serve to retell many aspects of these twenty years in Brazil, in our attempt to seek a final understanding of that period. And we are certain that the cartoonist's role is to tell the saddest part of the story.[11]

These anthologies really do tell only part of the story, because they are always a selection of the drawings published during the previous historical period. I thus decided to compare the images selected for the anthologies with the whole set of political cartoons published in the newspapers I consulted. Since the study's perspective focused on ARENA's view, I observed the cartoons accordingly. It is highly revealing that precisely the political cartoons that complexify ARENA's condition as a political party were not reedited in the volumes of the 1980s. In other words, they were excluded from the selection for the historical memory in book format, which has a long life, unlike the original newspapers.

The analysis of political cartoons depicting ARENA is one of the countless paths for reflecting on the social memory that was ultimately consolidated on the party. Such analysis provides a way to intertwine and tie together the threads of political history with the threads of history of art, drawing on a metaphor by Ségolène Le Men,[12] who studied the work of Honoré Daumier, the great French caricaturist who was considered the forerunner of modern political cartoons. From 1830 to 1875, Daumier produced caricatures of French authorities for illustrated magazines such as *La Caricature* and *Le Charivari.* His pen's main targets were members of Parliament, ministers, and King Louis-Philippe himself. In studies on Daumier's work, Ségolène Le Men shows how the artist's initial reference was portraits of the salons, later shifting to images produced by daguerreotypes and photographs.

According to Le Men's studies, the caricature aspired to be a sort of historical painting. It inaugurated a certain version of the grand genre, a version linked to current events. With Daumier, the derisory and burlesque caricature witnessed a heroic and glorious mode. His lithographs rose to the importance of grand art (usually reserved for painting or sculpture) and were no longer relegated to the status of lesser art.

Thus, since the nineteenth century there was a strong link between humour and the press in the European countries and in the main Brazilian cities, and political cartoons were always produced for periodicals.[13] Le Men assigned to the genre the roles of satire, art, and journalism, considering it an important element in the establishment of a public sphere. From this perspective, the illustrated journal serves as a sounding box, publicizing the debates in Parliament through lithographic reproductions of the political cartoons. Through caricature, Daumier proposed an alternative to the analysis of the debates waged in the French Legislature; another form of publicity for such debates and also for artistic practices. The caricature combines its satirical and artistic functions with a journalistic mission.

In the mid-twentieth century, political cartoons no longer merely played the role of communicating the politicians' image to the reader public, as in the nineteenth century. But they continued to link politicians to readers by making fun of public officials. According to studies on political cartoons in Brazil, their historical origins are intermingled with those of comic strips.[14] The cartoonists' reference was the world of comic strips, whose aesthetic appears to be the main trend in political cartoons published in the press since the nineteenth century. Many of the Brazilian artists did not work only with political humour, but also developed story characters for comic strips and advertising posters, a burgeoning field since the 1950s.[15] Since that decade, the visual communications media increasingly expanded the field of action for cartoons, making it indispensable to understand how the images also transmit meanings.[16]

My analysis of the political cartoons depicting ARENA is premised on the concept of art as a social practice. This methodological perspective opens a broad field of studies for historians, who see works of art as portrayals that result from social practices. One of the main elements in this methodological perspective is the concept of intertextuality, a fundamental contribution by Mikhail Bakhtin, found at the centre of current debates. The concept of intertextuality, originally applied to linguistic studies, posits that a text's analysis can only be performed based on other texts. The concept assumes that a work is never autonomous, since every discourse or text is a phenomenon of cultural communication that cannot be understood independently of the social situation in which it occurs.[17] For the historian's craft, the concept of intertextuality represents a contribution in the field of internal critique of primary sources. The aim is to work not only with the multiplicity of sources in each study, but to seek the relations among the diversity of funds consulted.

The dictionary *Dicionário Aurélio*, a standard reference in Brazilian Portuguese, defines "political cartoon" (*"charge"* in Portuguese) as a "burlesque and caricatural pictorial representation that satirizes an idea, situation, or person" (Ferreira, 1999). "Caricature" is defined as a "drawing which, by its stroke and choice of details, accentuates or reveals certain ridiculous aspects of a person or fact", as a "deformed reproduction of something" or "a ridiculous person based on appearance or manners".[18] A "cartoon" itself is a "humorous drawing that records or criticizes persons, situations, or events, real or imaginary: a graphic anecdote".[19]

Political cartoons are always an intertext. They are a counter-discourse that necessarily demands interlocution, not explicitly presenting all the elements needed to understand the message. In jokes, comic strips, and political cartoons, there is always information that has to be read between the lines (or strokes). It is this absence that lends force to the joke. In the case of political cartoons, their reading implies knowledge of the issues in the political conjuncture, the names and faces of public men, the meaning of the metaphors, gestures, and facial expressions in the local culture. All of this, in turn, qualifies the political cartoon as a narrative of its time that expresses shared values and ideas in a certain context.

2 Newspapers and political cartoonists

During Brazil's dictatorship, various periodicals published political cartoons, in both the mainstream press and the so-called alternative press. There is a very rich world of political cartoons produced under the dictatorial regime, criticizing various political aspects, often transformed into characters, like the military officer, the censor, the torturer (depicted in various drawings as a hangman), and the capitalist (identified in some illustrations by his coat and tails and top hat), among others. Importantly, however, in the current study the criterion for selection of political cartoons was the depiction of political parties of the time. Thus, some excellent work by important artists of the time were not included in the study, since they did not focus specifically on the parties.

ARENA was portrayed in numerous drawings published in the mainstream newspapers *Jornal do Brasil*, *O Estado de S. Paulo*, and *Correio da Manhã*. Contrary to what one might suppose, the newspapers from the so-called alternative or "midget" press published few political cartoons on the subject of party politics, as I discovered in a search in the alternative weeklies *O Pasquim*, *Movimento*, and *Opinião*. To study the portrayals of ARENA, I only analyse the production published in the mainstream newspapers, since I wanted to observe the image communicated to a broader readership rather than to specific niches like the readers of the alternative press (which had assumed a militant role against the regime) or even the weekly news magazines such as *Veja*, which reached a more select readership.[20]

Based on my reading of the mainstream newspapers, I selected a series of political cartoons for this study. They span the years from 1965 to 1979 and were published starting with the moment of extinction of the former political parties by the AI-2 on 27 October 1965 until the extinction of ARENA and MDB in November 1979. Each political cartoon was interpreted as a unit, but at the same time each one constituted an element within a series elaborated here on political parties under the dictatorship. Thus, the main focus of the analysis is precisely the series as a whole, the set of selected images rather than each iconographic element per se.[21]

The political cartoons generally refer to certain conjunctures that impacted the country's party system. Some facts were fundamental in these scenarios: AI-2 (1965); the 1966 elections; AI-5 (1968); Complementary Act No. 54 (1969); the 1970 elections; regulation of the Organic Law on Political Parties (1971); the 1974 elections; the "April package" of 1977; the 1978 elections; and the extinction of ARENA and MDB in 1979. The moments selected for analysis of the sources correspond to the months in which elections were held and those in which laws were implemented that directly modified the country's political and party system. The series of political cartoons features various portrayals of ARENA in these different conjunctures, suggesting an extensive web of meanings involving ARENA, as well as its relations with MDB, the government, and voters.

In a systematic reading of the weekly lampoon *O Pasquim*, one of the periodicals that made history in opposition to regime, the theme of partisan politics practically never appears. The main topics addressed by the tabloid included literature, music, theatre, cinema, customs, programs, and problems in the city of Rio de Janeiro. Meanwhile, the newspapers *Movimento* and *Opinião* published interviews and reportage on national politics. The journalists' perspective was one of critique rather than ridicule, and many editions featured interviews by *Arenistas* on the political conjuncture, the National Congress, and state governments. Both these papers also frequently published caricatures of politicians from both ARENA and MDB.

On the other hand, in Brazil's mainstream newspapers, political cartoons occupied an outstanding place throughout the regime. *Jornal do Brasil* had several political cartoonists, all highly respected artists in this area: Chico Caruso, Henfil, Lan, and Ziraldo. Yet the political cartoons in *Jornal do Brasil* did not always address national politics, nor did they always occupy featured places in the newspaper. In 1964, the political cartoons dealt with themes related to the city of Rio de Janeiro and were published in *Caderno B* (the newspaper's culture and entertainment section). Starting in 1966, they began to mainly address national politics and were moved up to the main news section, where they occupied a prime place, from pages 6 and 10, generally next to the editorials and conversing with them.

In *Correio da Manhã*, from 1965 to 1969, page 6 consisted of the editorial, background articles by such journalists as José Lino Grunewald and Hermano Alves, and political cartoons by artists like Fortuna, Mem de Sá, Arnon, Senna, and Claudius. But *Correio da Manhã* stopped publishing political cartoons on national politics starting in 1969, probably due to the ruthless censorship. That same year the newspaper was rented out, and it closed down entirely in June 1974.[22]

On the eve of the AI-5, political cartoons by Claudius and Mem de Sá in *Correio da Manhã* were quite critical of the latest measures by the dictatorship. During the month of December 1968, various political cartoons were published on the standoff between the President of Brazil, who was determined to purge then-National Deputy Márcio Moreira Alves, and the Chamber of Deputies. In a political cartoon by Claudius, for example, then-Minister of Justice Gama e Silva pushes President Costa e Silva towards the bonfire of the purge and convening the extraordinary session of Congress.[23] On the day after the vote, cartoonist Mem de Sá drew the heads of the Chamber of Deputies under the inscription *Libertas Quae sera Tamem* ("Freedom, Although Late", the rallying cry of the eighteenth-century insurgents from Minas Gerais that were the forerunners of Brazil's independence from Portugal, and currently the motto on the Minas Gerais state flag – T.N.)[24] Some political cartoons like this one, on the vote that denied authorization to the regime to try Deputy Moreira Alves, emphasized the incident as a reaction by Congress to the Executive, to be celebrated: *Freedom, Although Late.*

On the days immediately following the AI-5, few newspapers continued to publish political cartoons, due to the censorship. After 14 December, the cartoons in *Correio da Manhã* no longer made references to the country's political conjuncture, and starting on the 21st of that month they were no longer published at all until late 1968. In *Jornal do Brasil*, throughout the year 1969, no cartoons were published on national politics. Page 7 of the main news section featured cartoons by Lan on local problems in the city of Rio de Janeiro, such as stench from the Rodrigues de Freitas Lagoon,[25] roadway traffic,[26] problems with telephone services,[27] the hazards of paddle ball rackets on Rio's beaches,[28] the summer heat wave,[29] and construction work for the underground.[30] There were also some reasons for joy occupying that space in the newspaper, with cartoons on Carnival[31] and football, or more specifically the Flamengo football team,[32] the cartoonist's favourite.

In *O Estado de S. Paulo*, from the AI-5 to January 1969, no political cartoons were published on the national situation, only drawings referring to international news or more generic topics such as Christmas or Carnival, probably because the newspaper had been under prior censorship since 13 December 1968. In early December, *O Estado de S. Paulo* published an editorial stating that the government should conduct a constitutional reform to restore autonomy to Congress. The Executive was also urged to reformulate party life and modify the national security and press laws. Finally, after an editorial entitled *Instituições em frangalhos* (*Institutions in Shreds*), analysing the political crisis in the wake of the Márcio Moreira Alves affair, the newspaper's edition was seized in the middle of the night. But in early 1969, the cartoons on national politics started to be published again.

At times of heaviest censorship and repression, Brazil's mainstream newspapers stopped publishing cartoons on politics. Only the traditional *O Estado de S. Paulo* maintained its political cartoons throughout the regime. The cartoonists only covered other subjects for a short period, immediately after the AI-5, but they soon returned to Brazil's political scenario. This fact is important, since various studies on *O Estado de S. Paulo* find that the 1964 movement had sparked a veritable euphoria in its newsroom. However, there was no longer such enthusiasm in the following years, although the support remained for certain measures by the government. Even so, the "*Estadão*" (as it is nicknamed) suffered prior censorship from 13 December 1968, with the decree of the AI-5, until January 1975. During this period the journalists' stories were screened by a government censor in the newsroom itself or in the offices of the Federal Police Department.

From 1965 to 1979, the main cartoonists in *O Estado de S. Paulo* were Hilde Weber and Edmondo Biganti. Both were immigrants. Hildegard Weber had come to Brazil from Hamburg, in northern Germany, in 1933[33] and Edmondo Biganti from the Umbria region of Italy in 1954. In the period following 1964, Hilde was in charge of the cartoons on Brazilian national politics, while Biganti mainly covered the international news, occasionally touching on the Brazilian scenario. The political cartoons were not always published on the same page, but on some of the pages on national politics (pages 3, 4, or 5 of the main news section).

Edmondo Biganti was born in 1918 in Italy. In 1956 he began to contribute to *O Estado de S. Paulo* as a political cartoonist. His illustrations had won several awards in contests in Europe. He was also a painter, doing water colours on Brazilian motifs such as Rio's favelas and the baroque churches in Ouro Preto, Minas Gerais.

Artist Hildegard Weber was born in 1913 in Waldau, Germany. Before moving to Brazil, she studied drawing and painting at the School of Graphic Arts in Hamburg. In Brazil, besides creating political cartoons and caricatures for the press, she participated as an artist in countless collective and individual exhibits, including consecutive editions of the São Paulo International Biennial. By the 1960s, Hilde was already an internationally renowned caricaturist. In 1960, she won the international prize for political caricatures from the California Newspaper Association, and in 1962 she was awarded the gold medal for caricatures from the Liberal Journalists' Salon in Rio de Janeiro.

Hilde was married to journalist Cláudio Abramo, secretary-general of *O Estado de S. Paulo* until 1963. From 1933 to 1962, she lived in Rio de Janeiro and collaborated with various periodicals from Rio and São Paulo, notably Carlos Lacerda's *Tribuna da Imprensa*. In 1962 she moved to São Paulo, where she worked for *O Estado de S. Paulo* and *Jornal da Tarde* until her retirement in 1989.[34]

Other great names in this cast of caricaturists are Ziraldo Alves Pinto and Reginaldo Fortuna. Ziraldo was born in 1932 in Caratinga, Minas Gerais. In 1954, he began working for the newspaper *Folha de Minas*, and in the following years he published drawings in magazines such as *A Cigarra* and *O Cruzeiro*. He began collaborating with *Jornal do Brasil* in 1963. Besides political cartoonist, Ziraldo is a writer, painter, poster designer, and journalist. He was arrested in 1968 following the AI-5. That year his work was awarded at the International Oscar for Humour in the 32nd International Caricatures Salon in Brussels and with the Merghantealler, the top freedom of the press prize in Latin America.[35]

Reginaldo Fortuna was born in the state of Maranhão, Brazil. He began collaborating with the leading Brazilian magazines and newspapers in the 1940s, including the magazine *Senhor* in its inaugural phase. He was a political cartoonist for the newspaper *Correio da Manhã* from 1965 to 1969. Besides political cartoonist, he was a graphic designer, chronicler, and editor, having worked in the Brazilian press for

45 years.[36] In 1969, precisely after the AI-5, Ziraldo, Fortuna, and others left the mainstream press and founded *O Pasquim*, one of the most prestigious periodicals in the country's alternative press.

3 A history of ARENA in political cartoons

The images of ARENA displayed in the political cartoons clearly correspond to the historical periods built on the analysis of various sources, including documents in the ARENA National Committee's archives, the congressional debates, and the textual production in Brazil's mainstream press.

Soon after the AI-2 was decreed and before the creation of ARENA and MDB, several drawings were published on the government's intervention in the party system. These drawings clearly reveal the perception that the new parties would not be founded on a blank slate, and that they even pointed to partisan continuity in the new organizations. The cartoons in *O Estado de S. Paulo* only included drawings of PTB and PSD, both depicted as male figures or animals. The material published in October and November 1965 allow glimpsing the party preferences: PSD and PTB are portrayed quite critically, while there is not a single cartoon on UDN. Meanwhile, PSD and PTB are either foxes (Figure 6.1) or manipulators of the new parties' organization (Figure 6.2). Some of these portrayals are extremely partial, not only because they target PSD and PTB, but because the images reinforce the idea that the political parties are swindlers, dissimulators, or manipulators, when in fact they remain the same (the acronyms appear on the characters, but crossed out). As a whole, these images express the feeling that the parties display negative attitudes. They are situated in the field of "guile" or "cunning", which can also be considered a strategy to resist extinction via institutional decree. At the same time, there is a highly revealing silence on the main actor responsible for the extinction of the political parties in activity from 1946 to 1965, as well as on UDN, the principal party that conspired in the 1964 coup d'état.

One of the cartoons, with the title *Independência, ou nada . . .* (*Independence, or nothing . . .*) (Figure 6.3), addresses quite literally the position of PSD members vis-à-vis organization of the new parties, since the image refers to the difficulty of certain *Pessedistas* in "burying" the party's acronym. Senator Amaral Peixoto, then-chairman of the PSD National Committee, appears as a ghost over his party's tomb. In the newspaper articles from the same period, the *Pessedistas* officially voiced their opposition to the parties' extinction and their goal of maintaining the party's acronym and independence in relation to the government instituted by the 1964 movement.

Figure 6.1 Edmondo Biganti, *O Estado de S. Paulo*, November 6, 1965, 4.

Figure 6.2 Edmondo Biganti, *O Estado de S. Paulo*, November 14, 1965, 4.

Independência, ou nada...

Figure 6.3 Hilde Weber, O *Estado de S. Paulo*, November 30, 1965, 4.

In *Correio da Manhã*, the cartoons by Fortuna were highly critical of the parties' extinction. One provides a caustic interpretation of the decree's goal: "It's to leave just two parties: UDN and IPM"[37], a reference to the main party that backed the 1964 coup (UDN) and to the *Inquéritos Policiais Militares* (*Military Police Inquiries*) installed in its wake. In another cartoon, entitled *Baixado o Ato 2* (*Act 2 Decreed*), Fortuna makes a list of the purged parties.[38]

After the elections in 1965 and the unfavourable results for UDN in the state governments of Rio de Janeiro and Minas Gerais, various drawings by Arnon and Fortuna in *Correio da Manhã* deride the federal government for its difficulty in accepting the victory of politicians that did not identify with the 1964 movement. One cartoon by Arnon asks: "Tell me, does the law they passed apply to the ineligibles or to those who cannot be sworn in?"[39] Fortuna illustrates Brazil's "Novo Dicionário" ("New Dictionary", a sort of punning newspeak), in which *possesso* [literally "irate"] means "he who cannot stand to see a *posse* [the inauguration of an elected official]".[40] The same Fortuna wonders about the ambiguities of the prevailing political regime in which there are both direct and indirect elections: "The advantage of this amendment, which allows a return to pork-barrel nepotism, is obvious: if there were a public admissions exam for deputy, the distinguished colleague would never pass".[41]

It was not until 1966 that cartoons began to be published on the new party organizations created after AI-2 and Complementary Act No. 4

(AC-4) were decreed. Throughout this study, I have contended that there were three distinct periods in ARENA's history, which can also be identified clearly in the cartoons on the party. The first period starts with the party's founding on 30 November 1965 and lasts until the AI-5, on 13 December 1968. The AI-5, besides marking the shutdown of the National Congress and state legislatures, represents in ARENA's history the apogee of the crisis between the party and the government, since several *Arenistas* in Congress voted against the authorization for the Executive to purge National Deputy Márcio Moreira Alves (MDB – GB), as discussed previously.

The initial years of activity for ARENA and MDB were times of lack of definition. Even the politicians themselves harboured doubts on the continuity of the new acronyms founded as organizations with "attributions of political parties, while these are still not established", according to the *Ato Complementar n. 4* (AC-4). The political cartoons reveal at least two lines of thinking on the new parties. The newspapers frequently focused on the lack of identity in ARENA and MDB, both unknown to Brazilian politicians and Brazilian society as a whole. Biganti drew a cartoon in 1966 in which ARENA and MDB are depicted as a man with two heads, as if the two parties were one and the same (Figure 6.4). The lack of clearly defined party identities can also help explain why they were portrayed so rarely at the time.

Figure 6.4 Edmondo Biganti, O *Estado de S. Paulo*, October 16, 1966, 4.

Another watershed was clearly partial to MDB. Already in 1966, Fortuna, in *Correio da Manhã*, showed that he was very certain of the difference between the two parties, signalling thumbs-down on the votes for ARENA,[42] or ridiculing its meagre voter preference in Rio de Janeiro: "Our heartfelt thanks to ARENA, who gave us so little work during the vote count".[43] Aware of the purges of national deputies from MDB decreed by Marshall Castello Branco in late 1966, Senna drew a gallows to show readers where the opposition members were speaking from.[44] Meanwhile Fortuna noted that, "If the purges continue, we will have a unique contest: no gladiators, just the Arena [sic]".[45]

ARENA's second period in the political cartoons starts with the AI-5 and lasts until the 1974 elections. There was initially great uncertainty as to the existence of ARENA and MDB, not least because from the AI-5 until Complementary Act No. 54 of 20 May 1969, the Brazilian National Congress was closed and ARENA was inert. The AC-54 established new rules for party organizations and ended this period, indicating the resumption of party activity, albeit partial. The two parties appear frequently in the cartoons starting in January 1969. Thus, from January to May, the undefined situation of institutions of political representation was the predominant theme in the cartoons in *O Estado de S. Paulo,* the only mainstream newspaper that was publishing them at the time. The cartoonists depict quite precisely the predominant lack of definition as to the party's future. The best expression of the impasse is the cartoon in which ARENA, depicted as a lady, weeps at a crossroads as she looks in several different directions: call to order, extinction, reorganization, or reaction (Figure 6.5).

Figure 6.5 Edmondo Biganti, *O Estado de São Paulo*, May 4, 1969, 4.

There are images on Daniel Krieger's resignation as chairman of the National Committee and his replacement by Senator Filinto Müller. Other cartoons point to the inevitable changes: ARENA depicted as a woman in a plastic surgeon's waiting room; there are also allusions to meetings, so often postponed, to discuss the party's future.

From 1970 to 1974, the parties reorganized and acted under heavy restrictions which were attenuated in a certain sense by the measures for the election campaign in November 1974. During the campaign, politicians from both ARENA and MDB felt that there was a certain freedom of expression, at least as Brazil had not seen for years. It was no coincidence that the cartoons on national politics multiplied.

The third period identified here marked the sharpest competition between ARENA and MDB, lasting from the 1974 elections to the extinction of both parties on 29 November 1979. The victory by MDB in the senatorial elections was one of the most striking events in the history of the dictatorship and of the two parties. The visible change in the series is that starting with these elections, ARENA's identity is depicted in opposition to the MDB. A recurrent topic is precisely the struggle for votes. Based on the metaphor of competition, the cartoonists depict the two parties as opponents in fields of sporting contests or even fistfights. Besides the metaphor of sports contests, during election periods the cartoons address the theme of election returns. In some cases, the agenda is the interpretation of election results, the object of debates among politicians, pundits, and voters in general. For example, after the 1974 elections, when MDB elected more senators than ARENA, Hilde shows the latter's difficulty in comprehending the result. The artist portrays ARENA as a lady with spectacles, her hair in a bun, struggling to put a jigsaw puzzle together. In the background, a mocking MDB enters the scene.[46] In another cartoon, in the same spirit, ARENA appears as a woman with a hat and MDB as an obese man. The two are in a rowboat, and since MDB is much heavier, ARENA is tilted high and dry, unable to row. The election results in 1978 were much tighter. Thus, ARENA and MDB are portrayed as men in a wrestling match. One says, "I won", and the other, "I vanquished".[47]

Party reform was discussed openly in both the National Congress and the press in 1978 and 1979, and the politicians from ARENA and MDB dealt with the subject at length. There are several drawings on the parties' extinction, done by different cartoonists, and it is interesting that they were all based on the metaphor of death. In these scenes, the acronyms of the political parties extinguished in 1965 reappear, just as suggestions by politicians of the time are remembered in statements to the press and in letters sent to the ARENA National Committee.

One of the cartoons depicts a demonstration, a march, in which the banners feature possible names of new parties.[48] Next to the march is a funeral procession with coffins for ARENA and MDB and in the background, the ghosts of the parties banned in 1965: PSD, PS, PDC, and others. Another cartoon shows the government as a man opening a box in which there are several little men with the party acronyms PCB, PT, PI, PTB, PDR, and PXY, trying to scramble out. In the foreground are MDB and ARENA as two beaten and bedraggled men fallen on the ground, perhaps dead. There is even a series of cartoons with funeral wakes. In addition to the above-mentioned cartoons, others show such ceremonies. In *O Estado de S. Paulo*, Hilde drew a wake for ARENA, depicted as a woman. Several men are standing around the coffin, lamenting.[49] On the same page, right below, was the article entitled "Final Meeting and the Same Complaints".

Just a few days before the official demise of ARENA and MDB, Ziraldo was already predicting what the funeral vigil for the two parties would be like. A man calls out to the crowd trailing behind MDB's coffin: "Hey, guys! There's another dead body here!" ARENA's coffin looks abandoned, a sign of what was to come, since no one apparently wanted to keep vigil over the party's memory.[50] Not even the *Arenistas* wept over the acronym's impending death.

The cartoons portraying ARENA accurately describe a trajectory marked initially by the lack of an identity by temporariness. Soon after the AI-5, the organization began to be seen as a political party that was just as threatened as the MDB. Importantly, it was only after MDB's victory in the 1974 elections that ARENA began to be ridiculed and derided, starting a process of establishing a negative identity that would be increasingly consolidated in Brazil's political memory.

4 The personification of ARENA and its relations with the government

In the creation of cartoons, one of the principal resources is the transformation of metaphors from verbal language into concrete objects through images. In the illustrations on national politics produced during the dictatorship, the party issue was addressed suggestively through the parties' personification. ARENA was almost always depicted as a woman and MDB as a man.

This series of cartoons shares many common references with comic strips. One of the main ones is the transformation of ARENA and MDB into cartoon characters.

Interestingly, this type of portrayal is now rare in the cartoons published in Brazil's mainstream newspapers, perhaps because the parties' personification was an appropriate strategy in times of heavy press censorship. When cartoonist Biganti retired in 1984, he commented that his first years of work were quite significant, since they gave him "the opportunity to do caricatures of Adhemar de Barros and Jânio Quadros, polemical characters from an age that allowed the cartoonist greater freedom".[51] Meanwhile, the ARENA character was a providential character: a *persona* at once collective and fictitious, entailing no risk of encountering her on the streets as a flesh-and-blood politician. Therefore, certainly, it was less likely that a cartoonist would be accused of offending her honour.

The narrative solution of personifying ARENA as a woman harks to the moment of the party's creation, when the name *Aliança Renovadora Nacional* (conjugated in the feminine in Portuguese) was the object of debate and apprehensions among various formers members of the UDN, who were dissatisfied at creating a new party with another feminine name, which they viewed as indicative of weakness and other attributes associated with female gender stereotypes in Brazilian society. In 1965, after the extinction of the former parties and given the imminence of party reorganization, many agreed that the old *União Democrática Nacional* (UDN) was indeed obliged to change names, and that a male name should be chosen to replace it.[52] The commentary suggested that a female acronym was not appropriate for a political party, which is interesting, since in all my research on ARENA I only found one positive reference to the acronym. It happened during the debates over the extinction of ARENA and the creation of a new party. A sympathizer wrote to the chairman of the National Committee on 29 April 1979: "My dear Sarney, ARENA is a feminine name and ideal for a party".[53] As the saying goes, the exception confirms the rule.

In the cartoons on ARENA, one of the tricks to poke fun is precisely to associate the party with certain female stereotypes by depicting various situations. The character for ARENA appears cooking or in the plastic surgeon's waiting room. Portrayal of the party as a woman was complemented by drawing various women's accessories. ARENA always appears in a dress, with a handbag, sometimes with a flower in her hair, etc. However, the more critical drawings show her as a terribly ugly woman or even as a prostitute or blow-up doll, the object of the regime's desire (Figure 6.6).

The reference to comic strips appears in both the drawing style and in elements from that genre. One of the humorous motifs in several cartoons is the shift of partisan political issues to the world of household

Figure 6.6 Hilde Weber, *O Estado de S. Paulo*, April 16, 1977, 5.

and children's motifs. In some cartoons the parties star opposite ghosts or are depicted as children offering presents on Mother's Day (Figure 6.8). The politicians are also compared to schoolchildren racing to school on the first day of the school year.[54]

Interestingly, in most of the cartoons on political parties during the existence of the two-party system, ARENA and MDB appear with a third character: the government. In other words, this is a highly peculiar party system in which the "government" plays an independent part from the parties, while in principle a representative system of government should be formed by a party or coalition. The "government" is a character which does indeed favour ARENA in many cases, but this does not mean equating it to the party in any way. On the contrary, the cartoons problematize the relations between the "government" and ARENA, underscoring each one's individualities and specificities.

But unlike ARENA and MDB, the "government" was rarely personified, although it was occasionally depicted as a man looking like General Ernesto Geisel. The "government" was usually portrayed more diffusely, appearing with just its feet or hands or only with the word

Figure 6.7 Edmondo Biganti, *O Estado de S. Paulo*, May 7, 1969, 4.

"government" on a sign. This strategy suggests some difficulty in representing this political actor in cartoons, probably due to the censorship, again underscoring the differences between these political characters. ARENA could be personified and ridiculed, but the "government", consisting mainly of military officers, was largely spared in the illustrations published in the mainstream press. This differed markedly from the cartoons published in the alternative press and in the anthologies and collections with more limited circulation, which featured various caricatures of military officers, censors, and hangmen.

In this process of personification, the cartoonists often portrayed ARENA as a woman in trouble, a metaphor for situations the party frequently faced under the regime. The position of subordination to the government is depicted in various ways, and there is a clear difference between the cartoons published from 1969 and 1971 and those that appeared from 1974 onwards.

The cartoons published in the former period problematize the divergences between ARENA and the government, especially regarding the party's resistance to the Executive's orientation to grant authorization to try Deputy Márcio Moreira Alves in 1968. In early 1969, the cartoon entitled *Volta ao lar* (*Home Again*) shows a bedraggled ARENA returning to the government. There is also a caricature of Filinto Müller under an ARENA blanket.[55] The then-chairman of the National Committee was drawn sitting in a doorway with the sign "government". The fear of purges of *Arenista* congressmen also appears in a cartoon where ARENA is standing under an awning, holding her hand out to check whether rain is falling from the menacing overhead cloud of "PURGES".[56]

Only in the latter period, starting in 1974, ARENA appears stripped of her own will. Besides the personification as a woman, the party also appears as a string puppet in drawings by Lan and Ziraldo,[57] a balloon drawn by Hilde, and finger puppet by Ziraldo.[58] All these figures suggest that ARENA was manipulated by the government, variations on the recurrent metaphor of politicians as puppets in the hands of the military. Interestingly, in the usual metaphor of politicians as puppets, the manipulation is attributed to economic interests, but there are no such allusions in this case.

Equally important is that only ARENA was portrayed as a puppet, while MDB is depicted as more aware of its own political positions. This shows how the cartoon is actually an expression of opinion, recalling that many journalists/humourists working in the alternative press identified with the MDB. In this sense, cartoons allowed (and still allow) the dissemination of a certain political culture, transmitting complex messages synthesized in drawings. The cartoons' creation is thus informed by views of the parties and/or politicians that are profoundly incorporated by society.

The image of ARENA as a puppet (or variations thereof) may be quite amusing, but it is also an over-simplification. On the one hand, because ARENA did not fail to be a political opponent to the government, and had to be attacked. On the other, that image did not incorporate the social experience of the political actors that actually made ARENA function.

In this context, it is worthwhile to examine the work by Hilde during the period with the harshest repression, from 1969 to 1973. Her drawings succeeded in portraying the impasses experienced by the *Arenista* politicians, and Hilde may have succeeded precisely because of her perception that the true threat, which would lead to much more serious consequences in the long term, came from the Executive. After all, it was the government that kept the National Congress closed for 11 months. MDB's election defeats to ARENA were unfavourable results, but they were part of the political game and could be reversed, so they were no great surprise.

In the latter half of the 1970s, ARENA's representativeness (or lack thereof) was thus attributed mainly to the government. Most of the negative associations elaborated on the party focus on aspects of the peculiar political system built since 1965, in which Army officers occupied the office of President of the Republic and state governors and mayors of cities that were decreed national security areas were named by the federal Executive.

ARENA's electoral representativeness was always derided, because it referred exclusively to the discretionary measures by the Executive to favour it. Again, there is no perception and/or mention of a conservative electorate that would vote for a party in power, as if ARENA bore no relationship whatsoever to Brazilian society, as a creature totally derived from the Executive. Not coincidentally, many of these cartoons were published in the context of the "April package" of 1977, the set of reforms handed down by Constitutional Amendments No. 7 and No. 8.

The result of these measures would be summarized in the vision of an artificial growth of ARENA and shrinkage of MDB, as in a cartoon in which ARENA appears as an inflatable balloon shaped like a naked woman, hovering in the sky, tied to the National Congress building (Figure 6.6.). Suggestively, MDB also appears as a balloon, but deflated and on the ground. In a drawing by Ziraldo, ARENA and MDB are portrayed as boxers, but the cartoon's central figure is the referee, who appears in boxing gloves and dark glasses like those of President Ernesto Geisel.[59] He declares ARENA the winner while stomping on MDB's neck. In another cartoon, this one by Hilde, the government, depicted as a man, and ARENA as a woman fire a cannon called "reforms", but the shot backfires and hits them in the face. Right below this cartoon is the article: "Cariocas reject indirect elections",[60] highlighting the harmful effect of the "April package" for ARENA's electoral hopes in Rio de Janeiro. A clear dialogue between textual and visual language.

Other drawings predict the consequences of indirect elections to the Senate, either in the dispute for nomination to senator within the party (and probably with the President of the Republic), or suggesting that the next senators will be "swindlers". In another cartoon, several men worship, fan, kneel down to, and pray at the government's feet, depicted as a sitting man with only his feet and hands appearing. This cartoon illustrates the article: "Indirect Senate seat riles *Arenistas* in São Paulo".[61] In one, several men are carrying ARENA banners and armed with pick axes [a visual pun, since the word for pick ax in Portuguese, *picareta*, is also slang for swindler] are marching towards the Senate, indicating the widespread popular view of the so-called "bionic" senators.

Yet the ultimate derision for ARENA's political representation appears in the cartoons with references to election frauds. The criticism probably had some basis, but it should not be confused with total lack of representativeness, as the cartoonists certainly intended. In the weekly alternative newspaper *Movimento*, the distinction between the parties appears in a few illustrations. But in all of them, the artists openly ridiculed the votes for ARENA, either as a "magic trick with the blank votes" or as one of the specialties of a swindler who also forges news briefs, medical reports, and death certificates, procedures that some police officers, censors, and physicians performed during the dictatorship.[62]

In *Jornal do Brasil*, for example, there is a cartoon by Ziraldo parodying the Biblical passage of Christ on the cross. A man asks, "Hey, Ulisses [Guimarães, the MDB national chairman], if MDB is Christ, do you mean that ARENA-1 and ARENA-2 are the . . . ?"[63] Thus, by referring to the multiple tickets, ARENA-1 and ARENA-2, the cartoon suggests that all the *Arenistas* were thieves.

During the debates on party reform in 1979, the political cartoons suggest that the creation of the new parties would also be a manoeuvre by government. From Hilde's perspective, a man (government) opens a box with several little men trying to wiggle out (the new parties).[64] Another cartoon depicts the formation of a new government party as the work of the military, especially General João Figueiredo.[65] This illustration portrays Figueiredo as a tailor, properly armed with a scissors and tape measure, taking the measurement from the *"Arenão"* ("Big ARENA), as written on his tie, to cut a new suit. In 1979, "Arenão" or "João's party" was the nickname used by journalists for the party that would purportedly be organized by members of ARENA after the latter's extinction. This is another example of the view that the government parties under military regimes are generals' creations, overlooking or underestimating the autonomous careers of the politicians forming these parties and their ties to their constituencies.

5 Threats to political representation

There are also several cartoons addressing the government's interventions in the system of political representation, especially when the National Congress was shut down in 1968 and the parties were excluded from decision-making. Studies on the party system record the discussion by members of MDB on the party's possible dissolution,[66] a possibility that was also raised by the *Arenistas* under those circumstances. But it was not only the parties' future that was at stake. There was also a much larger impasse at that time, affecting the representative system as a whole.

A History of ARENA in Cartoons | 209

The most original images of ARENA in relation to the folklore built on the party were published in the context immediately following the decree of the AI-5. During this time, the ARENA character is definitely portrayed in the most humiliating situations, similar to that of MDB. The AI-5 thus placed ARENA and MDB in an extreme situation, and the cartoonists portrayed the experience shared by the two parties. This view has received little attention in the historiography of Brazil's dictatorship, and it reveals the kind of debate among politicians at that moment marked by uncertainty.

The narratives in cartoons thus show the various facets of that impasse: the phantom's shadow from the reform in the Organic Law on Political Parties, hovering over ARENA and MDB with a huge scissors (Figure 6.7); ARENA in a car bogged down and trying to help her: MDB, the Senate, and the Chamber of Deputies, all under the banner of the "political class";[67] and on *Mother's Day,* ARENA and MDB, shown as children, giving flowers to a woman, called "politics" (Figure 6.8).

Figure 6.8 Edmondo Biganti, *O Estado de S. Paulo*, May 13, 1969, 4.

In May 1969, in the wake of the decree of Complementary Act No. 54 (AC-54), the situation appeared to improve. The AC-54 established the calendar and rules for the political parties' national, regional, and municipal conventions, besides regulating the procedures for party membership. In a democratic regime, this would merely be a legal text, but given the great uncertainty surrounding the continuity of institutions of political representation, AC-54 sent a signal that the parties would not be extinguished and that there would be new elections. In the cartoons of this time, ARENA and MDB receive from the government's hands the AC-54 vaccine;[68] the parties are also depicted as shipwrecks glimpsing on the horizon the ship of the end of congressional recess coming to rescue them (Figure 6.9). During this period, the parties were portrayed as figures threatened in various ways (scissors, ghosts, vaccine, shipwrecks . . .), reflecting the institutions' extremely vulnerable conditions, suffering attacks or in situations of abandonment or fear.

Figure 6.9 Hilde Weber, O *Estado de S. Paulo*, May 28, 1969, 4.

During the years of heaviest repression, when disbelief in political representation predominated in Brazilian society, as reflected in the high rates of blank and null votes in the 1970 elections, what can be said of the possibility of re-democratization via the political parties? Still, Hilde continued to draw the parties confronting the AI-5. In early November 1970, a few days before the elections, the parties are shown facing the AI-5 in various ways, for example: MDB trying to force a door open (AI-5), with ARENA right behind, cheering him on.[69] Days later, however, in another cartoon, ARENA tosses the repeal of AI-5, democratic détente, *habeas corpus*, and amnesty into the trash basket, while MDB looks on from the background.[70]

The cartoons in O *Estado de S. Paulo* address various details from the debate on the Organic Law on Political Parties of 1971. This was a very specific but highly significant issue. Several years after the vote by *Arenistas* in Congress defying the government's instructions, and that resulted in the AI-5, the Executive attempted to control the ARENA caucus through legislation, without resorting to authoritarian measures that were alien to the institutions' proper functioning and without the political cost of closing Congress, as had happened before. Among the measures that forced ARENA to always vote the dictatorship's line, the most effective was the party loyalty law, established by Constitutional Amendment No. 1 of 17 October 1969. The party loyalty law was not regulated until 1971, with the passage of a new Organic Law on Political Parties.

There were several drawings on this issue at the time. ARENA is portrayed as a housewife grimacing as she smells the steam coming from a cooking pot labelled "Organic Law" or as a woman entering a surgical theatre for an extreme makeover.[71] MDB is also depicted together with ARENA, showing the common issues in both: the parties placing complaints on party loyalty in a ballot box.[72] The debate on regulation of party loyalty was portrayed as a clear intervention by the Executive in congressional competition. And the law aimed to weaken ARENA by further curtailing its autonomy.

The perception that there were various real threats to the representative system, already disfigured by the loss of congressional and judiciary prerogatives, points to the existence of a democratic resistance during the dictatorship, and which prizes the political parties. Not coincidentally, ARENA and MDB are portrayed side-by-side in this context, struggling to pull the "political class" out of a mudhole, together with the characters for the "Senate" and "Chamber of Deputies". The parties were also portrayed as children paying homage to "politics", on Mother's Day.

The study of the political cartoons published under certain circumstances shows that the artists depicted ARENA according to the most current analyses among journalists and also from the perspective of the politicians involved in the party. In many cases the cartoons even faithfully illustrated the news.[73] The references to public statements by politicians from ARENA are often quite direct and can be found in articles published next to the cartoons themselves. Importantly, such references were not generally ironic. The cartoonist did not cite certain positions or opinions in order to criticize or contradict them. This practice indicates that the cartoonist not only followed the newsroom's agenda, but even the approaches and nuances in the articles. The portrayals of ARENA alluding to the party members' views on existing policy alternatives at given moments assume acknowledgement of the party as an effective political actor. Likewise, the frequency of cartoons portraying the party issue indicates that the newspaper and/or artists acknowledge the parties' relevance in Brazil's national political scenario.

Thus, as mentioned, the messages produced by the cartoons are profoundly related to other texts published in the newspapers. On the one hand, to the newsroom's agenda and the orientation of the newspaper's own articles and editorials. As Beth Brait noted, on the pages of newspapers, the same theme is multiplied with different voices (front headline, editorial on the second page, cartoon, news story, etc.).[74] The cartoonists acted as chroniclers of party quarrels, often employing the same metaphors used elsewhere in the paper, but since they worked with non-verbal language, they turned the metaphors into images. The personification of ARENA through the drawing of a woman is the transcription of the party's anthropomorphization through non-verbal language.

The cartoons portray ARENA and MDB in quite similar fashion. The cartoonist situates them in the same plane, and according to the theme, they appear either as partners or opponents. This perspective differs considerably from the political humour on ARENA after détente, the tone of which was to deride the party as a political actor, which has become its most widespread image, reiterated by cartoonists, political scientists, and the press.

By comparing the images produced by the humorous depictions and other texts – speeches, correspondence, internal party documents, articles published in the press itself – one finds a great coincidence between the themes and the images produced on ARENA. This shows how the political issue was a source for cartoonists, who did not produce portrayals divorced from that context. This may not appear very evident at the first reading of current cartoons, but it implies an effort at contextualization when study portrayals produced many years ago.

My analysis of situations depicted in the cartoons reveals political alternatives that are often forgotten or overlooked, as time passes, by the events' contemporaries and even by those directly involved in those events. This is a key point in the history of Brazil's two-party system, since the literature is heavily marked by the teleology of the search for evidence of MDB's success and ARENA's failure since the two parties were founded, as well for the certainty that the two-party system would be temporary. The analysis of the portrayals in ARENA in various conjunctures thus indicates a diversity of possible consequences for this history.

ARENA's history as a joke in the newspapers of the 1990s clashes starkly with the news and the cartoons published in the 1960s and 70s in the same periodicals. One of the fundamental differences is that even the humour of the time considered ARENA a political actor and recorded the existence of various paths to be chosen by the *Arenistas*. The series of cartoons reveals ARENA as a party in action, with a much more complex trajectory than the recurrent anecdotes on the party consolidated in the hegemonic memory of the 1980s. This is because the portrayals of ARENA in the 1980s and 90s reiterated the image of ridicule or freakishness, stripping the party of any valid logic. This contrast appears as a clue to the peculiar relationship Brazilian society has established with its authoritarian past, between a political party's memory and its history.

Final Remarks
Political Party and Scapegoat

The image consolidated on ARENA is limited to a group of despicable politicians, the butt of countless jokes, and a scam as a political party. In studying a theme from the history of the present that is so controversial for a major part of Brazilian society, it proved essential to reflect on the memory that was built for that party. In this sense, examining the facts' contemporary sources allowed a more complex understanding of the party's organization, in addition to a reflection on the dynamics of this memory's construction beginning with the political détente and during the 1980s, when there was widespread repudiation of the military and the dictatorship in Brazil.

There are many negative references to ARENA, to the point of questioning whether that organization could even be considered a political party. If, on the one hand, these questions, shaped on a large scale by an anti-party and anti-congressional ideology, are common for Brazil's political parties, ARENA is an extreme case because the country was living under a dictatorship. This questioning is also part of the party's own history. Different actors such as MDB, the press, and the military accused ARENA of being "weak", "flawed", "artificial", or even of not exactly being a political party. However, such accusations were an important part of the political clashes in which these actors were vying for the legitimacy of their political representation. Nor was such questioning alien to the politicians that formed the party. The documents produced over the course of ARENA's activities contain endless discussions on its partisan political identity, as well as many clashes over electoral legislation, candidacies, and party loyalty. In other words, the *Arenistas* themselves questioned their own organization's performance due to the limitations imposed on party activities by the dictatorship.

This study on ARENA thus shows that far from being mutually exclusive propositions, the *political party* facet and the *scapegoat* facet are constitutive for the organization, proving to be a false dilemma. ARENA both acted as a political party, obviously considering the peculiarities of political activities under a dictatorship, and it was transformed as well, through a work of memory, into a scapegoat, beginning with the transition to a democratic regime.

The Brazilian dictatorship has two major scapegoats: the military and ARENA. The military are the brute force, the rudeness, the ignorance. It is the image of the "gorilla" that comes to haunt the Armed Forces, according to the language of the time. ARENA is an inverse scapegoat: because it is weak, laughable, has no power whatsoever. If, on some occasions, even the military in the Executive broadcast this image, the party could be ridiculed by everyone, by the oppositionist press or by its congressional opponents. The military and the government could not be attacked head-on, but ARENA could.

However, the reduction of ARENA to ridicule implied silence on society's participation in the 1964 movement and support for the regime for many long years. ARENA did not exist as an abstract entity, but as the result of practices of thousands of people across Brazil: voters, sympathizers, militants, and politicians. ARENA is thus representative of a major part of the history of political parties in Brazil, as well as their peculiarity. The party's membership consisted initially of a generation of politicians with longstanding careers and trained a large share of the following generation when the alternatives were limited to it and MDB. Even under a regime of exception, ARENA, like MDB, allowed holding elections in all the country's municipalities. Political parties are indispensable institutions for organizing elections, channelling a wide range of conflicts into electoral disputes.

ARENA is not devoid of representativeness, because many people voted for the party even with alternatives such as voting for MDB, voting null or blank, or abstaining. The *Arenistas* in Congress, in turn, even with their limited prerogatives, exercised their activities in the National Congress, the state legislatures, and the city councils. The party participated both by acting and by remaining silent. In the National Congress, the strategy of omission can be seen through the failure to appear for certain congressional sessions, preventing the necessary quorum for a vote, for example. There was heterogeneity among its politicians from 1965 to 1979. In light of the diversity of shades among the *Arenistas*, the party's members of Congress suffered some impositions by the Executive while arduously defending others.

It is thus essential to perceive that the creation of ARENA and MDB and their maintenance required the continuity of organizational practices (which are also cultural practices) during those years of dictatorial rule. Based on the successive interventions in the liberal institutions of political representation by the Executive, consisting mainly of military officers, many *Arenistas* defended the prerogatives of Congress and the activity by political parties. In this sense, by attempting to maintain their activities as professional politicians, they defended the institutions, which were extremely important for finally achieving the country's re-democratization.

Glossary of Political Parties

ARENA   *Aliança Renovadora Nacional* (National Renewal Alliance); *"Arenistas"*
The National Renewal Alliance (ARENA) was created in 1965 with the purpose of supporting the government instituted by the civilian-military *coup d'état* in 1964. The majority of the *Arenistas* consisted of professional politicians formerly affiliated with the UDN and PSD.

MDB   *Movimento Democrático Brasileiro* (Brazilian Democratic Movement); *"Emedebistas"*
The Brazilian Democratic Movement (MDB) was created in 1965 with the purpose of serving as opposition to the government instituted by the civilian-military *coup d'état* in 1964. The majority of the *Emedebistas* consisted of professional politicians formerly affiliated with the PTB and PSD.

MTR   *Movimento Trabalhista Renovador* (Labour Renewal Movement)
The Labour Renewal Movement (MTR) was created in 1960 by a dissident group from the PTB led by National Deputy Fernando Ferrari.

PDC   *Partido Democrata Cristão* (Christian Democratic Party)
The Christian Democratic Party (PDC) was founded in 1945 following the *Estado Novo* dictatorship (1937–1945). In Brazil, however, the PDC did not receive institutional support from the Catholic Church. Its main leaders included members of the Catholic University Youth (JUC).

PDR   *Partido Democrático Republicano* (Republican Democratic Party)
The Republican Democratic Party (PDR) was never actually created. After then-Vice-President Pedro Aleixo was prevented from taking office as President of Brazil in 1969, he left ARENA and began defending the creation of a new party, PDR, an alternative to ARENA and MDB.

PDS *Partido Democrático Social* (Social Democratic Party)
Following the party reform in 1979 and the extinction of ARENA and MDB, the majority of the politicians affiliated with ARENA regrouped in the Social Democratic Party (PDS). Its main leaders included José Sarney and Paulo Maluf.

PL *Partido Libertador* (Liberator Party)
The Liberator Party (PL) was founded in 1945 following the *Estado Novo* dictatorship (1937–1945). Most of its leaders were former members of the old Liberator Party (which had been extinguished in 1937) and opponents of the Getúlio Vargas government. From 1945 to 1964, the PL established a coalition with the UDN on various occasions.

PMDB *Partido do Movimento Democrático Brasileiro* (Party of the Brazilian Democratic Movement)
The Party of the Brazilian Democratic Movement (PMDB) was created in 1979 after the party reform that extinguished ARENA and MDB. Forced to change names, the MDB merely included the word "Party" at the front of its new name. The new organization is a continuation of the extinct MDB.

PR *Partido Republicano* (Republican Party)
The Republican Party (PR) was founded in 1945 following the *Estado Novo* dictatorship (1937–1945) and consisted mainly of former members of the old *Partido Republicano Mineiro* (PRM), or Minas Gerais Republican Party, extinguished in 1937. From 1945 to 1964, the PR formed a coalition with the UDN on several occasions.

PRP *Partido de Representação Popular* (Popular Representation Party)
The Popular Representation Party (PRP) was founded in 1945 following the *Estado Novo* dictatorship (1937–1945) and consisted mainly of former members of the *Ação Integralista Brasileira* – AIB (Brazilian Integralist Action), a fascist-inspired movement extinguished by Getúlio Vargas in 1938. The main leader of the PRP was the well-known integralist Plínio Salgado.

PRT *Partido Rural Trabalhista* (Rural Labour Party)
The Rural Labour Party (PRT) was created in 1958, succeeding the Republican Labour Party (PRT), with the aim of promoting labour ideals and practices in the Brazilian countryside.

PSD   *Partido Social Democrático* (Democratic Social Party); *"Pessedistas"*
The Democratic Social Party (PSD) was founded in 1945 following the *Estado Novo* dictatorship (1937–1945) and consisted mainly of political leaders from the Getúlio Vargas (1930–1945) government, such as intervenors and mayors. From 1945 to 1964, PSD was the majority party in the National Congress. The main *Pessedista* leaders included Amaral Peixoto and President Juscelino Kubitschek (1956–1960).

PSP   *Partido Social Progressista* (Progressive Social Party)
The Progressive Social Party (PSP) was created in 1946, following the *Estado Novo* dictatorship (1937–1945), by Adhemar de Barros, former intervenor and later elected governor of São Paulo. From 1945 to 1964, the PSP won a series of elections in São Paulo running against PSD, UDN, and PTB, the largest political parties in Brazil.

PST   *Partido Social Trabalhista* (Social Labour Party)
The Social Labour Party (PST) was founded in 1945 following the *Estado Novo* dictatorship (1937–1945). From 1945 to 1964, the PST consisted of dissidents from the PSD, with which it formed coalitions on various occasions.

PTB   *Partido Trabalhista Brasileiro* (Brazilian Labour Party)
The Brazilian Labour Party (PTB) was founded in 1945 following the *Estado Novo* dictatorship (1937–1945). The party consisted mainly of labour unions and political leaders from trade unions and the Ministry of Labour, Industry, and Commerce. The main PTB leaders included Presidents Getúlio Vargas (1930–1945, 1951–1954) and João Goulart (1961–1964).

PTN   Partido Trabalhista Nacional (National Labour Party)
The National Labour Party (PTN) was founded in 1945 following the *Estado Novo* dictatorship (1937–1945). Like the PTB, it consisted mainly of politicians connected to the Ministry of Labour, Industry, and Commerce, joined over time by dissidents from the PTB. In 1960, the party elected the President of Brazil, Jânio Quadros (1961).

PFL   *Partido da Frente Liberal* (Party of the Liberal Front)
The Party of the Liberal Front (PFL) was founded in 1985 by dissidents of the PDS due to disputes for the candidacy in the presidential elections. Its main leaders were Governors Antônio Carlos Magalhães and Marco Maciel.

UDN *União Democrática Nacional* (National Democratic Union); *"Udenistas"*

The National Democratic Union (UDN) was founded in 1945 following the *Estado Novo* dictatorship (1937–1945). The UDN initially convened socialist and liberal leaders opposed to the Getúlio Vargas dictatorship. When the socialists left the party, the UDN was consolidated as the principal opposition party to the developmentalist and pro-labour public policies implemented by the PSD and PTB. Its main leaders were Governors Magalhães Pinto and Carlos Lacerda.

Notes

Introduction

1 Bolívar Lamounier, "Representação política: a importância de certos formalismos," in *Direito, cidadania e participação*, ed. Bolívar Lamounier (São Paulo: T. A. Queiroz, 1981).
2 Aurélio Buarque de Hollanda Ferreira, *Dicionário Aurélio Eletrônico* (Rio de Janeiro: Nova Fronteira, 1999. CD-ROM).

1 Political Memories of ARENA

1 Machado de Assis, José M. "Casa Velha" in *Obra Completa* (Rio de Janeiro: Nova Aguilar, 1997), 1002.
2 Interview with *Pasquim*. *Apud* Maria V. M. Benevides, *A UDN e o Udenismo* (Rio de Janeiro: Paz e Terra, 1981), 134.
3 Henry Rousso, "Pour une Histoire de la Mémoire Collective: l'après-Vichy," in *Histoire Politique et Sciences Sociales*, ed. Denis Peschanski, et al. (Brussels: Éditions Complexe, 1991), 245–246.
4 Michel Offerlé, *Les Partis Politiques* (Paris: PUF, 1987).
5 Pierre Nora, "Gaullistes et communistes", in *Les Lieux de Mémoire. Les Frances I*, ed. Pierre Nora (Paris: Gallimard, 1992), 347–393.
6 Rousso, "Pour une Histoire", 255.
7 Offerlé, *Les Partis*, 6.
8 Offerlé, *Les Partis*, 10.
9 *Folha de S. Paulo*, May 3, 1995.
10 Interview with *Pasquim*. *Apud* Benevides, *A UDN*, 134.
11 Tancredo Neves used this expression in an interview. *Apud*. David Fleischer, "A Transição para o Bipartidarismo Legislativo," paper presented at the 3rd Annual Meeting of ANPOCS, *mimeo*, 1979.
12 *Jornal do Brasil*, February 7, 1995.
13 The party was created with the name Revolutionary National Party, which was then changed to Party of the Mexican Revolution, and in 1946 it was renamed the Institutional Revolutionary Party (PRI). Torcuato S. di Tella. *Historia de los Partidos Políticos en América Latina, siglo XX* (Buenos Aires: Fondo de Cultura Económica, 1994), 49.
14 Ziraldo A. Pinto, *1964–1984: 20 Anos de Prontidão* (Rio de Janeiro: Record, 1984).
15 Carlos Castello Branco, vol. 1, *Os Militares no Poder* (Rio de Janeiro: Nova Fronteira, 1977).
16 Otávio Dulci, *A UDN e o Anti-populismo no Brasil* (Belo Horizonte: UFMG/PROED, 1986), 13.

17 Bolívar Lamounier, *Voto de Desconfiança* (Petrópolis: Vozes, 1980).
18 Francisco Weffort, "A Vitória Inchada da ARENA," *Opinião*, November 27–December 4, 1972.
19 Maria C. C. de Souza, *Estado e Partidos Políticos no Brasil: 1930–1964* (São Paulo: Alfa-Ômega, 1990).
20 Serge Berstein, "Les partis," in: *Pour une Histoire Politique*, ed. René Rémond (Paris: Seuil, 1988).
21 Kinzo, *Oposição*, 225.
22 Daniel Aarão Reis Filho, *Ditadura, esquerdas e sociedade* (Rio de Janeiro: Zahar, 2000), 71.
23 Beatriz Kushnir, *Cães de Guarda: Jornalistas e Censores, do AI-5 à Constituição de 1988* (São Paulo: Boitempo, 2004), 36.
24 The interviews were published in three books organized by Maria Celina D'Araújo, Gláucio Ary Dillon Soares, and Celso Castro: *Visões do Golpe* (Rio de Janeiro: Relume-Dumará, 1994). *Os Anos de Chumbo* (Rio de Janeiro: Relume-Dumará, 1994). *A Volta aos Quartéis* (Rio de Janeiro: Relume-Dumará, 1995).
25 An. Cam. Dep. 2 (1976): 5204.
26 An. Cam. Dep. 4 (1978): 8391.
27 "Summary of the government's New Year's message to the population, broadcast by the National News Agency on December 31, 1968, on radio and television" in Arthur da Costa e Silva, *Pronunciamentos do presidente* (Brasília: Presidência da República, Secretaria de Imprensa e Divulgação, s/d), 479–483.
28 Nelson Rodrigues, *A Cabra Vadia* (São Paulo: Companhia das Letras, 1995), 279.
29 Sérgio Buarque, "Partido ou bode expiatório," *Movimento*, July 14, 1975, 4.
30 Bolívar Lamounier and Raquel Meneguello, *Partidos Políticos e Consolidação Democrática: o Caso Brasileiro* (São Paulo: Brasiliense, 1986), 21.
31 Serge Berstein, "L'Historien et la Culture Politique", *Vingtième siècle: Revue d'histoire* (1992): 67–77.
32 Lei n° 4740, July 15, 1965. Lei Orgânica dos Partidos Políticos (Organic Law on Political Parties).
33 Angela C. Gomes, "Política: História, Ciência, Cultura e Etc," *Estudos Históricos* 9 (1996), 59–84.
34 Angela C. Gomes, "Os Paradoxos e os Mitos: o Corporativismo faz 60 anos," *Análise e conjuntura* 6 (1991).
35 Souza, *Estado*, 27.
36 Antônio Lavareda, *Democracia nas urnas* (Rio de Janeiro: Rio Fundo Editora, 1991).
37 Argelina Figueiredo, *Democracia ou reformas?* (São Paulo: Paz e Terra, 1993).
38 Maria H. M. Alves, *Estado e oposição no Brasil: 1964–1984* (Petrópolis: Vozes, 1984), 95.

39 Philippe Schmitter, "The Portugalization of Brazil".
40 Wanderley G. dos Santos, "A Práxis Liberal no Brasil: Propostas para Reflexão e Pesquisa" in *Ordem Burguesa e Liberalismo Político*, ed. Wanderley G. dos Santos (São Paulo: Duas Cidades, 1978), 67–117.
41 Francisco Weffort, "Democracia e Movimento Operário: Algumas Questões para a História do Período 1945–1964," *Revista de Cultura Contemporânea* 1 (1979).
42 Weffort, "Democracia e Movimento", 10.
43 Lamounier, "Representação Política".
44 Alfred Stepan, *Authoritarian Brazil* (New Haven and London: Yale University Press, 1973).
45 Bolívar Lamounier, "O Brasil Autoritário Revisitado: o Impacto das Eleições sobre a Abertura," in *Democratizando o Brasil*, ed. Alfred Stepan. (Rio de Janeiro: Paz e Terra, 1988), 88.
46 Lamounier, *Voto*.
47 Lamounier, "O Brasil Autoritário", 113.
48 Sebastião V. Cruz and Carlos E. Martins, "De Castello a Figueiredo: uma Incursão na Pré-história da 'Abertura'" in *Sociedade e Política no Brasil pós-64* ed. Bernardo Sorj and Maria H. T. Almeida (São Paulo: Brasiliense, 1984), 44.
49 Pierre Bourdieu, *O Poder Simbólico* (Lisboa: DIFEL, 1989), 175.
50 Bourdieu, *O Poder Simbólico*.
51 Max Weber, *El Politico y el Cientifico* (Madri: Alianza Editorial, 1996).
52 Offerlé, *Les Partis*, 33.
53 Offerlé, *Les Partis*, 33.
54 Alexis de Tocqueville, *De la Démocracie en Amérique*, J.P. Mayer ed. (Paris: Gallimard, 1968). *Apud* Elisa Reis, *Processos e escolhas: estudos de sociologia* (Rio de Janeiro: Contra Capa Livraria, 1998), 87.

2 A Time of Conspiracy and Misgivings (1964–1966)

1 An. Cam. Dep. 2 (1964): 143.
2 According to Luís Carlos Prestes, in the 1930s "it was easier to build the Communist Party in the barracks than in the factories". Dulce Pandolfi, *Camaradas e Companheiros: História e Memória do PCB* (Rio de Janeiro: Relume-Dumará, 1995), 110.
3 Maria Celina D'Araújo, *Sindicatos, Carisma e Poder* (Rio de Janeiro: Fundação Getúlio Vargas, 1996).
4 Benevides, *A UDN*, 127.
5 Francisco Viana, *Daniel Krieger* (Brasília: Senado Federal/Dom Quixote, 1982).
6 D'Araújo, *Visões do Golpe*, 82.
7 Benevides, *A UDN*, 130. D'Araújo, *Visões do Golpe*, 89.
8 An. Cam. Dep. 2 (1964): 152.
9 An. Cam. Dep. 2 (1964): 141.
10 An. Cam. Dep. 2 (1964): 141.
11 "Ministros de Goulart sem mandatos," *Jornal do Brasil*, April 9, 1964, 5.

12 "UDN rejeita proposta de Levi para cassação," *Jornal do Brasil*, April 4, 1964, 5.
13 "Líderes contra cassações," *Jornal do Brasil*, April 4, 1964, 1.
14 "Ademar exige cassação," *Jornal do Brasil*, April 5–6, 1964, 1.
15 These deputies aimed to try the former Goulart cabinet members under Articles 48 and 139 of the National Constitution and related provisions in the Chamber's internal rules and statutes. "Ministros de Goulart sem mandatos," *Jornal do Brasil*, April 9, 1964, 5.
16 "Amaral Neto faz lista para cassar," *Jornal do Brasil*, May 1, 1964, 1.
17 "Governo cassa mandatos e suspende direitos de 35 gaúchos,". *Jornal do Brasil*, May 8, 1964, 3.
18 "Oposição à cassação de mandatos gera suspeita de fechamento do Congresso," *Jornal do Brasil*, April 5–6, 13.
19 "Deputado irá até a ONU para defender mandato," *Jornal do Brasil*, April 14, 1964, 1.
20 "Mineiros cassam mandatos," *Jornal do Brasil*, April 9, 1964, 8. "Cearenses cassam mandatos," *Jornal do Brasil*, April 10, 1964, 3.
21 "Senadores denunciam abusos e violências," *Jornal do Brasil*, May 23, 1964, 5.
22 "Doutel de Andrade diz que do jeito que está é melhor fechar de vez o Congresso," *Jornal do Brasil*, April 5–6, 1964, 13.
23 "Milton pede ao Congresso que resista," *Jornal do Brasil*, April 7, 1964, 4.
24 "Câmara convoca suplentes dos ex-deputados," *Jornal do Brasil*, April 11, 1964.
25 "Ex-ministro dá tiros na Câmara," *Jornal do Brasil*, April 12–13, 1964, 1. According to the newspapers, this took place in the State of Guanabara: "Deputados se despedem na Assembleia Legislativa em ambiente de lágrimas," *Jornal do Brasil*, April 15, 1964, 5.
26 "Deputado irá até a ONU para defender mandato," *Jornal do Brasil*, April 14, 1964, 1.
27 "Suspensos esperam direitos," *Jornal do Brasil*, April 19–20, 1964, 1.
28 "Governo cassa mandatos e suspende direitos de 35 gaúchos," *Jornal do Brasil*, May 8, 1964, 3.
29 "Deputado irá até a ONU para defender mandato," *Jornal do Brasil*, April 14, 1964, 1.
30 "Senadores denunciam abusos e violências," *Jornal do Brasil*, May 23, 1964, 5.
31 "Denúncias agora só com provas," *Jornal do Brasil*, May 23, 1964, 1.
32 "Cassação só virá com provas indiscutíveis," *Jornal do Brasil*, May 29, 1964, 3.
33 "Juraci acha cassação de Juscelino necessária como quebrar ovos para omelete," *Jornal do Brasil*, June 24, 1964, 4.
34 Vianna Filho, *O Governo*, 101–102.
35 Benevides, *A UDN*, 130.
36 Vianna Filho, *O Governo*, 103.

37 Castello Branco, vol. 1, *Os Militares*, 88.
38 "Juizes eleitorais condenam falta de autenticidade dos partidos políticos," *Jornal do Brasil*, August 7, 1964, 5.
39 Castello Branco, vol.1, *Os Militares*, 602.
40 JM 65.08.27 CMJ
41 *Apud*: Kinzo, *Oposição*, 28.
42 José B. T. Salles, *Milton Campos, uma Vocação Liberal* (Belo Horizonte: Vega, 1975), 199.
43 Vianna Filho, *O Governo*.
44 Salles, *Milton*, 210–214.
45 *Jornal do Brasil*, October 28, 1965, 16.
46 "Hamilton Nogueira concita deputados a protestarem contra o segundo Ato," *Jornal do Brasil*, October 30, 1965, 4.
47 "UDN foi o único dos grandes que não falou da extinção," *Jornal do Brasil*, October 28, 1965, 16.
48 "Viagem de Castelo desmente reabertura militar," *O Estado de S. Paulo*, November 25, 1965, 3
49 "Hamilton Nogueira concita deputados a protestarem contra o segundo Ato," *Jornal do Brasil*, October 30, 1965, 4.
50 "Desolação com liquidação das siglas", *Diário de Notícias*, October 29, 1965, 4.
51 "Reação dos líderes partidários," *Diário de Notícias*, October 28, 1965, 4.
52 "O PSD não pretende de deixar de ser PSD," *Jornal do Brasil*, October 28, 1965, 16.
53 "Reações dos líderes partidários," *Diário de Notícias*, October 28, 1965, p. 4.
54 "Líderes aguardam ato complementar para a formação de novos partidos," *Jornal do Brasil*, October 29, 1965, 4.
55 "Castelo recusa sugestões de encontro com coronéis," *Jornal do Brasil*, November 26, 1965, 6.
56 "Novo partido," *Jornal do Brasil*, November 25, 1965, 3.
57 "Resistência ao bipartidarismo," *O Estado de S. Paulo*, November 4, 1965, 3.
58 "Fórmulas: dissidência e partidos estaduais," *Diário de Notícias*, November 4, 1965, 4.
59 "Pessedistas se dividem e asseguram existência do partido da oposição,". *Jornal do Brasil*, November 27, 1965, 4.
60 "Quadro político fruto do ato está praticamente delineado," *O Estado de S. Paulo*, November 27, 1965, 3.
61 "Senador pede suspensão do Ato n° 4 por cinco meses," *O Estado de S. Paulo*, November 26, 1965, 4.
62 "Oposição em dificuldade para formar novo partido," *Jornal do Commércio*, November 22–23, 1965.
63 "Adauto acha aceitáveis as exigências dos lacerdistas para ingressar na ARENA," *Jornal do Brasil*, December 16, 1965, 3.

226 | Notes to Chapter 2

64 "ARENA e Movimento não se transformarão em partidos depois das eleições de 1966," *Jornal do Brasil*, December 8, 1965, 4.
65 "Ata da reunião do Gabinete Executivo Regional da Aliança Renovadora Nacional da Guanabara. Aos seis de julho de mil novecentos e sessenta e seis, sob a presidência do deputado Adauto Lúcio Cardoso . . . É apresentada e lida pelo ministro Danilo Nunes uma carta do ministro Venancio Igrejas, na qual argumenta favoravelmente à aceitação dos membros do PAREDE como componentes da ARENA". ARENA 66.01.20 op/a pasta 1.
66 "ARENA é tema de fundo," *Jornal do Brasil*, December 19, 1965, 3.
67 ARENA 65.11.30 op/co.
68 ARENA 65.11.30 op/co.
69 ARENA 65.11.30 op/co.
70 ARENA 65.11.30 op/co.
71 ARENA 65.11.30 op/co.
72 "Quadro político fruto do Ato está praticamente delineado," *O Estado de S. Paulo*, November 27, 1965, 3.
73 Carlo Ginzburg and Carlo Poni, "O Nome e o Como: Troca Desigual e Mercado Historiográfico," in *A Micro-história e Outros Ensaios*, ed. Carlo Ginzburg (Lisboa: DIFEL, 1991), 169–178.
74 ARENA 66.06.17 op/d.
75 ARENA 65.08.31 cor/cg pasta 1.
76 Sérgio Miceli, "Carne e Osso da Elite Política Brasileira Pós-30," in *História Geral da Civilização Brasileira*, ed. Boris Fausto (Rio de Janeiro: Bertrand Brasil, 1991), vol. 10.
77 According to Dulci, in the studies on political parties, based on the diagnosis of their inauthenticity, "the topics that stand out are patronage, clan politics, oligarchical power network, corporatism, seen as capable of leading the analysis to the essence of political cleavages. From this perspective, the political parties were viewed as the sums of political machines rather than as agents of representation and promotion of class-type interests, and precisely for this reason, devoid of greater meaning for understanding Brazilian politics. The contrast between 'patronage politics' and 'ideological politics', underscored by many authors, constitutes the classic illustration of this point of view", Dulci, *A UDN*, 13.
78 See: *Revista Brasileira de Ciência Política* (1966–1979).
79 "Partidarismo," *Jornal do Brasil*, June 1, 1971, 10.
80 Lamounier, *Voto de Desconfiança*, 10.
81 Maria M. R. N. Neves, "Ruptura Institucional e Consolidação Política: Mato Grosso e a Hegemonia Arenista," *Dados*, 32 (1989), 373.
82 Fábio Wanderley Reis, *Política e Racionalidade* (Belo Horizonte: UFMG, 2000) 2ª ed.
83 December 14, 1965. Arquivo Particular Luís Vianna Filho. Arquivo Nacional (AN).
84 December 14, 1965. Arquivo Particular Luís Vianna Filho. Arquivo Nacional (AN).

85 Gomes, "Os Paradoxos", 13.
86 ARENA 65.08.31 cor/cg.
87 ARENA 65.08.31 cor/cg.
88 ARENA 65.08.31 cor/cg.
89 ARENA 65.08.31 cor/cg.
90 ARENA 65.08.31 cor/cg.
91 ARENA 65.08.31 cor/cg.
92 ARENA 65.08.31 cor/cg.
93 ARENA 65.08.31 cor/cg.
94 ARENA 65.08.31 cor/cg.
95 ARENA 65.08.31 cor/cg.
96 ARENA 65.08.31 cor/cg.
97 ARENA 65.08.31 cor/cg.
98 ARENA 65.08.31 cor/cg.
99 ARENA 65.08.31 cor/cg.
100 ARENA 65.08.31 cor/cg.
101 ARENA 65.08.31 cor/cg.
102 ARENA 65.08.31 cor/cg.

3 A Time of Uncertainty and Divisions (1966–1968)

1 ARENA 66.05.26 / 2 op/cp.
2 René Dreifuss, *1964: a Conquista do Estado* (Petrópolis, Vozes, 1981).
3 Reis Filho, *Ditadura*.
4 Último de Carvalho. *Aliança Renovadora Nacional*, ARENA, instalação solene em 31 de março de 1966 (Brasília, Câmara dos Deputados, 1967).
5 Último de Carvalho, *Aliança Renovadora Nacional*.
6 ARENA 66.05.26/2 op/cp.
7 ARENA 66.05.26/2 op/cp.
8 Wanderley G. dos Santos, *Regresso* (Rio de Janeiro, Opera Nostra, 1994).
9 ARENA 66.05.26/2 op/cp.
10 ARENA 66.05.26/2 op/cp.
11 Krieger, *Desde*, 206.
12 Speech by Deputado Ernani Sátiro at the ARENA convention on 26 May 1966. ARENA 66.05.26 / 2 op/cp.
13 ARENA 66.05.26 / 2 op/cp.
14 Speech by Deputado Ernani Sátiro at the ARENA convention on 26 May 1966. ARENA 66.05.26 / 2 op/cp.
15 ARENA 66.05.26/2 op/cp.
16 ARENA 66.05.26/2 op/cp.
17 ARENA 66.05.26/2 op/cp.
18 ARENA 66.05.26/2 op/cp.
19 Arquivo Particular Luís Vianna Filho (Arquivo Nacional / RJ).
20 "Adauto reafirma apoio da UDN ao governo federal e rebate crítica a Campos," *Jornal do Brasil*, September 20–21, 1964, 4.
21 Célio Borja, *Célio Borja* (Rio de Janeiro, Fundação Getúlio Vargas/ALERJ, 1999), 7.

22 Luiz Fernando Mercadante, "Há liberdade no Brasil?," *Realidade*, September,1966, I, n°6.
23 Carlos Castello Branco, "Coluna do Castelo", *Jornal do Brasil*, October 4, 1966, 4.
24 An. Cam. Dep. 23 (1966): 13.
25 An. Cam. Dep. 23 (1966): 347.
26 "ARENA se solidariza com Castelo e apóia recesso," *Jornal do Brasil*, October 22, 1966, 1.
27 "Nada contra Adauto," *Jornal do Brasil*, October 22,1966, 6.
28 "Adauto encerra campanha da ARENA afirmando que não deixa de crer na revolução," *Jornal do Brasil*, November 12, 1966, 3.
29 "ARENA não crê na derrota de Adauto mas amigos já a consideram possível," *Jornal do Brasil*, November 18, 1966, 4.
30 "Adauto vê no voto apoio a cassações," *Jornal do Brasil*, November 17, 1966, 1.
31 "Adauto, a afirmação pela renúncia," *Jornal do Brasil*, March 11, 1971, 3.
32 "ARENA dirá em votação secreta quem prefere para presidir o Congresso," *Jornal do Brasil*, January 8, 1967, 3.
33 Lamounier, "Representação Política".
34 "Coisas da Política," *Jornal do Brasil*, October 12, 1966, 6.
35 *Jornal do Brasil*, September 7, 1966 to October 12, 1966.
36 Carlos Castello Branco, "Auro e Adauto outra vez de mãos dadas," *Jornal do Brasil*, October 5, 1966, 4. Carlos Castello Branco, "Auro e Adauto não se dão por vencidos," *Jornal do Brasil*, October 7, 1966, 4.
37 Krieger, *Desde*, 240.
38 Elio Gaspari, *A Ditadura Envergonhada* (São Paulo, Companhia das Letras, 2002), 136.
39 "Revogação do AI-2 volta a ser reclamada por Adauto," *Jornal do Brasil*, October 30–31, 1966, 6.
40 Viana Filho, *O Governo*, 454.
41 "Auro diz que omissão é bonito mas trás ônus," *Jornal do Brasil*, December 13, 1966, 3.
42 "Auro diz que omissão é bonito mas trás ônus," *Jornal do Brasil*, December 13, 1966, 3.
43 Afonso Arinos, *Planalto (Memórias)* (Rio de Janeiro, José Olympio, 1968), 279.
44 An. Const. 1967. 4 (1967): 487.
45 An. Const. 1967. 4 (1967): 488.
46 An. Const. 1967. 4 (1967): 488.
47 An. Const. 1967. 6 (1967): 501.
48 Humberto de Alencar Castello Branco, *Discursos, 1965* (Brasília, Secretaria de Imprensa da Presidência da República, s/d), 286.
49 An. Const. 1967. 6 (1967): 501.
50 An. Const. 1967. 6 (1967): 501.
51 An. Const. 1967. 6 (1967): 501.

52 An. Const. 1967. 6 (1967): 501.
53 An. Const. 1967. 6 (1967): 501.
54 An. Const. 1967. 6 (1967): 503.
55 An. Const. 1967. 4 (1967): 568.
56 An. Const. 1967. 4 (1967): 613.
57 An. Const. 1967. 4 (1967): 621.
58 An. Const. 1967. 4 (1967): 655.
59 An. Const. 1967. 6 (1967): 418.
60 An. Const. 1967. 6, (1967): 420–422.
61 An. Const. 1967. 6, (1967): 422.
62 An. Const. 1967. 4 (1967): 120.
63 An. Const. 1967. 4, (1967): 826.
64 An. Const. 1967. 6 (1967): 827.
65 An. Const. 1967. 6 (1967): 417.
66 An. Const. 1967. 6 (1967): 417.
67 An. Const. 1967. 6 (1967): 418.
68 An. Const. 1967. 4 (1967): 120.
69 An. Const. 1967. 4 (1967): 121.
70 An. Const. 1967. 4 (1967): 121.
71 An. Const. 1967. 4 (1967): 782.
72 An. Const. 1967. 4 (1967): 782.
73 *Jornal do Brasil*, January 21, 1967, 3. The following members of Congress signed the manifesto accompanying the vote: Herbert Levy, Alvaro Catão, José Humberto, Vasco Filho, Lauro Cruz, Horácio Bethônico, Ferraz Egreja, Manoel Taveira, Britto Velho, Norberto Schmidt, Nicolau Tuma, Flores Soares, Lyrio Bertoli, Alde Sampaio, Elias Carmo, Francelino Pereira, Nogueira de Rezende, Aniz Badra, Ossian Araripe, Segismundo de Andrade, Paulo Freire, Cardoso de Menezes, Dnar Mendes, Gilberto Faria, Bias Fortes, Pedro Vidigal, Francisco Elesbão, Hermes Macedo, Albino Zeni, Diomício Freitas, Paulo Montans, Rafael Rezende, Elias Nacle, Zacarias Seleme, Braga Ramos, Heitor Cavalcanti, Padre Medeiros Neto, Carneiro Loyola, Amintas de Barros, Celso Murta, Milo Cammarosano, Plínio Costa, Pedro Zimmerman, Emílio Gomes, Gabriel Hermes, Aécio Cunha, Henrique Turner, Saldanha Derzi, Hary Normaton, Cantídio Sampaio, Monteiro de Castro, Bagueira Leal, Dulcino Monteiro, João Calmon, Rachid Mamed, Broca Filho, Leão Sampaio, Osni Régis, João Cleofas, José Meira, Campos Vergal, Tufy Nassif, Cunha Bueno, Lacorte Vitale, Aroldo Carvalho, Arnaldo Nogueira, Oceano Carleial, Dyrno Pires, Floriano Rubim, Euclides Triches, Minoro Miyamoto, Abel Rafael, Adrião Bernardes, Paulo Pinheiro Chagas, Wilson Falcão, Souto Maior, Mário Gomes, Abraão Sabbá, Yukishigue Tamura, Ivan Saldanha, Clodomir Millet, Henrique de La Rocque, Ezequias Costa, Lisboa Machado, Francisco Scarpa, Janary Nunes, José Esteves, Wanderley Dantas, Pereira Lúcio, Armando Carneiro, Leopoldo Perez, Teotônio Neto, José Carlos Guerra, Nonato Marques, Walter Passos, Dias Lins,

Costa Lima, Flávio Marcílio, Arruda Câmara, Ormeo Botelho, Plínio Salgado (and five more illegible signatures).
74 An. Const. 1967. 4 (1967): 472.
75 "Congresso aprova carta com os relógios parados," *Jornal do Brasil*, January 22–23, 1967, 1.
76 Castello Branco, vol. 1, *Os Militares*, 643.
77 "Coisas da Política," *Jornal do Brasil*, January 24, 1967, 6.
78 Krieger, *Desde*, 251.
79 An. Cam. Dep. 10 (1968): 421.
80 An. Cam. Dep. 10 (1968): 421.
81 An. Cam. Dep. 10 (1968): 421.
82 An. Cam. Dep. 10 (1968): 425.
83 An. Cam. Dep. 10 (1968): 430.
84 An. Sen. 8 (1968): 558.
85 Castello Branco, vol. 2, *Os Militares*, 359.
86 Fabiano Santos, "Microfundamentos do Clientelismo Político no Brasil: 1959–1963", *Dados* 38 (1995): 459–496.
87 Document preparded by Daniel Krieger, addressed to General Costa e Silva, June 1968. Krieger. *Desde*, 310.
88 Krieger, *Desde*, 270.
89 In 1937, during the *Estado Novo*, Daniel Krieger went into exile in Uruguay. From 1945 to 1946, he chaired the UDN state committee in Rio Grande do Sul. In 1947 he was elected national deputy in the Constitutional Congress. In 1954 he was elected to his first term in the Senate through a coalition between UDN, PSD, and PL to face the PTB candidate, João Goulart. In 1962 he was reelected through a coalition of parties in opposition to PTB: UDN, PSD, PL, PSP, and PDC. Abreu, *Dicionário*.
90 An. Cam. Dep. 9 (1968): 949.
91 Castello Branco, vol. 2, *Os Militares*, 366.
92 An. Sen. 8 (1968): 555.
93 An. Sen. 8 (1968): 556.
94 Krieger, *Desde*, 310.
95 Krieger, *Desde*, 310–311.
96 ARENA 68.07.02 op/cp.
97 ARENA 66.05.26/2 op/cp.
98 ARENA 66.05.26/2 op/cp.
99 ARENA 66.05.26/2 op/cp.
100 ARENA 66.05.26/2 op/cp.
101 ARENA 66.05.26/2 op/cp.
102 "Exame da conjuntura político-partidária e sugestões para o seu aperfeiçoamento (Por Arnaldo Cerdeira)" 26/6/1968 ARENA 66.05.26/2 op/cp.
103 ARENA 66.05.26/2 op/cp.
104 An. Sen. 10 (1968): 595.
105 An. Sen. 10 (1968): 596.
106 An. Sen. 10 (1968): 596.

107 An. Sen. 8 (1968): 357.
108 The records of the Senate and Chamber of Deputies published various debates between members of ARENA and MDB on the invasion of the University of Brasília. There are detailed reports on the "Márcio Moreira Alves affair" in the following publications: Krieger, *Desde.*; Márcio Moreira Alves, *68 Mudou o mundo* (Rio de Janeiro, Nova Fronteira, 1993). Zuenir Ventura, *1968 o ano que não terminou* (Rio de Janeiro, Nova Fronteira, 1988).
109 Moreira Alves, *68*, 151.
110 Krieger, *Desde*, 333.
111 Moreira Alves, *68*, 149.
112 Krieger, *Desde*, 335.
113 Diógenes da Cunha Lima, *O Homem que Pintava Cavalos Azuis: Djalma Marinho* (Brasília, Câmara dos Deputados; Rio de Janeiro, Forense Universitária, 1982), 41.
114 Kinzo, *Oposição*, 117.
115 "Líder do governo não sabe explicar," *Correio da Manhã*, December 13, 1968, 3.
116 "Derrrubada cassação na Câmara por maioria absoluta: 216 x 141," *Correio da Manhã*, December 13, 1968, 1.
117 *Jornal do Brasil*, December 13, 1968, 3.
118 "Povo na Câmara cantou hino nacional," *Correio da Manhã*, December 13, 1968, 2.
119 *Correio da Manhã*, December 13, 1968, 1.
120 An. Cam. Dep. 3 (1969): 251.
121 An. Cam. Dep. 3 (1969): 251.
122 Alberto Dines, *Histórias do Poder* (Rio de Janeiro: Editora 34, 2000), 337.
123 According to Márcio Moreira Alves, Daniel Krieger and Raphael de Almeida Magalhães tried to the end to dissuade the Executive from requesting the authorization. Moreira Alves, *68*, 149.
124 The document was signed by Senators Gilberto Marinho, Daniel Krieger, Milton Campos, Carvalho Pinto, Eurico Resende, Manoel Vilaça, Wilson Gonçalves, Aloísio de Carvalho Filho, Antônio Carlos Konder Reis, Ney Braga, Mem de Sá, Rui Palmeira, Teotônio Villela, José Cândido Ferraz, Leandro Maciel, Vitorino Freire, Arnon de Mello, Clodomir Millet, José Guiomard, Waldemar Alcântara, and Júlio Leite". *Correio da Manhã*, January 7, 1969.
125 Krieger, *Desde*, 343.
126 "Mensagem ao povo brasileiro, transmitida pela Agência Nacional, na noite de 31 de dezembro de 1968, através de uma rede de rádio e televisão," *In:* Costa e Silva, *Pronunciamentos*, 479–483.
127 Krieger, *Desde*, 314.
128 Gaspari, *A Ditadura Envergonhada*.

4 A Time of Silence and Reorganization (1969–1973)

1. An. Cam. Dep. 3 (1969): 251.
2. Kenneth Serbin, *Diálogos na Sombra* (São Paulo: Companhia das Letras, 2001).
3. "Krieger e 21 senadores protestam contra AI-5," *Correio da Manhã*, January 7, 1969, 11.
4. "Costa divulgará a resposta a Krieger," *O Estado de S. Paulo*, January 8, 1969, 3.
5. "Condenada à sepultura," *Correio da Manhã*, May 9, 1969, 4.
6. "Informes deixam políticos perplexos," *O Estado de S. Paulo*, May 9, 1969, 3.
7. "Contra a extinção," *Correio da Manhã*, May 10, 1969, 4.
8. "ARENA faz meeting e Executiva pede renúncia coletiva," *Correio da Manhã*, March 19, 1969, 2.
9. "Novo partido divide políticos," *Correio da Manhã*, January 5, 1969, 3.
10. "Filinto se recusa a reunir a ARENA," *O Estado de S. Paulo*, January 31, 1969, 4.
11. "Contra a extinção," *Correio da Manhã*, May 10, 1969, 4.
12. *O Estado de S. Paulo*, January 4, 1969, 3.
13. "Radicais da ARENA – MG são por renúncia," *Correio da Manhã*, March 6, 1969, 2.
14. "Cerdeira procura Filinto para ver mudanças na ARENA," *Correio da Manhã*, March 11,1969, 2.
15. "Filinto veta reunião da ARENA antes de uma reunião política. *Jornal do Brasil*, April 8, 1969, 3.
16. ARENA 66.01.20 op/a pasta 2.
17. "Examinada a situação da ARENA," *O Estado de S. Paulo*, January 18, 1969, 4.
18. "CGI inicia hoje suas atividades," *O Estado de S. Paulo*, January 7, 1969, 4.
19. "Quatro Cantos," *Correio da Manhã*, January 7, 1969, 7.
20. "Quatro Cantos," *Correio da Manhã*, January 23, 1969, 7.
21. "Informe JB," *Jornal do Brasil*, April 5, 1969, 10.
22. "Vácuo político," *Correio da Manhã*, May 4, 1969, 4.
23. Castello Branco, vol. 2, *Os Militares*, 187.
24. "Rondon: recesso político também," *O Estado de S. Paulo*, January 3, 1969, 4.
25. "Governo deseja manter a ARENA," *O Estado de S. Paulo*, January 10, 1969, 3.
26. "Ministro da Justiça prega reforma dos poderes fortalecendo Executivo," *Jornal do Brasil*, May 24, 1969, 5.
27. ARENA 65.08.31 cor/cg pasta 3.
28. Arthur da Costa e Silva. *Pronunciamentos do Presidente* (Brasília: Secretaria de Imprensa e Divulgação, [s.d]).
29. "Müller vai tomar pulso da ARENA," *O Estado de S. Paulo*, May 24, 1969, 3.

30 "Müller vai tomar pulso da ARENA," *O Estado de S. Paulo*, May 24, 1969, 3.
31 "Rondon define reabertura," Jornal do Brasil, May 27, 1969, 3.
32 "Rondon define reabertura," *Jornal do Brasil*, May 27, 1969, 3.
33 "Ministro da Justiça prega reforma dos poderes fortalecendo Executivo," *Jornal do Brasil*, May 24, 1969, 5.
34 *Jornal do Brasil*, April 2, 1969 p. 4.
35 "Resistência contra Rondon aumentou," *O Estado de S. Paulo*, November 21, 1969, 3.
36 *O Estado de S. Paulo*, January 2, 1969, 3.
37 Mello, *A Revolução*, 813.
38 "Recesso pode ir além de março," *O Estado de S. Paulo*, January 7, 1969, 3.
39 "Estuda-se critérios para as cassações," *O Estado de S. Paulo*, January 5, 1969, 3.
40 *Discursos da III Convenção Nacional da ARENA, em 20 de novembro de 1969* (Brasília: ARENA, 1970), 22.
41 The AI-16 of 14 October 1969 declared vacant the office of President of the Republic and scheduled new indirect elections. In this same act, the ARENA National Committee was called to a meeting with the powers of a national convention to choose candidates for President and Vice-President. ARENA 66.01.20 op/a.
42 *Discursos da III Convenção*, 21.
43 Linha de comportamento partidário. ARENA 68.06.25 op/cp.
44 An. Cam. Dep. 1 (1969): 345.
45 An. Cam. Dep. 1 (1969): 346.
46 F.J.L. Costa and Lucia Klein, "Um Ano de Governo Médici," *Dados* (1972): 173.
47 "Julgamento é precipitado," *O Estado de S. Paulo*, November 21, 1969, 3.
48 Starting in 1969, as the majority leader, Cantídio Sampaio played a role that had belonged previously to mythical figures from the UDN, such as Afonso Arinos. Cantídio Sampaio was a military officer, elected national deputy for the first time in 1962 on the PSP ticket. He served as secretary of public security in the Adhemar de Barros' government until 1966, when the governor of São Paulo was purged from office. In Sampaio's opinion, the "revolution" was essentially *Udenista*: "We had bit parts, while they played the leading roles." Abreu, *Dicionário*.
49 An. Cam. Dep. 1 (1969): 81–82.
50 An. Cam. Dep. 3 (1969): 164.
51 An. Cam. Dep. 3 (1969): 165.
52 Decreto-lei n° 1063, October 21, 1969.
53 "Medidas iriam a ex-governadores," *O Estado de S. Paulo*, January 1, 1969.
54 An. Cam. Dep. 1 (1969): 1075.
55 "Filinto deseja reduzir propaganda eleitoral gratuita em rádio e tv," *Jornal do Brasil*, March 24, 1970, 3.

234 | Notes to Chapter 4

56 ARENA 70.05.13 op/rb pasta 1.
57 ARENA 70.05.13 op/rb pasta 1.
58 ARENA 70.05.13 op/rb pasta 1.
59 ARENA 70.05.13 op/rb pasta 1.
60 Em 1962, José Lindoso elegeu-se deputado federal pela coligação entre UDN e PSD (seu partido) e em 1966 foi eleito pela ARENA. Abreu, *Dicionário*.
61 ARENA 70.05.13 op/rb pasta 1.
62 ARENA 70.05.13 op/rb pasta 1.
63 ARENA 70.05.13 op/rb pasta 1.
64 In 1954 he was the first mayor elected to the city of Curitiba and one of the founders of the Christian Democratic Party (PDC), on whose ticket he was elected national deputy in 1958 and governor of Paraná in 1960. Abreu, *Dicionário*.
65 ARENA 70.05.13 op/rb pasta 2.
66 ARENA 70.05.13 op/rb pasta 2.
67 ARENA 70.05.13 op/rb pasta 2.
68 Timothy J. Power, "The Political Right and Democratization in Brazil" (PhD diss., University of Indiana, 1993).
69 "Objetivo do sistema é enquadrar a ARENA," *O Estado de S. Paulo*, June 11, 1971, 3.
70 Joaquim Nabuco, *Um Estadista no Império* (Rio de Janeiro: Topbooks, 1997), 766.
71 Renato Lessa, *A Invenção Republicana* (Rio de Janeiro: Vértice, 1988).
72 *Apud* Power, "The political right", 61.
73 Margaret S. Jenks, "Political Parties in Authoritarian Brazil" (PhD diss., Duke University, 1979), 21.
74 Castello Branco, vol. 3, *Os Militares*, 472.
75 ARENA 70.05.13 op/rb pasta 1.
76 Edilson Távora was elected national deputy for the first time in 1958 under the Democratic Coalition, consisting of the UDN, PSP, PRP, PR, and PTN. He was reelected in 1962 under the Union for Ceará alliance, consisting of UDN and PSD. Abreu, *Dicionário*. Reunião realizada em 23/6/1971. ARENA 70.05.13 op/rb pasta 2.
77 ARENA 70.05.13 op/rb pasta 2.
78 "Coisas da Política," *Jornal do Brasil*, June 11, 1971, 6.
79 ARENA 70.05.13 op/rb.
80 ARENA 70.05.13 op/rb.
81 ARENA 70.05.13 op/rb.
82 ARENA 70.05.13 op/rb pasta 2.
83 ARENA 70.05.13 op/rb pasta 2.
84 Parecer da comissão encarregada de analisar o relatório político e financeiro do partido. ARENA 72.02.09 op/cp.
85 ARENA 66.05.26/2 op/cp.
86 ARENA 70.05.13 op/rb pasta 3.
87 ARENA 70.05.13 op/rb pasta 3.

88 ARENA 70.05.13 op/rb pasta 3.
89 ARENA 70.05.13 op/rb pasta 3.
90 ARENA 70.05.13 op/rb pasta 3.
91 ARENA 70.05.13 op/rb pasta 3.
92 An. Cam. Dep. 2 (1972): 528.
93 An. Cam. Dep. 2 (1972): 530.
94 An. Cam. Dep. 2 (1972): 944.
95 An. Cam. Dep. 2 (1972): 965.
96 An. Cam. Dep. 3 (1972): 289.
97 Amaral de Souza had belonged to the youth wing of PSD in Rio Grande do Sul state, in 1952 was vice-president of the National Student Union (UNE), elected state deputy in 1962 under PSD, elected national deputy in 1966 under ARENA, reelected in 1970, and name deputy governor of his state in 1974. Abreu, *Dicionário*.
98 An. Cam. Dep. 3 (1972): 309.
99 Etelvino Lins de Albuquerque was intervenor in the state of Pernambuco in 1946, senator under PSD (1946–1952), governor of Pernambuco (1952–1955), justice of the Federal Accounts Court (TCU) (1955 – 1959), national deputy (1959–1963), justice of the TCU (1963–1969), and national deputy under ARENA (1971–1975). Abreu, *Dicionário*.
100 An. Cam. Dep. 3 (1972): 447–448.
101 An. Cam. Dep. 19 (1973): 795–796.
102 An. Cam. Dep. 19 (1973): 796.
103 Alain Rouquié, "Desmilitarización y la Institucionalización de los Sistemas Políticos Dominados por los Militares en América Latina," in *Transições do regime autoritário: primeiras conclusões*, ed. Guillermo O'Donnell and Philippe Schmitter (São Paulo: Vértice, 1988).
104 "Gente e notícia," *Jornal do Commércio*, May 28, 1969, 3.
105 "A carta-renúncia subirá amanhã," *O Estado de S. Paulo*, January 26, 1969, 3.
106 "Stenzel: esquerdas vivem dos liberais," *O Estado de S. Paulo*, January 29, 1969, 4.
107 "Reação contrária à decisão do senador," *O Estado de S. Paulo*, March 7, 1972, 3.
108 "Reação contrária".
109 "ESG ainda busca a doutrina política," *O Estado de S. Paulo*, March 4, 1972, 4.
110 "ESG ainda".
111 "ARENA busca os ideólogos," *O Estado de S. Paulo*, March 2, 1972, 4.
112 ARENA 66.05.26/2 op/cp pasta 2.
113 ARENA 66.05.26/2 op/cp pasta 2.
114 ARENA 66.05.26/2 op/cp pasta 2.
115 ARENA 66.05.26/2 op/cp pasta 2.
116 ARENA 66.05.26/2 op/cp pasta 2.
117 ARENA 66.05.26/2 op/cp pasta 2.
118 ARENA 66.05.26/2 op/cp pasta 2.

119 An. Cam. Dep. 25 (1971): 508.
120 "Stenzel: MDB copia 'banda de música' dos udenistas," *Correio da Manhã*, May 19, 1971, 2.
121 An. Cam. Dep. 2 (1969): 87.
122 An. Cam. Dep. 2 (1969): 98.
123 An. Cam. Dep. 2 (1969): 100.
124 An. Cam. Dep. 2 (1969): 100.
125 An. Cam. Dep. 25 (1971): 510–511.
126 An. Cam. Dep. 6 (1973): 639.
127 An. Cam. Dep. 6 (1973): 639.
128 An. Cam. Dep. 6 (1973): 639.
129 An. Cam. Dep. 9 (1973): 765.
130 An. Cam. Dep. 9 (1973): 768.
131 An. Cam. Dep. 1 (1973): 594–595.
132 An. Cam. Dep. 2 (1973): 228.
133 An. Cam. Dep. 4 (1973): 809–810.
134 An. Cam. Dep. 2 (1973): 227.
135 An. Cam. Dep. 8 (1973): 212–213.
136 An. Cam. Dep. 8 (1973): 212–213.
137 An. Cam. Dep. 2 (1973): p. 230.
138 An. Cam. Dep. 2 (1973): p. 230.
139 Rodrigo P. S. Motta, *Em Guarda Contra o Perigo Vermelho* (São Paulo: Perspectiva/FAPESP, 2002).
140 "Censura leva crise ao STF; Adauto sai," *O Estado de S. Paulo*, March 11, 1971, 1.
141 "Censura leva."
142 "Supremo já providencia aposentadoria de Adauto," *Jornal do Brasil*, March 12, 1971, 3.
143 "Supremo já providencia aposentadoria de Adauto," *Jornal do Brasil*, March 12, 1971, 3.
144 "Saída de Adauto divide opiniões," *O Estado de S. Paulo*, March 12, 1971, 40.
145 "Saída de Adauto."
146 "Gallotti: Adauto foi pessimista," *O Estado de S. Paulo*, March 11, 1971, 20.
147 "Beau geste," *O Estado de S. Paulo*, March 12, 1971, 3.
148 "Adauto, a afirmação pela renúncia," *Jornal do Brasil*, March 11, 1971, 3.
149 "Aleixo lança o terceiro partido ainda este mês," *Jornal do Brasil*, March 2, 1971, 1.
150 An. Cam. Dep. 2 (1971): 630.
151 "Filinto alerta arenistas contra criação do PDR," *Correio da Manhã*, May 20, 1971, 2.
152 Milton Campos, *Testemunhos e Lições* (Brasília: Senado, 1976), 293.
153 *O Estado de S. Paulo*, March 9, 1972, 3.
154 *O Estado de S. Paulo*, March 9, 1972, 3.

155 "Os encapuçados passam à crítica," *O Estado de S. Paulo*, September 23, 1972, 3.
156 "Os encapuçados passam à crítica," *O Estado de S. Paulo*, September 23, 1972, 3.
157 "Nos desmentidos, a marca da realidade," *O Estado de S. Paulo*, September 12, 1972, 3.
158 An. Cam. Dep. 14 (1972): 375.
159 An. Cam. Dep. 14 (1972): 380.
160 An. Cam. Dep. 22 (1972): 26–27.
161 An. Cam. Dep. 14 (1972): 382–383.
162 An. Cam. Dep. 14 (1972): 374.
163 Geraldo Freire (ARENA – MG). An. Cam. Dep. 20 (1973) 423.
164 Ildélio Martins was an attorney, civil servant, labour judge, auditor of the Military Justice system, functionary of the Ministry of Labour, Industry, and Commerce, and national deputy under ARENA. Abreu, *Dicionário*.
165 An. Cam. Dep. 4 (1973): 776.
166 An article from the Chamber of Deputies' bylaws, transposed from Constitutional Amendment no. 1.
167 An. Cam. Dep. 8 (1973): 154.
168 An. Cam. Dep. 8 (1973): 155.
169 An. Cam. Dep. 20 (1973): 425.
170 An. Cam. Dep. 20 (1973): 425.
171 An. Cam. Dep. 23 (1972): 1046.
172 An. Cam. Dep. 25 (1972): 887.
173 "Hora de transição pede ação cautelosa," *Jornal do Brasil*, November 11, 1973, 4.
174 "Reforma de Flávio Marcílio prevalece só nos pontos aprovados pelo governo," *Jornal do Brasil*, November 14, 1973, 3.
175 "Marcílio acha políticos otimistas," *Jornal do Brasil*, November 15, 1973, 3.
176 Lucia Klein, "Pós-64: A Nova Ordem Legal e a Redefinição das Bases de Legitimidade," in *Legitimidade e Coação no Brasil Pós-64*, ed. Lucia Klein and Marcus Figueiredo (Rio de Janeiro: Forense, 1978), 35.

5 The Time of Political Détente (1974–1979)

1 ARENA 66.05.26/2 op/cp.
2 Borja, *Célio*, 264.
3 An. Sen. 3 (1977): 417.
4 An. Sen. 3 (1977): 417.
5 An. Sen. 3 (1977): 423.
6 Klein, "Brasil," 72.
7 Kinzo, *Oposição*, 156–157.
8 "Célio não vê nenhuma apatia," *Jornal do Brasil*, October 3, 1974, 3.
9 "Arenistas pedem ao TSE que reconsidere restrições à divulgação dos candidatos," *Jornal do Brasil*, October 1, 1974, 4.
10 Celso Castro and Maria Celina D'Araújo, *Dossiê Geisel* (Rio de Janeiro: Fundação Getúlio Vargas, 2002).

238 | Notes to Chapter 5

11 "Abstenção pequena inquieta a ARENA," *Jornal do Brasil*, November 16, 1974, 1.
12 Bolívar Lamounier, "O Voto em São Paulo, 1970–1978," in *Voto de desconfiança*, ed. Bolívar Lamounier. David Fleischer, "Renovação Política – Brasil 1978: Eleições Parlamentares sob a Égide do Pacote de Abril," *Revista de Ciência Política* 23 (1980).
13 Francelino Pereira, *Castelinho: o Reinventor do Jornalismo Político no Brasil* (Brasília: s/e, 2001). Castro, *Dossiê Geisel*. Armando Falcão. *Tudo a Declarar* (Rio de Janeiro: Nova Fronteira, 1989).
14 "Política voltando a ser tema de politicos," *Jornal do Brasil*, November 29, 1974, 4.
15 Ana Lagoa, *SNI, como Nasceu, como Funciona* (São Paulo: Brasiliense, 1983).
16 Celso Castro, "As Apreciações do SNI," in Castro, *Dossiê Geisel*.
17 "Airon atribui a derrota à 'ação predatória de diversos governadores'," *Jornal do Brasil*, November 29, 1974, 4.
18 "Coluna do Castelo," *Jornal do Brasil*, November 16, 1974, 4.
19 "Célio Borja credita vitória à escolha de bons nomes," *Jornal do Brasil*, November 18, 1974, 4.
20 "Eurico Resende diz que dar o voto à oposição não representa contestação," *Jornal do Brasil*, November 6, 1974, 3.
21 "Petrônio saúda MDB como um partido forte," *Jornal do Brasil*, November 17, 1974, 2.
22 An. Sen. 11 (1974): 481.
23 An. Sen. 11 (1974): 154.
24 An. Sen. 11 (1974): 154.
25 An. Sen. 11 (1974): 154.
26 An. Sen. 11 (1974): 157.
27 An. Sen. 11 (1974): 159.
28 An. Sen. 11 (1974): 155.
29 An. Sen. 11 (1974): 160.
30 *O Estado de S. Paulo*, April 13, 1975.
31 *O Estado de S. Paulo*, June 7, 1975.
32 *Veja*, July 2, 1975.
33 Maria Celina D'Araújo and Celso Castro, *Ernesto Geisel* (Rio de Janeiro: Fundação Getúlio Vargas, 1997).
34 Elio Gaspari, *A Ditadura Derrotada*, 323.
35 Borja, *Célio*, 186.
36 Abreu, *Dicionário*.
37 The newspaper coverage shows the context in which this ruling was handed down. Shortly before the trial was to begin, four military policemen were positioned near the table where the judges were sitting: "Never have the police taken this ostensive position in the Supreme Court. Chief Justice Eloy Rocha, as soon as he learned of this, ordered the soldiers to leave the courtroom immediately and only allowed the lieutenant to remain, since he was in civilian clothing." The trial lasted six hours. *Jornal do Brasil*, October 11, 1974, 3.

38 Passarinho, *Um Híbrido*, 452.
39 Passarinho, *Um Híbrido*, 452.
40 "Petrônio nega rebeldia dos senadores da ARENA," *Jornal do Brasil*, September 2, 1975, 4.
41 "Edígio vê aplicação do Ato 5 como hipótese," *Jornal do Brasil*, July 1, 1975, 3.
42 "Edígio admite AI-5 para cassar Campos," *Jornal do Brasil*, July 1, 1975, 1.
43 "Renúncia é o meio que evita cassação," *Jornal do Brasil*, July 1, 1975, 3.
44 "Falcão empossa interventor de Rio Branco," *Jornal do Brasil*, April 23, 1975, 1.
45 *Jornal do Brasil*, April 24, 1975, 4.
46 ARENA 66.05.26/2 op/cp.
47 ARENA 66.05.26/2 op/cp.
48 ARENA 66.05.26/2 op/cp.
49 ARENA 66.05.26/2 op/cp.
50 ARENA 66.05.26/2 op/cp.
51 ARENA 66.05.26/2 op/cp.
52 ARENA 66.05.26/2 op/cp.
53 ARENA 68.06.25 op/cp pasta 3.
54 ARENA 68.06.25 op/cp pasta 3.
55 ARENA 68.06.25 op/cp pasta 3.
56 ARENA 68.06.25 op/cp pasta 3.
57 ARENA 68.06.25 op/cp pasta 3.
58 Diário do Congresso Nacional, April 26, 1975. *Apud*: Marly S. Motta, *Grandes Vultos que Honraram o Senado* (Brasília: Senado; Rio de Janeiro: Fundação Getúlio Vargas, 1996), 85.
59 ARENA 66.05.26/2 op/cp pasta 5.
60 ARENA 66.05.26/2 op/cp pasta 5.
61 ARENA 66.05.26/2 op/cp pasta 5.
62 ARENA 66.05.26/2 op/cp pasta 5.
63 ARENA 65.08.31 cor/cg pasta 20.
64 "Bonifácio revela no Rio que não sabe nada sobre cassações de mandatos," *Jornal do Brasil*, January 5, 1976, 3. "Geisel cassa mandatos de deputados paulistas," *Jornal do Brasil*, January 6, 1976, 1.
65 "Bonifácio revela no Rio que não sabe nada sobre cassações de mandatos," *Jornal do Brasil*, January 5, 1976, 3.
66 "Geisel cassa mandatos de deputados paulistas," *Jornal do Brasil*, January 6, 1976, 1.
67 Borja, *Célio*, 207.
68 Armando Falcão, *Tudo*, 390.
69 ARENA 65.08.31 cor/cg.
70 ARENA 65.08.31 cor/cg pasta 36.
71 ARENA 65.08.31 cor/cg pasta 25.
72 ARENA 65.08.31 cor/cg pasta 25.
73 ARENA 65.08.31 cor/cg pasta 25.

Notes to Chapter 5

74 ARENA 65.08.31 cor/cg pasta 25.
75 ARENA 65.08.31 cor/cg pasta 25.
76 An. Cam. Dep. 3 (1977): 992–993.
77 ARENA 65.08.31 cor/cg pasta 59.
78 "JK sepultado em Brasília," *Folha de S. Paulo*, August 24, 1976, 1.
79 ARENA 65.08.31 cor/cg.
80 An. Cam. Dep. 3 (1977): 992–993.
81 Yet the President, according to the notes in Heitor Ferreira's diary, "amicably banned publication of the book Luiz Vianna Filho had written about the Castello Branco government, to prevent the revelations by the former Chief of Staff from opening wounds among the military". This shows Geisel's understanding of the possible repercussions from Senator Luís Vianna Filho's words. Gaspari, *A Ditadura Derrotada*, 231.
82 An. Sen. 3 (1977): 417.
83 An. Sen. 3 (1977): 417.
84 An. Sen. 3 (1977): 417.
85 Senator Luís Vianna Filho had researched the life and work of his fellow Bahian, Ruy Barbosa, having published several anthologies of his work, such as: Ruy Barbosa. *Trabalhos Diversos* (Rio de Janeiro: Casa de Rui Barbosa, 1957).
86 An. Sen. 3 (1977): 417.
87 An. Sen. 3 (1977): 418.
88 An. Sen. 3 (1977): 424.
89 An. Sen. 3 (1977): 424.
90 Substitutivo Accioly Filho, artigo n° 119, letra h. Anna Lucia Brandão, *A Resistência Parlamentar Após 1964* (Brasília: Senado Federal, 1984).
91 Brandão, *A Resistência*.
92 Kinzo analyses in MDB's action in detail in *Oposição e Autoritarismo*. Congress voted on the bill "in the first round on 29 March 1977, with 237 ayes and 155 nays. It was thus rejected, since it failed to reach the constitutional quorum. Second vote on 30 March that same year, with 241 ayes and 157 nays. Rejected for the same reason." Falcão, *Tudo*, 352.
93 "Geisel fará reforma política no recesso," *Jornal do Brasil*, April 2, 1977, 1.
94 "Petrônio comunica recesso aos colegas," *Jornal do Brasil*, April 2, 1977, 4.
95 "Krieger reafirma esperança em Geisel," *Jornal do Brasil*, April 1, 1977, 19.
96 "Passarinho recorda frase de Castelo," *Jornal do Brasil*, April 1, 1977, 19.
97 Passarinho, *Um Híbrido*. According to Armando Falcão, "In the political area, Geisel usually listened to the following: ... Falcão; ... Golbery; president of the Chamber of Deputies, Célio Borja, first, and Marco Maciel later; president of the Senate, Magalhães Pinto first, and Petrônio Portela later; leader in the Chamber, José Bonifácio de Andrada (whom I had nominated); leader of the Senate, Petrônio Portela, first, and Eurico Resende later; chairman of ARENA, Petrônio Portela, first, and Francelino

Pereira later. They formed the Policy Council, whom the head of government convened occasionally at the Presidential Palace." Falcão, *Tudo*, 327–328.
98 *Jornal do Brasil*, April 4, 1977, 1.
99 *Jornal do Brasil*, April 5, 1977, 3.
100 ARENA 65.08.31 cor/ger.
101 Decree-law no. 1540 of 14 April 1977 regulates the composition and functioning of the Electoral College for electing state governor. Decree-law no. 1541 of 14 April 1977 establishes multiple tickets for elections to senator and mayor. Decree-law no. 1543 of 14 April 1977 regulates election to senator as provided in paragraph 2, article 41, of the Federal Constitution.
102 Passarinho, *Um Híbrido*, 451. "Cariocas rejeitam indiretas," *O Estado de S. Paulo*, April 24, 1977, 5. "Vaga indireta no Senado agita os arenistas de São Paulo," *O Estado de S. Paulo*, April 22, 1977, 5.
103 An. Cam. Dep. 3 (1977): 1843.
104 Kinzo, *Oposição*, 193–195.
105 Ernesto Geisel, *Discursos 1977* (Brasília: Assessoria de Imprensa da Presidência da República, 1978).
106 "Arenistas enchem o salão do Alvorada," *Jornal do Brasil*, December 2, 1977, 3.
107 "Arenistas enchem o salão do Alvorada," *Jornal do Brasil*, December 2, 1977, 3.
108 "Geisel diz que quer acabar com o AI-5," *Jornal do Brasil*, December 2, 1977, 1.
109 "ARENA revela euforia e MDB prefere posição mais discreta," *Jornal do Brasil*, December 2, 1977, 5.
110 An. Cam. Dep. 4 (1978): 7179.
111 Among other measures on the eve of the repeal of the AI-5, other acts pertaining to bans were revoked by Decree no. 82960 of 29 December 1978; the General Commission for Investigations (CGI), created after the AI-5 on 17 December 1968, was also repealed by Decree no. 82961 of 29 December 1978.
112 An. Cam. Dep. 4 (1978): 5663.
113 An. Cam. Dep. 4 (1978): 5663.
114 An. Cam. Dep. 4 (1978): 7178–7179.
115 An. Cam. Dep. 4 (1978): 7178–7179.
116 "Francelino contesta MDB sobre vitória nos centros mais politizados," *Jornal do Brasil*, November 19, 1976, 3.
117 "Marco Maciel acha que eleição indireta é tão democrática como direta," *Jornal do Brasil*, April 5, 1977, 4.
118 "Arenistas fazem movimento a favor de eleição direta," *Jornal do Brasil*, April 6, 1977, 4.
119 An. Cam. Dep. 4 (1978): 506–507.
120 An. Cam. Dep. 4 (1978): 506–507.
121 An. Cam. Dep. 4 (1978): 506–507.
122 An. Cam. Dep. 4 (1978): 506–507.

123 An. Cam. Dep. 4 (1978): 506–507.
124 An. Cam. Dep. 4 (1978): 506–507.
125 An. Cam. Dep. 4 (1978): 506–507.
126 An. Cam. Dep. 4 (1978): 506–507.
127 An. Cam. Dep. 4 (1978): 506–507.
128 ARENA 66.05.26/2 op/cp.
129 ARENA 66.05.26/2 op/cp.
130 ARENA 78.04.08 op/cp.
131 ARENA 78.04.08 op/cp.
132 ARENA 78.04.08 op/cp.
133 ARENA 66.05.26/2 op/cp.
134 ARENA 65.08.31 cor/cg pasta 67.
135 "Congresso rejeita a Emenda de Montoro com abstenções da ARENA e de 5 emedebistas," *Jornal do Brasil*, October 17, 1978, 4. These three senators did not appear for the indirect election to President of the Republic.
136 "Figueiredo eleito oferece a conciliação," *Jornal do Brasil*, October 16, 1978, 1.
137 Fleischer, "Renovação Política".
138 Oscar Niemeyer, "Brasília 79," *Correio Braziliense*, January 4, 1979, 1.
139 *Veja*, January 17, 1979, 12. *Apud*: Ciambarella, A. "Anistia Ampla, Geral e Irrestrita": a Campanha pela Anistia Política no Brasil (1977–1979). (Masters Thesis, Universidade Federal Fluminense, 2002), 112.
140 *Jornal do Brasil*, March 7, 1978, 2.
141 An. Cam. Dep. 5 (1979): 1287.
142 An. Cam. Dep. 5 (1979): 1287.
143 An. Cam. Dep. 1 (1979): 646.
144 "Senadores arenistas vão ampliar projeto de anistia," *Jornal do Brasil*, August 2, 1979, 4.
145 "Projeto de anistia é intocável," *Folha de S. Paulo*, August 22, 1979, 1.
146 Decreto nº 83936, September 6, 1979.
147 Reis, *O eleitorado*. Kinzo, *Oposição*.
148 Luís H. Bahia, Olavo Brasil and César Guimarães, "O perfil social e político da nona legislatura," *Jornal do Brasil*, April 22–24, 1979.
149 Fleischer, "Renovação Política", 82.
150 "Movimento para a extinção dos partidos continua vivo," *Jornal do Brasil*, April 7, 1975, 2.
151 ARENA 66.05.26/2 op/cp pasta 5.
152 ARENA 65.08.31 cor/cg pasta 38.
153 ARENA 65.08.31 cor/cg.
154 ARENA 65.08.31 cor/cg.
155 Kinzo, "Novos Partidos", 238.
156 ARENA 79.05.22 op/rb.
157 ARENA 79.05.22 op/rb.
158 ARENA 79.05.22 op/rb.
159 ARENA 79.05.22 op/rb.
160 ARENA 79.05.22 op/rb.

161 ARENA 79.05.22 op/rb.
162 ARENA 79.05.22 op/rb.
163 ARENA 79.05.22 op/rb.
164 Kinzo, "Novos".
165 ARENA 65.08.31 cor/cg.
166 ARENA 65.08.31 cor/cg.
167 ARENA 65.08.31 cor/cg.
168 Kinzo, *Oposição*.
169 ARENA 66.05.26 el/pe pasta 13.
170 An. Sen. 2 (1975): 278.
171 An. Cam. Dep. 4 (1978): 8391.
172 An. Cam. Dep. 2 (1976): 5204.
173 An. Cam. Dep. 4 (1978): 5663.
174 An. Cam. Dep. 4 (1978): 10823.
175 An. Cam. Dep. 5 (1979): 458.
176 ARENA 78.04.08 op/cp.
177 ARENA 66.05.26/2 op/cp pasta 5.
178 An. Cam. Dep. 4 (1978): 523.
179 ARENA 65.08.31 cor/cg.
180 ARENA 79.05.22 op/rb.
181 ARENA 79.05.22 op/rb.
182 ARENA 79.05.22 op/rb.
183 ARENA 79.05.22 op/rb.
184 ARENA 79.05.22 op/rb.
185 ARENA 79.05.22 op/rb.
186 ARENA 79.05.22 op/rb.
187 ARENA 79.05.22 op/rb.
188 ARENA 79.05.22 op/rb.
189 ARENA 65.08.31 cor/cg pasta 85.
190 ARENA 65.08.31 cor/cg pasta 85.
191 ARENA 65.08.31 cor/cg pasta 85.
192 ARENA 65.08.31 cor/cg pasta 83.
193 Kinzo, *Oposição*, 209.
194 *Estado de Minas Gerais*, January 19, 1980, 2. *Apud*: Maria F. J. Anastasia "O Partido Democrático Social e a Crise da Ordem Autoritária no Brasil" (Master Thesis, Universidade Federal de Minas Gerais, 1985), 39.

6 A History of ARENA in Cartoons

1 On the commemoration of the 30th anniversary of the AI-5, see: Daniel Aarão Reis Filho, "O Ato Institucional n° 5, sociedade e ditadura ao sul do Equador," *Jornal da Tarde*, December 12, 1998, 4.
2 Sebastião Nery, *Folclore Político Brasileiro* (Rio de Janeiro: Politika, 1973). *Folclore Político, 3* (Rio de Janeiro: Record, 1976). *Folclore Político, 4* (Rio de Janeiro: Record, 1982).
3 Millôr Fernandes, "Quando os Políticos se Divertem," in *Folclore Político Brasileiro* ed. Sebastião Nery (Rio de Janeiro: Politika, 1973), 4.

4   Lucia Grinberg, "*Fotopotocas*: Fotografia e Cultura Política no Início dos Anos 1960" (Final paper, Universidade Federal Fluminense, 1993), 15.
5   Alzira A. Abreu, "Jornalistas e Jornalismo Econômico na Transição Democrática," in: *Mídia e Política no Brasil*, ed. Alzira A. Abreu, et al. (Rio de Janeiro: Fundação Getúlio Vargas, 2003).
6   Nery, *Folclore Político 2*.
7   Antônio Callado, "Posseiro Fortuna," in *Aberto para Balanço: 95 Charges do Correio da Manhã, 1965 e 1966* (Rio de Janeiro: Codecri, 1980).
8   Darcy Ribeiro, *Aos Trancos e Barrancos: Como o Brasil Deu no que Deu* (Rio de Janeiro: Guanabara Dois, 1985).
9   Elias T. Saliba, *Raízes do Riso* (São Paulo: Companhia das Letras, 2002).
10 Mônica P. Velloso, *Modernismo no Rio de Janeiro* (Rio de Janeiro: Fundação Getúlio Vargas, 1996), 91.
11 Ziraldo A. Pinto, *1984: 20 anos de Prontidão* (Rio de Janeiro: Record, 1984).
12 Ségonele Le Men, "La Représentation Représentée," in *Daumier et les Parlementaires de 1830 à 1875* (Paris: Assemblée Nationale, 1996).
13 Saliba, *Raízes*.
14 Luís G. Teixeira, *O Traço como Texto* (Rio de Janeiro: Fundação Casa de Ruy Barbosa, 2001), 7.
15 Renato Ortiz, *A Moderna Tradição Brasileira* (São Paulo, Brasiliense, 1991).
16 Antônio Ribeiro de Oliveira Jr., "A Imagem Como Discurso," in *Também com imagem se faz história. Cadernos do ICHF* 32 (1990), 24.
17 Beth Brait, "As Vozes Bakhtinianas e o Diálogo Inconcluso," in: *Dialogismo, Polifonia, Intertextualidade*, ed. Diana L. P. Barros, et al. (São Paulo: Edusp, s/d).
18 Ferreira, *Dicionário Aurélio Eletrônico*.
19 *Koogan/Houaiss.Enciclopédia e Dicionário Ilustrado* (Rio de Janeiro: Edições Delta, 1993), 337.
20 See: Maria P. N. Araújo, *A Utopia Fragmentada* (Rio de Janeiro, Fundação Getúlio Vargas, 2000). Bernando Kucinski, *Jornalistas e Revolucionários* (São Paulo, Scritta, 1991). Maria H. T. Almeida and Luiz Weis, "Carro-zero e Pau-de-arara: o Cotidiano da Oposição de Classe Média ao Regime Militar" in: *História da Vida Privada no Brasil*, ed. Lilian M. Schwartz (São Paulo, Companhia das Letras, 1998) v. 4.
21 Ciro F. S. Cardoso, "Iconografia e História," 1 *Resgate* (1990): 9–17.
22 Jefferson de Andrade and Joel da Silveira, *Um Jornal Assassinado: a Última Batalha do Correio da Manhã* (Rio de Janeiro: José Olympio, 1991). Ainda sobre o *Correio da Manhã*, ver Gil V. V. Oliveira, "Imagens Subversivas: Regime Militar e o Fotojornalismo do *Correio da Manhã*" (Master thesis, Universidade Federal Fluminense, 1996).
23 *Correio da Manhã*, December 9, 1968, 6.
24 *Correio da Manhã*, December 13, 6.
25 *Jornal do Brasil*, November 3, 1969, 7.
26 *Jornal do Brasil*, January 9, 1969, 7.

27 *Jornal do Brasil*, May 2, 1969, 7.
28 *Jornal do Brasil*, January 23, 1969, 7.
29 *Jornal do Brasil*, January 21, 1969, 7.
30 *Jornal do Brasil*, May 9, 1969, 7.
31 *Jornal do Brasil*, January 22, 1969, 7.
32 *Jornal do Brasil*, January 18, 1969, 7.
33 Fernando Pedreira, "O Brasil nas charges de Hilde," in: *O Brasil em charge: 1950–1985*, ed. Hilde Weber (São Paulo: Circo Editorial, 1986).
34 "Hilde Weber", last modified February 7, 2019, http://enciclopedia.itaucultural.org.br/pessoa23325/hilde-weber
35 "Ziraldo: a biografia", last modified February 7, 2019, https://www.ziraldo.com/historia/biograf.htm
36 Gilberto Maringoni, "Forte Fortuna," 26 *Teoria & Debate* (1994).
37 *Correio da Manhã*, May 29, 1965, 6.
38 *Correio da Manhã*, November 2, 1965, 6.
39 *Correio da Manhã*, December 3, 1965, 6.
40 *Correio da Manhã*, December 4, 1965, 6.
41 *Correio da Manhã*, December 21, 1965, 6.
42 *Correio da Manhã*, March 13, 1966, 6.
43 *Correio da Manhã*, November 20, 1966, 6.
44 *Correio da Manhã*, November 20, 1966, 6.
45 *Correio da Manhã*, November 11, 1966, 6.
46 *O Estado de S. Paulo*, November 30, 1974, 4.
47 *O Estado de S. Paulo*, November 18, 1978, 10.
48 *O Estado de S. Paulo*, November 26, 1978, 4.
49 *O Estado de S. Paulo*, November 7, 1979, 2.
50 *Jornal do Brasil*, November 23, 1979.
51 "Morre em São Paulo aos 82 anos o chargista Edmondo Biganti," *O Estado de S. Paulo*, October 1, 2000.
52 "Reações dos líderes partidários," *Diário de Notícias*, October 28, 1965, 4. The last chairman of UDN, Deputy Ernani Sátiro, confirmed that the new party would have a male acronym. *Diário de Notícias*, October 29, 1965, 4.
53 ARENA 65.08.31 cor/cg pasta 78.
54 *O Estado de S. Paulo*, August 1, 1979, 2.
55 *O Estado de S. Paulo*, May 1, 1969, 4.
56 *O Estado de S. Paulo*, May 5, 1969, 4.
57 Pinto, *1964–1984*.
58 Pinto, *1964–1984*.
59 *Jornal do Brasil*, April 15, 1977.
60 *O Estado de S. Paulo*, April 26, 1977, 5.
61 *O Estado de S. Paulo*, April 22, 1977, 5.
62 On the newspaper reviews, see: Kushnir, *Cães*.
63 *Jornal do Brasil*, 14 August, 1979.
64 *O Estado de S. Paulo*, August 31, 1979, 2.
65 *O Estado de S. Paulo*, November 8, 1979, 4.

246 | *Notes to Chapter 6*

66 Kinzo, *Oposição*.
67 *O Estado de S. Paulo*, May 8, 1969, 4.
68 *O Estado de S. Paulo*, May 23, 1969, 4.
69 *O Estado de S. Paulo*, November 5, 1970, 4.
70 *O Estado de S. Paulo*, November 10, 1970, 4.
71 *O Estado de S. Paulo*, June 9, 1971, 4.
72 *O Estado de S. Paulo*, June 6, 1971, 4.
73 There are many examples. The cartoon illustrates the article: "Vaga indireta no Senado agita os arenistas de São Paulo," *O Estado de S. Paulo*, April 22, 1977, 5. Below the cartoon was the article: "Cariocas rejeitam indiretas," *O Estado de S. Paulo*, April 26, 1977, 5. The cartoon illustrates the article: "Portella e Ulysses negam diálogo," *O Estado de S. Paulo*, April 27, 1977, 5.
74 Brait, "As vozes", 26.

References

1. Sources

1.1 Archives
CPDOC/FGV, Rio de Janeiro.
Arquivo do Diretório Nacional da ARENA
Arquivo Juraci Magalhães
Arquivo Nacional, Rio de Janeiro.
Arquivo Luís Viana Filho

1.2 Newspapers
O Correio da Manhã, Rio de Janeiro.
Diário de Notícias, Rio de Janeiro.
O Estado de S. Paulo, São Paulo.
Jornal do Brasil, Rio de Janeiro.
Jornal do Commércio, Rio de Janeiro.
Movimento, São Paulo.
Opinião, São Paulo.
O Pasquim, Rio de Janeiro.

1.3 Official Documents
Anais da Câmara dos Deputados. Brasília: Câmara dos Deputados, 1964–1979.
Anais do Senado Federal. Brasília: Senado Federal, 1964–1979.
Anais da Constituição de 1967. Brasília: Senado Federal, 1967.
Atos complementares 1 a 45. Brasília, Senado Federal, 1969.
Ato Complementar n° 54, de 20 de maio de 1969. Convenções partidárias, eleições de Diretórios e sua composição, recursos para a justiça eleitoral. Brasília, [s.e], 1969.
Castello Branco, Humberto de A. Discursos. 1965. Brasília: Secretaria de Imprensa da Presidência da República, s/d.
Geisel, Ernesto. Discursos. 1977. Vol. IV Brasília: Assessoria de Imprensa da Presidência da República, 1978.
Silva, Arthur C. Pronunciamentos do presidente. Brasília, Secretaria de Imprensa e Divulgação, [s.d]. 2 v.

1.4 Memories and Biographies
Aleixo, José C. B. Pedro Aleixo (1901–1975): Itinerário de um Liberal. Belo Horizonte: Imprensa Oficial, 1986.
Alves, Márcio M. 68 Mudou o Mundo. Rio de Janeiro: Nova Fronteira, 1993.

Borja, Célio. *Célio Borja*. Rio de Janeiro: Fundação Getúlio Vargas/ALERJ, 1999.

Campos, Milton. *Testemunhos e Ensinamentos*. Rio de Janeiro: Livraria José Olympio Editora, 1972.

D'Araújo, Maria C., Gláucio Soares, and Celso Castro. *Visões do Golpe: a Memória Militar sobre 1964*. Rio de Janeiro: Relume-Dumará, 1994.

D'Araújo, Maria C., Gláucio Soares, and Celso Castro. *Os Anos de Chumbo: a Memória Militar sobre a Repressão*. Rio de Janeiro: Relume-Dumará, 1994.

D'Araújo, Maria C., Gláucio Soares, and Celso Castro. *A Volta aos Quartéis: a Memória Militar sobre a Abertura*. Rio de Janeiro: Relume-Dumará, 1995.

D'Araújo, Maria C. and Celso Castro. *Ernesto Geisel*. Rio de Janeiro: Fundação Getúlio Vargas, 1997.

Dulles, John W.F. *Castello Branco, o Presidente Reformador*. Brasília: UnB, 1983.

Dines, Alberto, Florestan Fernandes Jr., and Nelma Salomão. *Histórias do Poder: 100 anos de política no Brasil*. Rio de Janeiro: Editora 34, 2000.

Falcão, Armando. *Tudo a Declarar*. Rio de Janeiro: Nova Fronteira, 1989.

Franco, Afonso A. M. *Planalto (Memórias)*. Rio de Janeiro: José Olympio, 1968.

Krieger, Daniel. *Desde as Missões*. Rio de Janeiro: José Olympio, 1976.

Lima, Diógenes C. *O Homem que Pintava Cavalos Azuis, Djalma Marinho*. Brasília: Câmara dos Deputados; Rio de Janeiro: Forense Universitária, 1982.

Magalhães, Juraci. *Minhas Memórias Provisórias*. Rio de Janeiro: Civilização Brasileira, 1982.

Mello, Jaime P. *A Revolução e o Governo Costa e Silva*. Rio de Janeiro: Guavira, 1979.

Passarinho, Jarbas. *Um Híbrido Fértil*. Rio de Janeiro: Expressão e Cultura, 1996.

Salles, José B. T. *Milton Campos, uma Vocação Liberal*. Belo Horizonte: BDMG Cultural, 1994.

Viana, Francisco. *Daniel Krieger: um Liberal na República*. Brasília: Senado Federal/Dom Quixote, 1982.

Vianna Filho, Luís. *O Governo Castelo Branco*. Rio de Janeiro: José Olympio, 1975.

Vilela, Teotônio. *A Pregação da Liberdade: Andanças de um Liberal*. Porto Alegre: LPM, 1977.

2. Articles, Books, and Theses

Aarão Reis Filho, Daniel. *Ditadura Militar, Esquerdas e Sociedade*. Rio de Janeiro: Jorge Zahar Editor, 2000.

Abreu, Alzira A. "Jornalistas e Jornalismo Econômico na Transição Democrática." In *Mídia e Política no Brasil: Jornalismo e Ficção*, edited by Alzira A. Abreu, Fernando Lattman-Weltman, and Mônica Kornis, 13–74. Rio de Janeiro: Fundação Getúlio Vargas, 2003.

Abreu, Alzira A., Israel Beloch, Sérgio Lamarão, and Fernando Lattman-Weltman. *Dicionário Histórico-Biográfico Brasileiro: 1930–2000*. Rio de Janeiro: Fundação Getúlio Vargas, 2001. CD-ROM.
Almeida, Maria H. T. and Luiz Weis. "Carro-zero e Pau-de-arara: o Cotidiano da Oposição de Classe Média ao Regime Militar." In *História da Vida privada no Brasil: contrastes da intimidade contemporânea*, edited by Fernando Novaes, and Lilian Schwartz, 319–410. São Paulo: Companhia das Letras, 1998. v. 4
Alves, Maria H. M. *Estado e Oposição no Brasil*. Petrópolis: Vozes, 1984.
Anastasia, Maria F. J. O Partido Democrático Social e a Crise da Ordem Autoritária no Brasil (1979–1984). Masters Thesis, Universidade Federal de Minas Gerais, 1985.
Andrade, Carlos D. and Ziraldo A. Pinto. *O Pipoqueiro da Esquina*. São Paulo: Círculo do Livro, 1981.
Andrade, Jefferson de and Joel da Silveira. *Um Jornal Assassinado: a Última Batalha do Correio da Manhã*. Rio de Janeiro: José Olympio, 1991.
Aquino, Maria A. *Censura, Imprensa, Estado Autoritário (1968–1978): o Exercício Cotidiano da Dominação e da Resistência: O Estado de S. Paulo e Movimento*. Bauru: EDUSC, 1999.
Araújo, Maria P. N. *A Utopia Fragmentada*. Rio de Janeiro: Fundação Getúlio Vargas, 2000.
Beiguelman, Paula. *O Pingo do Azeite: a Instauração da Ditadura*. São Paulo: Perspectiva, 1994.
Benevides, Maria V. M. *A UDN e o Udenismo: Ambigüidades do Liberalismo Brasileiro (1945–1965)*. Rio de Janeiro: Paz e Terra, 1981.
Berstein, Serge. "Les Partis." In *Pour une Histoire Politique*, edited by René Rémond, 49–85. Paris: Seuil, 1988.
Berstein, Serge. "L'historien et la culture politique," *Vingtième Siècle: Revue d'Histoire* 35 (1992): 67–77.
Brandão, Anna L. *A Resistência Parlamentar após 1964*. Brasília: Senado Federal, 1984.
Brait, Beth. "As vozes bakhtinianas e o diálogo inconcluso." In *Dialogismo, Polifonia, Intertextualidade*, edited by Diana L. P. Barros and José L. Fiorin, 11–27. São Paulo: Edusp, 2003.
Bourdieu, Pierre. *O Poder Simbólico*. Lisboa: DIFEL, 1989.
Callado, Antonio. "Posseiro Fortuna." In *Aberto para Balanço. 95 Charges do Correio da Manhã, 1965 e 1966*. Rio de Janeiro: Codecri, 1980.
Cardoso, Ciro. F. S. "Iconografia e História." *Resgate* 1 (1990): 9–17.
Castello Branco, Carlos. 3 vols. *Os Militares no Poder*. Rio de Janeiro: Nova Fronteira, 1977–79.
Castro, Celso. "As Apreciações do SNI." In *Dossiê Geisel*, edited by Maria C. D. Araújo and Celso Castro, 41–62. Rio de Janeiro: Fundação Getúlio Vargas, 2002.
Ciambarella, Alessandra. "Anistia Ampla, Geral e Irrestrita: a Campanha pela Anistia Política no Brasil (1977–1979)." Master Thesis, Universidade Federal Fluminense, 2002.

Costa, Fernando J. L. and Lúcia Klein. "Um ano de governo Médici," *Dados*, 9 (1972): 156–221.

Cruz, Sebastião V. and Carlos E. Martins. "De Castello a Figueiredo: uma incursão na pré-história da abertura". In *Sociedade e Política no Brasil pós-64*, edited by Bernardo Sorj and Maria H. T. Almeida, 13–61. São Paulo: Brasiliense, 1983.

D Araújo, Maria C. "Ouvindo os Militares: Imagens de um Poder que se foi." In *Entre-vistas: Abordagens e Usos da História oral*, edited by Marieta de M. Ferreira, 147–172. Rio de Janeiro: Fundação Getúlio Vargas, 1994.

D'Araújo, Maria C. *Sindicatos, Carisma e Poder*. Rio de Janeiro: Fundação Getúlio Vargas, 1996.

Dreifuss, René A. *1964: a Conquista do Estado*. Petrópolis: Vozes, 1981.

Dulci, Otávio S. *A UDN e o Antipopulismo no Brasil*. Belo Horizonte: UFMG, 1986.

Dulles, John F. *Castelo Branco: o Presidente Reformador*. Brasília: UnB, 1983.

Fernandes, Millôr. "Quando os Políticos se Divertem." In *Folclore Político Brasileiro: 350 Histórias da Política Brasileira*, edited by Sebastião Nery, 4. Rio de Janeiro: Politika, 1973.

Ferreira, Aurélio B. de Hollanda. *Dicionário Aurélio Eletrônico*. Rio de Janeiro: Nova Fronteira, 1999. CD-ROM.

Figueiredo, Argelina C. *Democracia ou Reformas?* São Paulo: Paz e Terra, 1993.

Fleischer, David. "Renovação política – Brasil: 1978. Eleições parlamentares sob a égide do pacote de abril," *Revista de Ciência Política*. 2 (1980): 57–82.

Gaspari, Elio. *A Ditadura Envergonhada*. São Paulo: Companhia das Letras, 2002.

Gaspari, Elio. *A Ditadura Derrotada*. São Paulo: Companhia das Letras, 2003.

Ginzburg, Carlo and Carlo Poni, "O Nome e o Como: Troca Desigual e Mercado Historiográfico." In *A Micro-História e Outros Ensaios*, edited by Carlo Ginzburg, 169–178. Lisboa: Difel, 1991.

Gomes, Angela M. C. "Política: História, Ciência, Cultura e etc," *Estudos Históricos* 9 (1996): 59–84.

Gomes, Angela M. C. "Os Paradoxos e os Mitos: o Corporativismo Faz 60 anos," *Análise e Conjuntura* 6 (1991): 49–63.

Hippólito, Lúcia. *De Raposas e Reformistas: o PSD e a Experiência Democrática brasileira, 1945–64*. Rio de Janeiro: Paz e Terra, 1985.

Jenks, Margaret S. *Political Parties in Authoritarian Brazil*. PhD diss., Duke University, 1979.

Kinzo, Maria D. G. *Oposição e Autoritarismo: Gênese e Trajetória do MDB*. São Paulo: IDESP/Vértice, 1988.

Kinzo, Maria D. G. "Novos Partidos: o Início do Debate." In: *Voto de Desconfiança: Eleições e Mudança Política no Brasil, 1970–1979*, edited by Bolívar Lamounier, 217–265. Petrópolis: Vozes, 1980.

Klein, Lucia. "Pós-64: A Nova Ordem Legal e a Redefinição das Bases de Legitimidade." In *Legitimidade e Coação no Brasil Pós-64*, edited by Lucia

Klein and Marcus Figueiredo. Rio de Janeiro: Forense-Universitária, 1978.
Kucinski, Bernardo. *Jornalistas e Revolucionários*. São Paulo: Scritta, 1991.
Kushnir, Beatriz. *Cães de Guarda: Jornalistas e Censores entre o AI-5 e a Constituição de 1988*. São Paulo: Boitempo, 2004.
Lagoa, Ana. *SNI, Como Nasceu, Como Funciona*. São Paulo: Brasiliense, 1983.
Lamounier, Bolívar. "O Brasil Autoritário Revisitado: o Impacto das Eleições Sobre a Abertura." In *Democratizando o Brasil*, edited by Alfred Stepan, 83–134. Rio de Janeiro: Paz e Terra, 1988.
Lamounier, Bolívar. "Representação Política: a Importância de Certos Formalismos." In *Direito, cidadania e participação*, edited by Bolívar Lamounier, Francisco Weffort, and Maria V.M. Benevides, 230–266. São Paulo: T. A. Queiroz, 1981.
Lamounier, Bolívar. *Voto de Desconfiança: Eleições e Mudança Política no Brasil, 1970–1979*. Petrópolis: Vozes, 1980.
Lamounier, Bolívar and Raquel Meneguello. *Partidos políticos e consolidação democrática*. São Paulo: Brasiliense, 1986.
Lavareda, Antônio. *A Democracia nas Urnas*. Rio de Janeiro: Rio Fundo, 1991.
Le Men, Ségolène. "La Représentation Représentée." In *Daumier et les parlementaires de 1830 à 1875*, 25–85. Paris: Assemblée Nationale, 1996.
Lessa, Renato. *A Invenção Republicana*. Rio de Janeiro: Vértice, 1988.
Levi, Giovanni. "Sobre a Micro-História." In *A Escrita da História*, edited by Peter Burke, 133–162. São Paulo: Unesp, 1992.
Machado de Assis, José M. "Casa Velha." In *Machado de Assis: Obra Completa*, 998–1044. Rio de Janeiro: Nova Aguillar, 1997. vol. 2.
Miceli, Sérgio. "Carne e Osso da Elite Política Brasileira Pós-30." In *História Geral da Civilização Brasileira*, edited by Boris Fausto, 557–556. Rio de Janeiro: Bertrand Brasil, 1991. vol.10.
Motta, Marly S. *Grandes Vultos que Honraram o Senado*. Brasília: Senado; Rio de Janeiro: Fundação Getúlio Vargas, 1996.
Motta, Rodrigo P. S. *Em Guarda Contra o Perigo Vermelho: o Anticomunismo no Brasil (1917–1964)*. São Paulo: Perspectiva/FAPESP, 2002.
Motta, Rodrigo P. S. *Introdução à História dos Partidos Políticos Brasileiros*. Belo Horizonte: UFMG, 1999.
Nabuco, Joaquim. *Um Estadista do Império*. Rio de Janeiro: Topbooks, 1997. 5ª Ed.
Neves, Maria M. R. De N. "Ruptura Institucional e Consolidação Política: Mato Grosso e a Hegemonia Arenista." *Dados* 32 (1989): 363–388.
Nora, Pierre. "Gaullistes et Communistes." In *Les Lieux de Mémoire. Les Frances I*, edited by Pierre Nora, 347–393. Paris: Gallimard, 1992.
Offerlé, Michel. *Les Partis Politiques*. Paris: Presses Universitaires de France, 1987.
Oliveira Jr. Antônio Ribeiro de. "A Imagem Como Discurso," In Antonio Ribeiro de Oliveira Jr. and Ciro F. S. Cardoso. *Também com imagem se faz história. Cadernos do ICHF* 32 (1990): 1 – 38.
Oliveira, Gil V. V. "Imagens Subversivas: Regime Militar e o Fotojornalismo do *Correio da Manhã*." Master Thesis, Universidade Federal Fluminense, 1996.

Ortiz, Renato. *A Moderna Tradição Brasileira*. São Paulo: Brasiliense, 1991.
Pandolfi, Dulce. *Camaradas e Companheiros: História e Memória do PCB*. Rio de Janeiro: Relume-Dumará/Fundação Roberto Marinho, 1995.
Pereira, Francelino. *Castelinho: o Reinventor do Jornalismo Político no Brasil*. Brasília: Senado Federal, 2001.
Pinto, Ziraldo A. *1964–1984: 20 Anos de Prontidão*. Rio de Janeiro: Record, 1984.
Power, Timothy J. *The Political Right and Democratization in Brazil*. PhD diss., University of Indiana, 1993.
Reis, Elisa. "O Estado Nacional como Ideologia." In *Processos e Escolhas: Estudos de Sociologia Política*, edited by Elisa Reis. Rio de Janeiro: ContraCapa Livraria, 1998.
Reis, Fábio W. "O eleitorado, os partidos e o regime autoritário brasileiro." In *Sociedade e Política no Brasil Pós-64*, edited by Bernardo Sorj and Maria H. T. Almeida, 91–131. São Paulo: Brasiliense, 1983.
Reis, Fábio W. *Política e Racionalidade: Problemas de Teoria e Método de uma Sociologia Crítica da Política*. Belo Horizonte: UFMG, 2000. 2ª ed. revista e atualizada.
Ribeiro, Darcy. *Aos Trancos e Barrancos: Como o Brasil Deu no que Deu*. Rio de Janeiro: Guanabara Dois, 1985.
Rodrigues, Nelson. *A Cabra Vadia*. São Paulo: Companhia das Letras, 1995.
Rouquié, Alain. "Desmilitarización y la Institucionalización de los Sistemas Politicos Dominados por los Militares en América Latina." In *Transições do Regime Autoritário: Primeiras Conclusões*, edited by Guillermo O'Donnell and Phillipe Schmitter, 171–211. São Paulo, Vértice, 1988.
Rousso, Henry. "O Arquivo ou o Indício de uma Falta," *Estudos Históricos* 9 (1996): 85 – 91.
Rousso, Henry. "Pour une Histoire de la Mémoire Collective: l'après-Vichy." In *Histoire Politique et Sciences Sociales*, edited by Denis Peschanski, Michael Pollak, and Henry Rousso, 244–264. Brussels: Éditions Complexe, 1991.
Saliba, Elias T. *Raízes do Riso*. São Paulo: Companhia das Letras, 2002.
Santos, Wanderley G. *Ordem Burguesa e Liberalismo Político*. São Paulo: Duas Cidades, 1978.
Santos, Wanderley G. *Regresso*. Rio de Janeiro: Opera Nostra, 1994.
Schmitter, Philippe. "The *Portugalization* of Brazil?" In *Authoritarian Brazil*, edited by Alfred Stepan, 179–232. New Haven: Yale University Press, 1973.
Serbin, Kenneth P. *Diálogos na Sombra: Bispos e Militares, Tortura e Justiça Social na Ditadura*. São Paulo: Companhia das Letras, 2001.
Souza, Maria C. C. *Estado e Partidos Políticos no Brasil*. 1930–1964. São Paulo: Alfa-Ômega, 1990.
Teixeira, Luís G. S. *O Traço como Texto: a História da Charge no Rio de Janeiro de 1860 a 1930*. Rio de Janeiro: Fundação Casa de Rui Barbosa, 2001.
Tella, Torcuato S. di. *Historia de los Partidos Políticos en América Latina, siglo XX*. Buenos Aires: Fondo de Cultura Económica, 1994.

Velasco e Cruz, Sebastião and Carlos E. Martins. "De Castello a Figueiredo: uma incursão na pré-história da 'abertura'" In *Sociedade e Política no Brasil Pós-64*, edited by Bernardo Sorj and Maria H. T. Almeida, 8–90. São Paulo: Brasiliense, 1983.

Velloso, Mônica P. *Modernismo no Rio de Janeiro*. Rio de Janeiro: Fundação Getúlio Vargas, 1996.

Weber, Max. *El Politico y el Cientifico*. Madri: Alianza, 1996.

Weffort, Francisco. "Democracia e Movimento Operário: Algumas Questões para a História do Período 1945–1964." *Revista de Cultura Contemporânea* 2 (1979): 3–11.

Index

1964 movement
  Adauto Cardoso's support for, 76
  Aliança Renovadora Nacional (ARENA), 1, 8, 12, 67, 71, 131
  Brazilian literature on, 14
  Brazilian society support for, 18, 71–2
  O Estado de S. Paulo newspaper, 194
  impact on the political field, 28
  Mexico's PRI comparison, 10
  military role, 16, 67–8
  Partido Social Democrático, 9
  purges (Castello Branco government 1964), 31
  referred to as a revolution, 71
  torture denials, 135

Aarão Reis Filho, Daniel, 14–15
abertura see détente (*abertura*)
Abi-Ackel, Ibrahim, 184
Abramo, Cláudio, 195
Abreu, Alzira A., 12
AC-4 (1965), 40–1, 45, 198–9
AC-26 (1965), 41
AC-54 (1969), 106–7, 108, 119–20, 192, 200, 209–10
Acre State Legislature, 154
Agência Nacional, 99
Agostini, Angelo, 187
Agripino, João, 35
AI-2 *see* Institutional Act No. 2 (AI-2) (1965)
AI-5 *see* Institutional Act No. 5 (AI-5) (1968)
Albuquerque, Theódulo de, 46, 126, 166
Aleixo, Pedro
  Castello Branco's presidential term, 35
  Constitution (1967) drafting, 80, 81, 109
  criticism of military intervention in politics, 142
  as former *Udenista*, 30, 43, 64
  indirect elections, 74–5
  leaves ARENA, 138, 140
  liberal exit strategy for the dictatorship, 138
  Manifesto dos Mineiros, 75
  military contacts, 30
  military distrust of, 109
  new government party, 43
  Partido Democrático Republicano, 140
  prevented from taking office as President, 109, 116, 138, 140
  as UDN liberal, 64
Aliança Renovadora Nacional (ARENA), 217
  1964 movement, 1, 8, 12, 67, 71, 131
  adesismo, 2, 8, 63, 183
  amnesty, 172
  autonomy, 16, 102, 106, 120, 121, 130, 131
  bylaws, 44, 45, 120, 121
  caricatures in alternative press, 192
  cartoon portrayal as a woman, 185, 201, 202, 203, 205–6, 211, 212
  Castello Branco government purges (1966), 76
  clichés on, 6
  Complementary Act No. 54, 107
  Congress office meetings, 117–20
  Congressional debates, 16, 86–7, 95, 146
  Congressional prerogatives, 142
  Constitution (1967) drafting, 80, 82–3, 84, 85–8
  Costa e Silva government purges (1968–1969), 110, *111*
  creation of (1965), 10, 42, 44–65, 203
  defunct parties members, 42, 45, 46
  derisory image of, 7, 16, 17–18, 65, 71, 185
  détente period, 3, 146–8
  as dictatorship scapegoat, 214–15
  "easement" ("*distensão*") project, 146
  elections (1966), 12
  elections (1970), 11, *12*

Index | 255

elections (1974), *12*, 146, 147, 148–51, 173, 201
elections (1978), *12*, 171
extinguished (1979), 8, 147, 184, 192, 201–2
as a feminine name, 203
founding of, 71–5
Geisel's criticism of, 151–2
as "government party", 16, 71, 179–80, 181–3
historiography of, 11–18
"hooded ones", 140, 141
inaugural session (1966), 71
indirect elections, 82–3, 122–3, 125–6, 127–30, 149–50, 154, 167, 170
Institutional Act No. 5 (AI-5), 3, 97, 103, 152, 209, 210
Joint Committee on Constitutional Reform, 80, 81–2
Krieger's resignation as party chairman, 91–2, 201
leadership, 131–8
liberalizing the dictatorship, 146
Márcio Moreira Alves affair, 16–17, 96–7, 98, 102, 105–6, 109, 155, 205
membership diversity, 3, 13, 71, 95, 123, 130, 170, 172, 174, 215
membership political experience, 13–14, 28, 47, 55
memories of, 6–7, 8–10, 189, 214–15
military distrust of, 107
multiple tickets, 12, 41, 45–6, 61, 91–2, 98, 107
municipal committees, 10, 66, 68, 69, 124
municipal conventions, 125, 126
municipal executive boards, 45, 68
municipalities autonomy, 29, 88–90
National Committee candidates, 55–60
National Committee established, 44
National Committee members, 47, *48–54*, 55, 55, 60, *112–13*
National Committee's political reorientation, 113–14
National Convention (1966), 72–4
National Convention (1968), 93–4, 113–14, 161
National Convention (1969), 113–14
National Convention (1972), 125, 126
National Convention (1975), 154–7, 180
National Convention (1978), 168–9, 180
national conventions, 16, 45

National Executive Board, 44, 45, 46, 47, 93, 108, 109, *112*
National Security Act, 167
negative image of, 8, 13–14, 156, 202, 214–15
newspaper reports, 8–9, 10, 103, 104, 105–6
objectives of, 44–5
organizational structure, 107
party loyalty issue, 16, 118–22, 141, 160–1, 211
party reform, 173–7, 184, 201–2
party size, 63
party's founders, 46–7
personification as cartoon characters, 202–4
political capital, 9, 27, 39, 115–16, 156, 170, 184
political cartoons, 10, 185, 189, 190, 191–2, 196–213, *199*, *200*, *204*, *209*, *210*
political disputes, 60, 170
political reforms, 160–71
political representativeness, 1–2, 8, 12, 14, 16, 207–8
professional politicians, 47, 55, 73–4, 92, 183
PSD association, 61–2, 64–5, 72, 176
as a "pseudo-party", 13
purging of Wilson Campos, 154
"redeemed ones", 140
relations with Castello Branco government, 63–4
relations with Costa e Silva government, 91–101, 102–9, 113–14
relations with ESG, 132
relations with Geisel government, 145, 146–7, 155–8, 180
relations with Médici government, 120, 125, 126, 157
reorganization (1969–1973), 107–10
ridicule of, 6, 18, 106, 202, 213, 215
rifts, 102, 103–4
Rio Branco mayor indirect elections, 154
self-determination issue, 155–6
shutting down threat, 103–5, 107
state committees, 10, 65, 66, 69, 110, 124
state conventions, 45, 124, 125, 126, 169
state executive boards, 45, 68
state party committees' leadership, 122–3

Aliança Renovadora Nacional (ARENA) *(continued)*
  subordination and subservience image, 8, 11, 151, 154–6, 180, 205
  as "Yes Sir! Party", 12–13, 14–15, 16, 151, 178–84
  see also Arenistas
Aliança Renovadora Nacional (ARENA)
  National Committee archives, 65–9
  ARENA documents not filed, 103
  congressional caucus meetings, 145
  "Constitutional Affairs" series, 69
  "Correspondence" series, 66–8
  Costa e Silva government purges (1968–1969), 110
  "Elections" series, 68
  membership in the extinct parties, 28
  Organic Law on Political Parties (1971), 118–21, 124–5
  "Party Organization" series, 68–9
  as source material, 3, 196
Almeida, Tabosa de, 80
Almeira, Cardoso de, 136–7
Álvares, Élcio, 125, 128, 136
Alves, Hermano, 193
Alves, Márcio Moreira, 95–8
  Aliança Renovadora Nacional, 16–17, 96–7, 98, 102, 105–6, 109, 155, 205
  Arenistas, 16–17, 97, 98, 103, 108, 199
  O Estado de S. Paulo editorial, 194
  Movimento Democrático Brasileiro, 96–7, 98
  political cartoons, 193, 205
  press reports, 97, 105–6, 194
  pretext for decreeing the AI-5, 97, 100, 102, 109–10
Alves, Maria Helena Moreira, 21
Amaral Neto, 32, 174
Amazonas, 156
Anais da Câmara dos Deputados, 4, 178
Anais do Congresso Nacional, 143
Anais do Senado, 4, 178
Anaisda Constituição de 1967, 4
Andrade, Auro de Moura, 76, 79, 80, 87
Andrade, Carlos Drummond de, 187
Andrade, Doutel de, 32
anti-communism, 67, 138
Aragão, Moniz de, 142
Aragarças, military rebellion, 30
Araújo, Henrique Fonseca de, 163
Arbage, Jorge, 166–7, 172
ARENA *see Aliança Renovadora Nacional* (ARENA)

Arenistas
  "1964 revolution" supporters, 101, 108
  Adauto Cardoso's resignation, 139
  alternative press interviews, 192
  amnesty, 172
  anti-communism, 135
  ARENA as "government party", 181–3
  ARENA shutting down threat, 104–5
  ARENA subordination to the government, 154–6, 180
  ARENA as "Yes Sir! Party", 178, 179–83
  censorship, 136–8
  Complementary Act No. 54, 107
  Congress floor emptying strategy, 76, 91, 98, 215
  Congressional debates, 16, 86–7, 95, 152
  Congressional prerogatives, 143–5
  Constitution (1967) drafting, 85–8
  Constitutional Amendment No. 1 (1969), 115, 116
  "Correspondence" to National Committee, 66–8
  Costa e Silva government purges (1968–1969), 110
  criticism of *Emedebistas*, 134
  criticism of liberalism, 133–4
  criticism of military intervention in politics, 141–2
  defence of the government, 70
  elections (1974), 147, 148, 150, 157
  electoral legislation, 102, 145, 170
  Falcão Act (1976), 159
  Freire's speech (1966), 72–3
  Geisel government purges, 153, 158
  governor disputes, 149
  images of the "monster" and phantoms, 147
  indirect elections, 73, 128, 154, 167, 170
  ineligibilities decree, 115, 116
  Institutional Act No. 5 (AI-5), 104, 133, 134, 152, 154, 165–6
  liberalizing measures adoption, 182
  Márcio Moreira Alves affair, 16–17, 97, 98, 103, 108, 199
  multiple tickets, 98, 107
  municipal elections (1976), 158–9, 160, 167
  National Congress recess, 164–5
  Organic Law on Political Parties (1971), 121

Partido Democrático Republicano, 140
party loyalty issue, 122, 160–1
party reform, 173–4, 175–7
PDS members, 184
political cartoons, 206, 208
as the political class, 23, 110, 125
political culture of, 66
political reforms, 160–1, 164–6, 167, 169, 170–1
"politics of the governors", 123
purging of Wilson Campos, 154
representative democracy, 44, 130, 183
as a "revolutionary", 67
societal distrust of, 26
as subservient latecomers, 8
"subversion" threat, 133, 134, 137
Superior Electoral Court petition, 148
torture issue, 135
see also Aliança Renovadora Nacional (ARENA)
Arinos, Anah, 35
Arinos de Mello Franco, Afonso
 Castello Branco's presidential term, 35
 Constitution (1967) drafting, 78, 80–1, 82–3, 86, 87
 military contacts, 30
 as UDN legal scholar, 30
 as UDN liberal, 2, 35, 64, 233*n*
Armed Forces *see* military
Arnon (cartoonist), 193, 198
Arraes, Miguel, 67
Attorney General, 138–9, 167

Bacelar, Rui, 121
Bahia State Union of Mayors, 127
Bakhtin, Mikhail, 190
Baleeiro, Aliomar
 Castello Branco government purges (1964), 33
 dissident voice of, 3
 elections (1965), 36–7
 Institutional Act No. 5 (AI-5), 142
 liberal exit strategy for the dictatorship, 138
 support for Castello Branco government, 75–6
 as UDN legal scholar, 30
Barbosa, Antônio Fernandes, 46–7
Barbosa, Ruy, 136, 138, 142, 161, 240*n*
Barros, Adhemar de, 31–2, 63, 104, 184, 203
Belo Horizonte, 104
Beltrão, Hélio, 93
Bernardes Filho, Arthur, 47

Bernardes, Juarez, 128–9
Berstein, Serge, 19
Biganti, Edmondo, 194–5, 197, 199, 199, 200, 203, 205, 209
"*bigorrilhos*", 35
Bley, João Punaro, 47
Bonifácio, José, 160, 164, 165, 172
Borja, Célio, 147, 148, 150, 153, 158
Bornhausen family, 60
Bourdieu, Pierre, 24, 25, 26, 27, 60
Braga, Luiz, 124–5
Braga, Nei, 121, 234*n*
Brait, Beth, 212
Brant, Fernando, 156
Brasília
 demonstrations, 171, 173
 Kubitschek's death, 159–60
 Niemeyer's architectural projects, 171
Brasília University, 95
Brazilian Committee for Amnesty, 172
Brazilian Communist Party (PCB), 22, 30, 120, 171, 202
Brazilian Democratic Movement (MDB) *see Movimento Democrático Brasileiro* (MDB)
Brazilian Empire (1822–1889), 18–19
Brazilian Institute of Social and Economic Analyses (IBASE), 188
Brazilian Labour Party *see Partido Trabalhista Brasileiro* (PTB)
"Brazilian miracle", 103, 129, 138
Brazilian National Congress *see* National Congress
Brazilian Revolution (1930), 18, 86
Brazilian Socialist Party (PSB), 38
Brito, Oliveira, 32, 80
Brizola, Leonel, 177
Broad Front (*Frente Ampla*), 77
Brossard, Paulo, 165, 178–9
Buarque, Sérgio, 18
bureaucratic power, 90
Buzaid, Alfredo, 114, 124

Caderno B newspaper section, 193
Callado, Antônio, 187
Calmon, Pedro, 32
Camões, Luís de, 186
Campos, Aluísio, 146, 155–6
Campos, Francisco, 78
Campos, Milton
 ARENA identity, 157
 ARENA National Committee member, 47
 Castello Branco government purges (1964), 34
 Constitution (1967) drafting, 78

258 | Index

Constitutional Amendment No. 1 (1969), 115
criticism of military intervention in politics, 142
Institutional Act No. 2 (AI-2), 37
Institutional Act No. 5 (AI-5), 116
institutional political issue, 23
liberal exit strategy for the dictatorship, 138
marginalization of the "political class", 116
as Minister of Justice, 34, 37
party–government relations, 116, 117
as pro-regime politician, 23
resignation as Minister of Justice, 37, 161
as UDN liberal, 2, 35, 64, 115
Campos, Siqueira, 124
Campos, Wilson, 153–4
Capanema, Gustavo, 9, 34, 47, 55, 64
Cardoso, Adauto Lúcio
1964 movement supporter, 76
Castello Branco government posts, 75
Castello Branco government purges (1964), 31
Castello Branco government purges (1966), 76–8
Castello Branco government supporter, 75–6
Constitution (1967) drafting, 79, 80, 87–8
coup d'état (1964), 30–1
criticism of military intervention in politics, 142
death of (1974), 140
democracy in Brazil, 75, 76
indirect elections, 76
Institutional Act No. 2 (AI-2) (1965), 75, 76, 79
joins ARENA, 75
liberal exit strategy for the dictatorship, 138
military contacts, 30
new government party, 43
PDR affiliation, 140
removal from Congress, 77, 87–8
resignation as president of the Chamber (1966), 77, 139–40, 158
resignation as Supreme Court justice (1971), 138–40
as Supreme Court justice (1967–1971), 77–8, 87–8, 138–9
as UDN legal scholar, 30, 75, 78
as UDN liberal, 2, 64
Careta magazine, 187
La Caricature magazine, 189

caricatures, 187–8, 189, 190, 191, 195, 205
Carlos, J., 187
Carneiro, Levi, 78
Carneiro, Nelson, 115, 151
Caruso, Chico, 193
Carvalho, Aloísio de, 32, 115, 142
Carvalho Neto, Raimundo Barbosa de, 104
Carvalho, Último de, 71–2, 83
Castello Branco, Carlos (journalist)
Castello Branco government purges (1964), 34
Castello Branco's presidential term, 35
Constitution (1967) drafting, 83, 86, 87
elections (1974), 149–50
ineligibilities decree, 116
Krieger's resignation, 92
Mexico's PRI, 10
municipal autonomy, 90
political party reform (1964–1966), 19, 36
"politics of the governors", 123
Castello Branco government (1964–1967)
Congressional support for, 73, 76
Constitution (1967) drafting, 77–88, 109
elections, 64, 69
formation of a new party system, 40–3
Institutional Act No. 2 (AI-2), 18, 37–9, 79
National Congress recess (1966), 77
new government party, 43, 63
party reform, 36–40
party–government relations, 63–4
political purges (1964), 31–4, 93–4, 99
political purges (1966), 75–8, 79, 93–4, 200
Presidential term extension, 34–6
state government elections (1965), 36–7, 42–3
Supreme Court (STF) position, 77–8, 87–8, 138–9, 142
Udenistas in government, 30
Castello Branco, Humberto de Alencar (President)
ARENA's National Executive Board, 46
political contacts with *Udenistas*, 30
as self-proclaimed *Udenista*, 30
views on Adauto, 77
Castro, Celso, 15
Catholic Church, 102–3
Caulos (cartoonist), 187

Cavalcanti, Luiz, 153, 157
Cavalcanti, Temístocles, 78, 109
CCJ (Committee of Constitution and Justice), 96, 109
censorship, 15, 102, 136–8, 140, 186–7, 193, 194
Cerdeira, Arnaldo, 94, 104, 105, 110
CGI (*Comissão Geral de Investigações*), 34, 105
La Charivari magazine, 189
Chaves, Aureliano, 168
Christian Democratic Party *see Partido Democrata Cristão* (PDC)
Cícero, Paulino, 158
A Cigarra magazine, 195
Circo Editorial publishing house, 188
Claudius (cartoonist), 193
Clube Militar, 31
Codecri publishing house, 188
Coelho, Levindo Ozanam, 60
Coelho, Lopo, 106
Collares, Alceu, 136
Comando Revolucionário, 33
comic strips, 186, 190, 191, 202, 203
Comissão Geral de Investigações (CGI), 34, 105
Committee of Constitution and Justice (CCJ), 96, 109
Communist Putsch (*Intentona Comunista*), 135
Complementary Act No. 4 (AC-4) (1965), 40–1, 45, 198–9
Complementary Act No. 26 (AC-26) (1965), 41
Complementary Act No. 54 (AC-54) (1969), 106–7, 108, 119–20, 192, 200, 209–10
Conselho de Segurança Nacional (National Security Council), 109, 110
Constitutional Amendment No. 1, 114, 115–16, 118, 211
Constitutional Amendment No. 2, 127–9, 143
Constitutional Amendment No. 7, 165, 207
Constitutional Amendment No. 8, 165, 207
Constitutional Amendment No. 9, 35, 81
Constitutional Amendment No. 11, 166, 171, 175
Cordeiro de Farias, Osvaldo, 30
Corrêa, Oscar Dias, 32, 39, 84–5
Corrêa, Villas-Boas, 6, 8–9
Correio da Manhã newspaper

Márcio Moreira Alves affair, 97, 105
political cartoons, 191, 193, 195, 198, 200
Costa e Silva, Arthur da
ARENA reorganization, 107–8
ARENA shutting down threat, 107
ARENA support, 104
illness and death, 109
Krieger's reinstatement as ARENA chairman, 94
political cartoons, 193
Presidential candidacy, 73
Presidential indirect election, 73–5, 76, 81–3
relations with Krieger, 91, 92
speeches on ARENA, 16–17
UDN contacts, 30
Costa e Silva government (1967–1969)
disregard for politicians, 99–100
Institutional Act No. 5 (AI-5), 2, 29, 67, 99–100, 102, 103, 109–10
local government autonomy, 88–91
Márcio Moreira Alves affair, 16–17, 95–6, 98, 193
National Congress recess (1968–1969), 67, 97, 100, 105, 106, 110, 114, 206, 208
party–government relations (1966–1968), 91–101, 102–9, 113–14
political class, 99–100, 102, 108, 110
purges (1968–1969), 95–9, 110, *111*, 114
Costa, Octávio, 30
coup d'état (1964), 29, 30–1, 70–1, 196, 198
Coutinho, Florim, 143, 168
Couto Filho, Miguel, 46
O Cruzeiro magazine, 195
Cunha, Osmar, 89

Dantas, Santiago, 32
Dantas, Tourinho, 127
D'Araújo, Maria C., 15–16
Daumier, Honoré, 189, 190
decreto-lei (decree law), 84–5, 86
Delfim Netto, Antônio, 100
democracy
Brazilian society's view of, 1, 18
Cardoso's views on, 75, 76
Freyre's critique of, 133
political parties instrumental concept of, 21, 22
Second Brazilian Republic (1946–1964), 22
social memory, 14
see also representative democracy

260 | Index

Democratic Social Party (PSD) *see*
    Partido Social Democrático (PSD)
Denys, Odilo, 30
Derzi, Saldanha, 89
détente (*abertura*)
    access to information, 148
    Aliança Renovadora Nacional
        (ARENA), 3, 146–8
    amnesty bill, 171–3
    enabling of, 22
    Geisel's proposals, 144, 152, 156, 161
    images of the "monster" and phantoms, 147
    party reform, 171, 173–7
    studies of, 1, 14, 146–7
Dicionário Aurélio, 191
dictatorship (1964–1985)
    armed resistance, 14, 102, 131
    historiography of, 27–8
    Kinzo's studies, 14, 23
    military's view of, 15–16
    oppositionist press, 15
    political associations, 9
    rebellion against (1968), 15
    relations with Brazilian society, 14–18
    representative system, 14
    research studies on, 11
    "simplified architecture" of, 14, 18
    social memory of, 14–16, 18, 65, 185
    specificities of, 23
    studies on, 14–18, 22–3
    subordination and subservience to, 8, 11, 151, 154–6, 180, 205
    see also Castello Branco government (1964–1967); Costa e Silva government (1967–1969); coup d'état (1964); Figueiredo government (1979–1985); Geisel government (1974–1979); Médici government (1969–1974); military
Dines, Alberto, 98
Dulci, Otávio S., 11, 226*n*
Dutra, Eurico Gaspar, 9, 30, 46
Dutra, Milton, 32, 33

"economic miracle", 103, 129, 138
Edígio, Paulo, 152, 154
Editora Inúbia publishing house, 140
elections (municipal), 12, 90, 158–9, 160, 167
elections (National Congress 1966), *12*, 43, 192
elections (National Congress 1970), 11, *12*, 192, 210

elections (National Congress 1974)
    ARENA defeat, *12*, 146, 147, 148–51, 173, 201
    Chamber of Deputies, 11, *12*
    MDB victory in Senate, 11, *12*, 14, 148–9, 150–1, 201, 202
    political cartoons, 192, 201
elections (National Congress 1978), *12*, 167, 171, 192, 201
elections (state government 1965), 36–7, 42, 198
electoral legislation, 41, 45, 102, 107, 145, 165, 170
Emedebistas
    ARENA leadership criticism of, 134
    ARENA as "Yes Sir! Party", 178
    ARENA's subordination to government, 154
    censorship, 136
    Congressional debates, 16, 95
    Geisel government purges, 153
    indirect elections for state governments, 128
    Judiciary reform bill, 163
    party loyalty issue, 160
    societal distrust of, 26
    see also Movimento Democrático Brasileiro (MDB)
Ermírio de Moraes, José, 32
Escola Superior de Guerra (ESG), 30, 131, 132, 183–4
Espírito Santo, 47, 60, 156
O Estado de S. Paulo newspaper
    Adauto Cardoso's resignation, 139
    ARENA as "government party", 179
    censorship, 136, 137, 194
    formation of the new parties, 41
    Márcio Moreira Alves affair, 194
    political cartoons, 185, 191, 194–5, 196, *197*, *198*, *199*, 200, *200*, 202, *204*, *205*, *209*, *210*, 211
    Villas-Boas Corrêa's articles, 8–9
Estado Novo dictatorship (1937–1945), 9, 18, 19, 75

Fadul, Wilson, 32
Fagundes, Aldo, 136
Fagundes, Seabra, 78
Falcão Act (1976), 159, 165
Falcão, Armando, 158, 163
Faraco, Daniel, 115, 117, 128, 136, 137, 138
Farias, Cordeiro de, 142
Fascist Party, 120
Feliciano, Antônio, 46, 80
Fernandes, Célio, 166, 179, 180

Fernandes, Millôr, 186, 187
Ferraz, José Cândido, 39
Ferreira, Aurélio B. de Hollanda, 191
Ferreira, Benedito, 114
Ferreira, Heitor, 240*n*
Figueiredo, Argelina, 21
Figueiredo, Argemiro de, 92
Figueiredo government (1979–1985)
  amnesty, 171–3
  liberalization policy, 171
  party reform, 171, 173–7, 201
  party reform law, 183–4
  party–government relations, 146
Figueiredo, João Baptista, 168, 171, 208
Figueiredo, Petrônio, 115
Filho, Accioly, 80, 81–2, 83, 162–3, 170
Filho, Santos, 179
First Republic (1889–1930), 20, 22, 64, 122, 187
Fleischer, David, 122–3, 171, 174
Folha de Minas newspaper, 195
Folha de S. Paulo newspaper, 8, 95
Fon-Fon magazine, 187
Fonseca, Deodoro da, 161
Fonseca, José Carlos, 119
Fontes, Geremias, 104
Fortes, José Francisco Bias, 60
Fortuna (cartoonist), 187–8, 193, 195–6, 198, 200
Fotopotocas magazine, 186
Franco, Augusto do Prado, 60
Franco, Walter Prado, 60
Freire, Geraldo
  ARENA convention (1966), 72–3
  ARENA convention (1969), 114
  ARENA leader in Chamber of Deputies, 96, 115, 141
  ARENA shutting down threat, 104
  censorship, 137, 138
  Florim Coutinho slander case, 143
  government intervention in the party system, 72–3
  Institutional Act No. 5 (AI-5), 137, 143–4, 152
  liberal democracy, 137
  Márcio Moreira Alves affair, 96, 103
Frente Ampla (Broad Front), 77
Frente Parlamentar Nacionalista, 32
Freyre, Gilberto, 132–3
Furtado, Alencar, 136, 153
Furtado, Celso, 168

Gallotti, Luiz, 139
Gato, Marcelo, 153, 157

Geisel, Ernesto
  "ARENA is government" speech (1975), 157
  authoritarian personality, 153
  criticism of ARENA, 151–2
  inaugural speech, 158
  Kubitschek's death, 159
  MDB's election victory (1974), 149
  political cartoons, 204, 207
  Presidential inauguration (1974), 107
  purging of Wilson Campos, 153–4
  speeches on ARENA, 16
  Vianna Filho's book on Castello Branco government, 240*n*
  views on the "political class", 151
Geisel government (1974–1979)
  "April package", 165, 171, 192, 207
  Constitutional Amendment No. 11, 166, 171
  disregard for politicians, 151
  elections (1974), 11, *12*, 14, 146, 147, 148–51
  indirect elections, 149–50, 154, 170
  Institutional Act No. 5 (AI-5), 152, 154, 157–8, 160, 165–6, 167, 171, 172
  Judiciary reform bill, 162–3
  National Congress recess (1977), 152, 160, 162, 163–5, 167
  party loyalty issue, 152, 160–1
  party reform, 169, 201
  party–government relations, 145, 146–7, 155–8, 180
  political reforms, 144, 146, 148, 151–2, 156, 160–71
  purges, 153–4, 157–8
General Inquiries Commission (CGI), 34, 105
Getulismo, 61, 62, 177
O Globo, 17
Goiânia City Council, 174–5
Gomes, Eduardo, 30
Gomes, Severo, 168, 169
Gonçalves, Wilson, 46, 80, 84
Goulart, João, 14, 29, 30–1, 42, 71, 72
Grunewald, José Lino, 193
Guanabara, 35, 77
Guanabara State Legislature, 104
Guiomard, José, 92
Guizzo, Martinho Herculano, 178

Heck, Silvio, 30
Henfil (cartoonist), 187, 188, 193
Hippólito, Lúcia, 20–1
"hooded ones", 140, 141
Horta, Pedroso, 135

262 | Index

Human Rights Council, 33
Hungria, Nelson, 142

IBASE (Brazilian Institute of Social and Economic Analyses), 188
Informe JB, 61, 106
Institutional Act No. 2 (AI-2) (1965)
  Adauto Cardoso's support for, 75, 76, 79
  Castello Branco government, 18, 37–9, 79
  elimination of direct elections, 41
  elimination of existing parties, 19, 20–1, 28, 45, 76, 192
  indirect elections for state governors, 167
  party acronyms banned, 176, 177
  political cartoons, 192, 196, 198–9
  revoking of articles 14 and 15, 79
  União Democrática Nacional, 37, 38
Institutional Act No. 5 (AI-5) (1968)
  Aliança Renovadora Nacional, 3, 97, 103, 152, 209, 210
  Arenistas, 104, 133, 134, 152, 154, 165–6
  Baleeiro's condemnation of, 142
  Bonifácio's defence of, 165
  Costa e Silva government, 2, 29, 67, 99–100, 102, 103, 109–10
  Costa e Silva government purges (1968–1969), 110
  Freire's speeches, 137, 143–4, 152
  Geisel government, 152, 154, 157–8, 160, 165–6, 167, 171, 172
  literature on, 14
  Márcio Moreira Alves affair, 97, 100, 102, 109–10
  Milton Campos's opposition, 116
  Movimento Democrático Brasileiro, 152, 209, 210
  National Congress revocation bill, 146
  political cartoons, 192, 193, 199, 209, 210
  Ramos's description as a "punitive recess", 126
  repeal of, 165–6, 167, 171, 172
  Rio Branco mayor indirect elections, 154
Institutional Revolutionary Party of Mexico, 10, 221*n*
Intentona Comunista (Communist Putsch), 135
intertextuality, 190, 191

Jacareacanga, military rebellion, 30
Jaguar (cartoonist), 187

Jenks, Margaret, 123
Jorge, J.G. de Araújo, 143
Jornal da Tarde, 195
Jornal do Brasil newspaper
  Castello Branco government purges (1964), 31
  Castello Branco government purges (1966), 75
  Castello Branco's column, 149
  Constitution (1967) drafting, 86
  Márcio Moreira Alves affair, 97
  marginalization of Brazil's politicians, 141
  National Congress recess, 164
  national movement plans, 43
  new government party, 43
  party reform, 174
  political cartoons, 191, 192–4, 195, 208
  purging of Wilson Campos, 153
  Villas-Boas Corrêa's articles, 8–9
Jornal do Commércio, 43, 131
journalism *see* newspapers
Julião, Francisco, 67
Jurema, Abelardo, 32

Kalume, Jorge, 158–9, 171
Kinzo, Maria Dalva Gil
  Brazilian dictatorship, 14, 23
  Brazil's political regime (1945–1964), 90–1
  Falcão Act (1976), 159
  gubernatorial elections, 169
  party reform, 175
  principal characteristic of ARENA and MDB, 13
  two-party system, 13, 42, 46, 98
Klassman, Marcos, 153
Klein, Lúcia, 13, 148
Konder family, 60
Krieger, Daniel
  as ARENA chairman, 46, 55, 91
  ARENA chairman re-election, 93, 94
  ARENA chairman resignation, 91–2, 201
  ARENA convention (1966), 73
  ARENA convention (1968), 113–14
  Castello Branco's presidential term, 35
  Constitution (1967) drafting, 80, 81, 87, 88, 91
  criticism of military intervention in politics, 142
  détente, 147
  dissident voice of, 3, 141
  elections (1974), 150
  as "hooded one", 141

indirect elections, 76
Institutional Act No. 2 (AI-2), 38, 79
Institutional Act No. 5 (AI-5), 103
as leader of the government, 91
leadership qualities, 98
liberal exit strategy for the dictatorship, 138
Márcio Moreira Alves affair, 96, 103
military contacts, 30
National Congress recess, 163
party–government relations, 113–14
political career, 230*n*
political cartoons, 201
praise for Teotônio Vilela, 156–7
purging of Wilson Campos, 153
relations with Costa e Silva, 91, 92
relations with Gama e Silva, 98
resignation as government leader in the Senate, 96, 115
right for ARENA Senators to disagree, 141
state-level parties, 41
as UDN legal scholar, 30, 91
as UDN liberal, 2, 30, 35, 64, 115
Kubitschek government (1956–1961), 30, 118
Kubitschek, Juscelino ("JK")
death of (1976), 159–60
loss of political rights, 35–6
national movement plans, 43
Pessedista leader, 30, 82
possible purge target, 34
Presidential candidate (1955), 30, 37
Kushnir, Beatriz, 15

Labour Renewal Movement (MTR), 217
Lacerda, Carlos, 30, 35, 36, 43, 187, 195
Lacerda, Flávio Suplicy, 47
Lacerda, Maurício, 131
Lamounier, Bolívar
ARENA creation, 13
Brazilian dictatorship, 22
détente, 22
elections (1970), 11
formalisms in representative democracy, 130
political liberalism studies, 21
political party instability, 18–19
representative system, 14
two-party system, 62
Lan (cartoonist), 187, 193, 194, 206
Lavareda, Antônio, 21
Le Men, Ségolène, 189, 190
Lembo, Cláudio, 175
Lemos, Plínio, 60

Levi, Giovanni, 26
Levy, Herbert
ARENA subordination to government, 180
ARENA's new name, 184
Castello Branco government purges (1964), 31, 32
Constitution (1967) drafting, 85–6, 87
criticism of military intervention in politics, 141, 142
dissident voice of, 3, 141
as "hooded one", 141
institutional political issue, 23
liberal exit strategy for the dictatorship, 138
marginalization of Brazil's politicians, 141
as pro-regime politician, 23
liberal political institutions, 20, 29, 131, 133–4, 137
Liberator Party (PL), 43, 63, 65, 88, 177, 218
Ligas Camponesas, 67
Lima Filho, Oswaldo, 32, 83
Lima, Jarbas, 159
Lindenberg, Carlos Fernando Monteiro, 60
Lindoso, José, 120
Lins, Etelvino, 129, 235*n*
Linz, Juan, 13
Lixto, K., 187
local government autonomy, 88–91
localism, 90
Lopes de Souza, Ney, 153
Lott, Henrique, 30
Louis-Philippe, King of France, 189
LPM publishing house, 188
Lucena, Humberto, 84
Lupion, Moisés, 82

Macedo Soares, Edmundo, 47
Machado de Assis, José M., 6
Machado, Expedito, 32
Maciel, Leandro Maynard, 60
Maciel, Lysâneas, 153
Maciel, Marco, 171
Magalhães, Jairo, 124
Magalhães, Juracy, 34, 36–7, 38, 60, 161
Magalhães, Rafael de Almeida, 43
O Malho magazine, 187
Marches for Family and Freedom, 15, 67, 72
Marcílio, Flávio, 144, 167
Marinho, Djalma, 33, 80
Marinho, Josaphat, 32, 81, 94, 96

Mariz, Antônio, 119, 120
Mariz, Dinarte, 154
Marquezan, Nelson, 166, 179
Martins, Carlos Estevam, 23
Martins, Ildélio, 143, 237*n*
Mato Grosso, 62, 89
MDB *see* Movimento Democrático Brasileiro (MDB)
Medeiros Silva, Carlos, 79, 88, 109
Médici, Garrastazu
  ARENA convention (1969), 113
  "Brazilian solutions to Brazilian problems", 132
  Márcio Moreira Alves affair, 95
  "politics of the governors", 123
  Presidential candidacy, 116
Médici government (1969–1974)
  ARENA leadership, 133
  Chamber of Deputies internal rules, 144
  Congressional prerogatives, 144
  defenders of formalisms, 138
  Freyre's defence of, 133
  indirect elections, 122–3, 125–6, 127–30
  National Congress leaders, 115
  party–government relations, 120, 125, 126, 157
  "politics of the governors", 122–31
  torture accusations, 133
Meneguello, Raquel, 13, 18
Mesa Diretora, 32
Mesquita Filho, Júlio de, 136
Mexico, Institutional Revolutionary Party, 10, 221*n*
Miceli, Sérgio, 60
Miguel, Nazir, 134–5
military
  1964 movement, 16, 67–8
  ARENA's founders, 46–7
  candidacy to indirect elections, 73
  as dictatorship scapegoat, 215
  distrust of ARENA, 107
  images of the "monster" and phantoms, 147
  Krieger's analysis, 147
  Márcio Moreira Alves affair, 95–6, 109–10
  National Congress recess (1968–1969), 110
  national security role, 89
  new party system created, 14, 23, 63–4
  origin of the AI-5, 99, 102
  political activity, 23–4, 26
  political capital, 116
  political cartoons, 205, 208

political détente, 146–7, 152
relations with politicians, 26
relations with politicians (1946–1964), 30
relations with politicians (Castello Branco government), 63–4
relations with politicians (Costa e Silva government), 91–101, 102–9, 113–14
relations with politicians (Geisel government), 145, 146–7, 155–8, 180
studies on, 11, 18, 23–4
subordination and subservience to, 8, 11, 151, 154–6, 180, 205
torture issue, 102–3, 135
"tutorship power", 20
view of ARENA, 16–17
view of dictatorship, 15–16
see also Castello Branco government (1964–1967); Costa e Silva government (1967–1969); coup d'état (1964); dictatorship (1964–1985); Figueiredo government (1979–1985); Geisel government (1974–1979); Médici government (1969–1974)
Military Club, 31
Millet, Clodomir, 117–18, 123
Minas Gerais
  ARENA formation, 63
  ARENA leaders, 47, 55, 60
  ARENA party leaders' resignation, 105
  ARENA shutting down threat, 104
  eighteenth-century insurgents, 193
  elections (1965), 198
Montoro, Franco, 154, 162, 170
Mosca, Gaetano, 116
Motta, Rodrigo Patto de Sá, 12–13
Mourão, Olímpio, 30
Movimento Democrático Brasileiro (MDB)
  accusations against ARENA, 98
  amnesty, 172
  ARENA as "government party", 16
  ARENA as "Yes Sir! Party", 16, 151, 178
  Arenista "Correspondence" to National Committee, 67
  censorship for books and periodicals, 138
  Congressional debates, 16, 95
  Congressional prerogatives, 142
  Constitution (1967) drafting, 81, 83, 87

Constitutional Congress campaign, 69
criticism of military intervention in politics, 142
defunct parties members, 42, 45, *46*
diversity of members' party origins, 13
elections (1966), *12*
elections (1970), 11, *12*
elections (1974), 11, *12*, 14, 148–9, 150–1, 201, 202
elections (1978), *12*, 171
electoral growth, 177, 178
electoral possibilities, 22
extinguished (1979), 147, 184, 192, 201–2
Florim Coutinho slander case, 143
formation as opposition party, 41, 42
Geisel government purges, 157
indirect elections for state governments, 128
Institutional Act No. 5 (AI-5), 152, 209, 210
Judiciary reform bill, 163
Kinzo's thesis on, 23
Krieger's resignation, 92
liberalizing the dictatorship, 146
literature on, 14
Márcio Moreira Alves affair, 96–7, 98
Movimento newspaper ties, 17
municipal elections, 12
municipalities autonomy, 88, 89
National Congress reopening (1969), 115
party loyalty issue, 211
party reform, 173–5, 177, 201–2
party reform law, 183
party size, 63
party–government relations, 94
personification as cartoon characters, 202–3
political cartoons, 199, *199*, 200, 202–4, 206, 207, 209–11, *209*, *210*, 212
"Portella mission" on political reforms, 160
PSD association, 9
PTB politicians, 41
Rio Branco mayor indirect elections, 154
"*sub-legendas*" (multiple tickets) bill, 12, 91
as "Yes! Party", 12–13, 14–15, 178
see also Emedebistas
Movimento newspaper, 17–18, 191, 192, 208
Movimento Trabalhista Renovador (MTR), 217

Müller, Amaury, 153
Müller, Filinto
ARENA acting chairman, 105
ARENA assistant chairman, 46
ARENA chairman, 105, 126, 127, 132, 144, 201
ARENA leader in the Senate, 115, 141
ARENA link to ESG, 132
ARENA National Convention (1968), 93, 94
ARENA National Convention (1972), 126
ARENA reorganization, 108
and the *Arenistas*, 117
Castello Branco's presidential term, 35
Complementary Act No. 54, 107, 108
Constitution (1967) drafting, 88
constitutional amendments, 127
death of (1973), 144
election advertising on radio and television, 116
Estado Novo posts, 9
initiatives to strengthen ARENA, 131–2
Krieger's reinstatement as ARENA chairman, 94
Krieger's resignation, 92
leadership authorized by the dictatorship, 3
Márcio Moreira Alves affair, 103, 108
National Congress recess, 105, 106
Partido Democrático Republicano, 140
party loyalty issue, 121
party–government relations, 126
political cartoons, 201, 205–6
PSD affiliation, 42, 64
two-party system, 42
Müller, Gastão, 176
multiple tickets *see* "*sub-legendas*" (multiple tickets)
municipal autonomy, 29, 88–91
municipal elections, 12, 90, 158–9, 160, 167

Nabuco de Araújo, Joaquim, 122
Nascimento, Milton, 156
National Congress
amnesty bill, 173
Arenistas strategy of omission, 76, 91, 98, 215
autonomy, 120, 131, 144
closed by the Estado Novo coup d'état, 19
Complementary Act No. 54 (AC-54), 106, 200

National Congress *(continued)*
  Congressional debates, 4, 12, 16, 86–7, 95, 146, 152, 162, 172, 173, 178
  Congressional prerogatives, 124, 126, 142, 143–5, 167, 183
  Congressional recesses (Castello Branco government), 77
  Congressional recesses (Costa e Silva government), 67, 97, 100, 105, 106, 110, 114, 206, 208
  Congressional recesses (Geisel government), 152, 160, 162, 163–5, 167
  Congressional records, 4
  Congressional sessions, 4, 95, 215
  Constitution (1967) drafting, 79, 80, 83, 84, 87, 88
  Constitutional Amendment No. 1, 114, 115–16, 118, 211
  Constitutional Amendment No. 2, 127–9, 143
  Constitutional Amendment No. 7, 165, 207
  Constitutional Amendment No. 8, 165, 207
  Constitutional Amendment No. 9 (1964), 35, 81
  Constitutional Amendment No. 11, 166, 171, 175
  constitutional amendments (Castello Branco government), 35, 37
  constitutional amendments (Geisel government), 160, 162, 164, 166
  constitutional amendments (Médici government), 143
  elections (1966), *12*, 43, 192
  elections (1974), 11, *12*, 14, 146, 147, 148–51, 173, 201, 202
  elections (1978), *12*, 167, 171, 192, 201
  immunity issue, 143–5
  Institutional Act No. 2 (AI-2), 18
  Institutional Act No. 5 (AI-5), 67, 97, 133, 134, 199, 200
  new party system, 40
  party loyalty, 122
  party reform, 201
  political reforms bill, 161
  purges (Castello Branco government 1964), 31
  purges (Castello Branco government 1966), 76
  purges (Geisel government), 153
  reopening (1969), 106, 110, 113–16
  votes on bills to revoke, 146

National Democratic Union (UDN) *see* União Democrática Nacional (UDN)
National Intelligence Service (SNI), 15, 95, 149
National Labour Party (PTN), 219
National News Agency, 99
National Renewal Alliance *see* Aliança Renovadora Nacional (ARENA)
National Security Act, 166, 167
National Security Council (*Conselho de Segurança Nacional*), 109, 110
National Security Law, 143, 146
Nationalist Congressional Front, 32
Nery, Sebastião, 186, 187
Neves, Maria Manuela Renha de Novis, 62
Neves, Tancredo, 9
newspapers
  dictatorship period, 15
  humorous tradition of, 185–6
  political cartoons, 185–96
  social memory of Brazil's dictatorship, 185
  as source material, 4
  see also individual newspaper titles
Niemeyer, Oscar, 171
Nogueira, Hamilton, 38
Nonato, Orozimbo, 78

Offerlé, Michel, 7, 24, 25, 60
Oliveira, Adolfo de, 139
Opinião newspaper, 140, 191, 192
Organic Law on Political Parties (1965), 36
Organic Law on Political Parties (1971), 118–21, 122, 124–5, 192, 211

Pacheco, Rondon
  ARENA caucus meeting (1970), 117
  ARENA chairman of National Committee, 114
  ARENA convention (1969), 113, 114
  ARENA Executive Board chairman, 108–9
  ARENA secretary-general, 46, 55
  ARENA shutting down threat, 107
  Constitution (1967) drafting, 109
  elections (1966), 55
  as governor of Minas Gerais, 118
  leadership authorized by the dictatorship, 3
  Márcio Moreira Alves affair, 103
  military trust in, 109
  party–government relations, 108, 113, 114, 155

political career, 108–9
"politics of the governors", 123
as UDN legal scholar, 108
Padilha, Raimundo, 46, 83, 86, 93–4
Palmeira, Rui, 80
Paraíba, 60, 119
Paraná state, 82
Pareto, Vilfredo, 116
Partido da Frente Liberal (PFL), 8, 10, 219
Partido de Representação Popular (PRP), 72, 218
Partido Democrata Cristão (PDC), 217
 ARENA association, 72
 ARENA National Committee, 47
 Institutional Act No. 2 (AI-2), 38
 political cartoons, 202
Partido Democrático Republicano (PDR), 140, 202, 217
Partido Democrático Social (PDS), 8, 10, 176, 184, 218
Partido do Movimento Democrático Brasileiro (PMDB), 14, 218
Partido Libertador (PL), 43, 63, 65, 88, 177, 218
Partido Republicano (PR), 47, 63, 72, 218
Partido Rural Trabalhista (PRT), 218
Partido Social Democrático (PSD), 219
 1964 movement, 9
 Accioly Filho's career, 82
 ARENA association, 61–2, 64–5, 72, 176
 ARENA National Committee, 47, 55
 ARENA's history, 9
 Castello Branco government purges (1964), 33, 34
 Castello Branco's presidential term, 35–6
 coalition with PTB, 30, 37
 congressional alliances (pre–1964), 72
 Constitution (1967) drafting, 80
 election results, 37
 electoral coalitions, 61
 extinguished (1965), 65, 67
 founding of, 20, 67
 fragmentation of, 20
 Institutional Act No. 2 (AI-2), 38–9
 MDB association, 9
 military contacts, 30
 organizational structure, 42
 party acronym loss, 38–9
 party reform (1964–1966), 36, 37, 38–9
 party reform (1979), 174, 176, 177
 political capital, 9, 42

political cartoons, 196–7, *197, 198,* 202
 restoration of, 176
 two-party system, 40, 41–3
 Último de Carvalho's influence, 71
 Youth Wing, 20
 see also Pessedistas
Partido Social Progressista (PSP), 47, 63, 65, 72, 219
Partido Social Trabalhista (PST), 176, 219
Partido Socialista Brasileiro (PSB), 38
Partido Trabalhista Brasileiro (PTB), 219
 ARENA association, 72
 ARENA National Committee, 47
 base for the opposition party, 41
 Castello Branco government purges (1964), 32–3, 34, 99
 Castello Branco's presidential term, 35
 coalition with PSD, 30, 37
 election results, 37
 extinguished (1965), 65
 founding of, 20
 Institutional Act No. 2 (AI-2), 38–9
 João Batista Ramos's political career, 118
 mass rallies, 31
 MDB formation, 41
 military contacts, 30
 party acronym loss, 38–9
 party reform (1964–1966), 36, 37, 38–9
 party reform (1979), 177
 political cartoons, 196, *197*, 202
 in Rio Grande do Sul, 61
Partido Trabalhista Nacional (PTN), 219
Party of the Brazilian Democratic Movement (PMDB), 14, 218
Party of the Liberal Front (PFL), 8, 10, 219
party loyalty issue, 16, 83, 118–22, 141, 152, 160–1, 211
O Pasquim weekly lampoon, 9, 188, 191, 192, 196
Passarinho, Jarbas
 amnesty, 172–3
 ARENA National Executive Board, 46, 108
 Constitutional Amendment No. 8, 165
 defence of ARENA, 180
 elections (1974), 150–1
 indirect elections, 170
 Márcio Moreira Alves affair, 98
 political reforms, 169, 171

268 | Index

Passarinho, Jarbas *(continued)*
  purging of Wilson Campos, 153
  re-democratization, 163–4
  support for Krieger, 98
patronage practices, 8, 63, 90–1
PCB (Brazilian Communist Party), 22, 30, 120, 171, 202
PDC *see Partido Democrata Cristão (PDC)*
PDR (*Partido Democrático Republicano*), 140, 202, 217
PDS (*Partido Democrático Social*), 8, 10, 176, 184, 218
Peasant Leagues, 67
Peixoto, Ernani do Amaral, 39, 40, 122, 151, 196
Pereira, Francelino
  ARENA clichés, 6, 9–10
  ARENA convention (1975), 157
  ARENA National Committee chairman, 157, 158
  elections (1978), 167
  indirect elections, 170
  multiple tickets, 158
  Partido Democrático Republicano (PDR), 140
  party reform, 164, 169, 175
Peres, Glênio, 153
Perez, Leopoldo, 46
Pessedistas
  ARENA membership, 9, 10, 45, 63
  control of new government party, 42–3
  dispute with *Udenistas*, 42, 61, 63
  political cartoons, 196–7
  two-party system, 42–3
  see also Partido Social Democrático (PSD)
PFL (*Partido da Frente Liberal*), 8, 10, 219
Pinheiro, Israel, 60, 104
Pinochet, Augusto, 153
Pinto, Bilac, 30
Pinto, Carvalho, 93, 115, 142
Pinto, Francisco, 153
Pinto, José de Magalhães
  ARENA convention (1978), 168, 169
  ARENA National Committee member, 47
  candidacy to President of Brazil, 168, 181
  elections (National Congress 1970), 55
  indirect elections, 170
  Institutional Act No. 5 (AI-5), 158
  institutional political issue, 23
  military contacts, 30

party reform, 36
political cartoons, 186
  as pro-regime politician, 23
PL (*Partido Libertador*), 43, 63, 65, 88, 177, 218
PMDB (*Partido do Movimento Democrático Brasileiro*), 14, 218
political capital
  Aliança Renovadora Nacional, 9, 27, 39, 115–16, 156, 170, 184
  gubernatorial candidacies, 115–16
  Partido Social Democrático, 9, 42
  União Democrática Nacional, 9, 39
political cartoons
  Aliança Renovadora Nacional (ARENA), 10, 185, 189, 190, 191–2, 196–213, *199*, *200*, *204*, *209*, *210*
  Correio da Manhã newspaper, 191, 193, 195, 198, 200
  O Estado de S. Paulo newspaper, 185, 191, 194–5, 196, *197*, *198*, *199*, 200, *200*, 202, *204*, *205*, *209*, *210*, 211
  the "government", 204–8
  Jornal do Brasil newspaper, 191, 192–4, 195, 208
  Movimento Democrático Brasileiro (MDB), 199, *199*, 200, 202–4, 206, 207, 209–11, *209*, *210*, 212
  newspapers, 185–96
  Organic Law on Political Parties (1971), 211
  party loyalty issue, 211
  party reform, 201–2, 208
  political representation threats, 208–13
political class
  Arenistas, 23, 110, 125
  Costa e Silva government (1967–1969), 99–100, 102, 108, 110
  disregard for, 99–100, 102, 149
  Geisel's views on, 151
  indirect elections, 128
  marginalization of, 116
  political cartoons, 209, 211
  versus state governors, 125
political field, 23, 24–6, 27, 28, 64, 125, 183
political humour, 186, 187, 188, 190
political institutions, 20, 27–8, 29, 106, 131, 133–4, 137
political liberalism, 21–2
political parties, 217–20
  authenticity of, 11, 19, 29
  Brazilian society's view of, 1
  concept of, 7

extinguishing of (1965), 19, 20-1, 28, 29, 36, 37-40, 65
extinguishing of (1979), 8, 147, 184, 192, 201-2
as a field of forces, 25
First Republic (1889-1930), 20, 64
formation of a new party system (1965-1966), 40-3
history in Brazil, 18-21
identity, 70
instability, 18-19
institutionalization of, 20
liberal institutions, 20
members' behaviour, 27
objectives, 70, 162
oligarchical origins, 60-1, 63-4
Organic Law (1965), 36
Organic Law (1971), 118-21, 122, 124-5, 192, 211
organizational structure, 64
party loyalty issue, 16, 83, 118-22, 141, 152, 160-1, 211
political representation, 19
reform (1964-1966), 36-40
representative democracy, 25
Second Brazilian Republic (1946-1964), 20, 21, 22
state-level parties, 41
studies of, 27
see also *individual political parties*; two-party system
political prisoners, 102, 135, 173
political problematics, 26
political purges (Castello Branco government 1964), 31-4, 93-4, 99
political purges (Castello Branco government 1966), 75-8, 79, 93-4, 200
political purges (Costa e Silva government 1968-1969), 95-9, 110, *111*, 114
political purges (Geisel government 1974-1979), 153-4, 157-8
political representation
Aliança Renovadora Nacional, 1-2, 8, 12, 14, 16, 207-8
attacks on, 19
authenticity of, 11, 19, 29
Brazilian society's view of, 1
part as a "collective brand", 7
political cartoons, 208-13
professional politicians, 24
see also representative democracy; representative systems
Popular Representation Party (PRP), 72, 218
Portella, Jayme, 109

Portella, Petrônio
amnesty, 171, 172
ARENA chairman, 144
ARENA convention (1969), 114
ARENA convention (1975), 154-5, 156
ARENA subordination to the government, 154-5
censorship, 136
constitutional reform bill committee (1973), 144
elections (1974), 150
indirect elections, 170
institutional political issue, 23
liberalization policy, 171
Márcio Moreira Alves affair, 155
National Congress recess, 163
National Security Act, 166
Niemeyer's Brasília architectural projects, 171
party reform, 171, 174
party-government relations, 154-5
political reforms, 152, 160, 163, 165
as pro-regime politician, 23
purging of Wilson Campos, 153-4
Rio Branco mayor indirect elections, 154
Power, Timothy, 121
PR (*Partido Republicano*), 47, 63, 72, 218
Prado, Hamilton, 117
press censorship, 15, 102, 136-8, 140, 186-7, 193, 194
Prestes, Luis Carlos, 67
Prieto, Arnaldo, 105, 109
professional politicians, 23-6
Aliança Renovadora Nacional, 47, 55, 73-4, 92, 183
Brazilian society's negative view of, 1
Progressive Social Party (PSP), 47, 63, 65, 72, 219
PRP (*Partido de Representação Popular*), 72, 218
PRT (*Partido Rural Trabalhista*), 218
PSB (*Partido Socialista Brasileiro*), Institutional Act No. 2 (AI-2), 38
PSD see *Partido Social Democrático* (PSD)
PSP (*Partido Social Progressista*), 47, 63, 65, 72, 219
PST (*Partido Social Trabalhista*), 176, 219
PTB see *Partido Trabalhista Brasileiro* (PTB)
PTN (*Partido Trabalhista Nacional*), 219

Quadros, Jânio, 203
Queiróz, Ademar de, 30

Radmaker, Augusto, 116
Ramos family, 60
Ramos, João Batista, 118, 119–20, 125–6
Reale, Miguel, 109, 132
Realidade magazine, 76
Record publishing house, 188
"redeemed ones", 140
Reis, Antônio Carlos Konder, 80, 82, 84, 85
representative democracy
  Arenistas, 44, 130, 183
  consolidation of, 23, 26
  First Republic (1889–1930), 64
  founding principles, 183
  as highly valued, 75
  historical experience of, 25
  maintenance of the electoral system, 91
  municipal autonomy, 90–1
  political party system, 25
  professional politicians, 25
  see also democracy; political representation
representative systems
  Arenistas, 130
  authenticity of, 11, 19, 29
  congressional recesses, 106
  dictatorship (1964–1985), 14
  First Republic (1889–1930), 20, 64
  formalisms, 1, 130, 133, 149
  fundamental principles, 116, 145
  important mechanisms of, 131
  maintenance of, 73, 91, 101, 163
  political cartoons, 204, 208–13
  sorites speech by Nabucode Araújo, 122
  threats, 208–13
  see also political institutions; political representation
Republican Democratic Party (PDR), 140, 202, 217
Republican Party (PR), 47, 63, 72, 218
Resende, Eurico
  Adauto Cardoso's resignation, 139
  ARENA leader in the Senate, 162, 163
  Constitution (1967) drafting, 79, 80, 81
  elections (1974), 150
  Institutional Act No. 2 (AI-2), 38
  Judiciary reform bill, 163
  municipalities autonomy, 89–90
  Vianna Filho's criticism of the political system, 162

Revolutionary Command, 33, 78
Ribeiro, Darcy, 187–8
Ribeiro, Jair Dantas, 32
Ribeiro, Nina, 135–6, 167
Rio Branco, 152, 154
Rio de Janeiro city, political cartoons, 193, 194
Rio de Janeiro state
  Adauto Cardoso's career, 75
  elections (1965), 198
Rio de Janeiro State Committee, 104
Rio Grande do Sul, 61, 88, 156, 177
Rios, Airon, 129–30, 149, 174
Rocha, Eloy, 238*n*
Rodrigues, Martins, 81
Rodrigues, Nelson, 17
Roma, João, 103, 109
Rosseti, Nadyr, 153
Rousso, Henry, 6–7, 65
Rural Labour Party (PRT), 218

Sá, Mem de, 64, 88, 92, 193
Salles, Campos, 122
Salles, Claudino, 172
Sampaio, Cantídio
  censorship, 136
  defence of ARENA, 180
  indirect elections, 128
  Institutional Act No. 5 (AI-5), 97, 134–5, 152
  leader in the Chamber of Deputies, 115
  party–government relations, 141–2
  political career, 233*n*
  torture accusations in documentary, 135
Santa Catarina, 60
Santa Catarina State Committee, 178
Santos, Rui, 136
Santos, Wanderley Guilherme dos, 21
São Paulo
  ARENA formation, 63
  Costa e Silva government purges (1968–1969), 110
  Teatro de Arena, 6
São Paulo State Committee, 104, 175
Sarazate, Paulo, 30, 46
Sarney, José
  ARENA archives, 3
  Castello Branco government purges (1964), 31
  Constitutional Amendment No. 11, 166
  party reform, 175, 176, 183–4
  Teotônio Vilela's view on politics, 156–7

Sátiro, Ernani, 38, 40, 60, 70, 73, 90, 245n
Schmitter, Philippe, 13, 21
Senhor magazine, 195
Senna (cartoonist), 193, 200
Sergipe, 60
Silva, Golbery do Couto e, 63, 152, 171, 184
Silva, Luís Antonio da Gama e
  ARENA reorganization, 108
  Constitution (1967) drafting, 109
  derision of liberalism, 131
  Márcio Moreira Alves affair, 96, 193
  political cartoons, 193
  political reforms, 114
  relations with Krieger, 98
Silva Neto, Augusto Lins e, 147, 159, 160–1, 167–8, 180, 181
SNI (National Intelligence Service), 15, 95, 149
Soares, Airton, 179
Soares, Flores, 80, 84, 89
Soares, Gláucio Ary Dillon, 15
Sobrinho, Nelson Fabiano, 153, 157
social demand, 11
Social Democratic Party (PDS), 8, 10, 176, 184, 218
Social Labour Party (PST), 176, 219
Souza, Amaral de, 129, 235n
Souza, Herbert de, 188
Souza, Maria do Carmo Campello de, 13, 20
Stenzel, Clóvis, 104, 131, 134
STM (Superior Military Tribunal), 15
Storni, Alfredo, 187
"*sub-legendas*" (multiple tickets)
  Aliança Renovadora Nacional, 12, 41, 45–6, 61, 91–2, 98, 107
  Complementary Act No. 54, 107
  injustice of, 12
  Movimento Democrático Brasileiro, 12, 91
Superior Electoral Court (TSE), 107, 148
Superior Military Tribunal (STM), 15
Superior War College (ESG), 30, 131, 132, 183–4
Supreme Court (STF)
  Adauto Cardoso's position, 77–8, 87–8, 138–9, 142
  Adauto Cardoso's resignation, 138–40
  Florim Coutinho slander case, 143
  Francisco Pinto's trial, 153, 238n
  Judiciary reform bill, 162–3
  National Security Act, 167
  Niemeyer's architectural projects, 171
  number of sitting judges, 38

Tavares, Aurélio de Lira, 95
Távora, Edilson, 124, 234n
Teatro de Arena, 6
terrorism, 128, 133–4
Tito, Marcos, 153
Tocqueville, Alexis de, 27
Toledo, Maurício, 124, 127
Torres, Vasconcelos, 80
Torres, Weimar, 89
torture, 75, 102–3, 135–6, 153
Tribuna da Imprensa periodical, 195
TSE (Superior Electoral Court), 107, 148
two-party system
  central ideas of, 95
  creation of, 13, 40–3
  electoral competition studies, 11
  end of, 173
  Kinzo's studies, 13, 42, 46, 98
  meaning to the electorate, 62
  Partido Social Democrático (PSD), 40, 41–3
  União Democrática Nacional, 40–1, 42–3

Udenistas
  ARENA members, 9, 10, 45, 63
  ARENA party leaders' resignation, 105
  Castello Branco government purges (1964), 31–2
  control of new government party, 42–3
  dispute with *Pessedistas*, 42, 61, 63
  military contacts, 30
  moral reserve, 100
  two-party system, 42–3
União Democrática Nacional (UDN), 220
  Adauto Cardoso's membership, 75
  ARENA association, 9, 61–2, 64–5, 72
  ARENA National Committee, 47, 55
  bacharéis (legal experts), 30, 75, 78, 84–5, 91, 108
  as base for the government party, 41
  Castello Branco's presidential term, 35, 36
  congressional alliances (pre-1964), 72
  Constitution (1967) drafting, 80
  coup d'état (1964), 196, 198
  election results, 37
  electoral coalitions, 61
  extinguished (1965), 65, 203
  founding of, 20, 66
  Gomes's nomination, 30
  gubernatorial elections (1965), 36–7, 198
  Institutional Act No. 2 (AI-2), 37, 38
  "Marching Band" strategy, 134, 139

Udenistas
  opposition to Getúlio Vargas, 66
  party acronym loss, 39
  party reform (1964–1966), 36–7, 38
  party reform (1979), 174, 176, 177
  political capital, 9, 39
  political cartoons, 196, 198
  two-party system, 40–1, 42–3
  Villas-Boas's views on, 9
  see also Udenistas
United Nations, 33

Valadares, Benedito, 47, 64
Valle, Edmundo Jordão Amorim do, 46
Vargas, Getúlio, 9, 31, 66, 82, 83
  Getulismo, 61, 62, 177
Vargas, Ivete, 39
Vargas, Lenoir, 33
Veja magazine, 192
Velasco e Cruz, Sebastião, 23
Velho, Britto, 43, 80, 83, 84, 85
Veloso, Gil, 32
Veríssimo, Luís Fernando, 10
Viana, Aurélio, 94, 95
Viana, Francisco, 98
Vianna Filho, Luís
  amnesty, 172, 173
  ARENA convention (1968), 113–14
  ARENA creation, 63
  ARENA subordination to the government, 180
  book on Castello Branco government, 240*n*
  Castello Branco government purges (1964), 34
  Castello Branco's presidential term, 34–5
  constitutional reform, 94
  détente obstacles, 147
  municipal "intervenors", 75
  party–government relations, 113–14

political career, 60, 161
political parties' objectives, 162
political reforms, 161–2
Ruy Barbosa anthologies, 240*n*
value of politics and politicians, 94
Vidigal, Pedro, 97–8
Vieira, Heribaldo, 80
Vieira, Laerte, 142
Vilaça, Manuel, 80
Vilella, Teotônio, 156–7, 159, 166, 170, 173, 180

Weber, Hilde (cartoonist)
  ARENA depicted as a woman, 201, 202, 207
  ARENA vs. MDB, 201, 207, 210
  Arenista politicians, 206
  biography, 195
  O Estado de S. Paulo cartoons, 194, 198, 202, 204, 210
  Institutional Act No. 5 (AI-5), 210
  party reform, 208
  personification of ARENA, 206
Weber, Max, 24, 60
Weffort, Francisco, 12, 21, 22
Wesson, Robert, 122–3

Zancaner, Orlando, 150
Ziraldo
  20 Years at Attention, 189
  ARENA vs. MDB, 207
  biography, 195
  comparison of ARENA and PRI, 10
  demise of ARENA and MDB, 202
  Fotopotocas magazine, 186
  Jornal do Brasil cartoons, 193, 208
  O Pasquim newspaper, 196
  personification of ARENA, 206
  as political editorialist of Brazil, 187